P9-AGD-082

Emotional Intelligence Mastery Bible

—7 BOOKS in 1— Emotional Intelligence, Improve Your People Skills, Accelerated Learning, How to Analyze People, Overthinking, Manipulation, Dark Psychology

Social-Emotional Academy

© Copyright 2020 - All rights reserved.

The content contained within this book may not be reproduced, duplicated or transmitted without direct written permission from the author or the publisher.

Under no circumstances will any blame or legal responsibility be held against the publisher, or author, for any damages, reparation, or monetary loss due to the information contained within this book. Either directly or indirectly.

Legal Notice:

This book is copyright protected. This book is only for personal use. You cannot amend, distribute, sell, use, quote or paraphrase any part, or the content within this book, without the consent of the author or publisher.

Disclaimer Notice:

Please note the information contained within this document is for educational and entertainment purposes only. All effort has been executed to present accurate, up to date, and reliable, complete information. No warranties of any kind are declared or implied. Readers acknowledge that the author is not engaging in the rendering of legal, financial, medical or professional advice. The content within this book has been derived from various sources. Please consult a licensed professional before attempting any techniques outlined in this book.

By reading this document, the reader agrees that under no circumstances is the author responsible for any losses, direct or indirect, which are incurred as a result of the use of information contained within this document, including, but not limited to, — errors, omissions, or inaccuracies.

Table of Books:

Table of Contents

Emotional Intelligence

9

Emotional Intelligence

Improve Your Social Skills and Emotional Agility For a Better Life, Success At Work and Happier Relationships. Discover Why it Can Matter More Than IQ (EQ 2.0)

Introduction

The study of emotion has been around for several centuries, as far back as when Plato wrote: "All learning has an emotional base." During the early centuries, it was commonly thought that emotions affected humans negatively. Many elites of that era believed a man would do better if he wasn't held back by emotions. Many believed that man was a slave to his emotions. Unfortunately, many still do. A quick burst of anger prompting a violent act that would be regretted later on, or a bout of depression driving a promising high-spirited youth to suicide are examples of the negative effects of emotions of humans. The emotion was part of man, but it was considered man's obstacle to achieving much more.

The 90s saw a shift in how emotions are perceived. A growing body of research continues to prove that emotion, once considered a limitation, holds substantive value.

In the 1950s, the "Human Potential" movement was sparked by Abrahams Maslow's paper which explained how humans could enhance their emotional, spiritual, physical and mental capacity. This movement saw human emotion as a strength rather than a weakness. This was considered a great celebration of humanism and opened the door to further study into the power of human emotions.

In 1990, Peter Salovey and John Mayer published an article titled "Emotional Intelligence" which states that emotional intelligence is a scientifically testable intelligence. Although the term 'emotional intelligence' was first used in 1964 by Michael Beldoch, it remained a relatively unknown concept until 1995, when Daniel Goleman, in his book titled "Emotional Intelligence", wrote extensively on the subject. The concept of Emotional Intelligence has been widely used ever since.

Various research studies on the concept of emotional intelligence have established it as an easily perceivable trait in people. Emotional Intelligence is important in making great decisions and in daily interaction with other human beings.

Studies have shown that high emotional intelligence is linked to great mental health, leadership skills, healthier approaches to relationships and better job performance.

People with good emotional intelligence are often known to have accurate perceptions of themselves as they are highly self-aware individuals. They often know what they are feeling and know how to express their feelings. These people can also easily understand the experiences and feelings of others. They are generally emotionally balanced people with fewer regrettable actions. They seem to always make calculated decisions and are rarely taken over by their emotions. They always pay attention to themselves and to others. Developing high

14

emotional intelligence is a great step towards self-development.

This book explains the concept of emotional intelligence and other surrounding concepts. It will help you understand how emotions affect daily life, how they affect personal and formal relationships and how they influence our decisions in varying situations. It also explains how we can be more emotionally intelligent by breaking down the key areas of emotional intelligence and suggesting ways to build competence in these areas.

Chapter 1: What Is Emotional Intelligence?

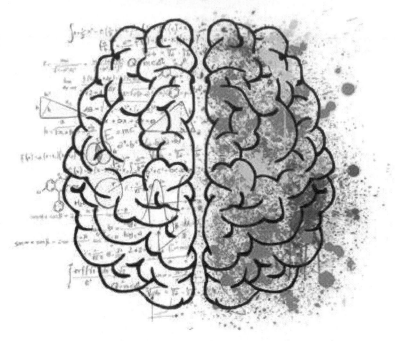

In simple terms, emotional intelligence is recognizing emotions and leveraging on emotional information in making healthy choices.

Emotional intelligence is the capacity to recognize our emotions and regulate them, to discern the emotions of others, and to differentiate between varying emotions, using this information to facilitate thoughts and behavior in order to achieve the desired results.

Since emotional intelligence involves recognizing emotions, it is important to have an understanding of what emotions are and what types of emotions there are.

What Are Emotions?

In 384-322 BCE, Aristotle described emotions as "those feelings that so change men as to affect their judgments, and that are also attended by pain or pleasure. Such are anger, pity, fear and the like, with their opposites."

These are mental states or feelings that occur spontaneously and not by intention. These feelings are often accompanied by physiological reactions. These occurrences are in response to our perception of what is happening or what we see or hear per-time.

Emotions help us understand our experiences. We would never know that the death of a loved one is a sad experience if we have never felt sadness. We would never know that someone destroying our lawn is an annoying experience if we have never felt angry. Feeling emotions help us categorize our experiences and react accordingly.

Positive emotions register an experience we are having or are about to have as good and worth having. When we say we look forward to the experience, it is not the experience we look forward to per sé. It is more the emotions associated with that experience that we look forward to having.

On the other hand, negative emotions alert us of unpleasant or potentially unpleasant experiences. We know we should do certain things or not do certain things if we would avoid such experiences. For example, when we are faced with a sudden threat, we feel fear of loss or pain. The emotion of fear triggers a fight or flight reaction. What we really are trying to avoid is the loss or pain, not the occurrence itself.

Without emotions, there would be no emotional intelligence and without emotional intelligence, we would not be able to tell precisely the kinds of experiences we want to have and the kinds we don't want to have.

According to author David G. Meyers, "Emotion is made up of three components; physiological arousal, expressive behaviors, and conscious experience."

Physiological arousal means the person feeling a particular emotion will become physiologically alert. This is a point where the sense organs are stimulated to perceive. Physiological arousal is primarily controlled by a part of the brain called the reticular activating system (RAS).

Expressive behavior refers to a behavioral reaction to the perception of what is happening, or to what is seen, heard or thought. This often involves verbal and non-verbal communication of a person's emotions.

Conscious Experience refers to the awareness of a person's environment, what he sees, hears and feels as well as his thoughts.

According to Paul Ekman, there are six basic emotions and they are anger, disgust, fear, happiness, sadness, and surprise. Robert Plutchik suggests there are eight. These eight he grouped into 4 pairs of polar opposites: joy and sadness, anger and fear, trust and distrust, surprise and anticipation.

Primary and Secondary Emotions

Emotions are grouped into primary emotions, secondary emotions, and tertiary emotions.

Primary emotions are the initial emotions felt in response to a perception. These emotions are fear, anger, sadness, joy, love, and surprise. These are the emotions you feel without thinking. They are instinctive feelings we don't plan to have. Imagine you are walking down the road in the company of a friend and a reckless cyclist runs into your friend. The emotion you likely instinctively feel is fear. Fear that your loved one may get hurt.

Primary emotions are often called transient because they disappear quickly and are replaced. They are replaced by secondary emotions and can be secondary emotions themselves.

Secondary emotions are an offshoot of primary emotions. These emotions replace primary emotions. The emotion of fear you felt when you saw your loved one getting knocked down by the reckless cyclist may be replaced by the secondary emotion of anger. You feel angry at the cyclist for causing someone you love pain.

There are so many emotions that it is considered impossible to list all emotions that exist, but below is a generally comprehensive list of human emotions and their meaning. This list contains the basic emotions, their meanings, and their related secondary and tertiary emotions. As you go through this list, try to remember times when you felt each of these emotions. Also, try to remember times when you witnessed someone else express each of the listed emotions. You can take as much time as you need.

Fear

Fear is an unpleasant feeling triggered by a sense of danger or a threat. It is the emotion we feel when we think something bad is going to happen. The primary trigger of fear is the perception of imminent pain. This could be physical pain: fear of bodily harm or hurt; or emotional pain: fear of loss, rejection or distress; or social pain: fear of disgrace, isolation or shame. We feel the emotion of fear not only for ourselves but for others as well. Fear for others can sometimes be more unpleasant to experience than fear for oneself. This is because we usually can't control what happens to others.

Fear ranges from a little scare accompanied by mild muscular tension to a paralyzing feeling accompanied by crippling muscular tension or numbness.

When we have a serious fear of a thing or an animal, it is called a phobia.

A secondary emotion relating to fear is "nervousness". Tertiary emotions relating to nervousness are anxiety, dread, uneasiness, tenseness, apprehension, and worry. Another secondary emotion relating to fear is "horror". Tertiary emotions relating to "horror" include panic, shock, hysteria, terror, fright, and alarm.

Sadness

Sadness is an emotional pain that occurs in response to disappointment, grief, loss, sorrow, and helplessness. It is a temporary state of melancholy and is a dominant emotion. Sadness is a natural and automatic emotion but when it is extreme and persistent, it could be a symptom of depression.

Sadness is a normal emotion like fear or happiness. The death of a pet, the loss of a job or even breaking our favorite china could trigger sadness. When that feeling persists and overwhelms us permanently, it could be an indication of a mental health problem and a person experiencing such should urgently seek professional help.

A secondary emotion relating to sadness is "suffering". Tertiary emotions relating to "suffering" are agony, hurt, suffering, and anguish. Another secondary emotion relating to sadness is "sadness" (we should keep in mind that primary emotions often show up as secondary emotions). Some tertiary emotions relating to the secondary emotion of sadness are depression, despair, hopelessness, gloom, glumness, sadness, unhappiness, grief, sorrow, woe, misery, and melancholy.

Surprise

Surprise is an emotion characterized by a sudden feeling of wonder or astonishment in response to an unexpected event or information. Surprises may be pleasant or unpleasant.

A secondary emotion relating to surprise is "surprise". Tertiary emotions relating to the secondary emotion of surprise are amazement, surprise, and astonishment.

Joy

Joy is a pleasant feeling of great pleasure and excitement. The emotional state of joy is characterized by feelings of contentment, happiness, gratification, satisfaction, and well-being.

A secondary emotion related to happiness is cheerfulness. Tertiary emotions relating to cheerfulness are amusement, bliss, cheerfulness, gaiety, glee, jolliness, joviality, joy, delight, enjoyment, gladness, happiness, jubilation, elation, satisfaction, ecstasy, and euphoria.

Zest

Tertiary emotions relating to the secondary emotion of zest are enthusiasm, zeal, zest, excitement, thrill, and exhilaration.

Contentment

Tertiary emotions relating to the secondary emotion of contentment are contentment and pleasure.

Pride

Tertiary emotions relating to the secondary emotion of pride are pride and triumph.

Optimism

Tertiary emotions relating to the secondary emotion of optimism are eagerness, hope, and optimism.

Enthrallment

Tertiary emotions relating to the secondary emotion enthrallment are enthrallment and rapture.

Relief

A tertiary emotion you may feel relating to relief is also relief.

Anger

Anger is a strong feeling of displeasure, annoyance or hostility triggered by external provocation. Anger is associated with feelings of antagonism towards someone, something or an idea. Anger can be directed at oneself. When a person is angry at himself, the feeling of antagonism associated with his anger is directed at the person feeling the emotion.

While anger, like sadness, is a natural and often automatic reaction. Anger causes increased blood pressure, heart rate, adrenaline and noradrenaline levels. Extreme anger can substantially impair judgment.

Although anger is a primary emotion, it often occurs as a secondary emotion because it is frequently preceded by a negative primary emotion.

Anger is sometimes used as a mechanism to distract oneself from negative emotions that are self-focused. This happens when people stimulate the emotion of anger, either consciously or not, so as to avoid feelings of pain or vulnerability.

Doing this takes their attention off themselves and their unpleasant state and directs it at a person, a thing or an idea. This is considered by the person to be a better state than the state of pain. Anger by itself often does not feel bad to the person feeling it. This is because anger is associated with feelings of justification, moral superiority and pride.

This does not deal with the pain or suppress it. What has happened is a shift of attention from the pain to the 'forced' anger. Once the anger wears off, attention reverts to the pain.

Some secondary and tertiary emotions relating to anger are aggravation, irritation, agitation, annoyance, grouchiness, grumpiness and exasperation. A tertiary emotion relating to exasperation is frustration.

Rage

Tertiary emotions relating to rage are anger, rage, outrage, fury, wrath, hostility, ferocity, bitterness, hate, loathing, scorn, spite, vengefulness, dislike, and resentment.

21

Love

Love is a strong feeling of affection towards a person, a thing or a thought. Love, like other primary emotions, is often not deliberate. It is a dominant emotion of affinity. Love is a positive feeling accompanied by pleasure and happiness.

A secondary emotion relating to love is affection. Tertiary emotions relating to affection are adoration, affection, love, fondness, liking, attraction, caring, tenderness, compassion, and sentimentality lust arousal, desire, lust, passion, and infatuation.

Chapter 2: The 5 Elements of Emotional Intelligence

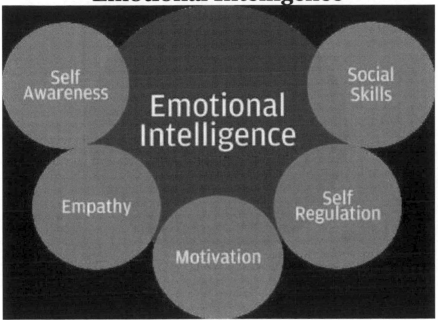

1. Self-awareness

2. Self-regulation

3. Motivation

4. Empathy

5. Social skills

First Element of Emotional Intelligence: Self-awareness

In simple terms, self-awareness is knowing oneself. This may bring to mind the popular Greek Maxim, "Know thyself", which perhaps most simply insinuates self-awareness. Self-awareness is being aware of one's unique self as independent of one's environment and in relation to one's environment. Self-awareness involves understanding the unique elements that makeup oneself.

In his book "Emotional Intelligence", psychologist Daniel Goleman defined self-awareness as "knowing one's internal states, preferences, resources, and intuitions."

One can further describe self-awareness as being aware of what you are thinking, doing and experiencing.

It is as simple as this: if you had an opportunity to live with a replica of yourself for a day, would you recognize how you think, your usual physiological and emotional response to varying situations, the kinds of judgments you make, your abilities, your preferences?

At the core of self-awareness is self-focus. The study of self-awareness is believed to have been pioneered by Shelley Duval and Robert Wicklund in 1972 when they proposed the self-awareness theory. They proposed that focusing on oneself as opposed to one's environment would enable people to compare themselves with their own internal standards. These standards will become the benchmark with which individual thoughts, feelings, and actions are judged. The disparity in a person's character and internal standard leads to dissatisfaction in oneself. This dissatisfaction will, in turn, make that person constantly seek self-improvement or behavioral change in a bid to match his internal standards. Self-awareness is considered one of the most important tools for self-control.

Second Element of Emotional Intelligence: Self-regulation

Self-regulation is the ability to positively regulate emotional reactions and manage impulses as they come in order to produce desired results. In other words, it is the ability to decide which response is best suited for an experience and to react accordingly.

It involves managing emotions, thoughts and actions, and controlling expression. Developing self-regulation skills involves self-awareness. It also involves stress-management and sound emotional judgment.

Self-regulation is like adding salt to food. You can only add enough for the amount and type of food. You cannot add an equal amount of salt to a plate of rice as you would five plates of rice. One plate will either be too salty or too bland. Self-regulation is like that. You cannot respond to every situation with the same emotional intensity. You either will be overreacting or under-reacting most of the time, and that will make life a lot more difficult to live: too salty or too bland.

Self-regulation is usually influenced by a person's temperament, experiences, ability to stay focused and manage distractions, awareness of self, values, empathy, etc.

According to Roy Baumeister, self-regulation is a mental activity fuelled by limited mental energy. When there is little mental energy for mental activities to draw from, it becomes difficult to self-regulate; this, he called, "the state of ego depletion".

Usually, a state of ego depletion will be followed by outbursts or mental breakdowns. An event or task that requires a lot of self-regulation can deplete mental energy and make it difficult to self-regulate during subsequent tasks. Also, a quick succession of events that are mentally draining will add up and deplete mental energy.

Third Element of Emotional Intelligence: Motivation

Murray Johanssen defined motivation as "the effort, the drive, the desire, and the energy a person uses to activate and maintain goal-driven behavior." In simple terms, motivations are why we do what we do, the reason for any behavior. They are the internal force that sets us on a path and keeps us on it. Motivation is always fueled by something or geared towards something: a desire or a kind of reward.

Types of Motivation

There are two types of motivation: intrinsic motivation and extrinsic motivation.

Intrinsic Motivation

Intrinsic motivation occurs when factors stimulating motivation in an individual are internal. This type of motivation is fuelled by an individual's belief system or satisfaction.

Intrinsic motivation could be a desire to be accepted by the people around us, knowledge, respect for authority, religious or anti-religious beliefs, moral gratification, and so on.

When you say, "I am just doing it for the fun if it", that is intrinsic motivation.

Extrinsic Motivation

Extrinsic motivation occurs when factors stimulating motivation in an individual are external. These motivation stimulating factors are external rewards separate from the activity done. For example, if you take on a job because you want more money, the job and the money are separate and the motivation is the money which is an external factor.

Some external factors that stimulate this kind of motivation include money, instructions from a difficult superior, organized activities, bonuses, trophies, fame, and so on.

Some believe that there is a third type of motivation, which is not so much a type of motivation but the lack of it. This is called 'amotivation'. Someone in a state of amotivation will display negligible or no traits of intrinsic or extrinsic motivation.

A person can have multiple sources of motivation which can spread across the two types. For example, if you decide to change jobs because you believe you may find another job fun and exciting, you are intrinsically motivated. Your intrinsic motivation may be backed by the extrinsic motivation to make more money.

Maslow Motivation Theory

The Maslow motivation theory is not the only theory of motivation, but it is the most influential and thus it is what worth a mention. It may also help you understand how your needs affect your emotional intelligence.

In the 1940s, Abraham Maslow, the renowned psychologist developed his theory of individual development and motivation. In his theory, he suggested that human beings have a hierarchy of needs which range from basic needs at the bottom of the hierarchy to more complex needs at the top. According to Maslow, human beings are wired to take actions to address their basic needs before seeking to address more complex needs.

At the bottom of Maslow's hierarchy of need is man's most basic need, the "physiological need" which includes food, water, and shelter.

Following man's physiological need is "safety", that is security.

That is followed by man's need for "love/belonging", that is, his need for intimate relationships.

Man's need for love is followed by his need for "esteem", this is a feeling of accomplishment.

Man's need for "esteem" is followed by his most complex need which is his need for "self-actualization", that is, achieving his full potential.

26

How the Hierarchy of Need Affects Motivation.

Man's needs are his motivator. He is first motivated to meet his basic needs. As those needs are met, they stop motivating him and his next needs on the hierarchy become his new motivator. Only needs that are yet to be met motivate people and man has the innate desire to meet all his needs by following this hierarchical order of needs.

Fourth Element of Emotional Intelligence: Empathy

Empathy is the capacity to understand someone else's experiences and to share their feelings. In simpler terms, it means putting oneself in another's shoes.

Unlike self-awareness, empathy is not focused on self, rather on the experiences of others while feeling the effect of that experience. Empathy does not mean one has to go through the experience of another person to understand how it feels, although empathy is sometimes associated with memories of similar past experiences.

Types of Empathy

Emotional Empathy

Cognitive Empathy

Compassionate Empathy

Emotional Empathy

Emotional empathy also called "affective empathy", occurs when the emotional state of others triggers a corresponding and appropriate emotional response in a person.

Daniel Goldman, in describing emotional empathy says it is "when you feel physically along with the other person, as though their emotions were contagious."

Cognitive Empathy

Cognitive empathy is understanding and seeing from the perspectives of others. Daniel Goleman describes it as "knowing how the other person feels and what they might be thinking. Sometimes called perspective-taking."

This type of empathy is intellectual. Cognitive empathy understands feelings on an intellectual level, not an emotional level. A person with cognitive empathy may know why other people are supposed to feel a certain way, such as why it is understandable that an old hard working businessman who lost his life savings is sad. Without emotional empathy, he wouldn't be able to share in the emotions of the businessman. When the businessman cries, he understands his tears but he doesn't feel the same emotion. What he feels is an intellectual connection to the businessman's pain, not an emotional one, which may make him seem detached.

Compassionate Empathy

Daniel Goleman identifies it using the term "empathetic concern". In describing this type of empathy, Daniel Goldman states that "with this kind of empathy we not only understand a person's predicament and feel with them but are spontaneously moved to help, if needed."

An individual with compassionate empathy goes beyond feeling the pains of others or understanding their experiences, he is also moved to take action when needed.

Social Skills

Social skills are specific skills that foster interpersonal relations. They are simply skills that help an individual relate adequately with others. Social skills are important tools and are useful skills in meeting new people, maintaining relationships, communicating effectively, getting needs met, interacting with different personality types and getting along in a community.

Some social skills include speaking clearly, giving constructive criticism, asking clear and direct questions, taking criticism, having a healthy sense of humor, managing disagreements, being helpful, speaking with an appropriate tone of voice, asking for help, asking permission, apologizing when wrong, taking "no" for an answer, speaking kindly, waiting in turn, conversational skills, listening, conflict management, teamwork, persuasion and influencing skills, etc.

Chapter 3: How Does EQ Differ From IQ?

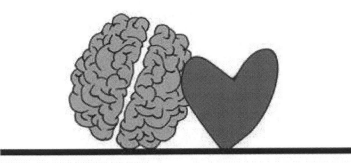

While EQ refers to a person's capacity to recognize, interpret and regulate emotions, IQ, which stands for intelligence quotient, are derivative scores aimed at determining how intelligent a person is. There are numerous standardized tests used in determining a person's IQ. IQ tests have helped in identifying individuals who are mentally challenged or those who are intellectual geniuses.

It was a once common belief that a high intelligence quotient was highly important to succeed in life and work. A growing body of research has proven that Emotional Quotient is more important in determining a person's success. In fact, it is 4 times more important than intelligence quotient. Studies show that successful life and work depends on 80% EQ and 20% IQ. This is very believable as interpersonal relations are a major driver in success.

Average IQ scores have improved by 25% while EQ scores have dropped by 25%. This will not necessarily result in an increase in the number of successful people in life and in career. It also will not necessarily result in an increase in the number of happy people. In fact, individuals with high EQ are more likely to be happier.

IQ does not guarantee success. Success is a product of a combination of several skills and competencies which are subsets of emotional intelligence as well as IQ. IQ is most effective when backed up by emotional intelligence just as emotional intelligence is most effective in achieving life goals when backed up by IQ. IQ on its own is considered by some psychologists as too narrow to encompass the vastness of intelligence.

Psychologist Howard Gardner stated that intelligence isn't a general all-encompassing ability, but rather there are varying intelligences, several of which an individual may have strengths in.

While IQ tells how intelligent a person is or can be, EQ tells us how well a person can understand his emotions and those of others. IQ may be an indicator of how well a person will perform academically, but EQ will indicate how well a person will manage relationships and lead other people since high EQ is not attainable without substantial levels of self-awareness, self-regulation, motivation, empathy and social skills.

An individual with high IQ may have the knowledge and cognitive skills necessary to finish a task but if he cannot interact with others in his work environment or if he cannot work in a team, he may find it difficult to climb up the career ladder fast enough. Also, a high IQ can be useless if emotions cannot be regulated. For example, an individual who needs to urgently solve a life-threatening problem may not be able to do so if he cannot manage his anxiety and stay calm, even if he has the necessary skills. While IQ is important, EQ will boost performance. In fact, many companies now conduct emotional intelligence tests during their recruitment process as well as organize emotional intelligence training for their staff.

Snarey and Vaillant in 1985, suggested that IQ wasn't much more a determinant of how successful an individual will become than his ability to manage his emotions and interact adequately with other people.

There have been renewed discussions on which is better: EQ or IQ. Those who speak for IQ seem to downplay the importance of emotional intelligence.

It has been said that it is risky to be emotionally competent, using Hitler as an example of someone who used emotional intelligence to manipulate his followers.

Psychologist Scott Geller, an expert in self-motivation, lists three questions that can be used to determine how self-motivated someone is:

Can you do it?

Will it work?

Is it worth it?

Answering all three questions in the affirmative is a good sign that a person is self-motivated.

According to Scott Keller, an individual needs to need to sincerely want the consequences of the action they take in order to be self-motivated and not just take an action only to avoid negative consequences.

Competence is vital in self-motivation as a competent individual will likely feel more motivated than someone who does not think he has the ability to complete the task. Answering all three questions above in the affirmative boosts the feeling of competence.

Being able to make autonomous decisions encourages self-motivation.

Also, having the support of people around you gives you a feeling that you can do what you want, that it will work, and that it is worth it.

Scott Geller based a substantial part of his research on Albert Bandura's work. Albert Bandura in 1981 said, "Self-motivation... requires personal standards against which to evaluate ongoing performance. By making self-satisfaction conditional on a certain level of performance, individuals create self-inducements to persist in their efforts until their performances match internal standards. Both the anticipated satisfactions for matching attainments and the dissatisfactions with insufficient ones provide incentives for self-directed actions" (Bandura & Schunk, 1981).

Cognition and emotion work hand in hand and cannot perform at their best without each other. We cannot make use of IQ to its fullest capacity if emotional intelligence is not available to help us understand people and emotions. We also cannot make adequate use of emotional intelligence if IQ is not available to help us make cognitive analysis and rational observation.

Emotions are natural and inborn; the ability to recognize and regulate emotions is learned and can be improved over time. EQ is made up of a collection of elements that deal directly with human emotions which can be better controlled by practice and learning. IQ, on the other hand, is inborn.

Although there are arguments for emotional intelligence as a more important element for success, IQ is still considered important, especially in academic achievement. An individual with a high IQ will often perform better in academics than an individual with a low IQ.

Chapter 4: Importance of Emotional Intelligence

Emotional Intelligence and Mental health

Emotional intelligence and mental health are directly linked. Studies show that mental disorders are associated with low emotional intelligence.

An individual in a state of depression finds it difficult to feel positive emotions. He is in a prolonged state of immense sadness or fear. Further studies have shown that patients being treated for depression have lower emotional intelligence scores. They find it difficult to recognize emotions and give adequate emotional responses. The study showed that depressed patients can't adequately discern changing emotional expressions. This is due to their difficulty in accepting positive emotions. As a result, they are likely to have a negative perception of even positive experiences. A depressed individual would likely be the only one on a team who thinks there's no reason to celebrate a remarkable achievement.

The study also showed that depressed patients tend to display less capacity in using emotions to facilitate thought.

According to Astrid Schütz and Sophia Nizielski, "Perso
depression are not generally worse at perceiving emotions; th
seem to be overly sensitive to positive ones. They may not have
deficits, but suffer from difficulties in managing negative emotions

Generally, a low level of competence in regulating and understanding
emotions is common among patients with a mental disorder.

It can be argued that all mental illnesses occur as a result of certain
emotional deficiencies as several symptoms of mental illness are
associated with emotional deficiency.

A study conducted by Astrid and Sophia aimed at deciding the emotional
competencies of patients with mental disorders namely: depressive
disorder, substance abuse disorder, and borderline personality disorder.
The results of their work showed that emotional problems were apparent
in all these patients.

Their study also involved a separate group of 94 individuals who had
never been diagnosed or treated for mental disorders. The three
categories of patients included 31 patients with unipolar depression, 19
patients with borderline personality disorder, and 35 patients with
substance abuse disorder. All individuals completed the German version
of the Mayer-Salovey-Caruso Emotional Intelligence test.

Test results showed that patients with unipolar depression performed
worse than individuals not diagnosed with depression. They showed less
competence in understanding emotions. These patients had difficulty in
identifying and separating varying emotions and, in turn, difficulty in
regulating them.

In patients with borderline personality disorder, the major symptom
found was systemic dysregulation. Mood swings, relationship instability,
self-destructive tendencies, and impulsiveness were common to patients
with this disorder.

They also displayed high sensitivity to negative emotions and positive
emotions. The tests proved patients with this disorder are competent in
detecting even subtle emotional expressions. According to Astrid and
Sophia, memory, learning and impulse control are impaired by
prolonged abuse of psychoactive substances such as cannabis, nicotine,
or alcohol.

Mental patients had remarkably low competence levels in certain aspects
of emotional intelligence such as understanding emotional information,
regulating emotions and using emotions to facilitate thought. Patients in
this group showed the lowest levels of emotional stability and all-around
emotional intelligence.

Generally, deficiency in emotional intelligence is linked to mental illness. Patients diagnosed with mental illness will experience improved conditions if they can improve on specific aspects of their emotional intelligence. This also means that a high level of emotional intelligence will help individuals guard against certain mental illnesses.

Self-management

Achieving our dreams can be a daunting task. It takes a lot of determination, sacrifice, self-development, relationship management, and other competencies that are required to navigate life. But self-management is important as it helps you make decisions about your behavior and regulate them as needed in order to achieve your goals.

The Effect of Self-confidence on Emotional Intelligence

Self-confidence is evident in an individual who has a positive attitude towards himself.

Self-confidence is a balanced attitude towards oneself in relation to his environment. The basic foundation of self-confidence is the belief an individual has that he can do any physiological or mental task needed to get the desired results.

A person with self-confidence is more likely to take on challenging tasks and complete them than someone who is not self-confident.

Self-confidence should not be confused with arrogance. While arrogance is sometimes called a kind of self-confidence or over-confidence, it is in reality, a display of certain deficits in emotional intelligence.

Arrogance stems from a feeling of superiority and entitlement. An arrogant individual displays superiority in an overbearing manner and can often be irritable. Arrogance is often accompanied by a desire to be admired and revered which makes the arrogant individual constantly trying to display superiority and importance. Individuals who are arrogant usually do not consider how their actions affect others. They do not perform well in interpersonal relationships as they tend to trigger negative emotions in other people.

Certain characteristics such as trying to force their perceptions on others (sometimes their perception of themselves), difficulty in apologizing, and difficulty in admitting a wrong are common to individuals who are arrogant.

One could argue that arrogance is an overdose of self-confidence stripped of self-regulation and empathy. An arrogant individual needs to learn and practice self-regulation and empathy to improve his overall emotional intelligence.

As opposed to a self-confident individual with high emotional intelligence who empathizes with people, understanding that people don't meet up to certain levels of success for varying reasons, while an arrogant individual sometimes claims superiority because he believes everyone who has not attained his level of success is simply inferior. This individual takes immense pride in his accomplishments and is constantly weighing his self-worth based on the accomplishments of others. When others have greater accomplishments than he does, it triggers prolonged negative emotions.

Arrogance is not always a product of confidence. It is sometimes the opposite. In some cases, arrogance is used as a mechanism to cover up insecurities and feelings of inferiority. As opposed to the expressions of confidence this individual may display, he generally has negative emotions about himself and displays physiological actions that he believes match the level of confidence he should have.

Low Self-confidence

Low self-confidence is often associated with a negative perception of oneself. Anxiety is a common emotion that dominates the feelings of an individual with low self-confidence. Low self-confidence, similarly to confidence, affects a person's physiological expressions. It can often be perceived in a person's voice or body language. Low self-confidence hampers a person's success as it is often associated with a deficiency in motivation. This means an individual with low self-confidence doesn't believe he is qualified to take on important tasks or to get the desired results. Such individuals have the tendency to be laid-back. This makes it difficult for them to reach their potential as they may constantly pass on tasks other self-confident individuals consider opportunities.

Individuals with low self-confidence are often not as efficient as individuals with healthy self-confidence even when they are more skilled.

Self-confidence inspires confidence in others. Individuals that are self-confident often make great leaders if they perform well in other areas of emotional intelligence. Self-confidence is usually perceived very quickly, even before a person speaks.

Aspects of Emotional Intelligence Displayed by Self-confident People

- Social skill: A self-confident individual interacts more confidently with other people. He is not constantly thinking about how he is perceived such that he cannot interact freely.

- Self-awareness: Being self-aware is a common trait of self-confident people. They know their thoughts and expressions.

- Self-regulation: Self-confident people are often good regulators of their emotions who know how to keep negative emotions at bay.

- Motivation: Self-confident people believe in themselves. They believe they have the necessary competence to achieve their goals. This enables them to see a task to completion.

Emotional Intelligence and Emotional Resilience

Emotional resilience is the capacity to adapt emotions to varying situations and manage stress while sustaining mental actions that give the desired results. Emotionally resilient people are great stress managers and are more likely to finish a mentally demanding task without breaking down. One element of emotional intelligence closely associated with emotional resilience is "self-regulation".

Living in the world with all its complexities can be physically tiring and mentally draining. Life itself seems a daunting task. Coping with the stress of work, the peculiarities of relationships and other complexities demands a lot of mental energy. How each individual reacts to these mental stressors is largely dependent on emotional intelligence. Emotional intelligence has a direct influence on motivation.

When an individual's capacity to self-regulate becomes impaired, he starts to experience a breakdown and gives in to the stress. At this point, the individual starts to become less productive and more irritable. The mental energy which fuels the mental task of self-regulation is depleted and he starts to lose hold of his emotions. He is more likely at this stage to make errors and make incorrect decisions. This is the state of ego depletion. Remaining in this state for a long time may be a sign of an inherent mental illness. To more effectively handle stress, it is important to build an aspect of emotional intelligence called emotional resilience.

36

Building better emotional resilience should be aimed at mastering techniques that help an individual avoid being affected by pressure, rather than how to recover from pressure when affected.

In building emotional resilience, there are a series of proven methods which help prevent tension and avoid a breakdown. Knowing which actions to take will reduce the likelihood of being pathologically affected by pressure.

It is not a quality that is either had or not. It is inherent in everyone but in varying degrees. Here are some characteristics that individuals with good levels of emotional resilience possess.

- Perseverance: Emotionally resilient people often stick to their objectives without giving up on their course. They do not abandon tasks due to pressure; rather, they see it to the end.

- Emotional-awareness: Emotionally aware individuals understand their emotions which helps in regulate them per-time. Emotional awareness is important as resilience is highly hinged on emotional-regulation.

- Emotional-regulation: The capacity to adequately regulate emotions in response to pressure is basically what emotional resilience is about. This competence helps an individual adequately determine his emotional reactions. Individuals with this trait have a sense of control and they understand that they are the ones who determine how life affects them.

- Motivation: This major element of emotional intelligence is a key trait common to emotionally resilient people. If you can manage your emotions adequately, you will be able to stay motivated as you have control over stressors that can influence your motivation. An emotionally resilient person is optimistic, thereby motivated.

Chapter 5: Emotional Intelligence and Leadership (Developing Important Emotional Skills)

Leadership and Self-awareness

Self-aware leaders can recognize their own emotions. They know how their actions and inactions affect other people. Self-awareness in leadership is cogent as it enables you to understand yourself and how events affect you. This is highly important for self-regulation which will aid decision making and stress management.

Self-awareness gives a leader an understanding of his strengths and weaknesses. This helps him gauge his limits and monitor his reactions during his highs and lows.

Self-awareness is also important for self-confidence which is an aspect of emotional intelligence needed in leadership.

Empathy

Being able to inspire faith and confidence in those who follow you is important in leadership. As a leader, you cannot efficiently inspire those who follow you if you do not share their feelings and understand them. People connect more easily with a person that understands their feelings and shows consideration.

As an empathetic leader, you care about what your team members are going through. You feel and understand their pain. Your feedback is constructive. Being compassionately empathetic, you help them cross individual hurdles, helping them develop into more skilled and emotionally developed individuals. This earns you their respect and loyalty.

Ways to Improve Empathy

Wear The Shoes of Others: It can be confusing when people display certain emotions we do not understand. We just cannot see why a person has broken down in tears or why they are sad. It is understandable. We did not experience what triggered their pain. But taking the time to think about their situation and how you would feel if you were in it is a good place to start in understanding their emotions.

Pay Attention To Non-verbal Cues: Also called 'body language', non-verbal cues are strong indicators of what people are feeling. In fact, studies have shown that humans communicate more nonverbally than verbally, even when they are actually speaking.

Non-verbal communication involves body language and tone of voice. While verbal communication communicates actual words, body language and tone of voice can help put those words into an emotional context.

Paying attention to non-verbal cues can help a person perceive and feel the emotions of others. It can help you as a leader to perceive what your team members really feel about an issue. You can tell when there is apprehension or when motivation is low. You can use this emotional information to facilitate adequate reactions.

Respond: People often feel better when someone else shares their emotions. It is always good to know someone understands how you feel. The best way to show that you understand how a person feels is by responding to the emotional cues he sends. Give verbal and non-verbal responses such as nodding when they speak or mirroring their emotional expression. Saying the right words is also a great way to respond to emotions. As a leader, doing this tells your team members that you are understanding and considerate. It makes you the kind of leader they want leading them.

Developing Social Skills

Social skills are important for effective communication. Communication is important in leadership as leaders need to communicate instructions, aims, and objectives as clearly as possible. Inadequate communication leaves team members confused or at worst, ill-informed. An ill-informed member of a team can cause substantial setbacks.

Social skills also help you as a leader to connect with members of your team individually and collectively. This skill is also important in conflict avoidance and resolution which are traits highly needed in good leadership.

Tips for Developing Good Social Skills

- Don't Run From Conflict, Manage It: Conflicts are inevitable in life. As long as there is more than one person in a space over a substantial period of time, conflict is bound to occur. A leader must know how to manage conflicts when they arise within his team and how to manage them until they are resolved. Conflicts are not always bad as when adequately managed, they can open doors to new possibilities and a better understanding of individuals. Conflict management and resolution is an important social skill.

- Learn to Communicate Better: Communication is regarded by most as the most important social skill. As a leader, you should learn to communicate your emotions and thoughts effectively through verbal and non-verbal expressions. Self-awareness is important here as it helps you recognize and understand the emotions you want to communicate.

- Praise People: A person deficient in social skills, self-regulation, and empathy will find it difficult to praise people. Doing this develops the aforementioned aspects of emotional intelligence. When you praise people, it builds their self-confidence and encourages them to warm up to you. Noticing good things about people is a good indicator that you care about them. No one loves to hang out with someone who is self-absorbed.

Self-regulation

Self-regulation, the capacity to regulate one's emotions and expressions, is a key trait important in effective leadership. Leaders competent in self-regulation and are often in control of their actions and emotions which keeps them level headed during high-stress tasks. Self-regulation coupled with empathy and social skills will make you into a leader that not only is a master at managing pressure, but also is adept at helping others manage pressure and self-regulate.

Leaders that self-regulate and are socially skillful are often able to stay on course, staying true to their values and objectives, while carrying everyone along.

Emotional Intelligence and Motivation

Motivation is important for leaders to be able to keep striving for the collective goal. It is the leader's job to bring his team to reach a goal. Sometimes, the entire team will feel unmotivated, this could be due to a major setback or multiple failed attempts at getting something done. A leader's competence in this area of emotional intelligence will suffice at times like this. Motivation with self-regulation, empathy and social skills can uplift low-spirited members of a team.

It is very important that a leader is self-motivated if he wishes to effectively motivate a group of people.

Ways to Improve Motivation

- Go Over the 'why' Once Again: Why are you doing what you are doing? Why did you take on the task? Why did you join the team? Why did you want the job? Going over why you wished to do something can help you remember the emotional state in which you were motivated to start what you are doing. This is why it is important to write your goals in such a way that reading it can energize you and keep you motivated.

- Access Your Motivation Level: Keep constant tabs on your level of motivation. Do not wait till your motivation level finds rest on the seabed before you seek ways to raise it from the dead. Constantly weigh your motivation. Are you as excited about working on the task today as you were yesterday? Do you still find the same amount of happiness engaging in the task as before? Do you still have a goal in mind?

- o Keep constant tabs so that when your motivation weakens, you can take appropriate actions to rejuvenate it before it gets too bad. This is another instance where competence in self-awareness and self-regulation skills comes in handy.

- Find the Good in the Bad: The difference between a person who has a generally good outlook on life and a person who does not is that while the person with a good outlook will often find something good in every situation, the other person is always focusing on everything bad about almost every situation they find themselves in. This does not mean the first person does not know that a situation is bad, it only means that he does not focus on the negative. Rather, he finds something positive about the situation to hold on to. He likely thinks, "This may be something small and unremarkable, but it is a good thing that has been birthed by this unpleasant situation."

  - o Finding something good about every situation will keep a leader positive and energized, reducing the likelihood of demotivation caused by emotional stress.

Experts in the field of behavioral psychology have formulated 3 major rules for understanding the motivation of a person. Though these rules might not be all-encompassing, they paint a clear picture of a person's self-motivation. The rules are in the mold of 3 questions asked below.

Can you do it?

Will it work?

Is it worth it?

A positive answer to these questions is a reasonable affirmation of a high level of self-motivation in any person.

Scott Keller postulated that to check the motivation of a person regarding any pursuit, such a person must have a positive feeling about the consequences of the action that's about to be taken. Thus, the motivation cannot be the avoidance of possible negative consequences that could result from taking the action.

Competence is key in assessing self-motivation as a competent individual would most likely feel confident about the likelihood of success in the task he is about to undertake. Providing positive answers to the questions above can also boost competence which has a positive effect on self-motivation.

Being able to make autonomous decisions encourages self-motivation.

Also, having the support of people around you gives you a feeling that you can do the task, that it will work, and that it is worth it.

Self-motivation stems from an internal standard of how things should be. When a person believes in a state of affairs so strongly that he can make decisions to pursue it, such a person would be self-motivated. Sometimes people find motivation in the circumstances of their birth or family background. Whatever the reason for the motivation, this strength is what propels a person to act. You might believe that a state of affairs should be present in your immediate environment but where such a belief is lacking in depth it might not spur you to act.

Chapter 6: Labeling Emotions

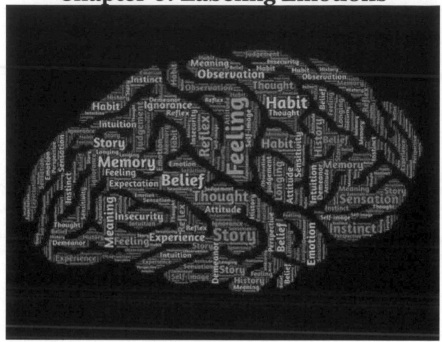

In building emotional intelligence, it is expedient that we develop competence in understanding emotions and labeling them appropriately. Being able to distinctly describe how we feel enables us to analyze our emotions more adequately. By making use of this information, we're able to regulate our emotions better.

The number of emotions that exist is so large that they can get confusing to distinguish. What makes it even more confusing are the similarities between several emotions. This makes recognizing and labeling emotions not nearly as easy as identifying our favorite celebrities. However, like identifying our favorite celebrities, we learn to identify emotions by learning what they look like and knowing what to call them. Understanding how you feel is only difficult if you have not developed the competence to do so. This competence can't be built without developing the right vocabulary.

One word and two-word descriptions like 'good', 'bad', 'awful', 'okay', 'alright' and so on, do not adequately label any emotions.

Developing competence in labeling emotions starts with a simple practice. Pay attention to how you feel and name it. What you call it must be distinctive enough to distinguish it from other emotions. Sad, angry, happy, regretful, afraid and so on, are distinctive labels that bring the memory of specific emotions to mind. They are unlike labels such as alright, awful, good, bad and so on. Each of these labels brings several feelings to mind. For example, you feel bad when you are sad. You also feel bad when you are rejected. Those two words: 'sad' and 'rejected', would have been more accurate labels.

The list below contains over 440 emotions and what they mean. You can always come back to this list to build your emotional vocabulary.

Absorbed - to be keenly interested in something.

Abhorrence - a feeling of disgust.

Acceptance - accepting the reality of a situation without seeking to change it.

Admiration - a feeling of respect and approval.

Adoration - to respect, rever, and admire.

Adrift - feeling lost or without cause.

Aching - a feeling of intense sorrow or desire.

Affection - a pleasant feeling of fondness or liking.

Afraid - a feeling of fear or apprehension.

Agitated - a feeling of worry or anxiety.

Agony - a severe feeling of physical or mental pain.

Aggravated - a feeling of annoyance or irritation.

Alarm - a feeling of fear caused by a sudden threat.

Alert - a feeling of readiness to deal with potent danger.

Alienated - a feeling of isolation.

Alive - the feeling of experiencing something while emotionally attached to it or to someone.

Alone - being without anyone.

Amazed - a feeling of pleasant surprise.

Amused - a feeling of entertainment or fun.

Anger - a feeling of annoyance.

Angst - a strong feeling of anguish about life.

Animated - the feeling of excitement which could be accompanied by dramatic expressions.

Animosity - a strong feeling of dislike and antagonism.

Animus - feeling of enmity.

Annoyed - feeling of displeasure, upset.

Antagonistic - a strong feeling of opposition.

Anticipation - a feeling of expectation.

Antipathy - a deep-seated feeling of distaste.

Antsy - a feeling of impatience, restlessness, and agitation.

Anxiety - a feeling of excessive worry or fear.

Apathetic - a feeling characterized by lack of concern and display of detachment.

Apologetic - a feeling of regretful acknowledgment of a wrong.

Appalled - feeling dismayed.

Appreciative - feeling gratitude or pleasure.

Apprehensive - feeling anxious about the future.

Ardor - great enthusiasm.

Arousal - feeling aroused, evoked, or awakened.

Astonishment - a feeling of great surprise.

Astounded - a feeling of shock.

Attachment - a feeling of fondness.

Attraction - a feeling of interest.

Aversion - a feeling of distaste towards something and a desire to avoid it.

Awe - a feeling of astonishment.

Awkward - feeling so embarrassed that you do not know how to react.

Baffled - surprise accompanied by an inability to understand or explain.

Bashful - feeling shy or timid, avoiding attention.

Befuddled - feeling confused and unable to think clearly.

Bemused - feeling confused or bewildered.

Betrayed - feeling pain because someone was disloyal to you.

Bewildered - deeply confused or perplexed.

Bitter - feeling deep anger or resentment.

Blessed - feeling gratitude for a privilege.

Bliss - feeling great happiness and contentment.

Blithe - a feeling of merriment or gladness.

Blue - a feeling of sadness.

Bold - feeling courageous and daring.

Bonhomie - a feeling of friendliness and excitement.

Boredom - a feeling of restlessness due to disinterest in one's surrounding.

Bothered - feeling concern about something.

Bouncy - very lively.

Brave - feeling the courage to deal with a threat and being ready to bear the pain.

Breathless - feeling utter amazement.

Brooding - showing deep concern about something.

Bubbly - feeling cheerful and in high spirits.

Buoyant - feeling cheerful and lively.

Burning - feeling extreme anger or hurt.

Calm - feeling relaxed or relieved.

Captivated - a feeling of deep interest.

Carefree - void of anxiety, worry, and responsibility.

Caring - a feeling of kindness and concern.

Cautious - feeling there's a need to be alert.

Certain - feeling deep assurance.

Chagrin - feeling upset due to failure or embarrassment.

Challenged - feeling that a particular opposition or difficulty will make you better.

Chary - feeling reluctant to do something.

Cheerful - feeling happy and optimistic.

Choked - feeling tough restraint against expressing something.

Choleric - feeling irritable.

Clueless - having no knowledge or understanding of a thing.

Cocky - feeling conceited or arrogant.

Cold - feeling detached and unemotional.

Collected - feeling calm under pressure.

Comfortable - feeling eased or relaxed.

Commiseration - feeling sympathy for the grief of others.

Committed - feeling attached and loyal to a person or thing.

Compassionate - feeling sympathy and concern for others.

Complacent - feeling satisfied in a situation or in one's ability that makes a person unmotivated.

Complaisance - wanting to please others by compliance.

Composed - feeling in control of one's feelings and expressions.

Compunction - a feeling of guilt that precedes or follows doing something wrong.

Confused - bewildered.

Courage - being able to do something frightening.

Concerned - a feeling of worry about something.

Confident - feeling convinced of your ability or of an outcome.

Conflicted - feeling torn between two or more decisions.

Consternation - a feeling of dismay that causes confusion.

Contemplative - feeling unsure.

Contempt - disregard.

Contentment - a feeling of satisfaction.

Contrition - the feeling of remorse.

Cordial - being warm and friendly.

Cowardly - lack of courage to face danger.

Crafty - being indirect or deceitful.

Cranky - a feeling characterized by being irritable.

Craving - a deep longing for something or someone.

Crestfallen - feeling of shame and embarrassment.

Cross - a feeling of annoyance.

Cruel - wanting to deliberately cause pain and difficulty for others.

Crummy - feeling miserable and worthless.

Crushed - feeling characterized by overwhelming disappointment or embarrassment.

Curious - feeling eager to know something.

Cynical - believing everyone is dishonest.

Defeated - feeling overcome by difficulty.

Dejection - feeling sad or depressed.

Delectation - feeling pleasure and delight.

Delighted - feeling great pleasure.

Delirious - feeling mentally disturbed such that it is difficult to speak or to think coherently.

Denial - a feeling of refusal to accept reality.

Derisive - showing contempt.

Desire - a feeling of deep longing or want.

Desolation - feeling of utter loneliness.

Despair - feeling there is no hope.

Despondent - losing hope and courage.

Detached - feeling aloof.

Determined - a feeling of resolve.

Detestation - a deep feeling of dislike.

Devastated - a feeling of utter pain.

Devotion - the feeling of commitment.

Disappointed - feeling displeasure in an occurrence.

Disbelief - unable to believe something.

Disdain - the feeling of disrespect.

Disgruntled - dissatisfied.

Disgust - the feeling of irritation.

Disillusioned - disappointment.

Disinterested - not showing interest

Dismay - anxiety caused by an unexpected occurrence.

Distaste - a deep feeling of disinterest.

Distracted - finding it hard to concentrate.

Distress - severe anxiety or pain.

Disturbed - being emotionally upset.

Doubtful - feeling unsure.

Downcast - feeling discouraged.

Drained - feeling of severed mental tiredness.

Dread - the feeling of utter fear, often in anticipation of something.

Dubious - feeling hesitant or feeling doubt.

Dumbfounded - shocked and perplexed.

Eager - a feeling of enthusiasm.

Earnest - feeling sincere.

Ease - feeling relief.

Ebullient - cheerful and full of energy.

Ecstatic - overwhelming joy.

Edgy - tense and irritable.

Elated - intensely happy.

Embarrassed - feeling shame and discomfort.

Empathic - feeling the emotions of others.

Energetic - feeling happy, optimistic and motivated.

Engrossed - feeling deeply interested.

Enlightened - increased understanding.

Enmity - feeling of opposition.

Enthralled - fascinated.

Enthusiasm - strong feelings of enjoyment or approval.

Envy - feeling displeasure at someone else's achievement.

Euphoric - feeling intense excitement.

Exasperated - frustrated and irritated.

Excitement - strong feelings of enthusiasm and eagerness.

Excluded - a feeling of being left out.

Expectant - feeling of anticipation.

Fascinated - strongly attracted.

Fatigued - feeling mental exhaustion.

Feisty - feeling aggression or a feeling of being lively and determined.

Fervor - a passionate feeling.

Flabbergasted - intense surprise.

Fondness - the feeling of interest, attraction, and love.

Foolish - feeling unwise.

Foreboding - feeling that something bad will happen.

Fortunate - feeling privileged.

Frazzled - a feeling of complete exhaustion.

Free - feeling of freedom.

Frightened - afraid.

Frustrated - a feeling of distress due to one's inability to do something.

Fulfilled - a feeling of accomplishment.

Furious - a feeling of intense anger.

Giddy - feeling extremely excited to the point of disorientation.

Glad - happy.

Gleeful - a feeling of exuberant or triumphant joyfulness.

Gloomy - a feeling of depression.

Goofy - feeling of harmless eccentricity.

Gratified - a feeling of satisfactory

Grateful - a feeling of gratitude.

Greedy - selfishly wanting more than you need.

Grief - deep sorrow.

Grudging - the feeling of giving or allowing something reluctantly.

Guarded - feeling cautious about a situation.

Guilt - an intense feeling of regret.

Happy - pleasant excitement.

Harassed - feeling stressed due to having too many things asked of you.

Hatred - the feeling of utter displeasure and antagonism.

Heartache - a feeling of anguish or grief due to loss.

Heartbroken - significant distress and sadness.

Helpless - feeling unable to do anything about a situation.

Hesitant - feeling unsure and slow to do something.

Hollow - a feeling of being empty or emotionally vacant.

Homesick - an intense longing for one's home.

Hopeful - a feeling that one's desires will be met.

Horrified - feeling utter fear.

Hostile - displaying strong antagonism and dislike.

Humiliated - feeling utter shame.

Humored - a feeling that others are agreeing only to keep one content.

Hurt - the feeling of pain.

Hyper - feeling hyperactive.

Hysterical - unable to control raging emotions.

Impatient - restless eagerness.

Incensed - feeling intense anger.

Indifferent - feeling not particularly interested.

Indignant - annoyance towards unfairness.

Infatuated - feeling of intense passion.

Inferior - feeling less than a person or a thing.

Inspired - encouraged, motivated.

Interested - having an interest.

Intimacy - feeling of close familiarity.

Intimidated - nervous due to uneasiness in a situation.

Intoxicated - feeling of extreme excitement.

Intrigued - aroused interest.

Invigorated - feeling energized.

Ire - anger.

Irritated - annoyed.

Isolated - a feeling of loneliness.

Jaded - lacking enthusiasm after having had too much of something.

Jealous - feeling of resentment towards someone's achievement.

Jittery - a feeling of fear.

Joy - happiness.

Jubilant - triumphant excitement.

Keen - a feeling of eagerness.

Lazy - unwilling to work.

Left out - excluded.

Nasty - longing to behave in an unpleasant or spiteful way.

Needy - in need or often feeling that one requires something from others.

Nervous - a feeling of agitation.

Neutral - not in support of one over another.

Lethargic - sluggish.

Liberation - freedom.

Lighthearted - a feeling of being happy and carefree.

Liking - affectionate interest.

Listless - lacking enthusiasm.

Lively - cheerfulness and fun.

Lonely - a feeling that one is alone.

Longing - a desire for someone or something.

Love - strong feelings of deep affection and caring.

Lucky - feeling that a good thing happened to you by chance.

Lust - strong sexual desire.

Mad - rage, anger.

Meditative - involving deep thought about something.

Melancholic - depressed.

Merry - a feeling of cheerfulness.

Mischievous - intending to cause trouble.

Miserable - utterly unhappy.

Mortified - an intense feeling of embarrassment.

Motivated - a feeling that one has a reason to act.

Moved - stimulated or caused to change one's opinion or behavior.

Mystified - bewildered.

Nonplussed - being so surprised one doesn't know how to react.

Nostalgic - sentimental longing for experiences that happened in the past.

Obsessed - inability to shift one's mind away from something.

Offended - annoyance due to something said or done

Optimistic - feeling hopeful about the future.

Outrage - intense anger.

Overwhelmed - emotionally drowned.

Pacified - relieved from anger.

Pain - a feeling of intense distress.

Panic - a feeling of sudden overwhelming fear.

Paranoid - irrational fear that people want to harm you.

Passion - intense and usually uncontrollable feeling.

Pathetic - miserable.

Peaceful - a feeling of calmness and assurance that all is well.

Pensive - feeling sad while in deep thought.

Chapter 7: Emotional Intelligence in the Workplace

In today's highly commercialized society, there is increased complexity and competition. The workforce is the forefront of this movement and developing a substantial amount of emotional intelligence can help one navigate these complexities. Whether you are an employer or an employee, possessing a high EQ can place you on a pedestal and allow you to fine-tune your skills to meet the ever growing world standards.

Getting a job ultimately means you will be integrated into a sphere where others would have varying interests and ideologies compared to yours. Therefore, the question of balancing conflicting interests arises. Your needs will differ and standards of how things ought to be done will be subject to a lot of discrepancies.

In the previous chapters, we discussed the importance of emotional intelligence as it relates to our individuality. In this chapter, we will discuss how EQ plays out in the workplace and why the lack of it can lead to complications and clashes. There exists a hierarchy of positions in any workplace, the vicissitudes of fate combined with the sheer force of hard work and consistency decides whatever position one hopes to occupy.

The epicurean ideology maintains that one must always remain in a job that provides happiness and a sense of fulfillment. While this is true, there is also the stark reality that we cannot all find jobs that would massage our egos and stimulate sensations of pleasure at all times. It is not alien that we should seek happiness along with the oftentimes bleak journey of life. But above all, our existence rests snugly on the basis of usefulness before happiness.

Some jobs can suck. To be frank, most jobs SUCK. A recent Forbes article reported that over half of Americans do not like where they work. It could stem from having an over-demanding boss or getting a paycheck that doesn't correspond to the amount of work you put in. While there are jobs that are mentally and physically exhausting to the point of being toxic– a major reference to 'The Devil Wears Prada', there is also the element of 'self' in some situations.

To survive, and not merely survive, but to flourish in a work environment, you have to be willing to constantly evaluate yourself. That job that seems awful and horrid beyond description may have a positive side which you unconsciously ignore because you are stuck in a vicious cycle of negativity. The most common complaint arises from the issue of stress and increased workload.

Stress takes a toll on our emotions, and emotions, in turn, can make us prone to transferring our aggression onto others, and consequently, strain our relationships with friends and family. It all plays out like a domino effect, with the first card taking root in your mind, in your emotions and how you handle them. According to the CDC's National Institute on health and safety, 29 to 40 percent of Americans are "extremely stressed" at work.

Stress is common in many jobs and it is difficult, albeit not impossible, to find a low-stress job. Considering the adverse effects of stress such as depression, anxiety, hypertension, diabetes and increased risk of heart disease, it is important for one to identify stressors and how to deal with them. Establishing boundaries, organizing your workspace, developing multitasking skills and speaking to your supervisor, can help to reduce stress levels.

Feelings of dissatisfaction and stagnancy can also arise in the workplace. There is a pressing need to do more and be more, and our jobs may not always be sufficient to satiate our need for a sense of fulfillment. Quitting your job is a crucial decision to take, and one needs the right amount of emotional intelligence to weigh the benefits and risks involved in such a venture.

Holding a managerial or executive position also requires one to be highly skilled in employing EQ in all aspects of work. The decision-making process does not necessarily have to be the sole responsibility of the leader or CEO, as employees or the board of directors may provide valid suggestions. This does not dispel the fact that most decisions are to be made by the leader in certain circumstances. There will be situations where you make the wrong decision and that results in devastating consequences for the institution. Your ability to bounce back and create stability amidst the crisis is also a subset of emotional intelligence.

How do you know you are doing enough? What standards do you compare your level of growth to? Are you constantly comparing your output to that of your colleagues, or are you completely absorbed in your work with a singularity of purpose? EQ affects our level of productivity in no small way. To raise the bar and increase our standards, there should be a definition of what those standards are and a clear vision of the goal you wish to achieve. EQ is essential in helping you ditch the totem pole syndrome and increase your output in a healthy way.

The benefits of team performance in a work environment can never be overemphasized. Working in synergy allows for the exchange of ideas and division of labor, which ultimately leads to increased output with reduced stress to the individuals involved. As much as there are benefits to group work, there are also disadvantages. Not everyone is receptive to the idea of working in groups, as they tend to do better when working alone.

However, this may not always be possible as some jobs require you to work in groups. When this occurs, emotional intelligence is crucial to establishing good communication between team members. EQ would also enable you to balance the needs of your workers with yours. EQ is also necessary for developing good work ethics and principles around the workplace. There is security in establishing a concrete set of values and principles that will not be violated in the workplace. It is also essential in helping one think out of the box to provide solutions to problems that the institution may face. Strategies to boost and employ EQ will be provided in the next chapter.

It is important to develop EQ as it permeates every aspect of the work process, and the lack of it can result in dire consequences. Picture yourself walking down a bush path with many pits dug all over the road. Your eyes would be essential in helping you avoid those pitfalls and dangers. But imagine walking on that same road with blindfolds on, with only your intuition to guide you. You would be prone to falling into one of those pits, and you would walk without sureness and direction because of the fear and uncertainty that would envelop you at that moment.

Working with a high IQ represents your intuition in this analogy. But combining your IQ and your EQ (which serves as your eyes), would result in even more desirous results than you could think of. Working without EQ can increase stress levels enormously and stress leads to decreased productivity – except your gears tend to work better under pressure, but it isn't advisable to work that way constantly.

A lack of EQ would lead to a skewed decision-making process and an incorrect approach to leadership duties. A boss with a lack of empathy would invariably produce employees who work without their heart in it.

Without taking the emotions of your employees into consideration, the quality of output produced would be affected. The remedy to this situation is to create an environment where enthusiasm is harnessed and kept at its peak. An eager approach to work produces greater results than a dull, monotonous and robotic process devoid of life.

Possessing empathy also means that you show sensitivity to the plight of your subordinates or colleagues. This involves making them feel heard, understood and human. Many world leaders have a high EQ and this has helped them surmount the impossible, as they have developed an understanding of human nature. In other words, high EQ is an asset in today's corporate world.

A high EQ helps in periods of conflict. A clash of ideas is inevitable in any work setting. Individuals all have various world views and you are only bound by what the institution hopes to achieve. Staying calm and being the mediator in times of conflict proves that you have good managerial skills, and may increase your prospects of getting a promotion.

In work, you are also expected to retain your cool and professionalism even with mounting pressure. A low EQ is a liability in this case, as you would be inclined to react to pressure negatively. Feelings should be kept in check in situations like this which may seem difficult to achieve if one does not possess EQ.

Interpersonal tension in teamwork could also be a trigger for one to react in unsavory ways. If one is averse to the idea of teamwork, he/she may tend to take either of these two extremes. The first is to isolate oneself from the process and refuse to make contributions. The second is to obstinately maintain that his/her idea is superior to that of the other team members and that he/she should be the only one employed in the process. This stems from a low EQ and little to no understanding of how to work in synergy.

Having a low EQ disrupts communicative processes. Communication is key to ensuring the smooth functioning of any organization. Lack of communication skills, especially listening skills, can lead to misunderstandings and misconceptions about the idea that is to be communicated. To work collaboratively, understanding the next person is essential. Reacting to mistakes by yelling or displaying passive-aggressive behavior can be destructive to your work life and may even get you fired.

A low EQ makes one resistant and vehemently opposed to change. A key feature of high emotional intelligence is an ability to remain open-minded and to welcome change. The organization will often undergo massive change and upheaval that would directly or indirectly affect the employees. One's response to change should be welcoming. An objective approach should be taken to situations that seem foreign.

Criticisms are also a part of learning in any work environment. A high EQ would help one understand that criticisms are meant to help him/her improve and not to stir up a malicious situation. As a leader or supervisor, a high EQ helps one give constructive criticism without being overly judgmental or having a propensity to dish out scathing remarks. A lack of emotional intelligence makes one averse to admitting a wrong and apologizing. This is detrimental to the progress of any organization, as it triggers feelings of resentment and suppressed anger.

Another disadvantage of having a low emotional intelligence is that it makes one apportion blame to other members of the team, even when one is in the wrong. It is the consequence of refusing to acknowledge a wrong.

In summary, having people with a high EQ in any organization is an asset, and sadly, the reverse is the case when surrounded by individuals with low EQ whether in the workplace or at home. A high EQ predisposes one to better interpersonal relationships, and an ability to react positively to unfavorable situations. In any corporate institution, understanding the personality and emotions of your fellow team players is a necessary skill to ensure productivity and efficiency.

The next chapter will focus on strategies to employ in order to improve emotional intelligence at work. On the bright side, it is never too late to develop a high EQ. Callous behaviors, exploitation of others, blatant disregard for the feelings of others, manipulation and arrogance, aren't the right characteristics of a leader. These may even indicate he/she is suffering from a repressed case of antisocial personality disorder (sociopathy), which can be extremely toxic to employees and subordinates.

Emotional intelligence, as previously mentioned, serves as our gateway to understanding how the 'software' of people around us operates. Getting a job propels you to establish a relationship with others. Therefore, it is imperative that we inculcate habits and principles to ensure that the relationship achieves the common goal for which it was created. □

Chapter 8: Strategies to Boost EQ in Our Jobs

Developing emotional intelligence like any other venture requires consistency and commitment. It may be slow and difficult at first, especially in areas where you need to employ self-regulation and restraint. But, it is not impossible and the outcomes of making this decision can improve all aspects of your life. Listed below are major strategies to employ in order to improve your level of emotional intelligence in the workplace.

- Develop communication and social skills

- Improve empathy

- Be receptive to feedback

- Identify your stressors and manage them outside work

- Maintain your enthusiasm

- Constantly evaluate your motives and approach to situations

- Develop self-awareness

Develop Communication and Social Skills

Communicative skills are important in the work environment, as it reduces tension, boosts interpersonal relationships, and creates an avenue for growth. As an employer, your subordinates should be able to approach you without fear or apprehension. Develop a welcoming attitude as this fosters communication. The next big idea that could determine the growth of the company to a large extent can come from an employee.

An important aspect of communication is the ability to listen without interference. An ability to receive the contributions of others without forcefully projecting your idea on them. Listening can bridge gaps and initiate understanding between team members. Emotional intelligence involves the ability to sit back, listen and then evaluate the information received on a screen of truth– the ability to discern. This quality would also ensure that you are level headed when faced with a critical decision. Listening, communicating and exchanging ideas also reinforce one with a lot of options, in the absence of one.

The art of persuasion is embedded in social skills. It is fundamental in many social situations such as conflict. Remaining calm and collected when conflict arises, avoiding office politics and drama, and providing solutions to problems can establish you as one who is well versed in human relations– which is proof of EQ. Understanding the art of persuasion can help in proposing ideas to your senior colleagues, as well as trying to win your teammates over to your side without being condescending.

Improve Empathy

As already established, a key feature of EQ is an ability to empathize. Empathy is basically the ability to understand the feelings and emotions of others. It means trying to mentally place yourself into someone else's situation. Empathy also involves listening to another person's point of view. It is easy to get absorbed in our work, without paying attention to our colleagues.

Being empathetic enables us to relate to the struggles of others and this initiates the feeling of being understood in the other party. When your colleagues feel a sense of security that stems from your understanding, they are motivated to overcome the situation more quickly than when they are left to shoulder the responsibility of recovery alone. In listening, we unlock an element of companionship and togetherness, which ultimately fosters teamwork.

As a supervisor or a leader in any capability, sharing personal experiences of your setbacks and how you overcame them can go a long way in reinforcing the spirit of trust in your employees, colleagues or subordinates. In sharing experiences, you attain the image of a team player and not just a boss whom they must tremble before. Empathy may be difficult to develop at first if you aren't naturally an empath. It may seem awkward trying to gauge your level of support and becoming invested in the lives of your employees. In the long run, the advantages always outweigh the disadvantages as a compassionate environment is an incentive to work hard.

As an employee, being empathetic to the plight of your colleagues can be draining as well. There is a tendency for some of your co-workers to take advantage of that peculiarity and constantly saddle you with work that should otherwise be theirs. Boundaries should be established in such instances. While you are willing to help out, remain firm in your decision to maintain your individuality and not bury yourself under the expectations of others.

Be Receptive to Feedback

A distinctive feature of high emotional intelligence lies in the ability to adapt and listen to what others have to say. Feedback is meant to be given at every point in our career. This is important as it helps us evaluate our position and pinpoint ways to improve our output. Giving feedback is an important aspect of communication.

Giving and receiving feedback can be a really tough conversation, as no one actually likes hearing something negative about their work. But this tough wall is something we must all scale as it is a fundamental instrument to our growth and could even be a bonding experience.

Our brains view criticism as a threat naturally. Therefore, without good self-esteem and self-awareness, it might be difficult to process the feedback as something useful and not merely a tool to incite animosity. Criticism will always be processed and stored more quickly than praise because our brains are wired to engage in what is called a negativity bias. It is possible to break out of this matrix, with self-awareness being the first step. In giving feedback, evaluate your motives. It should always stem from a desire to support, enhance, mentor or guide the individual to whom the feedback is addressed.

Since receiving feedback is a good thing for your career development, always remain approachable and receptive. Avoid being defensive and judgmental, and while listening, try to understand the point raised. Furthermore, reflect on what you hear and ask the opinion of trusted colleagues. You may also wish to ask for examples in which that particular correction was given and the outcome. In the event that you feel the critique wasn't constructive or was delivered in a brash manner, take a few moments to cool off and repeat the discussion at a later date.

Identify Stressors and Manage Them Outside Work

Stress in the workplace is inevitable. A small amount can even be great for your performance as it helps to keep you alert and improve your overall ability to surmount challenges. But there are situations where the stress gets out of hand, and it begins to affect your health, family, work and interpersonal relationships.

When it begins to take a toll on your productivity, confidence, and self-esteem, it is time to sit back and put things into perspective. Sometimes we can be extremely stressed without even knowing it, but those around us end up bearing the brunt of our aggression. Stress leaves you feeling irritable, anxious, depressed, and even apathetic. Sometimes stress can stem from a feeling that we aren't doing enough, dissatisfaction with our jobs, fear of getting sacked, or the pressure to make more money as the paycheck becomes inadequate due to pressing family needs. Even retaining a position without promotion and growth can drive one over the edge.

You can identify that you are stressed by keeping a journal of incidents that make you stressed and your reaction to those situations. This would help in keeping you focused. Also, decluttering your workspace can help to clear up your mind and give you a sense of control. Sometimes stress can originate from our colleagues or bosses. Establishing boundaries and having a proactive rather than a reactive stance can help reduce stress.

In a situation where something goes terribly wrong, reacting by yelling or ignoring everyone will only escalate the problem. But responding proactively always wins. Inculcating an exercise routine into your daily activities can help in relieving pent up energy. Understanding and gaining control over your mood and improving something as subtle as your nutrition can also help in alleviating stress. Lastly, reaching out to friends and family can help further combat feelings of stress.

Maintain Your Enthusiasm

Emotional intelligence is in tandem with demonstrating enthusiasm at work. An enthusiastic employee shows up at the appropriate time, is receptive to change and new ideas, and is willing to put everything into their work. Grit and determination is a subset of enthusiasm and these are invaluable when the institution enters into tough times.

Keep a positive and optimistic attitude while in the workplace. Positivity is infectious and this can enhance general productivity from everyone. Work doesn't always have to be corporate. Most times, people who work in a creative discipline suffer a stifled enthusiasm due to financial constraints. In this case, finding ways to reduce worry can help keep your enthusiasm top notch. This includes worry about outcomes and processes even before you set out to do the job.

If you hold an executive position, it is imperative that you maintain your enthusiasm at all times as it directly affects that of your employees. Celebrating successes can serve as an incentive to stimulate productivity. Also, select team members that are not only bounded by a common goal but also with a concomitant amount of energy as you. As a supervisor or leader, keeping your optimism high is very important when the going gets tough.

It is easy to get whirled into a boring routine, but try to make the work environment as fun and spontaneous as possible. A stimulating environment naturally improves enthusiasm. Drop random quotes for motivation, spring surprises, and make team members and employees participate in activities that increase productivity without posing stress. Taking surveys can also help to promote staff input.

Constantly Evaluate Your Motives and Approach to Situations

The ability to evaluate things in retrospect is one of the characteristics of emotional intelligence. What is the rationale behind every action you take? How do you react to praise, criticism, conflict, and changes? How did you react to such situations in the past and how can you improve your responses to create better outcomes?

Integrity in the workplace should never be compromised. Therefore, our actions should be backed up by principles and a solid reason. To lack a firm ethical foundation is to be prone to violating rules and involving yourself in unprofessional conduct. In the workplace, our motives for doing things should be thoroughly examined. Why are you giving that critique, why do you present yourself in that manner?

One's approach to situations is very critical in any professional sphere. Incidents will always occur, but your reaction to them determines whether they spiral into success or failure. As an individual in a position of power, understand the nature of people. Correct in private and praise in public. Provide support for your employees and make rewards achievable. This would boost the performance as well as the EQ of your employees in no small way.

Develop Self-awareness

Developing self-awareness is usually the first step of any program aimed at improving emotional intelligence. A step to improve your self-awareness in the workplace is to step out of your comfort zone. Leaving your comfort zone would enable you to harness hidden potentials and develop abilities you would have never thought possible. Another step is to identify your triggers and your reaction to situations, especially when under stress. In the workplace, self-awareness can go a long way in increasing your output and helping you avoid pitfalls.

In summary, emotional intelligence permeates every aspect of our lives: family, workplace, friends and even with total strangers. Our jobs indirectly define the course our lives take, and it is imperative that we remain level headed and smart when making decisions in the workplace. Interpersonal relationships demand that we create a balance between our needs and the needs of others and this pressure applies to the workforce as well. Managing stress, improving empathy, developing communication skills, being receptive to feedback, etc. can help in boosting EQ at any work environment you find yourself.

Chapter 9: Emotional Intelligence in Normal Life

Emotional intelligence is vital to our relationship with others and with ourselves. Daniel Goleman, the author of 'Emotional Intelligence', stated that eighty-five percent of our personal and professional success will be affected by EQ. Life deals us blows unexpectedly at every turn.

Have you ever wondered why some people seem to face this headlong, and others seem to crumble under the weight of it? Have you witnessed two people who face the same misfortune but have different levels of resilience? Emotional intelligence combined with other factors can determine, to a large extent, how fast you can bounce back when faced with unsavory situations.

One method of applying EQ to our everyday life is developing the art of assertiveness. Being on planet Earth and surrounded by so many people, we are bound to get into situations that will affect our person. Assertiveness involves possessing high self-esteem and self-confidence. In situations where we feel threatened or where our integrity is questioned, the appropriate reaction is to remain calm. This is achievable when we understand the reason for the other party's behavior.

Practicing mindfulness is a good way to boost EQ in our everyday life. Taking walks, practicing yoga and meditation, can help integrate one with his/her surroundings. Be aware of yourself, of the emotions you feel, and those of others. Taking deep breaths and grounding can help pass time when caught in aggravating situations.

Feel, do not suppress. Being emotionally intelligent does not require that you stifle or dismiss your emotions. Even the calmest and most collected persons experience their own share of overwhelming emotions. The difference lies in the outlet. Finding creative and healthy outlets instead of transferring our sadness, aggression and other negative emotions to others. It is normal to feel emotions, but do not bottle them up, and do not go on a hysterical spree.

In business, EQ is indispensable in negotiation talks. By controlling your emotions, communicating effectively and figuring out the mood, limitations, and peculiarities of the other party, you can successfully close deals in your favor. Emotions are often times displayed through body language, facial expressions, and other paralinguistic variables. Possessing a high EQ makes one sensitive to these changes, and being empathetic would determine to a large extent how you would apply this information.

In our daily activities, EQ would help you decipher if a particular problem stems from you or the other party. Sometimes we are the toxic person, and no matter how hard you try, you can't be great to everyone all the time. Man is inherently imperfect. Since self-awareness and self-regulation are thoroughly integrated into EQ, recognizing that you are the one at fault always comes handy in some conflict resolutions.

Show love and gratitude always. Appreciating what you have helps to reinforce emotional intelligence. Showing love and gratitude to those around you fosters understanding and togetherness. You can demonstrate empathy by paying the bus tickets of a total stranger or reaching out to support a colleague.

In interpersonal relationships, the level of compatibility between the EQ of the two individuals along with other factors determines the failure or success of the relationship.

Friendship

Emotionally intelligent individuals are endowed with impressive people skills. They have an uncanny ability to get along with everyone and provide calm to heated situations. Friends are a necessary part of our lives, no matter how introverted you tend to be. To develop your EQ, you need to understand the emotions of others, and this cannot occur through solo study. People react to situations in different ways and studying these reactions, their emotions, and their threshold is essential in knowing how to communicate with them in the future.

To allow a friendship to flourish, communication is essential. And by communication, we mean the ability to listen, to detect body language and to choose our thoughts and words in an emotionally intelligent manner. Maintaining a healthy amount of communication may be difficult at first, considering the fact that everyone is so busy nowadays. Video calls and texts aren't enough to provide the emotional intimacy we all deserve.

Cultivating the habit of reaching out to your friends would help boost your EQ by establishing emotional intimacy. We cannot always depend on our spouses for emotional intimacy. A good friendship where common interest is shared accrues in greater benefits for your mental health, emotions, and general well-being. Selecting friends who you have something to learn from, or who like you to a certain level– not to the point of sycophantic adoration, can help boost self-esteem and EQ.

Women are more likely to develop emotional intimacy than men because they are socially conditioned to be expressive and supportive. This brings in the aspect of communication. Communication involves listening and allowing yourself to be vulnerable in some cases, as well as speaking up. Because women tend to be more expressive, communication tends to be skewed. However, sometimes there exists a lack of trust. For example, when receiving a compliment, how do you know if she means it or is just being nice?

Trust is essential in communication. An assertive and emotionally intelligent individual is more likely to perceive the presence of trust or establish it strongly. Deeper communication and trust can clear all traces of misunderstanding. In friendships and even romantic relationships, the importance of trust can never be overemphasized.

Having or lacking trust in your friend or partner determines to a large extent how you would interpret their opinions and statements, and even their motives and intentions. Individuals with a high EQ are able to connect on a deep level, and this is because they have taken the initial pains to study those around them, and to ascertain if they are deserving of their trust and loyalty.

Question and filter the stories you hear on a table of truth. It is easy to always take the most often heard part as it gives feelings of security. But whatever you hear about a person should be subject to your scrutiny and understanding, especially when the person involved is close to you.

Celebrate positive emotions and moments. Giving yourself credits and rewards can help reinforce self-esteem and this spirals down into other aspects of our relationship with others. By seeing the good in yourself, it becomes easier to identify the good in others. Celebrating positive moments creates an avenue for more to come.

Parent-child Relationship

In parent-child relationships, emotional intelligence is essential. Children have emotions too, and it is imperative to commence an early education on their usage and importance. It is undoubtedly tough to raise a child. A high EQ can help when a child throws tantrums and tests the strength of your will and principles.

Parenting doesn't come with a 'one strategy works for all' instruction guide. In today's society, parents are expected to raise children who will make healthy decisions. It is even more difficult with the roof shattering divorce rates affecting modern marriages. Families have gotten more complicated and children often feel left out.

Emotionally intelligent families maintain a sense of identity and togetherness regardless of the situation. Family members stick up for each other despite sibling rivalry or moments of separation. In emotionally healthy families, children are allowed to express their opinions, and they are encouraged to speak up. Training your children to be vocal develops their assertiveness, which will help when they face the outside world.

Children should be allowed to voice their opinions. This can be fostered through making room for constructive arguments. Rules made by parents should be talked over. This would allow children to think for themselves and prevent an authoritarian stance by the parents. Their opinions are not only heard but validated.

Separation, divorce or the death of a loved one can be very devastating. The importance of EQ in such circumstances cannot be overrated. In the event of a separation, be aware and sensitive to the emotions of children involved. EQ would endow you with empathy, and resilience to bounce back from the loss, and carry others with you. EQ also comes in handy when you are directly involved in a toxic relationship. This point will be explained in the next chapter.

Being realistic and optimistic simultaneously is also a feature of emotionally intelligent families. Tough times are bound to happen, family members will become sick, lose their jobs, or do poorly at school. Responding proactively by having backup plans and being in tune with your emotions can help provide solutions.

To develop emotional intelligence in children, teach them to embrace negative feelings, as the problem does not lie in feeling, but in their reaction to those emotions. The adolescent period is often turbulent and may put a slight strain on the parents if not carefully handled. Family communication boosts connectivity and can provide a sense of security and stability for adolescents. Emotions tend to surge in this period, and adolescents are often confused.

It is a period where social pressure is at its peak, and they are faced with the burden of making the right decision. Parents are saddled with the responsibility of ensuring that their adolescent child is emotionally secure. Yelling at children has been proven countless times to be more damaging than spanking. When you constantly call them names, you tend to reinforce the idea that they are bad in their minds. Over time, they become numb to the yelling and put-downs.

As a parent, managing your emotions and curtailing impulsive behavior helps in creating emotionally stable children. Constant displays of anger through yelling and frequent outbursts result in children who resort to violence when they feel upset. Many children experience difficulties in articulating their thoughts and feelings. Trying to figure out activities that elicit a different range of emotions in them can help you understand where they are coming from. The next stage is to find solutions to the existing problem. A number of methods may fail, but remain optimistic and gather ideas from friends, family, or your family counselor.

Remember that being in touch with your emotions is not a sign of weakness. Children tend to express their intense feelings through crying and this may be difficult to watch, especially in public. Displays of anger like throwing tantrums or screaming in the middle of Walmart aren't a healthy response to negative emotions. Teach your child that it is not okay to hit or take out their anger or sadness on other people.

You can teach them to be in touch with their emotions by reflecting on their feelings. You could say, "I can tell that you are feeling sad right now." This would help them communicate their frustrations more easily. Establishing creative outlets around the home also helps channel their energy into something positive.

Creating an avenue for children to express their emotions encourages bonding and connectivity. To develop emotional intelligence in your child, understand their point of view and empathize.

Grief

Emotional intelligence can be applied in times of grieving. Nowadays, we place so many premiums on learning how to make better investments and improve our career that we forget to cultivate vital human skills. It is ironic for a society hinged on competency. People tend to shy away from grief, or are usually at a loss for words. Often times we are confused about whether to talk to a grieving person and offer succor or to keep quiet, sit still and let the storm pass.

We can't help or stop the loss of a loved one in many instances. And certainly, our friends do not want us to stay in that overwhelming state of shock and hurt associated with grieving. A curt "I'm sorry for your loss" doesn't always cut it, and may not help reassure the person grieving. Communication is essential in emotional healing. And to support a person who has lost a loved one, we have to communicate in such a way that we leave a path for them to talk openly, without being too pushy.

Body language and the simplest touches like a hug can help a person going through rough times. We can also offer to help, provide accommodation or assist in organizing the funeral if need be. Also saying reassuring statements like, "I'm really sorry you're going through this, how is everyone holding up? What's the most difficult thing right now?" has proven to be very helpful.

Offering to take them out is also a major step as people who grieve often have trouble eating, sleeping, or getting out of the house. If they are reluctant, do not push but try to use the power of persuasion to the best of your abilities. Bear in mind that the aim is not to fix the situation or speed up the process of healing, as it is unique to each individual. In the process of developing your EQ, you will come across people who do not need those phrases and would prefer to grieve in silence. In such instances, your presence is enough.

Sometimes, people who have lost a loved one may tend to suppress their feelings and shoulder the responsibility of others. They may be seen as bustling, brimming with energy, giving support to others and organizing, as if in a bid to get life back to normal. This suppressed grief will resurface months or years later, and often with ugly consequences. Learning the ability to spot that occurrence early usually accrues numerous benefits.

Suppressed grief may manifest in violent actions, decreased productivity at work, mental health issues, and irrational behaviors. When we are caught up in such situations, or when we spot a person manifesting such characteristics, we should take a step back, and breathe. As previously mentioned, negative emotions are not alien. They are part of being human.

Identifying our feelings and acknowledging them helps build our emotional resilience. Emotional resilience is indispensable in dark times as it helps us simply acknowledge the negative emotions, and bounce back into a more positive space. Grief can be relieved by using the SET (Simple Energy Technique). This involves tapping specific places–acupressure points, to help relieve pressure. Tapping the edge of your eyebrows and other points may seem awkward are first, but it has been proven to get emotions under control considerably.

Grief is often accompanied by denial and a strong unhealthy wish that things had turned out differently. A man who survived a car crash and lost his entire family may replay the scene over and over again in his mind. Replaying traumatic scenes may lead to an overwhelming sense of guilt and depression. If such a situation persists, reaching out to a therapist would be extremely helpful.

Most importantly, do not invalidate the experience of another person. Downplaying and failing to recognize the emotions of others is a sign of low emotional intelligence. Pain thresholds differ significantly between any two individuals, and acknowledging this peculiarity helps when stuck in situations that are completely foreign.

Chapter 10: Emotional Intelligence in Relationships

Emotional intelligence is invaluable if you aspire to have a long-lasting and healthy relationship. Trust, communication, loyalty, and commitment are frequently prescribed as the formula for a healthy relationship. The good news, however, is that EQ encompasses the entire spectrum of these qualities.

A relationship comprises of two individuals, bound by love, goals and perhaps a need for mutual fulfillment. People enter into relationships for various reasons that are valid, as long as there is an understanding and their reason is free from the intent to hurt. The most frequent reason is the need for companionship. In as much as we extol our personal space and self-love, human beings always demonstrate a propensity to meet and share little bits of ourselves with others.

In relationships, we all want our partners to act as our confidant and to give us a sense of dependability and lots of love. Considering the fact that it involves two individuals, who belong to different social strata, who have different experiences and world views, who were brought up by parents that most probably weren't like yours– things are bound to be slightly complicated.

Communication is needed to bridge the gap of existing differences. As already established, communication is a skill thoroughly understood and applied daily by people who possess high emotional intelligence. Creating a healthy relationship is a deliberate act. Therefore, in communicating with your partner, do not start off on an aggressive, defensive or contemptuous note.

Dr. John Gottman conducted research on couples and discovered that the first three minutes of a conversation determines its outcome. Basically, conversations which start out on a rash note usually end terribly. Sometimes the harshness doesn't stem from words but from demeanor, intent, and even silence. Sometimes, these behaviors are exhibited in reaction to previous incidents. It is for this reason that self-awareness and self-regulation (which involves understanding one's emotions) are of great importance.

In the politics of relationships, empathy is a profitable skill to have. By understanding the emotions and perspective of others, you experience a paradigm shift that can help resolve conflict amicably. In communication, there is listening, and in listening– the ever subtle but powerful art– you unlock a different realm of understanding and learning. You get to know your partner better and you get to understand the ability of compromise.

Compromise involves giving up your selfish interest when there is a conflict of wants and wills. In relationships, your partner will not always want the same thing or follow the same process as you. Conflict and strife can arise because of a discrepancy in interests. It could be from investments plans, interference from third parties, and even more serious issues like the decision to have a child or not, or differences in methods of raising a child. Inconclusive and differing decisions made by parents can have an adverse effect on a child.

Therefore, compromising for a greater good or to reach a unanimous consensus on issues is not a sign of weakness, but an indication of high emotional intelligence. The declivity of most relationships today arises from the inability to put the needs of others before ours, the wanton desire to satisfy our selfish interests first. The most unfortunate aspect of this is that the behavior presents itself like a cycle. People who have been hurt resolve to put themselves first too, in order to protect their space and emotions that were previously toyed with.

In a relationship where the parties involved have a high EQ, there would be empathy and subsequently, a balance of compromise. Since people are inherently flawed, your partner will always have characters that are not exactly pleasant to you. This is where tolerance comes in. Tolerance does not connote endurance and long-suffering at the detriment of your wellbeing. Instead, it presents with the ability to understand, bear with, adjust to, or overlook certain things– the minding of which will result in strife, or plunge the relationship into oblivion.

Emotionally intelligent couples are invested in building up the relationship. Because their impulsiveness is in check, they do not make threats they do not intend to carry out just to get what they want. For example, threatening to break up with or divorce their partner in order to manipulate and subject them into carrying out their wishes. They combine their individual identities and do not let their differences get in the way of what they have.

Being in a relationship does not translate into losing yourself– your individuality, uniqueness, and other things that make you, you. Self-awareness is applicable in this context. Holding on to yourself, but not in absolutism as you now share your life with another, is important in relationships. This establishes the concept of maintaining healthy boundaries.

Boundaries, aside from performing the function of preserving your individuality, help couples avoid the treacherous being that is infidelity. Sometimes, it is not a decision that has been planned and pondered upon, but it occurs as a gradual descent. Lack of emotional intimacy can lead to emotional dependency on a third party. Couples can get healthy feelings of companionship from friends and families, as emotional intimacy is not solely dependent relationship status.

But invariably, the bulk of one's source of emotional intimacy lies in one's partner, in most cases. Boundaries also help protect couples from forces and situations that threaten to separate them. It is like building a barricade, a bulwark, a united front against the forces that are toxic to the relationship. However, boundaries do not involve cutting off friends and families, although this is also a slight possibility if they prove to be toxic. Certainly, this decision would be made with mutual consent. Restricting one partner from having friends or maintaining family ties is a feature of emotionally manipulative partners.

Emotionally intelligent couples are aware of what motivates and drives each other, and they nurture this to the best of their ability. Couples with high EQ constantly motivate each other and fuel their individual passions. Since they are receptive to feedback and constructive criticism, they are capable of receiving critique without feeling like their ego is bruised. Couples correct each other in private and acknowledge each other's counsel and opinions.

Dr. Nichola Schutte proposed that emotionally intelligent individuals have the ability to self-monitor, and participate in perspective taking. This culminates in marital satisfaction if both couples possess high EQ. Since they have the ability to reflect, they can routinely go over ways to improve the relationship and pinpoint aspects where they aren't performing up to set standards. Couples in a purposeful relationship should have a vision of where they want to be, and how they want to get there. The ability to observe things in retrospect, to go over their previous goals, decisions and the reason for establishing that, helps to build long-lasting relationships.

Individuals with high EQ, understand the intricate relationship between thoughts, feelings, and emotions, and they regulate them accordingly. Thoughts have an effect on our emotions. Thus, a conglomerate of negative thoughts results in negative emotions and feelings. Regulating your thoughts, and constantly reinforcing positive thoughts, leads to positive and controlled emotions. Every day, be reminded of the reason why you love your partner, and why you have chosen to be with him/her. Also, tell them this as much as you can.

Not everyone is born with emotional intelligence inherent in them. It is therefore very possible to develop emotional intelligence, even if you are already in a relationship. Be deliberate about your actions. To be emotionally intelligent, recognize the effect your actions have on others, particularly your partner in this case. Sometimes, something seemingly flimsy like an unfulfilled promise can elicit feelings of hurt in your partner.

When your partner feels a certain way, for example, if your partner feels angry, it is your duty to find out why, the sequence leading to that reaction. William Glasser says all we can do is provide information to another person. Giving a listening ear and trying to figure out why, and the possible solutions to our partner's problems is an indication of how much we value them and the relationship.

In expressing our need for empathy, love, and attention, we should do it in such a way that your partner doesn't feel under attack. It is hard to feel sincere empathy when you are feeling attacked– you would most likely become defensive first because our brains and every cell in our body is naturally wired to protect us first. Trying to manipulate our partners to do as we please by introducing a guilt factor is dangerous.

By using their guilt as a tool against them, you prevent future occurrences of sincere empathy and positive actions. Why? This is because after providing your need in the short term, your partner would begin to question his/her worth to you, and his/her level of assertiveness. Thus, the situation would conflagrate into some sort of power play.

Using phrases like, "If you loved me, you would..." or, "You don't value this relationship enough, and that is why...", can be detrimental to the growth of any relationship. It is simply guilt-tripping and emotional blackmail because you know that they actually care. Self-awareness is also important in romantic relationships as articulating your own feelings and emotions prevents you from always putting the blame for how you feel on your partner.

Using a journal to keep track of these feelings helps in dealing with them. If you discover that you are always feeling that way– negative feelings in this case– and that it is usually escalated by the presence of your partner, then maybe it is time to address the situation in that sense. Inculcating the ability to manage your own emotions eases the burden on your partner to help you figure everything out. Remember that there is a fine line between loving and needing a person. Being needy connotes and utters dependency that stems from insecurity and low self-esteem.

Therefore, we should take responsibility for our feelings and ask for support from our partner, instead of expecting them to make us feel better automatically. We should ask ourselves how our partners feel, and how we can make them feel better. Also, the importance of communication cannot be overemphasized. Telling your partner what you want and what you feel helps to prevent the common habit of jumping to conclusions.

Unmet Emotional Needs

There is a tendency to project your unmet emotional needs from childhood on your partner. Growing up in a dysfunctional family or society, being tossed from one foster home to another– resulting in a lack of stability, can have adverse long-term effects. It may manifest as growing up and having unrealistic expectations from your partner. It is imperative to note that your partner is not responsible for your overall happiness.

It is your choice to be happy, and your partner can only do so much. His/her efforts may not be adequate to scratch the surface of what your subjective happiness entails. To heal and achieve the level of emotional fitness needed to move your relationship forward, you need to address the underlying issues that plague you emotionally. Only then can you develop a healthy, thriving relationship. You are primarily responsible for your happiness or feelings of resentment and negativity.

Emotional intelligence is integral to the success of any relationship. And frankly, it goes both ways. The two parties involved must possess a substantial amount of EQ in order for them to create a balance. A partner with a low EQ would feel averse to the expression of your feelings. This is because they are often clueless about how to handle such a situation, and the thought of sitting down evaluating and sorting through their emotions and yours scares them to no end.

Furthermore, an individual with low emotional intelligence tends to be emotionally unavailable. This is present as a major complaint in most separations. Often, it is a product of societal and social conditioning. Men are usually victims of 'emotion shaming'. They are taught to suppress their feelings and emotions as a mark of masculinity. Fortunately, emotional intelligence can be learned.

Developing emotional intelligence helps you understand your partner's needs, even if they are not vocal about it. Providing their needs even before they ask can help reinforce feelings of trust and love. It could be something as simple as providing a shoulder for them to cry on. Emotional availability makes it easier for our partners to open up to us and regard us as their confidant. Establishing trust in a relationship helps the relationship last longer.

Emotional intelligence helps you stay invested in your relationship. By cultivating empathy and avoiding the pitfalls that occur in most relationships, you will be able to better handle conflicts.

Spotting an Emotionally Abusive Partner

Emotional abuse, unlike physical or sexual abuse, is often difficult to detect and is undoubtedly more deadly in its subtlety. In the initial stages of the relationship, the abuser may project himself as caring and protective in a bid to win the trust, confidence, and love of the victims. This makes them susceptible to further abuse in the future.

Emotional abuse tactics include gas lighting– psychologically manipulating a person to the extent that they question their own sanity, and their ability to decipher reality–, stonewalling– a refusal to answer or cooperate–, and ignoring, deception, brash criticism, etc. It can be extremely traumatic, and victims often suffer from substance abuse, depression, PTSD, and other long-term psychological effects.

A sign that you may be in an emotionally abusive relationship is that you keep walking on eggshells around your partner. When you constantly evaluate yourself to know if you are enough, when you seek validation at every turn, when you second guess any decision you take and gauge it on the premise of your partner's approval and validation, you are most probably looped into an emotionally abusive relationship. Furthermore, if you see yourself feeling sorry about nothing and everything.

When the abuser constantly demeans and belittles you, self-doubt begins to creep in and you begin to actually believe that you are stupid, dumb, and incapable and that he/she is doing you a favor by being in a relationship with you. Apologizing for everything is a consequence of being tentative about everything you do around him/her. Abusers also tend to control their victims by using finances and sex. They withhold these things from you in order to 'punish' you.

This usually occurs after the abuser has stealthily drained you of your finances, or taken steps to make sure you are isolated from family and friends. As mentioned before, establishing boundaries as couples is necessary, but when it becomes one-sided, it results in a form of abuse. Another feature is that they suddenly withdraw and become cold. This may occur sporadically, and leave you feeling like you are doing something terribly wrong to warrant the silent treatment.

Your partner makes scathing remarks and labels them as jokes. When you react, they label you as being too sensitive and defensive. In reality, beneath every 'joke', there might be an element of truth. Also, emotional abusers would always downplay the achievements and exaggerate the flaws of the victims. Watch carefully how your partner reacts to positive happenings in your life. Do they regard it with disinterestedness, a sneer, or with a reminder that you had set higher bars to achieve?

They may also use the tool of comparison, comparing you to their ex's or even your close friends. They take advantage of your misfortunes and remind you of it every time in such a way that your confidence begins to diminish. Emotional abusers are like connoisseurs at manipulation. Despite their horrible behaviors, victims tend to feel sorry and make excuses for them. For example, blaming his impulsiveness and harshness on his traumatic childhood or the fact that he failed his ACT's multiple times.

Emotional intelligence can be used negatively. Most manipulators combine a high intelligence quotient with equally high emotional intelligence. Since they understand the dynamics of human nature and how emotions play, they can take advantage of their ability.

Manipulators play on fear, they exaggerate facts and situations in order to elicit reactions from you, that you would otherwise not exhibit. Because they know your emotional response to different circumstances, they twist and adjust the sails to their favor, in order for you to respond a certain way. To avoid this, carefully sift statements to understand if they are implying that you lack courage or any quality that would pressure you into proving yourself. In this situation, maintain your assertiveness. Know that it is completely okay to say no to demands that threaten to erode your moral principles or standards.

Emotional manipulators understand that we love to talk about ourselves a lot. Our achievements, experiences, and fears. They take advantage of this by asking multiple questions that would get you very thrilled to disclose information about yourself, while they refuse to reciprocate this action. This is dangerous as the information they garner will be used against you in the future. While there is absolutely nothing wrong with talking about yourself, ensure that there is a balance and that the individual you are relating the information to is trustworthy to an extent.

People are usually awestruck or intimidated by people they perceive as better than them, and they tend to suck up to them. Manipulators are aware of this, and they may present themselves as suave and debonair. Most are smooth talkers, with a good command of the English language. Their demeanor would hold you spellbound, and you would forget to take everything they say with a pinch of salt. Since it may be difficult to understand their lingo, you may fail to critically analyze what they say to you. Do not be afraid to tell someone to repeat a statement you don't understand.

Emotional manipulators often resort to the use of strong emotions. They exhibit negative emotions in order to make you react on the spur of the moment. To avoid this pitfall, practice the art of pausing before making any decision. They also give you little time to make a choice or decision. They give you an unreasonable amount of time, in order to force you to decide on an issue without weighing the consequences.

This won't come as a surprise, but emotional manipulators are deceitful. They spread rumors, lies, and implant negative ideas in the consciousness of others, for their selfish interest. To avoid being a victim of their deceit, don't take in everything they say, hook, line, and sinker. Screen what you hear on a filter of truth.

In the workplace, emotional intelligence can be used for dark and sinister purposes. It is important to note this as any mistake in the workplace can send your finances down the drain. We all have a dark side that is suppressed by conscience, morality, religion, and sociocultural factors. These manipulators appear completely normal and extremely talented on the surface, and sometimes you would be tricked into believing that you are the one being sentimental or even malicious.

They usually possess great verbal communication; they know the right people and can make you feel at ease. With their keen sense of empathy, they tend to steal your trust because they 'get you'. They promise a lot but fail to deliver.

In summary, emotional intelligence in intimate relationships is dependent on many factors. The compatibility of two individuals with the same level of EQ is important as past experiences shape our paradigm most of the time. A person who has charm and charisma may use this skill to get what he wants, and not necessarily in a bad way. A person with equally high emotional intelligence may detect this character as a sign of deception, especially if he/she has had a bad experience with an emotionally abusive lover who possessed charm and charisma.

Also, it is difficult for people to recognize the change in us when we improve our emotional intelligence. It is difficult also, for people with a long history together not to fall into old habits and behavior. Sometimes we are even appalled when we look back at the recklessness of our previous behaviors when we had low emotional intelligence.

In the workplace, with friends, with our family– particularly our partners and children, it is imperative that we apply emotional intelligence in everything we do. As humans, we are made of emotions and thoughts and feelings and these cascade into processes that we act out. Setting boundaries, displaying empathy, being receptive to feedback– even when dealing with our children, we have a lot to learn from them– anticipating the needs of our partner and exhibiting tolerance, selflessness, and self-regulation, can help improve our lives in a holistic sense.

Emotionally intelligent people understand that there are principles to all things, and this involves dealing with humans. They apply this knowledge judiciously to all aspects of their lives. Developing emotional intelligence is an important skill to learn (even though some people are born with that innate ability, it is possible to learn once you are committed) in today's society.

Chapter 11: Develop your EQ

Can EQ be developed? This question is important because of the significance of emotional intelligence to both every day and corporate living. It is a known fact that your emotions can either work for you or work against you. Being able to develop your emotional intelligence puts you on a pedestal where you can channel your feelings in the right direction. Hence, it is very important for you to know how to marshal your emotions.

When it comes to important discussions such as this, it will be unwise to depend on conjectures and popular opinions because they have a tendency to be misleading. You cannot afford to be carefree about the source of your information especially when you need information on something that can improve your life like emotional intelligence.

Requisite Skills for the Development of Your EQ

The best way to know whether it is possible to develop your EQ or not is to listen to experts in this important field of life. David Caruso and Peter Salovey, who are both professors and have researched extensively on emotional intelligence, affirmed that it is possible to develop your EQ. In "The Emotionally Intelligent Manager", their publication on emotional intelligence, they identified 4 vital skills you need to have before it will be possible for you to develop your emotional intelligence.

These 4 skills include:

- Being able to identify your feelings and those of other people around you.

- Being able to utilize your feelings in the guidance of your thoughts and reasoning process.

- Being able to grasp the way your emotions tend to change and grow during various unfolding events.

- Being able to remain objective and to use the information supplied by your emotions to make decisions and act accordingly.

You cannot develop your EQ when you struggle to identify your feelings. You should be able to tell exactly how you feel before you can know how to channel it the right way. You must be able to distinguish between bad, negative, and positive emotions because this is core to your EQ. You should be able to tell when you are feeling sad, for example, as that will help you ensure your decision making is not cluttered by that emotion.

You also need to be able to identify the emotions of others in order to know how to relate with them You should be able to say that a particular person is angry, for example, because that will help you know the kind of things to say to that person without adding "salt to injury". Once you can identify your various emotions and those of other people around you, you are ready to improve your emotional intelligence.

Being able to utilize your feelings in the guidance of your thoughts and reasoning process.

It is very vital that you are in charge of your emotions while reasoning and thinking. Imagine you are in a meeting with people who are interviewing you in view of employing you for your dream job and you receive a text. You read the text and it was your younger sibling calling you a fool. As long as you don't feel happy about the incident, you will be acting like a fool indeed if you flare up forgetting that you are in the middle of something important.

Therefore, your EQ can only be on the rise when you are able to lay hold of your emotions while thinking and reasoning. Failure to do that will make your emotions interfere with your thought process frequently and the resultant effect of such malaise is poor decision making.

Being able to grasp the way your emotions tends to change and grow during the various unfolding of events.

There are specific events that change your emotions rapidly. You must be able to identify such situations and plan accordingly. Once such situations occur, you will be able to caution yourself to avoid ruining a perfect day. There is a thin line between having a bad day and having a good day. It takes just one wrong decision to ruin your day sometimes. Being able to learn from the past is a display of intelligence.

The last time someone spoke ill of you publicly, how did you feel? What did you do? You need to identify such key moments in order to be in charge of your emotions. Your detractors can identify that Achilles heel of yours and use it against you. If people know that you will flare up when someone talks about your spouse in a way you don't like, they may use that to make you do something you will regret later.

Being able to remain objective and use the information of your emotions to make decisions and act accordingly.

Your emotions can move from positive to negative in no time; hence, you need to be able to stay objective in spite of how you feel. Doing what you feel like doing is being impulsive because you will wish you never did that when your sanity returns. People who are able to manage their emotions well have perfected the art of ensuring the way they feel does not determine how they act. Quality decision making is a product of a sound mind that harnesses emotional turmoil.

You must be able to tell yourself things like, "I know I am feeling like sleeping with that sexy lady but my commitment to my wife takes precedence. I won't do this." Such key moments are the differences between a quality life and a life full of regrets. Life will throw a lot at you but you must be able to identify what is best for you and what is good for you. The most important skill is being able to tell the difference between the two. Something might be good for you because of the short-term gratification but bad for your long-term happiness.

How to develop your EQ

Having recognized the skills you need to be able to develop your EQ, you

86

are ready for the next step which are the ways to go about the development of your EQ. Below are the ways you can develop your emotional intelligence:

Reduce Your Negative Emotions

An inability to reduce negative emotions does not bode well for you. I understand that it is easier said than done but it is not impossible. A key way to reduce your negative emotions is to evaluate the situation that has led to the way you feel. For example, no one likes to be criticized, especially when it is in the public sphere, but not all criticisms are destructive. You need to evaluate the profile of the person speaking and the validity of their claims.

Profiling the person will help you know why the person might be telling you the things he or she is telling you. Does this person have something to gain from this criticism? If people you know care about you criticize you, they are most likely only trying to help you improve. I know you would have preferred that the criticism is not public but it is practicing humility to accept what was said and improve.

Be Mindful Of Your Use of Words

You have to be careful regarding the things you say to people. You don't have to let out everything because you are angry. Words are like missiles and impossible to stop once released. You can choose to speak to people politely even when they don't rate you highly or speak less of you. They will remember your maturity when their sanity returns and will respect you for being noble when you have reasons not to be.

Put Yourself in People's Shoes Consistently

Empathy is the key to emotional intelligence. Don't you get angry because your boss speaks angrily at you and neglects the things you are going through? Don't always expect others to be as emotionally intelligent as yourself, always take the initiative. Also, learn to make excuses for other people. Instead of saying that your boss is such a terrible person, you can convince yourself that he or she might just be having a bad day.

Be Mindful of Things That Stress You Out

You need to also watch out for activities that tend to increase your stress level. Reduce these activities and you will be able to have fewer negative emotions that can cause you to make wrong decisions.

Be Assertive

It is not prideful to let people know the things you feel are unacceptable to you. Sometimes, people assume that others should know what they like and what they don't like. Making it clear to people around you that you don't like a particular thing will help them avoid doing those things to you.

They will have nothing to complain about if you rebuke them when they do those things because they have been warned. It is true that there are people that will do things you don't like just to annoy you, but clearly defining your likes and dislikes will help reduce such occurrences.

Be Open to the Opinion of Others

When you only hear your own voice, you cannot improve the quality of your life. There are times you did something or thought about something in a particular way and felt you are right but you realized you were wrong after seeking the opinion of someone else. Learn to ask for the opinion of others and compare and contrast. You will make better decisions this way and also gain the trust of others.

Be Patient

Learn to delay your decisions for as long as possible. Decisions made in a hurry will come back to haunt you. Take your time and think through before doing anything. You can speak to people you feel are in a better position to help you whenever you can. Some decisions look like no-brainers but you will realize that they are not in hindsight. Unless you definitely have to respond instantaneously, take your time because decisions made thoughtfully always have a higher chance of being right than the ones made immediately.

Chapter 12: Obstacles to the Improvement of EQ

There are things you need to be wary of because of the adverse effect they can have on the development of your EQ.

Once you are able to successfully navigate through these obstacles, you will be ahead of the curve when it comes to being emotionally intelligent.

Below are the challenges you need to surmount to rate high in emotional intelligence:

Not Realizing You Need to Change

Change is constant in life. However, it depends on the kind of change you are talking about. Change is constant because you will either get better or worse. Stagnancy does not really exist when it comes to human development; deterioration is what is constant when you are not getting better. In other words, positive changes are not constant, they demand to be deliberate and committed. It is, however, not possible to improve the quality of your life when you don't even realize or agree that you need to improve.

It is only after you have come to realize that you need to take purposeful steps to change your life that you can make the necessary changes. Hence, until you agree that you need to improve your EQ, you can never take any step to develop it. As much as it is good to have people around you that love you unconditionally, you need to be sincere with yourself to improve the areas of your life and to improve your EQ.

Not Being Ready To Change

It is one thing to realize and agree that you need to change; it is, however, a different thing entirely to be ready to pay the sacrifices attached to the positive change you crave. There are no free gifts in life. Every gift you receive was paid for by another person. No one can improve your life for you more than your own willingness to do that. Developing your EQ demands deliberate efforts that require your commitment.

Hence, don't just sit there and hope that a miracle will occur somewhere that will make you suddenly begin to improve. You must be ready to work your socks off. Thus, once you have agreed with yourself that you need to improve your level of emotional intelligence, you need to also start doing everything necessary to improve in the way you handle your emotions and those of the people that come your way.

Accepting Defeat

Some people have a deterministic view about life where they feel whatever comes their way is their lot. This view makes such people accept anything that comes their way and they rarely make any attempt to take deliberate steps or concise efforts to improve the quality of their lives. Such people will see their inability to manage their emotions effectively as just their 'personality'. This is their grand excuse for acting impulsively and having difficulties with maintaining excellent relationship with others.

I am not denying that your personality has a role to play in the way you behave, but there is a lot you can do to improve the way you act. Hence, you cannot afford to throw in the towel yet because there is still room for improvement. You can either chose to do nothing about your EQ or challenge yourself to make the necessary commitment to improving your emotional intelligence.

The Wrong Company

I am not talking about a firm, I am talking about the kind of people you have around you. You cannot grow beyond the kind of influence you have around you. When you surround yourself with negative people who don't care about the way they go about life, you will find it difficult to grow in the way you manage your emotions. Be around people who genuinely care about you as such people will accept you in spite of your deficiencies and help you grow.

They will not let you be contented with your flaws; they will work in tandem with you to help you grow and fulfill your potential. When you have such people in your life, don't let pride or offense set in and make you lose them. Value such people and see to it that the relationship continues to blossom. The quality of your life depends on such people.

Trying To Be Perfect

As much as it is important to ensure that you keep growing and getting better as a person, you will never be perfect. The faster you accept the fact that you are human and will flop once in a while, the better for you. Developing your EQ is not all about becoming a perfect person but improving yourself so as to improve the quality of your life. Hence, whenever you make a mistake, move on.

You will never be able to develop your EQ if you are trying to live a life that does not have any mistakes. What you need to do is to ensure that your mistakes decrease in frequency and that is the essence of being committed to developing your EQ. There is no one who does not make mistakes. Hence, you should not consider it an anomaly that you did something you should not have done.

Not Giving Room for Growth

This is particularly important if you function in one leadership role or the other. When I said "leadership role", I am not outrightly referring to being the C.E.O. of a company. As a father or mother, you are also a leader because you need to lead your children correctly. As a leader, you must be willing to give room for growth. In other words, as much as you want people to be productive and effective, you have to also allow them to make mistakes and learn from them.

Knowing when to be stern and when to pat people on the back is key to emotional intelligence. When you allow people to grow and become better, you will have a larger heart which is unconsciously developing your EQ. Therefore, you will not only harm the people you are leading when you don't allow them to grow, but you will also hamper your own growth as an individual.

Letting Every Opinion Matter

It is important to listen to the opinion of others but every opinion must not count to you. There will always be ridiculous people who have chosen to make you feel miserable. There is no one, no matter how good they are, that is disliked by absolutely no one. Hence, you will only be denying yourself the necessary room to develop your EQ when you take everyone who criticizes you seriously.

You must be able to know the difference between people who criticize you because they want you to become better as a person and people who are all out to bring you down. People who criticize you to bring you down will hammer on every fault and try to disrupt your rhythm. You must be determined to be focused and ignore such people. Trying to please such people is pointless because there is nothing you can do that will ever be good enough for them.

Being a Destructive Critic

You don't want people to talk you down just to distract you, you should also not do the same to others. When you are concerned about bringing others down, you will not be able to grow also. You will be too busy designing new techniques to attack others to come up with ideas to improve your own life. Not doing to others what you also don't want them to do to you is a simple but important life principle.

Get busy with improving your own life and developing your own EQ rather than saddling yourself with the task of bringing others down. Never forget that people only criticize those who have decided to go out there and do something important in life. No one criticizes people who don't do anything meaningful with their lives because such people don't count. It is hypocritical to want others to be kind to you while you are always ready to attack them when they make mistakes.

Getting Stuck in the Past

When you get stuck in the past, you will never be able to take advantage of the opportunities of today and the ones that will come your way in the future. I understand that you might have done things that make you feel like a complete idiot, but we all do that. When you talk to people you cherish and hold in high regard, you will realize that they have also made the wrong choices in the past. Hence, your case is not different.

It is when you have refused to forgive yourself and move on that you are truly making a mess of your life. You should treat your past as a lesson that will spur you to make better decisions in the future. There are endless opportunities to thrive and make the best out of your life but you will never be able to make use of these opportunities when you keep crying over "spilled milk".

Chapter 13: Practice Makes Perfect

You have been exposed to the meaning and importance of emotional intelligence all through this book. The skills you need to acquire and the things you need to do to develop your EQ have also been discussed extensively. In this last chapter, you will be introduced to some practical things you can do to improve the way you handle your emotions and those of others. These are not theories but simple things that have been practiced and attested to be effective by various people.

Below are some exercises that can help you master your emotions:

Always Have a Plan B

The reason you feel dejected and frustrated such that you take it out on others is probably because you know you don't have any other option apart from the current one. Hence, if the plan fails, you feel like your world is crashing down around you. You cannot afford to put all your eggs in one basket in life because life is way too risky for that kind of action. When you have a plan, you will always be afraid of the outcome of your decisions but having an alternative plan gives you peace of mind.

A plan B is not even good enough; you should have a plan B, C, D, E, F..., and Z. So, as you invest in that business, also look out for another business you can also invest your money in. In case you don't get the kind of yield you expect from that business, you will have another option you can look forward to. Some people see having other options as being afraid but that is not true. Having other alternatives is being shrewd. There will never be any time you will be at the mercy of anyone when you can access other options.

Stress Management Skills

Stress can make you anxious or nervous. It is okay to be anxious or nervous once in a while because of the sensitivity of a task you need to carry out. However, it becomes an issue when you are unable to perform as you ought because you are nervous. You can reduce anxiety by reducing your temperature. You can drink some cold water to help with this. You can also reduce the rate at which you consume caffeine to help with this.

Caffeine is a stimulant and can increase your anxiety level when not properly handled. Hence, you can stay off caffeine or reduce the quantity of your intake during periods when you need to handle situations that are tense. Simple things such as these will improve the way you handle yourself and others. The most important things in life are not necessarily complicated things but simple things you feel are too simple to be taken seriously.

Try Aerobic Exercises

Aerobic exercises can help you reduce fear and depression. You will be surprised to find out that you will be able to dissipate negative emotions as you move your body. Your calmness will return and you will be able to think clearly again. These exercises affect your heart rate and also make your circulatory system continue to function the way it ought to function. Examples of such exercises include taking a brisk walk or skipping with a jump rope.

Reduce the Use of Sentences That Begin With "You"

This comes in and when you feel that you are not getting what you deserve from a person or from a corporate body. Sentences that start with "you" during those moments often lead to pointing an accusing finger which makes people uncomfortable. You will be reducing your chances of getting what you want when you talk that way, especially to people who are superior and have the capacity to deny you or delay your entitlements.

By simply addressing the situation without pointing accusing fingers shows to them that you understand the situation in spite of the fact that you have not gotten what you want. Avoiding sentences that start with "you" will help you to avoid becoming defensive which pisses off people. When you are defensive, you will only see the faults of others and neglect yours. Instead of saying "you have not been listening to me", you can say "I would appreciate if you can hear me out please".

Those listening to you will also not be defensive when you don't point accusing fingers at them. They will want to hear you out and will most likely be ready to negotiate with you and even make compromises when they see that you are not making them responsible for the unpleasant situation you have found yourself in. This will not take anything from you, it will only allow you to reduce the rate of having to deal with negative emotions accusations often generate.

Take a Deep Breath During Tense Situations

There is no way you can escape having one or two difficult people in your endeavors in life. If you are lucky not to have such people as your spouse, they could be your boss or work under you. You will definitely come across such people at one point or the other. Hence, it is better to determine long beforehand what you will do when you come across such people rather than hope you will never have an encounter with them.

During tense moments when you feel like speaking in annoyance, learn to take deep breaths and slowly count to ten. You will have a better grip on your emotions when you do this. You will think about other means of resolving the situation during this moment and find an alternative dispute resolution rather than speak out of anger. Words spoken out of anger are usually "poisonous" and intended to hurt the other person.

Most times, even when you are in the right, you will end up regretting the things you say because you are angry. When you are angry, you are likely going to reveal secrets the person kept with you before your annoyance. You will go all out to hurt the person and this will not help you or the people around you.

Don't Hold Back Compliments

You will often be told not to let out negative emotions but it is equally important to let out positive emotions. I mean, always look out for opportunities to tell people good things about them. Tell people they have done well when they are doing well and mean it. When you tell people that they are doing well when they are not doing well, you are not helping them. It is mere flattery and they will eventually mark you out as an insincere person in the long run.

Hence, you don't have to go overboard. Simply look out for the right things they do and sincerely compliment them about those things. Let people around you know they are looking good. It helps boost their confidence and perceive you as a positive person. When you have a culture of telling people they are doing well when they do will make them open to hear you when you point out the areas that they need to improve. They will not see you as someone who is criticizing them to make them feel bad.

Listen and Truly Listen

It is one thing to listen hypocritically to people so that they will not accuse you of not listening to them, it is another thing to listen to people because you want to hear them objectively. There are different reasons that people listen. Some people listen so as to be able to find loopholes to attack the person they are listening to. You should not do this because it is not helpful. You will totally miss out on anything the person has to say that can help you get better.

You should listen to people because you are interested in whatever they have to say. Practicing active listening shows you are humble and don't see other people as nonentities. When people around you notice that you listen to them to combat them, they will be reluctant to tell you things even when they feel it will help you. They will also be reluctant to open up to you about themselves.

Conclusion

Without any controversy, if you have read the book attentively, you should have a good knowledge of what emotional intelligence is all about by now. You should not feel like a fish out of water when people talk about the art and practice of handling your feelings properly in order to make quality decisions. The painstaking approach to provide credible information taken towards writing this book guarantees that your knowledge level about emotional intelligence is improved considerably after reading the book.

However, any knowledge that cannot be used to improve your experience as a person is worthless. There is no point in reading a book that cannot help you make changes in your life. I am convinced that the reason you chose to read this book is that you felt convinced in your heart that it has contents that can help you excel in certain areas of your life. However, that purpose will be defeated if all you do with the knowledge you have garnered with this book is to tell people that you once read a good book on emotional intelligence.

The fact that you read a good book on emotional intelligence does not translate to being able to manage your emotions and those of others well. It is when you choose to internalize the ideas that have been passed across to you in a book that the book can make the desired impact in your life. Hence, I urge you to write down important tips to develop the EQ that you have learned in this book and start practicing them.

When you read a book that has quality content such as this book, people around you must be able to feel the impact. They should notice the changes and ask you what has happened to the old you. Let the impact of what you have learned appear in your attitude and behavior. When this happens, you will be able to recommend the book to others and they will also want to read it because they have seen how the book has affected your own life too.

There are still a whole lot of opportunities to improve the quality of your life as a person by getting better in your EQ. Never say never because it only ends when you decide to quit. Those who quit will never amount to anything tangible in life. Always look at the bigger picture and have a positive approach to life. A positive mindset will always spur you to look for means to get better. Your best days are ahead of you. Stay positive and keep growing.

Improve Your People Skills

How Breaking the Habit of Being Yourself, Boost Your Charisma To Become a Super Attractor, Take Control of Your Life and Learn Talking to Strangers So Anyone Can't Hurt You

Introduction

The following chapters will talk about how it's possible for anyone to learn to be more charismatic, how you need the proper mindset, inner energy, and warmth to come across to other people with confidence. We'll also discuss the importance of having *gratitude*, and having presence.

This book will cover the problems many of us face when dealing with social situations such as social anxiety, a critical inner voice, and common mistakes in body language and public speaking many of us make. If you think you are alone in struggling with these challenges, rest assured you are *not*. This book will help you overcome whatever's stopping you from being more charismatic with useful tips and advice from the experts.

Making the decision to learn to become more charismatic is in investment in your life—if you're ready to be more successful, more well-liked, and happier and more comfortable with yourself, then get ready for some positive change!

There are plenty of books on this subject on the market, thanks again for choosing this one! Every effort was made to ensure it is full of as much useful information as possible, please enjoy!

Chapter 1: What Is Charisma? An In-Depth Look

The etymology of the word charisma originated with the Greek *charis*, meaning grace. Charisma is the possession and utilization of grace, confidence, and charm; it doesn't veer into the ugly territory of arrogance or of conceit. Charisma is so delightful to the people effected by it, that a charismatic person will subconsciously cause the audience around him to mimic his inflections, body language, and movements. Rather some sort of occultish mind control—this is happening because it simply *feels good* to be in the company of a charismatic person. We want to feel what they are feeling because they genuinely look happy—and who doesn't want to be happy?

So what is it about charismatic people that charms us so? Here are three common traits exhibited by naturally charismatic people:

- Charismatic people feel *deeply*. Their emotions are real, genuine, and they're not afraid to show them to others.

- Charismatic people cause other people to feel what they're feeling. The form an emotional bond with others naturally.

- Charismatic people are immune to the effects of other charismatic people. They're simply not effected by them. This doesn't mean that their own empathy and/or respect flies out the window, but they possess their own personal strength and charm, and so are not easily swayed by the charm of others.

Some people are naturally charismatic, but if you want to be charismatic also, you'll be relieved to learn that approximately fifty percent of a person's charisma is usually *learned*. Yes, you can be taught to possess seemingly "natural" charisma!

You might think physical looks have a lot to do with whether or not someone is perceived as charismatic and likable. This is simply not true. You don't need a perfect, chiseled jaw, beach abs, blond hair, or to be a certain weight or height to be charismatic. Charisma comes from within—it's how we subconsciously connect with other people. In fact, sometimes people who don't exactly "fit" into a standard mold of physical attractiveness are the most charismatic, because they have *learned* how to bridge the distance and become successful in social situations, so that other people won't even have time to judge them on appearances. It's true that a person who is "ugly" inside, i.e. arrogant, rude, mean-spirited, distracted, or callous can be a 10 in looks, but most people won't find them particularly attractive, while someone who might not have a perfect body can win hearts wherever they go because they're *enjoyable to be around*. That is the seemingly "magical" power of charisma in action.

How do you know if you have the ability to exude charisma? Let's talk about something called charismatic potential.

Charismatic Potential

There are some lucky individuals who possess a great amount of what is called "charismatic potential", and they are able to quickly learn from other people by observing their charming behavior, positive body language, voice inflection, and emotional display. They are chameleon-like in a sense; charisma is an unspoken language, and these fortunate folks are able to pick up that language by the time they reach early adulthood, usually.

For the rest of us, it's important to remember that charisma is, by nature, a *learned* set of skills. There is no gate barring us from entering this world of success and popularity. We simply have to follow in the naturally charismatic person's footsteps, and do what they do, *see* what they see.

Marilyn Monroe was a perfect example of a person who understood how to tap into her own, natural charismatic potential. She was able to shift from her day-to-day persona of Norma Jean, to Marilyn, in a moment's notice. She would often playfully ask reporters and photographers if they wanted to "meet Marilyn" (to which they would all enthusiastically reply, yes!). Then with a subtle shift of posture, a touch of her hair, and a glorious smile, out would come the shining, powerfully charismatic Hollywood star. Marilyn understood the effect of her *feeling* glamorous would have on those observing her. You have to feel these positive emotions in order to project them towards other people, who will in turn feel them as well.

While Marilyn most definitely had natural beauty in her tool kit, throughout human history, so-called "plain" folks have risen to power and greatness, broken hearts and won wars, based on their own charismatic potential and the use of these clandestine tools of the human mind and heart.

There is one important thing we have to touch upon, before going any further. Learning and using charisma takes courage. It's natural to be afraid of social and public situations. Most of us are simply not taught to stand in front of a group of other people and win them over. That doesn't mean it isn't possible, however, and it also doesn't mean it can't be *enjoyable,* but you have to have some courage to take that first step towards learning to be more charismatic.

Throughout the process of learning to be more charismatic, you will have to undergo some self-exploration: you'll be looking at yourself beneath the microscope, so to speak, and that may at times be uncomfortable. Understand, however, that becoming more charismatic ultimately means you're going to be a happier person. The journey of self-discovery, (and scrutiny) will all be worth it in the end.

Having Presence

Try and recall the last time you attended a social event. Perhaps it was an office party that you felt obligated to go to in order to make a good impression on your managers, or maybe it was a hobbyist club's year-end party, or even your own family's Thanksgiving celebration.

At any point, if you remember talking with someone who was distracted, looking at their phone, looking away from you and around at other people, then you know what it's like to be engaged with someone who lacks *presence*. Presence is the number one ingredient of a person's charisma, after confidence. We simply don't want to be around people who aren't "there" for us; it feels cold, and it feels awkward. However what's even more surprising is how many of us are guilty of not being present; we spend too much time fiddling with our phones, checking emails, social media notifications, newsfeeds, and texts. To have better presence is incredibly easy—you'll boost your own as soon as you turn that phone off, and slip it into your pocket for the duration of the event, meeting, or even date.

Another way we might lack presence is through eye contact. This may not be easy for all of us—later on in the book we'll discuss being on the autism spectrum, Asperger's, and folks for whom so-called "normal" interaction is uncomfortable and/or awkward. Again, charisma is *learned*. Even if you start out with some natural setbacks to being charismatic, you can learn to overcome them. Additionally, people on the spectrum often have remarkable, natural tools that will *help* them navigate social settings, in ways that those of us not on the spectrum are not particularly good at.

Eye contact is a big part of being present. Taking cues from the other person helps take some of the burden out of it—when they look away, you can, too, then return to meeting their own eye contact a little earlier; they'll be charmed to find you're looking at them, and perhaps a little ruffled that they're not being present enough. In social interaction, we pick up cues from each other. The difference here is that the charismatic person *leads by example*.

Presence is all about *interest*. We all want other people to be interested in us; it's human nature. When we show others that we find them interesting, they're bound to listen to us for longer periods of time, remember us more vividly, and generally form a good impression of us. We tend to like people who want to hear what we have to say, who engage with us with enthusiasm, who do not simply "wait" for us to stop speaking so that they can get a word in. The charismatic person learns social cues that allow them to carry a conversation with a good, natural, give-and-take. Presence paves the way for this positive interaction.

Charisma may have the effect of getting others to like us, but it begins by us genuinely seeking to like others. Charisma is reciprocal; we receive triple-fold what we deliver.

Conversational Charisma

In a conversation, what should we talk about, and what if we're only *really* knowledgeable in a few, unusual areas? Being charismatic does not involve going back to school to tackle things we might have slept through in younger years (although further education can help), rather, conversational charisma often involves engaging with other people to *learn* what *they* know. People absolutely love to share their knowledge. Being a gracious listener with time to spare will boost your charisma through the roof.

Many of us instantly go on the defensive if we stumble on a fact we believed was true and someone points out its fallacy. This is a wrong technique, but it's natural, so we need to un-learn it in order to help our charisma potential. Ignorance in social settings need not be humiliating—the charismatic person takes this opportunity to connect with other people by graciously admitting their ignorance, and listening when the correct information is given. Asking questions, repeating phrases or facts to make sure you've got it right are all great ways to connect, engage, and delight the person or persons you're speaking with. These techniques are not just for the workplace: they are power tools in the social setting and will leave a good impression, every time.

Being charismatic means throwing some old, negative habits out the window. Judging other people is counter-intuitive to being charismatic. We are not always going to enjoy what others believe, what they practice, what they enjoy, or who they follow—however, if you were to look at these moments as potential learning experiences, you could still "turn on" your charisma and make it through the most socially land-mined territory while still leaving a good impression on those around you.

How to start a conversation. That's usually the toughest challenge for most of us. How do I begin? For starters, don't pick a subject that will make anyone feel uncomfortable. Nobody likes to talk about uncomfortable topics, generally, and you don't want to make a bad first impression that way. Nor do you want to stroll in and "wow" people with your knowledge on a subject. Only the person speaking ever believes that looks impressive—to everyone else, the biggest bore of the party just started talking!

An easy conversation-starter stems from the fact that people like it when you're nice to them. Not sugary-fake and flattery-based "nice", but genuine, straightforward, and humble. If you're truly strapped for what to say, here's a handy rule that will help:

The history/philosophy/metaphor rule is a tool used by improv comedians, and it's used to help bridge the gap when everyone's imagination has run completely dry. Say the topic of conversation has been diets. Suddenly, an awkward silence descends upon the group.

You might offer, "That reminds me of the time I tried the keto diet. I lost 20 lbs in a week but man, I sure missed potato chips." (History)

This statement can lead to something such as, "You know, I honestly think that a so-called diet should be just eating sensibly. I think the diet and fitness industry is making money off of our willingness to try new fads." (Philosophy)

Then, you can follow with, "Fad diets are like fashion trends. Bell bottoms didn't stay popular forever." (Metaphor)

Many of us try to begin a conversation with a stranger by asking them a question. This is a shot-in-the-dark technique, and can lead to a boring lull. Using the history/philosophy/metaphor rule instead is a sure bet.

You Can Boost Your Charisma By Strengthening These Areas

One of the universal things about people who possess great confidence and charisma is that by and large, most of them live with *purpose*. What their purpose truly is doesn't matter as much as they live have that purpose with conviction. This might seem to be a bit vague, but that's because the purpose and drive depends on the individual. What's woefully noticeable in social situations, however, is when someone lacks drive.

You do *not* have to proclaim your purpose to all who will listen, nor do you have to even make mention of it in conversation. A person's purpose is similar to a character's backstory in a novel: we may never hear about it directly from the author, but we sure notice when it's missing. When you walk into a room, you are projecting your energy to everyone else there. Your personal drive will fill out that energy, making it real, tangible, and interesting. Your purpose might be anything from the conservation of honeybees to being the biggest fan of the New York Jets, it doesn't really matter, as long as it matters *to you*.

So what do you do if you're currently without a purpose? That's easy— pick one. It doesn't have to be one you carry with you throughout your life, nor does it have to be of worldwide importance, sexy, or glamorous. Take some time to sit down and make a list of what you enjoy, and of what's important to you. Then in a neighboring column, strive to come up with ideas of how you can a) further the cause of one of these items, or

b) cultivate support for them, or c) if it's a personal goal, what are the first steps you can take to get closer to it and begin to achieve it?

Many people believe that being charismatic means you have to be perfect, and "on", all the time. Perfect doesn't work, however, because humans simply aren't perfect. If you fake it, other people will sense that. You can roll with the punches and ad-lib your lines, however—just be in the moment and *believe* in the moment. An important thing to get rid of, right now, right away, is shame. Shame does no good for anyone; it's the mental poison that makes everything harder, and that will erode your charisma. So when things get chaotic in a social situation, learn to stand in your comfort zone and in your power—never tell yourself, out loud or in your own head, "that was stupid of me". Get used to shrugging awkwardness off and have a good laugh about it. Laughter is contagious, too. When you spend even a fraction of a second self-analyzing and thinking what you just said was stupid, it *shows*. Your entire demeanor and facial expressions will reflect. You need to start learning, today, how to ditch the embarrassment and shame—those things must simply leave your personal, social vocabulary.

Practice body language. Proper eye contact is incredibly important. If someone stares into your eyes for too long, notice how that makes you feel. It probably makes you feel uncomfortable, right? Eye contact is not something you're going to master in a moment, or in one conversation, so you're going to have to go out and practice it. Wherever you happen to be, practice your eye contact: make sure that you a) don't hold it too long, b) don't look away too often, and c) don't look down. Looking down has the bizarre effect of making it look as if you're either ashamed, or hiding something. Neither of these things will contribute to your charisma.

Practice on the barista at your local coffee shop, your mail carrier, your waiter at a restaurant, anywhere you need to converse with a stranger in a casual setting, non-essential setting. In time, you'll get better at it, and be ready to use what you've learned in a more important situation.

If you're still uncomfortable with making eye contact, distract yourself with this trick: notice the color of the other person's eyes. Make note of the different shades of color in their irises. Doing this takes the discomfort and awkwardness out of the act of making eye contact by making it a cerebral practice rather than an emotional one, and by doing this, we instantly go from "creepy" to "pleasant".

Posture is important. This can be one of the most difficult areas to correct, and most of us are guilty of living with poor posture! The demands of sitting at a desk, or driving a vehicle, or sitting on our couches at the end of the day all create patterns of poor posture in our bodies. Remind yourself throughout your day to:

- **Shoulders back, and down.** It may feel as if you're jutting out your chest when in fact you're simply straightening your spine. If it feels awkward, it's because you're more used to slouching.

- **Head back.** Not tilted back as if you're looking up, but just gently pushed back. Part of poor posture is allowing our head to sit forward on our neck, and this contributes to a slouching spine.

- **Tuck your pelvis in** as much as you can comfortably. This will straighten the lower part of your spine.

- **Are your hands in your pockets?** If so, take them out, and let them be at your sides in a relaxed position.

Begin to notice physical expression in others, including animals. Notice how your dog wags her tail in a circular movement when you come home. Watch your cat stretch and flick his tail back and forth as he drinks water or eats. Notice your coworkers, neighbors, and other parents at the school PTO meeting—who attracts your attention the most? Usually those with the greatest vocabulary of physical movements and expressions. The most important of these? Smiling. Also, a little goes a long way—you don't want to seem performative or silly, but natural, and relatable. Nodding constantly, for instance, gives off an air of impatience, as if you're non-verbally saying "Enough already."

This is also where self-analyzing needs to come in. Many movements and habits we're not even aware of until we see ourselves perform them in a mirror. If you've lost touch with your body mid-conversation, take a second and focus on your toes, then work your way up your body, slowly. This is a good way to realize you've slipped back into poor posture, also.

This is also where something called "mirroring" comes in. Again, subtlety is key. If you gently mirror the physical cues your conversational partner is giving you, you will be pleasing them, and they will feel more comfortable around you.

Watch videos of famous actors and actresses during interviews, on the red carpet, and at award ceremonies. Pick and choose which aspects of their body movement and how they carry themselves physically would suit you, then practice these.

Physical and conversational charisma takes time to improve, so be patient with yourself, and notice how more in control you are during each new social event or gathering.

What Charisma Is Not

We've already covered how charisma is *not* arrogance, conceit, vast knowledge, a perfect body, or perfect anything, really. We don't connect with people at all when we act as if we're better than them—and conversely, we won't make a good impression if we self-deprecate and make fun of ourselves for the crowd's amusement.

Under social pressure, we might panic and think that telling as many jokes as possible is the way to go, and we'd be wrong—nothing is more awkward and alienating than a stand-up comic bombing during his set. There's a time and a place for everything. The way to connect with people is to constantly find common ground, and we do this both by offering similarities as well as by listening. It often takes a lot of listening to determine if a joke's going to be a hit, or not.

While we mentioned that *beginning* a conversation with a question is a potential risk, asking questions *during* a conversation is a great way to keep it going. The more you listen to someone, the greater sense you can get of the way they time their speech, so that you don't "step on" their words and accidentally interrupt them. If you find that the person speaks with very little to no breaks, you can try this technique: lift a finger (as if you're non-verbally saying "excuse me"), and say, "Question", then *ask your question*, and make sure it's pertaining to the exact thing the person was talking about before you paused them.

Think of talk show hosts. Some exist on the edge of what's morally correct, it's true, and seem to only incite the worst in their "guests", but the ones we truly love possess two things: an interest in their guests, and *control*. They deftly and appreciatively guide the conversation, asking questions, laughing at jokes, *connecting* to the human experiences being shared with them in the moment. Again, charisma involves being more interested in the people you're connecting with than being interested in yourself.

Chapter 2: Obstacles Many Of Us Face Regarding Charisma

Of course, if being charismatic were easy, everyone would do it. Let's talk about the obstacles many of us face regarding our charisma, learned or otherwise.

The Importance of Knowing Our Worth

This can be a very challenging task, and it's not necessarily our fault if we're out of touch with our own personal sense of value. Perhaps we were raised by a care-giver who put us down, or lived with a sibling who constantly berated us. Maybe we had a long-term relationship with a partner who was toxic, and who whittled away our self-esteem. Whatever the reason for your flagging self-worth, understand that a) it's not your fault and b) it is your responsibility to do something about it. Healing can take a lot of time, but that's no reason to ignore the need for it. The best time to start something new is today, and right now.

A frequent topic of debate is whether it's true that "we can do anything". For instance, not everyone's capable of becoming a prima ballerina or a professional quarterback. However, if we zero in on this statement, and add some detail to it, it's actually true, if:

- We make sure that our bodies are capable of the task, and discover if there's help to assist us.

- We take the time to do the work necessary to accomplish the "thing", and

- Make sure the thing is something we truly want to do.

You might not ever break into professional American football, but you could turn out to be an excellent football coach at your local Boys and Girls club, or even play in an amateur league. You might not ever perform the Nutcracker at Radio City Music Hall, but you can certainly perform in local events, strengthen your body, and achieve your dream of becoming a dancer. Even those without the use of their legs have ran in marathons, played basketball, or performed in dance concerts. The key elements here are *focus, will, and determination.*

Now let's focus on you. What have you achieved that is still a source of satisfaction and pride to this day? If you've not yet achieved anything you feel is worthy of respect, what would you *like* to achieve? Also, go back and look at things you might not consider achievements, but with a positive eye. Perhaps you're downplaying yourself and masking real, impressive accomplishments.

There are statements you need to make, right now, in order to better yourself and put yourself in the charismatic mindset. These aren't promises—promises can be broken, especially if we're making them to ourselves. These are *statements*:

- I have the potential to achieve great things. I was born with this potential, and no one can take it away from me.

- I will not remain idle in my daily life. I will move forward and be a person of action.

- Following action, I will also give myself permission to rest, and relax. Both action and rest are necessary ingredients to success.

- I will not allow myself to pity myself. There's nothing to pity about me. I am okay.

- I will shift my focus from other people I used to think were better, to myself. I am good enough.

- I will dare to question myself, in order to make sure I'm authentic in my endeavors and behavior. Questioning does not mean hating. I refuse to engage in self-loathing.

- I am going to tap into my potential and achieve more with it.

Understand that you will never please everyone. If you believe that you can, you'll soon learn that trying to please everyone pleases no one, and ignores important care of yourself. Make peace with this and realize that not everyone is for everybody else. It's a wide world out there. You will find the people that you connect with.

Your opinions matter, and they also may change, and that is okay. Don't hide yourself for fear of being unpopular. At the same time, have the strength to *examine* your thoughts and opinions when you gain information and other people's points of view. It's okay to concede that you were wrong, or ignorant of something. Admitting that shows greatness, humility, and a mind that's not afraid to learn and grow.

Pleasing other people is not the point of the game. If it happens, great! If it doesn't, that's okay. Desperation is something that naturally drives others away from us; when we show this in our need to please others, we actually drive them away. When you're not afraid to displease or even offend others with your opinions, it shows strength and confidence. Don't *try* to offend, or take joy in offending others, because that's extremely unappealing, however, when you refuse to change what's vital and *true* about yourself to impress others, that in itself is incredibly impressive. You will make the right connections with the right people when you stand up for yourself with both strength and integrity.

Integrity is the name of the game, and having integrity shows that you don't consider human interaction a game. Other people are just as important as you are; no one should ever be placed above or below someone else. When you are capable of empathy and can put yourself in another's shoes, your words and actions will maintain integrity, and other people will find it easier to relate to you, as well as have respect for you.

What happens when your values change, and you make choices or take action that you would never have in the past? You can still maintain integrity. Integrity simply means that you act and speak in accordance with what you believe, and beliefs change as we mature. Integrity can and should be maintained throughout our lives. Never let fear, your own ennui, or other people's threats coerce you into being corrupted.

Our Inner "Weather" And How It Effects Our Outer Presence

Getting back to our "presence", when we find ourselves in social situations, what's going on inside our heads at the time greatly effects how others perceive us. Later on in the book we'll discuss ways to cultivate happier mindsets and tackle charisma-killers such as anxiety, stress, and depression. Right now, let's focus on the immediate need for a clear, calm mind to project the best presence and maintain optimum charisma.

The nervousness you feel inside will be readily visible on the outside. Just like genuine joy, awkwardness is also contagious.

Refuse to feel shame. If you've made a mistake, it's perfectly acceptable and natural to feel *regret* regarding making that mistake.

Then, using our determination (if the mistake only effected us) or our empathy (if it effected someone else) we can strive to correct that mistake, or at least ensure that it never happens again. In social situations however, shame should be left at the door. It doesn't serve us, and has no place in the charismatic person's repertoire or vocabulary.

What happens when you say something that offends someone? For starters, do not immediately apologize. Stand your ground, not with arrogance, but with quiet strength. Listen to the other person and strive to learn what about your statement was offensive. See if you can learn anything from that person's point of view, and be thankfully vocal about it if you do. Make statements such as "I see where you're coming from." Then, if the emotions have cooled and you've made every effort to understand the other person, you may choose to offer an apology—but make sure you can do that with honesty. Stop adding "I'm sorry" into every other moment of a conversation. It's neither genuine, nor attractive.

Lastly, if you haven't done this enough already, start practicing the art of thinking for yourself. Don't just go along with the crowd. Examine the information you're given with an open mind, but don't be gullible. Become your own person.

Social Awkwardness Explained

When it comes to social awkwardness, there is a lot of *bad* advice out there. For starters, it doesn't matter if "everyone" has felt socially awkward at one point or another—that's not going to help you, not one bit. It also doesn't help to tell you to just "snap out of it" or imagine everyone in the room naked.

I mean, that would be even more awkward, right?

The art of social fluency takes practice. The most common reason people are socially awkward is because they are simply not in enough social situations to have acquired any practice or skills. If you want to be charismatic, you're going to have to do the work; there are no shortcuts.

Spending more time with people, you're going to begin to develop a sense of conversational and social rhythm: when to speak, and when to listen; when to tell a joke and when to keep the topic serious. If you spend most of your time alone, there's no way you're going to achieve this kind of intuitive interactional skill set. Watching actors in conversation might be a start, but we're also not always seeing characters at their best, and most importantly, *we* are not in the conversation—we're only watching it on the screen.

Anything you're skilled at—usually, unless you have a particular knack or gift in that certain area—you will have started out with some degree of awkwardness. Driving a car, writing a resume, mastering a video game, shaving, curling your hair—*it all takes patience and practice.* So resign yourself to the fact that if you want to be charismatic, you're going to need time, patience, and practice. Then approach this task with passion, because that will help too!

Muscle memory pertains to speaking, also. It also helps us with our facial expressions. We mimic each other all of the time, this is how babies learn to speak and express themselves, and this is how we learn to convey the emotions we feel—by watching other people. The more you work those muscles in a certain way to connect with a certain idea or emotion, the easier it will be, the more *natural* it will become, to express yourself with ease and grace in the future.

Social awkwardness comes when we don't exercise these muscles often enough. Spending too much time by ourselves can make these skills "rusty", or underdeveloped.

Determining Whether You're on the AS (Autism Spectrum), and Why It's Not a Bad Thing If You Are

Every one in fifty-nine people in the world will be born with autism. Male children are more apt to be on the autism spectrum than women. What is autism? For starters, it's not necessarily a setback. While approximately one third of people on the spectrum have some amount of intellectual disability and/or are non-verbal, others, such as those with Asperberg's Syndrome, do not. (Pronounced asz-*PURGER'S*). You see, autism is a *spectrum* of brain behavior and recognition. There are many different ways to be on the autism spectrum.

Asperger's is called a "high-functioning" placement of autism. One of the trademarks of having Asperger is having an acute interest bordering on obsession in a certain topic or topics. While this can be challenging during childhood (imagine an elementary school age kid trying to have in-depth discussions of World War II or cryptobiology and you'll get an idea), for adults, it can actually be quite an advantage. A kid obsessed with dinosaurs to the point of memorizing every bone of every species uncovered could have quite a career at a museum or professor of paleontology.

A trait that occurs in people with Asperger's is also a large vocabulary obtained at a young age. People with Asperger's may discover that they intimidate people with their knowledge and vocabulary, but ironically feel intimidated themselves by those people.

What's important to realize is that very often, people with Asperger's don't realize they have a "problem", generally speaking, until adulthood, and their behaviors and the way they look at the world is only labelled a problem by other people, or by themselves if they've been shamed for being awkward in social situations. People on the autism spectrum simply process the information that life gives them differently. That does not make them necessarily "stupid" or "weird". They often have mental and imagination-based gifts that people not on the spectrum do not possess.

However, having Asperger's can pre-dispose you to:

- Avoidance of eye contact (without even realizing it!). A classic sign is someone with Asperger's telling a story to someone, but looking past their shoulder or away while telling it, often making the listener ask, "What are you looking at?"

- Difficulty taking turns.

- Difficulty in making new friends.

- Being prone to conversations that revolve around yourself and your own interests.

- Occasionally, socially-inappropriate behavior. This usually stems from processing things differently, and often out of an attempt to be humorous in a social setting.

- Taking things literally and not understanding common social cues, such as high-fiving, or expressions like "sharp as a whip" to indicate intelligence.

- Some Aspie folks have heightened senses, such as the sense of smell, making those who wear too much cologne or perfume unbearable to be around.

- Finally, for someone with Asperger's, it may be difficult to express their impressions about things to non-AS people. Many people with Asperger's also have something called "synesthesia", where they see music in shades of colors, or can describe the flavor of something in number patterns or unusual choice of words. For these people, senses become combined or switched around.

Since there is a lot more awareness about the autism spectrum now, kids diagnosed early enough get special help at school, such as small classes where they meet once a day to go through "typical" social situations and learn good choices and responses that will keep them in the loop. And while becoming inauthentic to one's self is never a good idea, even to gain popularity, we all have social "tics" and quirks that can be worked through to make us engage with other people more comfortably and smoothy. People with Asperger's just sometimes need a bit more help in that area.

If you think you might have Asperger's, talking to your doctor or therapist, or taking an online test can help you determine whether the description fits you. Once knowing this about yourself, it can be easier zeroing in on the social skills you need to work on the most. Just remember, there is nothing shameful about being born on the autism spectrum. It's genetic, it's common, and people on the spectrum can live a full, vibrant, and fulfilling life.

If you are on the spectrum, or know that you have Asperger's, there are ways that you can get an edge on improving your social prowess. Begin by making a list of things that make you uncomfortable, socially. Separate them into these three categories:

- Things That Confuse Me (such as how to begin a conversation, tell a funny story)

- Things That Worry Me (such as the fact that you're not social enough, or what other people will think of you if you try to become more social)

- Excuses I Make To Avoid Being Social (such as taking on extra shifts at work, or binging an entire television series over a weekend)

Take a good, hard look at the things that worry you. If any of them sound silly, then that's a good thing! That means you're halfway towards eliminating them altogether. Underline or circle any of the worries that look less worrisome once you read them over.

Next, look at your excuses. Becoming more charismatic involves self-analyzing, and this is a challenging task for *everyone*, not just folks on the spectrum. Which of these excuses can be lessened (such as only watching three episodes per weekend of a show), and which would you be able to tackle first, so that over time, you slowly eliminate all of them?

Face your social fears, but do it slowly, one step at a time. There is no need to push yourself here—just *wanting* to get better at socializing is a step in the right direction. As long as you make steady progress, you will reach your goal.

Pay attention to when you try something new that landed on your list of "Worries". What happened when you tried it? How did everyone react? Chances are, it will not have been as bad, or not have been bad at all, as you first feared. Picture how you would react if you met someone who say, stumbled in their words or made an awkward joke. Would you have empathy for them, or would you ridicule them? Once you see that most people will opt to be kind in a social setting, it will be easier for you to reduce your fears in a realistic way.

Finally, if you exhibit any physical symptoms in social settings (or when you're preparing to go to one), such as feelings of panic, trouble breathing, sweating, increased heart rate or dizziness, consider talking to your doctor about trying anxiety medication or CBD. CBD is a non-narcotic derivate of the cannabis plant. It cannot make you feel "high" or intoxicated, but it has been proven to be an excellent tool in fighting anxiety and depression. Many people use it with good results, not just people with Asperger's.

Other steps to help in social settings include:

- Learning and understanding anything that's confusing to you. Reach out to a trusted family member or friend to discuss and even "practice" things that have baffled you in past social settings. Once you've tried a little in private, go out and see if you can gracefully get through these social cues in public, such as at a restaurant, at a library or store, on public transit, at a ball game.

- Learn the fine art of listening. Remember the tip to study the color of someone's eyes? This helps making eye contact comfortable for both the observer and the person being observed. When you listen to someone, give that person validation if they talk about their emotions. "When he raised his voice at me in front of everyone I felt so angry, and also ashamed." "Of course you did! I would, too." Ask the person questions to clarify anything they said.

- Keep your posture straight. If you need physical stimulation to stay focused, you can play with the straw of your drink or subtly tap one finger to your thumb at a time.

- If you're feeling overwhelmed, you can gracefully excuse yourself from the conversation by saying, "Excuse me for a moment. I'm enjoying talking with you, but I have to take care of something real quick." Remember to smile to leave them with a feeling of friendliness and warmth. They might reach out to shake your hand and say "Nice meeting you" or "It was a pleasure". Simply shake their hand, add a smile, and say "Same."

Finally, if you feel like having the support of a community would do you some good, seek out your local autism peer support group. There you can find others who are going through what you are, and who might have additional tips and tricks that have worked for them in social situations.

The Importance of Empathy

One of the biggest fears that haunts many of us in a social environment is the fear that we are being judged. Even if we think that we don't care about this, deep down, being painted unfairly or looked down upon is a very uncomfortable feeling. The key to never make someone feel this way in conversation is to make sure that you have *empathy*. You don't have to state that you empathize with them to let them know it's there—if you feel it, so will they. When you cultivate the ability to see things from someone else's point of view, it makes it easier to bridge the gap from your reality to theirs, and vice versa. Each of us lives and sees life in a unique way. We all may have similarities, but we all have something that's just slightly different about us as well. Having the mindset that being different is not only normal, but interesting and even delightful, will cultivate warmth between you and your conversational partner or group.

Chapter 3: How to Tap Into Advice From the Experts, and Outlast Your Vulnerability

When the late musician and artist Prince walked off the stage of his first big tour in 1979, the record company A&R folks had doubts he had enough charisma to make the tour worthwhile financially. In fact, they found him downright awkward! If you think of Prince's videos, concerts, and overall presence, the idea that someone would find him uncharismatic is a shock. When Prince was asked to warmup for Rick James' tour, the older, charismatic singer took Prince under his wing, and Prince—determined to learn the ropes—rose to the occasion: he observed James, and looked at performances by other artists he looked up to. *By the end of that tour,* it's said that Rick James felt a little intimidated by the younger star, his performance and command of the audience was that good. How did Prince go from awkward to amazing? He was determined, and he practiced, constantly.

This just goes to prove, however, that charisma is 50% *learned*. We all have our fears, hangups, and insecurities, but we can beat them and outlast them to bring out the bold, confident, happier person inside.

It might seem like a catch 22, but the two single things that enable charisma the most are confidence and warmth. Those two ingredients are nearly impossible to fake. What brings them naturally to the surface? Your experience, and your practice. The more you get out there and practice your "presence", the more you reach out and connect with people in the positive ways we've described, the more confidence and natural warmth you'll exude.

How to Get Started When You're Too Afraid You'll Fail

You might be saying now, well all of that is nice, but it's easier said than done. That's true: it's easier to talk about hard work than actually *do* the hard work. That doesn't mean you won't be able to do it. The first step is to understand what fears are holding you back, and the number one fear most people possess regarding self-improvement and confidence is the debilitating fear that they will fail.

Take a mental snapshot of where you are, right now. Whether it's your desk or position at work, or at home, or during your morning commute. Now, picture yourself in twenty years, same snapshot, just you—twenty years older. Is this a good image?

Fear is not what should be motivating you right now; fear usually cripples or depresses us. What should replace that fear is desire, and *belief*—belief in the potential that you still have within you, and the desire to see it come to fruition. The only thing holding you back is yourself.

The actual act of *feeling fear* can be dangerous, over time. The hormones secreted when we're afraid are the same that course through our bodies when we have a heart attack—and our bodies can often feel as if we were in cardiac arrest when fear grips us too tightly. Of course, there are times when fear is absolutely justified (a semi veering out of control towards your car on the highway), but the fear of failure need not be one of those times. For your own health, it's important to work on your fear/failure mindset *right now*:

- Immediately, today, in this moment—tell yourself that you are no longer afraid to fail. Failure leads to learning, and when we learn, we gain an edge over the competition. The acceptance of our own failure leads to bigger, better things, such as genuine warmth and gratitude. When we accept our own mistakes, we're also less prone to lose our tempers or judge others who make mistakes. All around, acceptance of failure is one of the healthiest choices you can make in your *life*.

- Never take it personally. When you fail, don't allow yourself to feel victimized or as if a target was painted on your back. Everybody fails! Top-selling authors have gotten hundreds of rejection letters; pro athletes stumble; CEO's make the wrong choice, and move on. The more you fail at first the bigger your successes will be in the future, if you choose to analyze the failure and gain knowledge from it.

- Every time you forgive yourself for failing, your self-esteem level shoots up. It might be hard for you to say, today, that you love yourself; that's not an easy thing to do for many of us. But you will subconsciously be saying just that when, after a failure, you say, "That's okay. I can learn from this and be better." That's self-love, and it builds your confidence exponentially every time.

- *DON'T STOP*. Don't let failure break your stride or disrupt your momentum. It's perfectly acceptable to rest and recoup, but don't take an extended hiatus because you failed. "Getting back on the horse" is a real thing. You have to get back in the game before fear, inactivity, and self-doubt take over.

- Talk to people that you trust. It's important not to go too long with your emotions bottled inside. People get shamed, especially men, for hanging on to "feelings". Well, that's nonsense—

everybody has feelings and emotions, and the most successful of us learn to process them, accept them, and share them with a confidante when we need to. Don't just tell yourself "get over it". Be the bigger person to yourself, and make peace with the fact that you are *not* an emotion-less robot. Charismatic people are in touch with their emotions—how else could they be able to connect to others, emotionally?

- Finally, *imagine* a scenario where you fail. Picture the consequences; they are often not nearly as bad as we feared. Challenge yourself to ask, not "what can go wrong?" but "what can go RIGHT?".

How to Give Your Social Skills a Tune-up

It can be difficult, even daunting, to take that first step towards socials skills mastery. There's no need to jump in feet first or tackle anything major right away. Ease yourself into being more charismatic by trying some of these techniques and tricks:

- **Use music to boost your morale.** If you're nervous before a social event, use classical, jazz, or even chilled-out classic rock to settle your anxiety and put yourself in a calm, collected, positive mood. If you're feeling less-than-pumped, put on tunes that elevate your emotions and put your thoughts in a more positive frame. If you're feeling down on yourself, use inspiration tracks to remember that you can do whatever you set your mind out to do. Play a favorite DJ mix to move you from hermit-mode to life-of-the-party winner.

- **Leave your comfort zone once in a while** by trying something new. Volunteering is a fantastic way to improve your social skills, learn new things, and practice what you've learned in a zero-pressure environment—plus, you'll good about doing something positive for the community. **Take a class** in something you've always wanted to learn, and take time to talk with other people in the class when you can. **Go to events at your local library,** another opportunity for pressure-free socializing.

- **Exercise your initiative muscle by making plans,** and sticking to them. Following through builds self-esteem because we learn we can count on ourselves. It also builds confidence because following through banishes fear. We begin to believe that what we say we'll do, we'll do—and that's a huge charisma boost.

- **Tap into meditation.** Try guided meditative exercises—where someone vocally guides you through the steps, a few minutes each day to cultivate a place of inner calm. Once the meditation becomes familiar, you'll find you can reach that calm place in the snap of a finger—essential when finding yourself in unexpected, awkward social situations.

- **Get some exercise.** Even walking at a comfortable pace for 20 minutes a day can help balance the mood of your mind: your body needs those good-feeling chemicals to function properly, and so does your brain. A constant influx of happiness hormones can banish a lot of anxiety and fear about social settings. Plus, you'll begin to feel better about your body, which will translate into your body language, instantly boosting your charisma levels.

- **Make a goal to face one of your fears.** This is a tough one, but the rewards are huge. Think of good you feel the last time you achieved something. Facing one of your fears will teach you that you have what it takes to rise to a challenge, or overcome an obstacle. Both your conscious and subconscious mind will carry that lesson for the rest of your life. Additionally, you'll foster empathy towards people who've either faced their fears, or are still struggling with doing so. This one's a tough task but it's worth it tenfold.

- **Tap into inner creativity.** The mind does not enjoy being idle. Sometimes, instead of feeding the brain with media, news, other people's opinions, we have to put something out into the world that's made of *us*. Creating something is a terrific exercise to gather your mind's skills into one unified focus. It doesn't have to be gallery-worthy or be able to sail across the Atlantic. Take some "me" time and work on something creative, just for what it does for your confidence and inner child.

- **Redesign your environment.** Take a look at your living space. Is it dark and cluttered, a place you just return to in order to crash after a long day? Now take a weekend and transform that pad into someplace that inspires you. How would a successful, happy person keep their living space? Bring in light, tidy up, set up a workout area or meditation spot. This space is your sanctuary, where you come home to build yourself back up. Act as if you're already successful, and soon you will be.

- **Use visualization every day.** Before a meeting, interview, social event, date—whatever the occasion, *visualize* it and imagine positive results. Professional dancers must *see* the moves they've not yet learned in their head before they can even begin to teach their bodies to master them. It's an important trait of successful people—learn to visualize the best outcome, and you'll up your odds of achieving great results.

- **Practice moving your body in a confident way.** Even when you're alone, or don't have a need to be "on", do it anyway! Muscle memory is a fantastic tool, and absolutely essential when it comes to changing your body language. Always focus on your posture, and practice developing a relaxed, confident poise.

- **"Now" is the most important time of all.** It's a good practice to look back at the past and recall positive memories, and it's important to imagine a positive future, but oftentimes we can get lost in switching back and forth from past to future while completely ignoring the present. Living in the present forces us to be the best we can be *right now*. Being mindful of what's happening in the moment can greatly improve your poise, confidence, and charisma.

- **Keep your focus outward.** When out among other people, focus on *them*. This will bounce back in your favor as they in turn focus on *you*. Introspection in a crowd projects awkwardness, as well as any negative emotions you might have tucked away, deep inside. So keep your mind out of itself and focused on the rest of the world. There's a lot to see, and you'll be interacting, learning, and growing while you do so.

- **Stick with positive people.** Learn to pick and choose who you spend your time amongst. Positivity is contagious, but so is negativity. If you form connections to people who have a positive outlook, you'll soon learn to look at life positively by proxy.

- **Curate the "newsfeed" of your daily social media.** Learn when to steer clear of negativity and bad news. Too much can wear on us like pollution or negative emotions. It's important to know what's going on in the world, but the human mind is so malleable, so impressionable, that you risk triggering anxiety or depression if you expose yourself to too much negative news.

- **Resist the urge to compare yourself to other people.** You are *you*, and there is no one else like you. The only person you should ever compare yourself to is who you were a year, five years, ten years ago—how have you grown? How have you improved, and what areas do you need to work on? What have you accomplished, big or small, and how can you focus on making yourself feel good about that?

How to Improve Your Speaking Skills

This can be one of the most challenging areas for many of us to improve upon, let alone master. Speaking skill excellence often gets overlooked in schools; the naturally extroverted kids stand out and rise up, while the shyer children remain on the sidelines, never having been given a chance or a lesson on how to join their more social peers.

Don't give up hope, however: learning good speaking skills is something anyone can accomplish, with determination and practice.

Here are some tips regarding practicing better speaking skills:

- **Don't judge yourself for being nervous; it's natural.** That doesn't mean you have to accept it! This is where practice takes our determination to the next level. Practice speaking in front of a mirror, to the person behind the counter at the dry cleaners, to your Uber driver, anywhere you can get some practice (without delaying someone or yourself), grab it. In time you will see your comfort level rising.

- **Prepare for your audience.** If you're going to be speaking to a crowd, or an important individual like a hiring manager, take some time to research them. Your words are for them, not for yourself—you can to yourself all day long at home. Discover how your audience views things, and tailor your words that viewpoint.

- **If you give a speech, you've got 30 seconds to hook your audience.** This is also why preparation is key; don't just try to wing it. Practice before the date.

- **Let yourself shine through.** Your personality is the best part of public and/or social speaking, so don't hide it. Be proud of you and let your inner qualities shine.

- **Ditch the "practice makes perfect" mentality.** Yes, we want you to *practice, practice, practice*, but understand that being human involves imperfection. Don't expect perfection from yourself: expect greatness. Even the best speakers, artists, professionals have flaws, and are not ashamed of them. If you stumble, just get up and keep going!

- **Use humor for instant connection.** Observe comedians: their stories are often based on simple, mundane aspects of every day life. As you go through your day, take notes of moments and situations that make you chuckle, then use these anecdotes for a clever shot of humor in a conversation.

The Power of Body Language

Over 90% of projected charisma is made up of non-verbal cues, i.e. body language. It's incredible how the human mind perceives the slightest detail without our even realizing it, but that's the reality of confidence, charisma, and communication.

Most of us are completely unaware of the messages we're sending with our posture, facial expressions, hand movements and bodies, so if you master these things, you gain a serious advantage in the social world.

The following are positive cues that make a good impression on your audience:

- **Firm handshake.** Many of us think this is a no-brainer, but many of us also get it wrong. Don't crush the other person's hand in a death grip and don't hold it too long. Think of it as stopping your car at a stop sign: come to a complete stop, pause, then drive. Grasp the other person's hand (allow the crook between your index finger and thumb to meet the other person's); hold firmly but comfortably, pause, then let go.

- **When seated:** Lean forward or sit up straight, allow yourself to gesture as you speak, make eye contact. This conveys you're invested in the conversation and the person or people you're talking to.

- **Watch the tone of your voice.** Keep it in the middle—don't lower it unnaturally to sound deeper, and don't let it slide upward as some of us do when we're home or in a casual setting. Comfortable and warm are the vibes you're aiming for with your voice.

- **Allow yourself to alter your facial expressions** per the context of what is being said. Avoid this mistake: don't look to the ceiling when something outrageous or frustrating is shared. The zombie eye-roll isn't flattering, but many of us need to "unlearn" this instinctive reaction, so don't feel bad if that's you as well. Remember to add genuine smiles where they're appropriate.

- **Pepper "nods" sparingly, but do use them.** Excessive nodding can come across as dismissive, but use them when you feel as if the conversation has come to a mutual agreement (this will hopefully happen more than once).

The following are habits that convey negative, subconscious emotions, so learn to avoid them:

- **Looking at a person who's not talking.** It's easy for many of us to find that our mind has wandered, and while you may not be actively *staring* at the person, looking at anyone but the speaker has a weird message that you're threatening that person. Try to be self-aware enough to catch if/when you do this, and quickly weed it out of your social body-vocabulary.

- **Don't look down; don't look up.** Keep your eyes level. You might let your gaze drop for a moment—that's natural, but when you look up, *re-engage*, whether it's with a nod, a smile, or a brief, spoken reiteration of what's just been said. It's okay to be human! Just be *present*.

- **Respect personal space.** This is a tricky one. If you were raised in the United States or are speaking with people who were, understand that American personal space is a lot more generous than what's practiced in other countries. Test the waters and make sure you're noticing if the other person backs up to add some room between you, then make sure you don't crowd them again. Don't apologize! Just move on from the awkward moment and keep the conversation going. The faux pas will soon be forgotten.

- **No need for eye contact during silences.** This is more to do with casual social settings, but when the conversation lulls, be comfortable within yourself and look at something else. Remember the history/philosophy/metaphor rule.

- **Don't cross your arms.** This is a self-comforting mechanism used by many of us, but leave it at the door during social events; it sends a message that you're guarded, bored, or disinterested.

- **No eye contact for longer than 5 – 7 seconds at a time.** Go over the limit and you run the risk of making the observed person uncomfortable.

- **Slouching.** The message this sends is anything from out of shape to subservient. It's a hard one to beat but give it your utmost attention—your spine will thank you and you'll save money on your chiropractic bill.

- **Fiddling with your fingers or objects.** If you're on the spectrum, you get a pass, but try to go as subtle with it as you can. If you're not, learn to control this habit during social or business situations.

- **Don't touch your hair or the back of your neck.** Two different situations: doing outside work (construction, yard work, community yard sale) vs. company function, social fundraiser, cocktail party. See the difference? In a social setting we're supposed to emulate a bit more poise, so try to avoid these casual physical cues. Playing with your hair (wrapping it around a finger) is also best left for movie night with friends.

- **This isn't the time for grooming.** Leave that piece of lint where it is until you can find a restroom; don't bite your nails or cuticles, and don't touch your face. Not only will avoiding these habits give an overall better impression, but keeping your hands away from your face and mouth will cut down tremendously on the number of times you get a cold or stomach bug.

- **Don't clear your throat too much.** People taking certain medications (such as blood pressure meds) can find they often get a dry throat. If that's you, have a glass of water, cocktail, or other beverage on hand. This presents an appealing image regardless , as long as you're not visibly intoxicated. Also: try to avoid saying "um" and "like" too much, as in "So like, we spoke to him yesterday and he said he was on board with the idea." The best way to get these verbal stutters out of your speech is to practice: speak out loud at home as if you were talking to someone else; if you use one of those filler-words, start over.

Chapter 4: Gratitude, Abundance, and Other Positive Mental States

The most important point, if you take away nothing else, is that to have charisma, there has to be an "inner you" that's feeling good. You can't fake happiness; people can see that pretension a mile away, and nobody wants to be around someone who isn't happy. It's not that they're judging you (well, maybe some of them are but that's their problem), it's that instinctively, we can feel unhappiness, and it scares us. So we move away from it and its source.

If you think happiness is merely another trick to gain you charisma, you need to think again: happiness and inner satisfaction is vitally important to your health, and to every aspect of your life. Those suffering from chronic depression are especially at risk for things because their mind's most essential defense mechanism is compromised; this is also why it's in extremely poor taste to judge someone for taking medication for their mental health. At least they are *trying*, and getting the help they need to win back some of the happiness and balance they lost.

However you don't have to suffer from chronic depression to be low on happiness. What we consider "being happy" is a combination of chemicals produced in the brain. This comes from a variety of sources and causes: a healthy, active body, a busy, engaged mind, but also a rested mind. Get used to the concept of "living well" if you want to portray confidence and charisma.

What defines "Living Well"? Not three houses, five cars, and a yacht, although that doesn't hurt. Living a good, satisfying life is as varied as there are people in the world: basically, living well depends on what you need and want from life, and figuring that out requires some tough honesty. Money buys freedom of choice, and peace of mind when it comes to being on top of bills, having left over for savings, being able to travel—but the accumulation of money in and of itself is only a means to an end. What do you want the "end" of your story to be?

Learning To Savor the Moment and the Experience

A good way to cultivate happiness in ourselves is to learn this important skill: *savoring*. One might immediately associate that with food, but it can be applied to any moment, any sensory input or experience that comes our way:

- Stepping out of the house to fetch the mail and feeling the morning sun on your face.

- Sitting in a park on your lunch break, watching the world go by and listening to the birds in the trees.

- Taking your car out for a weekend drive while listening to your favorite tunes.

- Laying your head on your pillow after a long but productive day.

- Having a passing, pleasant conversation with a stranger in a supermarket.

Life's not always about great, groundbreaking achievements, in fact, those are few and far between, typically, which is why they're so incredible and memorable. The *smaller* moments are what fill our lives, however, and if we rush past those in hopes of the groundbreakers, we're going to be missing a lot.

Learning to be *present* in the moment is a key to so many things: happiness, self-exploration, satisfaction, and greater *charisma*. People zero in and gravitate to those of us who are present. They want to know more and connect with this person. And why not? Present people are happy people, which leads us to the next sub-topic.

Happiness Is Contagious

As human beings and as inherently social creatures, we share a lot with each other even when we don't intend to or realize we're sharing. We pass information from person to person every day. One of the things we share the most are our emotions.

Take for example, a man pulling out of a parking lot and honking his horn at a pedestrian who dared walk in front of his car. He rolls down his window and gives that person a not-so-cordial piece of his mind before driving off. That person, in turn, feels a bit rattled but tries to shake the moment off, however while in the check-out line at the grocery store she can feel her impatience and anger rising as someone ahead of her slowly pays with a check.

Perhaps when it's her turn to check out and the cashier accidentally gives her incorrect change, she snaps, "Wow that is completely wrong. *Try again.*" Later in the day as the cashier boards the bus for home, he closes his eyes and pretends to sleep instead of offering an elderly man his seat, because *to heck with people.*

So the point of this is to state: emotions are contagious. We share them as quickly as we do words—faster, even. Emotions are written in our facial expressions, embedded in our tone of voice, in our body language, in the timber of the words we choose. So if you had a choice to share one emotion, which one would it be? The trick to this answer is that *you* have to feel the emotion first.

Of course you'd choose happiness—who wants to feel anger, rage, sadness or regret? When you cultivate happiness within yourself, it can begin as if you were holding a single candle. The wind is going to test that flame, and even put it out sometimes. With practice, however, you can relight it. With even more practice, your candle becomes a lantern, protected from the wind, impossible to snuff out.

Your happiness can be like that, too. Angry people may come and go, but you're inner fire burns on, and in doing so, draws people to it. That is the power of *charisma*.

Learn to Appreciate Yourself

A cornerstone of inner happiness is the skill of self-appreciation. You can get a head start on this important skill by setting time aside to make a list. Write down three to five things about yourself that you feel good about. Savor the positive emotions that come with recognizing these things.

Now, elaborate on this list by seeing if you can connect anyone else to these skills, traits, or achievements. Perhaps it was a parent or sibling, or foreman at a job site. Perhaps it was a professor in college, or an empathic coworker. Perhaps it was a best friend of two decades. Who contributed to the "you" you are today? Take time to relish the gratitude that comes from knowing those people helped you pave the way to the happiness of today.

Often, when we work on instilling happiness within ourselves and are practicing self-reflection, we also dig up painful or unpleasant memories or emotions. It's okay to think about these, as long as you're not going to let them linger. *Rumination* is the act of dwelling in the past, looking for places to lay blame for things going wrong; we often blame ourselves when we ruminate. Make the conscious decision to abandon this practice, in favor of gratitude and happiness. Building a powerful, confident self includes discarding that which hurts and undermines us.

Another good practice is at the end of each day, take time to consider the moments that were satisfying in some way, or that brought you happiness. If you found there weren't many of these, resolve to seek more happy moments tomorrow. Become an *active participant* in your daily life, seeking happiness, then taking the time to savor it once you find it.

Keeping a journal is a great way to be able to look back and realize you've had more good days than bad. In fact, decide today to stop labeling days as "bad"; unless a day is truly catastrophic, most days we consider "bad" were just full of obstacles and challenges. If we have enough self-belief and inherent joy within us, however, we can ride out those days without allowing them to get us down.

Cultivating Abundance

An abundance mindset is one in which you believe and live your life as if there is enough resources to go around. You don't focus on what you're lacking—you focus on what you have. You learn to get rid of fear or negative emotions when you spend money, and appreciate that you have money to spend. You are able to look around you and see that what you have is good, enough, and more will come. An abundance mindset is a bit like look at the glass-half-full, instead of worrying when the waiter will come to refill it.

Ways of thinking that promote abundance:

- You have control of your life and what happens in it.
- Your physical energy is relaxed but alert, present and mindful, patient and calm.

- Your emotional energy is balanced but engaged (empathy), and you come across as if you're invested in working on things that are bigger than just you. You care about things on a global scale. Your presence inspires others on some level. You meet every day with some excitement, and feel that good things are on their way.

- You can see multiple solutions to a problem, and what's more— you see opportunities and different paths, *rather* than problems and wrong turns. Your outlook is like someone cheerfully and effectively navigating rush our traffic, finding new routes, shortcuts, enjoying new scenery because you took a different way. This way of thinking leads you to realize *there is always a choice.*

Become mindful. Fine, but what does that mean, exactly? It means being present, being *here*, standing firmly at the point of *now*. Again, no rumination, and no dwelling in the future—it's important to have goals and dreams but we cannot *remain there*, or we might lose our way in the present. When you practice mindfulness, you're back in your body, back in your purpose, and you notice things. Being mindful is like being a defensive driver: you're not busy lost in thought or glancing at your phone because driving is important, and so is being alive!

Something interesting to know about being mindful: we often get hyper-focused on one thing. While that helps us hone skills and see projects to the end, when we don't take time to open our eyes to our surroundings and live in the moment, we tend to *miss* opportunities, learning, and important cues about other areas of our lives.

When you savor moments, live in the now, are grateful for what you've got and hopeful about what is on its way to you, then you are on your way towards happiness, abundance, and charisma.

Gratitude Is the First Step

Not everybody is well-suited for keeping journals. That being said, everybody is capable of journaling. While the thought of writing every day can be daunting for people who's interests lie elsewhere, remember this: you don't have to write anything deep, profound, worthy of the New York Times best-seller list. Writing a journal can be as mundane as writing a to-do or shopping list. It's almost the same thing when keeping a gratitude journal.

To really sink your teeth into living with gratitude, start a Gratitude Journal and list ten things you're grateful for every day. If you find yourself stuck, get into the small things, the fine details that make your daily life pleasant. Here's an example:

- I'm grateful to live in an apartment with air conditioning when this summer is reaching record-high temperatures.

- I'm grateful I found my favorite pen in that suit pocket this morning.

- I'm grateful that my dog doesn't tear up the house while I'm gone. I'm grateful for her company at night.

- I'm grateful that I haven't gotten sick yet this year.

- I'm grateful that my brother called the other day. I've missed him.

There does not have to be deep, sweeping statements of gratitude—that is not the point of a journal like this. The point here is to *notice the small things*, the things we all usually take for granted, because when we stop and notice them, suddenly that's:

- Living in the present.

- Living with gratitude.

- Appreciating the abundance in our lives.

- Living mindfully.

Use language that supports your mindset. Notice the words you choose. Are any particularly negative? Pay attention to what you choose to talk about. For some of us, sharing a common complaint has been a go-to ice-breaker. Realize, however, that when you connect with other people over negativity, you have no where to go from there. Positivity, however, will generally keep going, even if it veers into the negative for a moment. Remember—people gravitate towards *happiness*.

Not only does positive speech attract other people, but it's been proven to be good for your brain. Saying uplifting, confident, and empathic things on a regular basis is good for you—it will help you change your mindset if it's been too mired in negative thinking for too long.

Showing gratitude at work is a surefire way to promote positivity and exude confidence. Saying "thank you" doesn't cost a dime, but saying so adds to the general morale and happiness of the team or branch as a whole.

Build Up the Things You're Passionate About

Is there something (or more than one thing) that elates you, gets you excited with you think about? Tap into that passion; don't just keep it to yourself as something you like to daydream about. Find a way to incorporate a bit of that into your life, and watch it illuminate your confidence and charisma.

For instance, for someone who follows the great culinary competitions on television, it would be a good practice to find a way to corporate what is a passionate pastime into something they explore in their daily lives. If taking a cooking course isn't possible due to the demands of work and family, then take a look at the show's hosts—have they written any cookbooks? Who's style calls to you the most? Begin to learn, as an apprentice does, and let their passion guide you in the way a master guides a pupil. With this new passion-based hobby in your life, your energy, presence, and confidence will be felt by everyone you meet. Invite friends and family over for a dinner party; you'll have something to talk about in conversation—everybody loves to talk about food.

The Case For Daily Meditation

Regardless of age, gender, background or skill-set, anyone can find benefits in meditation. At the core of this practice is acceptance of self, and when practiced regularly, that acceptance of self extends to the world around the meditator. Meditation firmly anchors us in the balance of life; we give, and we receive. We become more than just the sum of our belongings and acquisitions. Eventually, regular meditation leads to an appreciation for our own well-being, and that well-being is the key to happiness. Meditation provides us with an easy, daily opportunity to bring a greater sense of well-being into our lives.

Choosing to begin to meditate is a personal choice, but it *can* be for everyone. If you're tired of feeling overburdened, physically and mentally exhausted, and/or sleep-deprived, however, then you'd be doing yourself a favor by giving meditation a try. Just one week of daily meditation—eight minutes a day—can bring such a turnaround in your outlook, odds are you'll never go back to living without it.

Meditation at first will seem *too simple* to be effective, but in time, you will learn that simplicity is often the most effective medicine. As you start to see the positive results, your confidence will gain a boost. You don't have to understand how meditation is doing this for you to enjoy the reality that's it making changes in your energy and psyche.

The mind and body are two parts of the same sum, and are interconnected. Meditation can help us heal one while simultaneously healing the other. The best part of meditation is that *you* are in control. Once you learn that, you can find the courage to let go of self-judgement, let go of a mindset of scarcity, of negativity, of fear, and of reaction.

Most of us know the popular expression, "Be the change you desire to see in the world." As you begin to *get better*—be that in dealing with healing an injury or illness, or just feeling better in your body, or perhaps by finally easing off the shackles of stress and anxiety—so will the environment you improve. The joy you have begun to cultivate within yourself will radiate out to everyone around you. Peacefulness begets peacefulness.

A more positive mind, and positive emotions. Studies have found that daily meditation has a profound effect on emotions, reducing anxiety and depression and increasing self-compassion in women who make meditation a part of their regular routine. Meditation works on the brain's natural *neuroplasticity*, which means the tissues of the brain can physically change over time, depending on the stimuli we feed it—if we subject it to stress and negativity on a regular basis, then the areas of the brain in charge of releasing stress hormones will increase in size. Meditation, on the other hand, slowly increases the areas of the brain that produce pleasure-inducing hormones, such as seratonin, which helps us relax and comprehend things more easily.

Learning to be in the moment mindfully effectively blocks the tendency to over-analyze and prevents thoughts from turning inward and becoming self-blame.

How do I meditate? Meditation is incredibly simple. There are books and websites devoted to it, but the core of all meditation begins with:

- good posture
- deep, proper breathing
- keeping one's free of thought

But wait, you might protest—is it not true that I "think, therefore I am"? Yes, were our brains to stop functioning, we would too—that doesn't mean we need immediate, extraneous thought crowding our conscious minds every minute of the day. There are deeper thought processes constantly stirring beneath the surface of our conscious mind that we are not readily aware of; as for the surface, we can benefit greatly by keeping that calm, simple, present, and mindful.

To get started with meditation, set aside ten minutes and find a comfortable place to sit. If you want to sit in a chair, make sure your arms can be in your lap or at your sides. Make sure your feet can be flat on the floor, and that your spine can be as straight as possible. Next, you can either close your eyes, or stare at a focal point such as a candle. Take a deep breath from your stomach—*do not move your shoulders up and down,* this is improper breathing. As a thought enters your mind, notice it (by thinking "I thought of work, just now"), then dismiss it. Categorize each thought briefly and quickly and let it fall from your mind like a leaf from a tree.

Ten minutes of this each day will have remarkable effects—try it this week, and see for yourself!

Practice Affirmations

Affirmations might be currently all the rage, but there's a reason they're so popular: *they work*. Words have power. It's simply a fact.

Think of something terrible someone said to you a long time ago: decades later, chances are those words still burn. On the other side of the coin, however, are positive, uplifting words: these, especially if spoken every day, can remap the brain and recharge the spirit. Affirmations rebuild us from within, making us better, making us stronger, and eventually more charismatic.

Some simple affirmations to say to yourself every day:

- I'm open to learning.

- I'm excited to see what today will bring.

- I'm interested in what other people have to say.

- I'm thankful for my thoughts and ideas.

- I hope for positive outcomes for both myself and others.

- I believe in the love inherent in the world.

- I can see the good in other people.

- I can see the good in myself.

You can say these affirmations in the morning when you start your day, as you're driving to work (after you've memorized some of them—don't read while you drive, of course), and during any difficult moment where you feel unsteady and need a calming focal point. The point of affirmations is to counteract any negative thoughts that might break through the surface of your mind. As soon as you feel that negativity barging in, meet it head-on with a positive affirmation.

Chapter 5: Making Excellent First Impressions

Research has proven that first impressions occur in the first thirty seconds of meeting someone—or less. Using what we know about the human mind, familiarity, visual cues, and mirroring behavior, we're able to gain some serious advantages in this area if we take enough time to prepare. Whether it's a simple matter of meeting the new neighbors, the crucial first meeting of a first date, a job interview, or finally meeting the new boss, you can step up your game and make their first impression and excellent one.

First, the Visuals...

This can be the most enjoyable or the most challenging, depending on the person. Some of us might take immediately to building the perfect outfit, the right colors and accessories, what looks most flattering and why, while others may stare at their closet and draw a complete blank.

Whatever your thoughts on fashion and grooming, understand that these tools exist to help us convey instant non-verbal information about ourselves to the viewer. If you think you don't want to care too much about the way you look, ask yourself—do you choose your words carefully, or do you say whatever random thought comes into your head, to anyone close enough to listen? If it's the former, than you can understand, fashionista or not, why appearance factors so highly in the subject of first impressions.

If you can't put an outfit together, don't be ashamed, just ask for help. People who enjoy this sort of thing also become *delighted* when asked to help the clothes-blind. Find someone who has a good understanding of the type of situation you're dressing for, as well as someone who's known you at least long enough to get a handle on your personality. You don't want to wander into a first date looking like someone who's in the midst of a mid-life crisis, nor do you want to dress like a retired golf-enthusiast if that's not anywhere near your personal mark.

Take stock of your entire wardrobe and see what items you might have overlooked. Many of us get stuck in the rut of wearing the same thing; there might be hidden gems in your closet that you've forgotten about.

Comfort plus excellent fit = success. You might not want to hear this, but going to a department store or higher end boutique has its advantages when first impressions matter. It's not the brand or the price tag—*it's the fit* and the quality. When clothes are mass-produced in the cheapest means available, they often end up ill-fitting, in materials that simply do not compliment the human body. Additionally, a department store or boutique often has higher-paid salespeople who can give honest advice on whether a garment works for your body or not. A note here: not every body is perfect, even the ones of the models we see in magazines and on tv. If a salesperson doesn't treat you and your body with respect, walk right out the door; they usually work on commission, and should know better anyway.

Consider using a tailor after you've found the perfect outfit. There's no reason you should put back a perfect pair of pants just because they're too long—if they fit you right in all the right places, consult a tailor to adjust the length, especially if the garment is high quality and you know it's going to be a good investment.

Power colors are a real thing—the human palette is incredibly varied, from skin and eye color to hair color. Any designer will tell you that certain colors compliment other colors. If the interviewer can't stop subconsciously noticing how your red suit clashes with your pink skin, you may not get the air time you need. Ask for help if you need some, and consider putting together a few looks and inviting friends to vote on them. (Share pictures of yourself *wearing* the looks so they can see if the colors are good on you).

Accessories are just as important as clothes. Especially in situations where you might be judged on how seriously you are about things—such as a job interview or meeting with a boss to discuss a promotion—wearing cheap or gawdy accessories can sabotage a potentially great outfit. Go with classic elegance if you're at a loss—it's a timeless style that can suit any personality or age group.

Finally, let's talk about hair. You might enjoy this topic even less than clothing, but it's just as important, if not even more so. Grooming is absolutely judged across the board, whether consciously or subconsciously. You don't have to be flamboyant or fancy (in fact it's better if you're not), but you do have to appear clean, controlled, and contained. If your hair is unruly, talk to a stylist about how best to get it under control. If your hair is thinning but your clinging on to those last, longer top wisps, now is the time to think about a sharp, short cut. If you've been wanting to dye your hair a wild color—go for it, just wait until after the important event. You never want to try a new style, cut or color immediately before an interview or first date. You'll need some buffer time to fix it if it didn't work out the way you'd anticipated, or to do it over completely if it was a disaster.

If you've gotten the same, sensible cut and style regularly, it's okay to do that the night or two before, since you're working with familiar territory.

When it comes to facial hair take some time and explore the culture of the company you're interviewing with. See if they have a website with any photos of employees. Do any of the men sport facial hair, and if they do, are they allowed to grow it out? If the culture is more casual than conservative and you've had a longer beard for a while, consider keeping it, but going in with it "tamed". Beard oil or even new beard "straightening" irons are easy to use and result in a good-looking, well-groomed beard.

If you're not sure of the company's policy on facial hair and you're not willing to shave (yet), trim your hair and look as neat as possible, then be sure to ask about the company's culture regarding facial hair. Frame it as "Can you share with me your firm's policy on facial hair, so I can better acclimate myself to the company culture?"

Some other things to consider: if you wear a wedding ring but perhaps it's grown tight, make sure you don't have a tan line in its place or wear a different, more casual ring in its place. Always turn your phone off—not just on vibrate—not only for interviews but also for first dates. Showing that you care and have respect goes a long way in making a fantastic first impression.

Have a Mental Destination Before You Embark

Many of us seem to just "go through the motions" when it comes to important events. That's for a couple of different reasons. We often feel pressure to get out there and "do something", even if that something is not necessarily the right thing for us.

Before going on a date, have some self-analyzing time. Is this what you really want? Is it what you need right now? Remember, there's another person invested in this. Going through the motions in this context does not only ourselves, but the other person a disservice. If you still want to go on that date but are just not sure if it's the right time for you, then by all means go—but make sure in the middle of the date (not the beginning, and certainly not the end) to talk about where you are at this point in life. It's okay not to be sure, just let the other person know that you appreciate their time with you and that you're enjoying yourself.

If you have been hoping to get back into dating to meet the right person, take some time to reflect on would help you build a happy future. What are you able to offer a new partner at this time? What are you hoping a new partner would bring to your life? Even if you don't broach these topics during the first date, having them in your thoughts will add to your authentic presence, and hopefully to the success of the date. What's more, if your date asks you about these things, you'll be ready with some answers, rather than caught with a mouth full of stuttering speech and nothing to say.

As for job interviews, many of us feel pressured to accept whatever opportunity lands on our lap. Beyond that, may of us are *desperate* for work—that is not an exaggeration in these modern times. If you know that you need to find work asap, but this job might not be the right fit for you, then you're going to have to make a hard choice. Being honest about this in the interview will most certainly not land you the job. So if you are successful and do get hired, have a plan of departure that commits at least three to six months to your new company before you leave for better opportunities. Always leave a good impression; jumping ship after a week or two will simply not accomplish that. In this highly competitive job market, regardless of position or field, good references are essential to give you a leg up on the competition.

If this is a job interview you've gone after with purpose, than congratulations on landing a foot in the door! The next step is to prepare yourself mentally: why do you want employment with this firm? What excites and interests you about the position and the work? Have this present in your thoughts when you go, so that you can share these ideas and goals with the interviewer.

During the Interview, Date, or Event

Now is the time to utilize the tips and tricks we covered earlier in the book. Smile authentically—many of us struggle with what is considered a truly "authentic smile", but the easiest trick in the book to achieve this is to simply have gratitude. What moments and situations bring out the genuine smile in the toughest nuts among us? Birthday cakes lit with candles, an unexpected gift, an embrace from a good friend, a sweet kiss from our partner, an enthusiastic puppy, a beautiful summer sunrise. Walking in to the situation, release the gratitude in your heart. You are in the right place at the right time, and you're thankful. Hold this emotion and release it when you first shake hands with the person you're meeting. Having gratitude will make it easy to smile with your mouth as well as your eyes.

Acknowledge and respect. If you're being interviewed by a group, make sure you get around to acknowledging everyone in the room with your eyes.

Be prepared, but wing it if that's more your style. Preparation can never go wrong, so always do that. However, some of us have an intriguing and engaging personal style that might be hampered by notes or pre-imagined answers, so allow the prep work to simply give you more confidence when you go off-script and answer authentically.

If there are objects within hand's reach, leave them alone. Salt and pepper shakers, paper weights, card holders—it may be tempting to subtly arrange these as you speak, especially to calm nerves, but do not. It sends the unspoken message that you're speaking because you must, not because you want to. Keep your hands free to gesture as needed, and give the person with you full attention.

Wait to speak. Even though you certainly want to show that you have initiative, this is not necessarily the time to take it. In any social situation it's vital to show the other person that you're listening: job interviews and first dates are perfect opportunities for this. In the case of the job interview, let the interviewer set the pace, then adjust your own tempo to that. In the case of a date, people love to talk about yourself: allowing the other person enough time to speak will teach you volumes about who they are, as well as allow you to gain major likability points.

Don't "upspeak". While more women seem to be brought up to speak this way—especially in cultures where women have to work harder to be heard, believed, and respected—men do it often as well. Upspeaking is where the end of all of your sentences swing "up", as if you were asking a question. It causes the impression that you're unsure, and seeking approval or validation.

It's a vocal tic just like peppering your sentences with too many "likes", "ums", and "you-knows". You can rid yourself of these habits by practicing at home, using a digital recorder or even your phone's video option. To practice, ask yourself this question:

"What are your goals for the next two years?"

Now record your answer. Don't write it down; allow yourself to improvise—that will bring out your nervous vocal habits the most. Listen to the playback and take note of any upspeak or vocal tics. Record again, this time with the goal of using less of these bad speech habits. If you have an interview in a week, practice for a few minutes every day, using different interview questions such as:

- If you get this job, what are your hopes regarding the position and the company?
- Tell me about one time that you used your skills and initiative to solve a problem on the job.
- What do you think your best qualities are? What are your worst*?

*Whenever someone asks about your worst qualities, frame the answer in the context of how much progress you've made in conquering these qualities, and what you've learned from the process.

Should you speak quickly, or slowly? Studies show that the faster a person speaks, the more often the listener perceives that they are mentally "quick", however, speeding through your sentences can backfire. Instead, mirror speed and speech patterns on your interviewers, subtly. This is why listening in the beginning of an interview is so essential.

Watch your pitch. If your voice is too high, it can come across as nervousness and transfer an overly-excited energy to the interviewer, who may become exhausted by it. If your voice is naturally high, simply allow yourself to be relaxed enough so that your voice is emanating from the lower part of your throat or chest, instead of up against the roof of your mouth. Recording yourself beforehand to practice is an excellent way to develop muscle-memory with your tone of voice.

Use that positive language! We covered the power of words and the importance of avoiding negative ones. Here is where that magic can come into play: using positive language in an interview not only makes a great impression, but it uplifts and energizes the interviewer. This is where the power of charisma comes beautifully into action. Own the emotions of the moment and ensure that they are positive and memorable.

Be honest, but don't throw yourself under the bus. If you don't know the answer to a question in an interview, don't pretend that you do. It's essential that you are your most authentic self here. Be gracious and confident, and above all do not draw attention to your shortcomings. If you look as if you're obsessed with your failures or faults, you're going to paint a picture of someone with low-confidence, and that is the opposite of what you hope to achieve.

Always follow up. Regardless of how well or poorly you felt the interview or date went, follow up with a simple note of thanks. Giving thanks is a courtesy that fewer people are practicing, and saying thank you makes a positive, humble impression every time. Someone out there is going to appreciate it, so make sure to do it!

Chapter 6: Navigating Tricky Social Situations

We've all been there. There's an event coming up, and either you *must* be there because of work, or family obligations, or because you simply promised you would and you don't want to come across like a person who doesn't keep their word, but you know it's going to be a rough time— potentially. Sometimes just the mixture of the crowd is a certain indication of troubled waters ahead, other times it's just one person who seems to spark unrest wherever he or she goes, but at the end of the day you just want to make it through the event with your dignity and confidence intact. So what can you do?

First of all, an important concept to begin to incorporate into your daily mindset is the fact that other people do not have control over us. While it's true that others *seem* to have the power to trigger certain reactions and emotions within us, the actual truth is that with enough practice, confidence, and presence of mind, *we* can be the ones in control of ourselves—and that includes emotional reactions.

You might ask, "How? How can I not react when somebody says something rude, hypercritical, or outrageous to me?" To that we say: *practice,* and poise. Poise just isn't a word evoking some sort of Hollywood-esque facade, and it isn't about a proper-fitting suit or dress, or body posture. Poise is keeping your head under pressure. Poise is about inner strength in the face of adversity.

For starters, get cracking on your forgiveness potential. The biggest diffuser of negative energy should come as no surprise: forgiveness. When we forgive, we gain back our power. What happens when we *do not* forgive? a) we hold on to the negative emotion the other person sparked in us, be it hurt, anger, judgement, disgust, and b) we send that emotion back to the sender, and to anyone around us as collateral damage. Now we're spreading negative emotions like wildfire! That certainly won't earn us any charisma points, will it? (D&D references notwithstanding).

If instead, we stand in our power when the other person releases the offensive or triggering statement, and simply say, "That's all right", we've dispelled that negative energy. We're like a lightning rod channeling electricity's potential destruction safely into the ground, where it can be spread out and rendered harmless. Not only are we effecting ourselves with power and calm, but our response can be an example to anyone else around us, and perhaps encourage them to forgive (and then move on from) the offending speaker.

It's important to understand that other people may not possess the same skills, and if others *do* react negatively to the original offensive speaker, it's best to gracefully move on to more positive waters. At least we did not allow the negativity to directly effects us, and I would call that a win.

Other forgiveness phrases include:

- I understand.
- I hear you.
- Noted (in a positive voice, as this can also sound dismissive)
- We are all different, of course.
- You are absolutely entitled to your opinion.
- Thank you for sharing your point of view.

If the person questions your response, such as "Oh really?", simply return with "Yes." Then perhaps excuse yourself and move on to a different group of people, or wait for someone else to pick up the conversation.

There's an alternate set of responses in the case of someone saying something that you know is deeply offensive to one or more persons in the room. In the case of prejudice or hate, it's a rare individual who will not instantly feel a negative emotion in response. At this point, your job is to refuse to add to the powder keg of the speaker's energy. Refuse to condone their words with a simple "I disagree", or "I would not share that here", and leave it at that. You may not be able to get this person to stop talking, but at least to those around you, you've quietly taken the side of being against hateful speech, while not contributing to the speaker's disruptive energy. Refuse to engage with them further.

Acceptance Gives You Freedom

Nobody in the world is perfect, which is good news, as it gives us freedom from believing that it's right to judge anyone else.

Learning to accept the fact that other people are different from ourselves is an important lesson, and it gives us great personal power when we achieve the acceptance state of mind. What's even more important is—extreme cases or instances aside—meeting and talking with someone who is vastly different from ourselves gives us a rare opportunity to expand our own understanding. When we set judgement aside and learn to

155

accept people for who they are, we open our minds to new information and new context, that we can often use later on when faced with a challenge our own perspective is stumped by.

Never pass up an opportunity to learn. All of life is a journey of awareness and opportunity.

Learn to look at disagreements as misunderstandings. When we remain in the pattern of "seemingly negative input = emotional response", it can be incredibly difficult to move from that point. We're stuck in a defensive position—where can we go from here? No one will ever back down, give up, and say "I'm sorry" simply because you think they're wrong, or that you are offended by their words. In addition, none of that's the point—we're not listening to the reasoning behind the words, we're not considering what brought this person to this moment of belief. All we hear is emotion, and that's what we're giving back. It's a useless, endless cycle, and it lowers everyone involved instead of showcasing their confidence and charisma.

If you take a moment and wait, center yourself and release that negative emotion, you might then see the person in front of you—unique, diverse, *different*, but also valid. Ask them to explain what they mean. Look for points of similarity between yourself and them. Offer up your own stories that might bridge the gap between the two of you. You'll be surprised at how often a non-negative reaction causes a conversation to become stronger, more neutral, and in the end, rewarding.

Initiating A Difficult Conversation

Studies show that in the workplace, employees are forced to navigate conflict related to managers or coworkers approximately 3 hours, at least, per week. Obviously it isn't easy to do a great job if you're mired in emotion and negativity. What's even more disturbing is that the study also revealed that more than one third of these employees left their jobs rather than deal with the conflict at all. How can this problem be better handled, or even handled at all?

Most of instinctively know when we *should* have a difficult conversation with someone—be it at work, in the family, or with a friend or a partner. If you're already feeling the pull to the do the right thing, then you need to it, no questions asked. But how to rise to the occasion successfully? You'll need the two things you've been working on cultivating for greater charisma first: empathy and social skill. There's going to be a lot of navigation to reach a mutually agreeable destination. You'll also need courage, which as well know is not the *absence* of fear, but the acknowledgement of it, then the choice to move forward despite it.

Before you reach out to have the conversation, do some mental preparation in anticipation of it. Ask yourself "what could be the person's motivation for their behavior, and how is their behavior causing this problem?" Even more importantly, ask yourself "how is their behavior-driven problem affecting the (company, family, our relationship). Get your thoughts on these two questions together, and take as much time as you need to have a central focus that you want to explore with the person, otherwise much of the initial conversation is simply going to be about discovery, and inevitably, defense. You'll go off on far fewer tangents if you have a mental map of the road ahead before you reach out to the person.

Know what your objective is before you enter the conversation.
You need to know what you want to accomplish before you start talking, otherwise the conversation is bound to become circular, and leave both parties hopelessly frustrated. Here's a checklist that can help organize your thoughts and goals:

- What is your best outcome to accomplish here?

- Is anything non-negotiable? Practice expressing this objectively.

- Plan on how you'll wrap up the conversation successfully.

- What action steps do you want to come out of this?

- What role do you want the other person to play regarding those action steps?

- Are you willing to support the other person after this conversation, and what support will you give, specifically?

Check your attitude at the door before the conversation begins. You're not on a hunt and you're not here to target; you need to approach this conversation with an inquiry-based frame of mind. If you've already made up your mind about what's been going on and how to fix it, then you're not going to be successful here. Just as a physician should have a long, thorough talk with their patient before deciding on treatment, so should you listen to the other person's point of view and experience before reaching out to propose a compromise and solution to any problems that have been occurring. Even if you *think* you know exactly what the problem is, respect for the other person demands you listen to their thoughts. You may discover something you hadn't realized or thought about previously, and the impression you make by showing empathy and respect can go a long way into healing any fissures or divides that may have existed between you.

Emotions, however, are a different story. We can't properly utilize empathy if we strip all emotions from ourselves and omit them from the conversation. We can, however, refuse to follow a particular direction of what is called the "wheel of emotions". In this particular emotional diagram, annoyance leads to anger which leads to rage, and so on. Knowing this, we can navigate the conversation back the other way. If emotions like shame, sadness, or regret lead to tears in the other person, we need to be strong enough not to judge them for that. Tears are *not* a sign of weakness, they're a sign of emotion, and we all have emotions so it's not our right to judge the next person for displaying them. Allowing the other person their emotional reactions puts us in a place of generosity and patience, and frames us in an empathic light.

If the other person does have a breakdown moment, we should acknowledge that this is perfectly okay, and allow them the time they need to collect themselves and return to the conversation.

If silence occurs, ride it out. Having difficult conversations is, well, *difficult*. We may need some time to collect our thoughts, and this is okay. Saying reassuring things like, "I can see how this could be difficult, and that's okay. Please take your time" can go a long way in making the other person feel respected and safe, and not pressured or put on the spot. Humans never react well when pushed into a position of defense, so make sure your body language and tone of voice don't contradict your words when you're trying to be reassuring.

Having high emotional intelligence, like charisma, is only partially inherent—most of it is learned. You can prove that yours is high, right now, in the midst of this difficult conversation. Knowing that years of built up trust can be destroyed in mere moments makes it essential to preserve the relationship as you near the end of the conversation. No amount of acquiescence or promises is worth losing the relationship. More time may be needed. Before you wrap things up, consider exploring how long changes could take to be initiated in the interest of both parties.

Don't be a hypocrite; preserve consistence. Never give one person a set of rules when another person doesn't have to follow that set of rules. If you think you're going to fool anyone, you're wrong—make sure that across the board, what applies to one applies to all.

Common Pitfalls We Might Encounter During a Difficult Conversation

Not everyone is going to be at their best when confronted in a difficult conversation, regardless of how objective, patient, and calm we are when approaching them. People sometimes adopt a defensive position because of their own fears and insecurities, and nothing we have said may be needed to trigger this. When people are in this position and trapped in a fear mentality, they may utilize something called a "thwarting ploy". Pay attention to these and be ready to respond correctly if they occur:

- Stonewalling. This technique used by fearful and/or manipulative people involves putting up roadblocks to a conversation, such as questioning the validity of each thing the other person says, refusing to answer questions, and making generalized statements such as "this is ridiculous" or "I can't believe this is happening". **How to disarm this tactic:** For starters, always acknowledge a thwarting ploy. You can say here, "I won't be able to help if you keep putting up roadblocks, and I want this to be resolved in a way that puts you at ease. It will be easier for us to move forward if we stick to the topic. I appreciate your cooperation with this."

- Sarcasm. Another defense mechanism, and one that can be acknowledged by saying, "I know this is a difficult subject, which is why it's best if we both keep our tone neutral. "

- Being unresponsive. You can say, "I'm not sure how to interpret your silence. Take your time with this, but when you're able to express yourself, I am here to listen to you."

Pay Attention to Where You're Having the Conversation

The name of the game is *neutral territory*. If you're talking to an employee and you're a manager, your office is not the most suitable place. If you're an employee talking to your boss, ask if there's a more discreet place to talk, such as a conference room or lounge. If you're talking to a partner, friend, or family member, suggest a quiet public place such as a coffee shop. This will help keep emotions under control as most people don't want to make a display in a public setting.

As for body language, remember to avoid the negative cues, such as arms crossed, tapping or fidgeting, and looking away from the person or staring for too long. If the person you're speaking to chooses to sit, you'll need to sit, also. If they prefer to stand, you've got a chance to avoid making them feel intimidating by sitting down.

Have an Idea of How to Start the Conversation

Never *surprise* someone by initiating a conversation without warning. Give the other person a heads-up; reach out for a time and place to talk. Be specific about what you'll be talking about without labeling it or being accusatory, such as "Hey I wanted to meet up and talk about what happened the other day in the meeting. What time is good for you?" or "Let's take some time tomorrow to clear the air about some things. I'd like to hear your opinions about it. Why don't we grab coffee?"

Many of us put off these difficult conversations because we're at a loss as to how to initiate them, but with enough preparation and thought, we can get these much-needed conversations started, and hopefully discover some solutions that benefit everyone involved. Make sure your tone of voice carries no sound of judgement or accusal, but merely inquisitiveness and discovery.

What To Do If You're Approached For a Difficult Situation

Sometimes we find ourselves on the other side of the table. Perhaps we slipped up and reacted inappropriately to criticism, disrupting a meeting or group work effort. For starters, at this moment your charisma and reputation are at stake—this might make you want to revisit that discarded emotion of shame, but now is not the time for regression. Bite down and don't let shame overwhelm you—*everybody* makes mistakes. How one processes those mistakes separates the leaders from the led.

Give the person you're wishing to speak with time to process and prepare. In other words, never ambush someone—you will *never* get the results you want this way, unless the results you want are purely negative.

How to Approach Your Boss With a Concern

What happens if you have an issue and you're the one needing to ask for a meeting?

Don't act out of emotion. Wait until you've had time to cool down. If your first reaction is to go on the war-path, you are doing yourself a grave disservice. Take time to assess the situation and what you want to get out of a meeting your manager or boss.

Understand that the bigger picture is important to management. A great manager will place themselves in an employees shoes for the purpose of empathy and understanding, but not every manager is a great one, and higher-ups are often overburdened by work load and lack of time. Therefore, even if your concern is strictly about you, such as a raise you thought you were entitled to, take time to frame your concern within the perspective of the work-group, branch, department, or company. If your raise was skipped this quarter, was that department-wide, and if so, is the company able to give a reason as to why the raises were delayed?

Speak logically, not emotionally. If you're angry that you didn't get a raise, that's valid, but don't frame your questions that way. Instead of saying "I'm furious that I've been skipped for a raise I was told was a sure thing", say instead "I'm sorry to have to talk about this with you, but my finances and budget didn't account for the lack of a raise I was assured was coming this quarter. Can we talk about why that didn't happen, and what can I do to support you as you solve this issue?" Make it seem as if you and your boss are part of a team—chances are he or she has had to look at things that way many times, so this could be familiar, comfortable territory. On a daily basis you may never have to go beyond your own personal language and perspective to get your job done satisfactorily, but understand that managers are trained to think in a different vocabulary, and when we mimic that vocabulary we place them more at ease. Rise up to their level for the best results that will benefit *you*. Erase class and position barriers by proving you can utilize both empathy and reason.

Speaking Critically In a Public Forum

White House press members get rattled in such situations, so how are you supposed to handle a scenario where you pose critical questions or statements in a large company or town meeting? If it sounds daunting, it is, for everyone from the pros to the amateurs. You can take the edge off the situation with some preparation, however.

Avoid trigger, aka emotion-based language. Standing up and calling something "wrong" "stupid" "idiotic" or a "waste of time" is the wrong way to go; you're sure to never get to the end of a perfect storm of criticism and reaction. Give people a chance to actually *hear* what you're saying by stripping all emotion from it. Speak logically and calmly. Know that even speaking this way, you will be met with criticism, potentially, and that criticism may not be constructive or objective. People most often respond with anger when it's a view they don't share. Promise yourself that you will retain your sense of poise and calm regardless.

Try to frame your statement in a way that acknowledges the majority. "I realize that many or most of us think this (frame the subject), however, I want to shed light on a possible outcome that I think may not be in the best interest of the (town, community, organization, company)." Don't stop, continue with proposed solutions you believe can help, then be prepared to really listen to what people are saying as they respond. Always reply to their responses and/or questions with a standard of *acknowledge what they said/propose alternative, or agree.*

If you keep your cool and remain centered, you may find more people coming over to your side and supporting your thinking on the matter.

How to Handle a Co-worker, Colleague or Peer Losing It

Here's where daily meditation comes in exceptionally handy. If you're side-swiped by another person's anger, *wait.* Hold your action and steady yourself as you allow that person's emotions to travel through you and out, just like random thoughts did while you were meditating.

It's human nature to mirror the attack and respond in kind, but avoid this at all costs.

For starters, there's no need to apologize right away or at all, depending on the accusation or comment. The first thing you need to do is understand the basis of what they're talking about, and understanding requires calm questioning. If the other person is too tied up in their emotions to think straight, cut through the confusion with a quick, neutral observation: "Listen. I'm not going to trade insults with you—that won't solve anything. I'm ready to listen when you're calm enough to discuss this." Suggest you meet another time to try and work things out.

The other person may absolutely reject meeting another time, and so it will be upon you to move forward. Keep neutralizing the emotions with your responses. If the statements truly felt out of the blue and like an attack, you can admit that, "I don't know how to respond just yet. This is unexpected. What should our next step be?" This way you haven't yet conceded (because you don't know yet if you should, at least until you discover the details of what the other person is upset about), and you haven't tried to placate them.

If, however, you know you're in the wrong, own it, immediately. Apologize, and resist the urge to grovel. Ask what you can do to help if after the apology the person appears to calm down.

Whatever you do, don't sidestep or avoid conversations that need to happen. You're in training to be more charismatic and successful. Dodging difficult situations is not only counter-intuitive to that goal, but it causes you to miss important, intensive training opportunities that can greatly improve your skill level.

Chapter 7: Exercises You Can Do to Improve Your Charisma

Here are some highly useful tricks and exercises you can try in your free time to help you get closer to your goal of achieving greater charisma.

While a total shift of attitude: from negative to positive, unsure to confident, greedy to grateful, out of focus to present takes time and a steady amount of determination and energy, exercises can help you fine-tune and hone your skills to really shine when you need to the most.

1. Exercise to Build Rapport

Humans are by and large emotion-driven beings. Very few of us use logic to guide us. When conveying charisma and confidence, you will not be successful unless people *trust you*. This is the essence of rapport.

Do this exercise with someone don't yet know. This may seem daunting, even scary, but they won't know it's an exercise—only you will. What's even better is that you're going to do the exercise in a low-pressure environment, such as the grocery store. This is going to take you to task regarding building instant rapport. If it doesn't work out the first time, try it again!

The meaning of genuine connection, is hard to put into words, but it's the same way we instantly know if something is inappropriate or even obscene—it's an instinctive, almost primal reaction. When you experience genuine connection with someone, these are a few of the signs you'll be looking for:

- a sudden, genuine smile or laughter that is mirrored in the eyes
- the sharing of a personal fact, feeling, or story
- the other person letting their guard down

When you are caught in a moment with someone else—and by caught I mean you are both in the same moment by coincidence, and cannot leave that moment, such as in a checkout line at a store, in an elevator, waiting at an airport gate, or on public transport—try to make brief conversation with them. This is much easier with someone who's the employee in a situation where you're the customer, of course. You can ask them how their shift is going, how life is treating them, or what they think of a product you're buying.

In a situation such as elevator, choosing a non-invasive question or topic is important, especially if you're male and the only other person is a woman. For the purpose of this exercise in those situations it's best to wait for another opportunity, as women are frequently on their guard around men they don't know, for obvious reasons. We don't want to make someone afraid or uncomfortable for the sake of an exercise.

However, if the person you're with is obviously happy (if they're smiling, for instance) you can ask them, "What's your secret to being in a great mood?" Make sure you're smiling as well so that you're not accidentally misunderstood as being sarcastic.

Look for some component of their answer that will help you create a conversation. Say for instance they answer, "I just like to be cheerful. My mom raised me to always look on the bright side", you can say, "That's a good way to look at life. Where were you raised?"

They might answer with "Maine. I'm going back home to visit in a month, I can't wait!"

When someone shares something personal such as this, then you know you've scored a win in the rapport exercise.

2. Exercises to Instantly Reduce Stress

Why do I need to reduce stress, in the middle of a book about improving my charisma? you might ask. The reasoning behind this is that we all carry stress, visibly, in our bodies, in our faces, and in our eyes. Other people can sense it from a mile away, and while happiness is contagious, so is anxiety and stress. We might not even realize we're holding on to stress, it's just that natural. However, if we learn instant tricks to let it go, we can shift that stress right out of our bodies before walking through a door to a party, date, meeting, or interview.

The breathe in calm, breathe out stress technique: Breathe is extraordinarily powerful. We need it to live and we breathe thousands of times a day without focusing on it or controlling it. When we choose to control it, however, breathe can be an effective tool to use in calming the mind and relaxing the body. Think about when you're at the doctor's for a simple checkup and she asks you to breathe so she can listen to your heartbeat. Unless we're feeling ill or out of sorts, this moment almost instantly calms us down, right?

In the cab, your car, the elevator, the lobby of the building—anywhere that you can do a series of slow, deep breaths without someone giving you the side-eye—breathe in through your nose, deeply. You'll know you've taken in enough breathe when your stomach pushes out, and always remember to keep your shoulders still. Healthy, natural breathing has everything to do with your diaphragm and nothing to do with your shoulders.

Hold the breathe for half a second. Imagine the fresh air you've just taken in surrounding and latching onto the stress in your body, then exhale through your nostrils and imagine the stress leaving your body, never to return. Do this again and feel the stress in your hands get pulled out of your body. Do it one more time, and this time imagine the stress leaving your face.

Facial exercise: Our faces can get exhausted, especially when we deal with other people all day long. Refresh your facial muscles by taking a moment in private (you can do this in front of the bathroom mirror at work or in a restaurant if you're not at home, or even in a bathroom stall), and moving your face in as many different positions as you can. It's going to look very silly when you do, but it works! Actors often do this before the director begins to shoot a scene, just to "reset" their face and deliver believable facial expressions.

3. The Instant Focal Shift

When entering a room, an instant rapport and charisma boost is to immediately shift your point of focus away from yourself and towards the others in the room. People notice when someone is giving them their full attention, and they respond positively to that. They also respond immediately to someone who seems to be distracted, disinterested, or caught up within themselves—and the response isn't a good one.

This is something many of us fail to consider when we walk into a meeting or interview. We're primarily focused on a) getting there, b) finding a place to sit, and c) gathering our thoughts together. In order to make an excellent impression, you need to get your thoughts together *before* you enter that room. Then, when you do walk through the door, acknowledge everyone in the room with your eyes. Try a genuine smile if and when you make eye contact with someone. Once you've acknowledged everyone, *that* is when you can look for a seat—usually, someone will pull out a chair or guide you to a seat that's empty, which is a great opportunity to start things out with a "Thank you."

Focusing your attention on to other people instead of yourself has the added benefit of moving your mind away from any nervousness, insecurities, or bad habits you might have—when you stop focusing on yourself, it's easier to project confidence, rather than exude anxiety.

4. Try A Powerful Pose

One of the fastest ways to hack the human brain and cause an inner upswing of confidence is through body language. A Harvard professor performed a study where volunteers were asked to assume poses of confidence, and poses of insecurity. When the volunteers posed confidently, their levels of cortisol, the hormone produced during times of stress, dropped, and their testosterone levels rose. The insecure poses had the opposite effect.

Want an instant confidence boost? Here are some physical poses to do to instantly raise confidence chemically in your brain:

- At your desk, lean comfortably back in your chair with your feet up, then fold your hands behind your head.

- Stand facing a table and lean forward to rest your weight on your hands—keep your palms down on the table's surface.

- Stand tall, feet apart, with your hands on your hips.

- Sit in your chair, then lean back. Cross one leg over the other leg's knee, resting your ankle on your knee. Again, hands are held behind your head, crossed and cradling it.

- Sit in your chair with your legs apart, and rest your arm across the back of an empty chair next to you.

5. Ask a Friend to Become Your Charisma Partner

So many of us are hesitant, even loathe to ask for help when it comes to feelings and emotions. Confidence *is* a feeling—and at first, when you're just learning to become more charismatic, it may be as easy to lose confidence as it is to gain it. Again, there should be no shame in this. Shame is a useless emotion and will only hold you back. By reaching out for help you are showing, *proving,* that you're a strong person who knows when they need some assistance. Strong people solve problems—weaker people ignore their problems because of their egos or their pride.

When your confidence is flagging, reach out to a trusted friend for help. Studies show that people who receive a boost from friends or peers enjoy long-term healing effects from such a connection, which in turn boosts their overall confidence. Conversely, you can be their lifeline when your friend needs help with their own confidence.

6. Use Music To Pump You Up

Music is an incredibly powerful tool when we want to give our brains a boost. Music can help the workday go by faster, can help a trip become more memorable, can connect us in large groups, and it allows us to tap into our deeper emotions. By listening to a high energy song, your seratonin and endorphin levels will naturally increase, your tension will lessen, and your confidence will rocket skyward. Studies have discovered that songs with a heavier bass line work the best in pumping us up—think of rock anthems or stadium dance songs. Make a short playlist that can become a go-to on days you need some help with confidence.

7. Adopt An Alter-Persona

At first you may think, wait, seriously? Pretend to be someone I'm not? Sort of, but actually, we're talking about being a different *version* of you. Celebrities, performers, and even mixed martial artists and professional wrestlers do this. It's okay to have different sides of yourself—that's totally natural. So consider cultivating the "big energy" version of yourself when you need a confidence pick-me-up.

One of the easiest ways to practice this energy-shift is to imagine a charismatic, powerful and present character, then *be* that character during your next work-related phone call. Ask yourself what would this character choose to do, what they would they sound like, and say?

After a while, you're going to develop and utilize your own charisma-based skill set, but playing a role in the interim can help you adopt some of your alter-ego's techniques and style.

8. Refuse to Allow a Less-Than-Awesome Self Image

This is such a widely overlooked problem that it's often the last thing we think about, although it should be our first! What's your self-image like? When you leave the house to conquer your day, do you feel just a little bit like an imposter? If your outer shell doesn't match your inner core, it's going to show. We want to come across as present, authentic, warm, and *real*. How can we do that if instead, our self-image is afraid, indisposed, unsure, and distorted?

Take some time to look inward. Be honest about what you see. Do you feel good about the image of you that you're imagining? If not, then it's time to take some steps:

- When you picture yourself, first picture your body. This may be uncomfortable for those of us with body-related hangups, such as our weight, our physique, our height, or an area of the body that we're self-conscious about. Next, imagine if a graphic artist used Photoshop to make you look better. See that improved image in your mind. This is *not* to allow you to feel bad about your current body. We have all seen living, breathing, examples of people with our *exact same* body type who we've thought looked terrific—this phenomenon happens all the time! The problem arises when we can't feel how those people look—the issue isn't a physical one, it's an *emotional* one. So use that inner graphic designer asap.

Now, every time you imagine how you look, see that improved image—soon you will emanate that and project it. That's how you'll be seen by others.

- Beyond your physical persona, how do you see your attitude, your personal power, your energy? If you see it all over the place or lagging, you can improve that as well, using your mind to re-draw that person you see. Imagine yourself confident, winning, being charismatic with others. Refuse to see the former image—the new image is your reality.

- Kick the negative thoughts right out of your head. This is serious! We discussed this earlier but it's *essential* to that better self-image that you follow through. The instant a negative thoughts pushes its way into your head, boot it out! Don't let it linger for a minute. You don't have the time or energy for that. Always...think...positive thoughts! An example: many of us have these instant reactions to frustrating problems: "This is too difficult" and "I can't", or "this is a bad day". Those are all self-defeating. They will literally make the situation harder for you. Pronouncing a day as "bad" will ensure that it's bad. Why settle for that when you have the power to change things with mere thoughts and words? Instead of "this is too difficult", say "I've got this" or "I can do this"--then give yourself the time you need to think it through, try different approaches, and get it done, and never be afraid to ask for help. Instead of saying "I can't", say "I will figure out a way". Instead of saying "this is a bad day", give yourself permission to say "this is a challenging day", and consider admitting that "I'll probably learn a lot from today".

- Learn about who *you are*. If you don't know yourself, than you'll be ill-equipped to defeat your own bad habits and thoughts. Knowing ourselves means learning about both the good and the bad. Once we do, we can utilize our strength and wisdom to change that bad to good.

- Be a person of *action*. Acting in a positive way will activate all the other areas of yourself, and trigger them to be positive as well. Positivity is essential to success when it comes to charisma and confidence. People become what they choose to *do*. Your choices build the future you, day by day. If you choose to live positively, you will become more positive, it's as simple as that.

- Choose to be kind and generous. You might think this is a little too hokey, but studies *prove* that when people choose to be kind, they grow more powerful. A kind act provides an instant surge in empathy and presence, which in turn, activates our charisma. Being generous taps into your feelings concerning abundance and gratitude. Choose to act with kindness and generosity when you can; soon, you'll get hooked on the positive feelings and feedback that comes from living this way.

- Become a lifelong student. Take time each day to practice something you want to be competent in; study things you want to retain. When you raise your competence level, it naturally transfers into your confidence.

- Slow your speech down. Not too slow, but not fast, either. People who speak too quickly are doing so because they're afraid they're going to run out of time, or the other person's attention, or both. When you speak with purpose, you *command* attention. Not in a forceful way, but in a way that shows you're speaking from a place of inner conviction and strength.

- Build your confidence by setting small, realistic goals, then achieving them. By doing this, you're proving to yourself that you're capable of achievement.

- Get rid of bad habits, one (small) habit at a time. Getting in the practice of both noticing your bad habits, and conquering them, will give you the confidence you need to tackle bigger habits that need to change. Try waking up a few minutes earlier each day, or walking an extra 15 minutes when you go out to exercise.

- Be a solution-based person. If your point of view tends to settle on the problems, such as "Okay I see what the problem is, it's (you describe the problem and stop there)", then it's time to shift focus and become the person who has an idea of how to solve the problem. Don't let the sentence end with the problem, instead, say "We can see that this is the problem, and I think doing (a, b, or c) is a way that we can try to solve it." When it comes to personal issues, take negative thoughts such as "I always procrastinate" and turn them around, instead saying "How can I learn to stop putting things off?" Then focus on the solution.

- Choose to volunteer in some capacity. This goes back to the being generous and kind, but it takes it a step further in that you're going to be around people who are unfamiliar to you (at first). This brings together the importance of generosity with the opportunity to practice your charisma skills.

9. Become an Intuitive Communicator

When someone is speaking to you, there are important techniques you should use. First, *never* try to anticipate their words or finish their sentences. Even if you know where their point is going, let it go there—this is their story to tell and you are showing them respect when you give them room to tell it in. Be *present* while listening—don't let your mind wander off to start formulating a response, because you haven't heard the whole point yet. Remember, charisma takes work, and being a good listener involves an investment of time and patience.

When the person is finished, wait a moment before responding. It can be helpful to ask them clarifying questions, or repeating back certain things they stated, adding a "is that correct?" to make sure they know you listened to them. If you respond *immediately* after they stop talking, they're going to know that you weren't really listening, but instead just waiting for your turn to speak, which is the opposite of empathic and charismatic, as well as disrespectful.

10. Work On Your Body, and Gain a Happier Mind

This may seem obvious, but many people fail to realize the instant impact any kind of physical activity has on the mind and positive hormone levels in the brain. Often, we ignore our body throughout the workday, and are just too tired to do anything physical once we return home. The simple fact is there is *always* time for exercise breaks, we just overlook them.

If you work for 40 minutes, then take a 5 minute break to stretch or lift free weights standing by your desk, in an 8 hour day you will have accomplished a decently-sized workout.

Movement, strength-building exercise, cardiovascular activities, and toning exercises all serve to support our charisma-building agenda of positive thinking, better posture, inner strength and gratitude. Don't ignore your body if you want to cultivate a more confident mind.

11. Refuse to Engage In Negative Conversation

One of the easiest ways to get people talking is to complain about something, however, you'll notice that if you do, the only people you've caught the attention of are the negative folks. This is *too easy*, so don't fall for it—refuse to begin conversations by pointing out the negative aspect of something.

Case in point: a father and son were standing in a long line at a Salvation Army store. The only cashier was patiently ringing up a full shopping cart's worth of garments for a Native American woman. While this was happening, the man in front of the the father and son was growing increasingly impatient: sighing loudly and looking around for someone to connect with in anger. The father refused to meet the other man's gaze, instead looking out over the racks of clothes beyond his son.

The woman checking out realized she'd need her husband's credit card, and that he was waiting in the car for her. She apologized and left the store to retrieve it. The line of customers waiting were respectfully silent, but the man in front of the father and son finally voiced his opinion that, "That is the most annoying customer I've ever seen in my life."

This time, the father allowed the man to make eye contact with him.

The father said, "You know, stores like these help a lot of folks. If someone wants to spend a lot of money here, I imagine that could only be helpful to the charity itself."

The angry man replied, "I'm entitled to my opinion. This is America."

The father nodded, and said, "That is true. And she was here first."

Nobody else spoke, but everyone else was listening. Who do you think the rest of the customers empathized with the most in this conversation? Perhaps some had sided with the angry man, but a better impression was made by the father.

12. The Importance of Boundaries

When navigating the social and business world, it is *essential* that we know our own personal boundaries, and are prepared to defend them. Being charismatic does not mean being a pushover. There's a fine line to walk between charm and acquiescence. A confident person does not sit idly by while someone else marches all over their personal space, ideals, ethics and values, and self-respect.

If you're starting your own business or have just landed a work-heavy new promotion, you might be tempted to forego all personal time or pleasure and just dive in, head-first. The trouble is you're on a fast-track to exhaustion. You need to learn to delegate; you also need how to say no, in a secure, non-threatening manner.

When framing a decline, state it simply and do not pile on the excuses why you aren't able to perform what's been asked of you at this time. Offer an alternative solution that is in everyone's best interests.

13. Don't Live For Validation From Others

It's important to win the respect of other people, but at the end of the day, nothing you do should be solely for the purpose of others' validation. You need to foster self-respect and a feeling of accomplishment. Those things come from within, not from the words of other people.

14. Don't Be Afraid to Become Passionate

Getting passionate about something lights a fire within you that others can see and admire. Don't be afraid to let yourself show what truly excites and motivates you in life. Hiding yourself creates the opposite effect of being charismatic.

15. Be True to Yourself

Finally, everything that you do should contain a reflection of who you are as a person. There are always more choices and opportunities. Don't live your life chasing someone else's dream; cultivate your own goals and dreams, then go after them. No one has the right to dictate how anyone lives their life. Life is an exciting journey, with reveals and hidden knowledge just for you—get out there and explore what intrigues you the most.

Conclusion

Thank for making it through to the end of *Improve Your People Skills*, let's hope it was informative and able to provide you with all of the tools you need to achieve your goals whatever they may be.

The next step is to take a look at your charisma-based goals and challenges. What information from this book can you use right away to start changing your attitude about things, and improving your own self-confidence? Change doesn't come overnight, but taking a first step will initiate a sweeping change across your entire attitude and outlook. Every great plan is simply a series of single steps. Don't put off the sense of accomplishment and personal satisfaction that comes from living your life with confidence, gratitude, and social success.

Finally, if you found this book useful in any way, a review is always appreciated!

Accelerated Learning

Advanced Strategies for Faster Comprehension, Systematic Expertise, Greater Retention: Becomes More Productive and Remember More

Introduction

Learning is always going to be a lifelong process. As a child you are conditioned to learn the fundamental principles involved in being a functional human being. You are taught how to walk, talk, run, jump, play, count, sing, dance, etc. As you get older, learning becomes increasingly more complex and challenging. However, you also know that failing to learn means failing to adapt. That's why you keep on encouraging yourself to do it.

It's something that we have to consistently incorporate into our daily lives if we are to continually grow and develop as people. It is vital that we make it a habit to learn new things every day if we want to be constantly prepared for the challenges that come our way. However, learning isn't always going to be an easy process for some. In fact, for a lot of people, learning can be a very slow, gradual, and grueling experience with a lot of speed bumps, hurdles, and challenges. Not everyone is going to be equipped with faculties for learning, and that is why some people end up getting left behind.

Undoubtedly, the modern day we live in is a cutthroat world. In any industry, people are scrambling to make it to the top of their respective fields. There are various power vacuums that are just waiting to be filled left and right, and only those who have the know-how are going to be able to fill those positions. It's all a matter of being able to equip oneself with the necessary tools that they might need to find success in life. That is exactly how learning plays a vital role in self-development and growth.

Charles Darwin explained it best in his Theory of Evolution. Only the strongest and fittest survive while the weak get left behind. This is a principle that has proven its authenticity time and time again throughout the history of human civilization. Those of us who are capable of adapting to our surroundings more quickly and effectively are the ones who are more likely to find success. Meanwhile, those who get a little too comfortable staying where they are will be the ones who will eventually falter. In spite of whatever circumstances one might have in life, people always have a choice whether or not to pursue opportunities for learning. Despite people's circumstances, people have the choice to seek out opportunities to learn. It's a level playing field for everyone, and it's all a matter of manifesting the will to act.

In the current state of our society, it's getting more and more difficult to stay ahead of the pack. Even though technology affords us with the tools that we might need to be armed with as we face everyday challenges, it can also serve as a major hindrance. You might think that technology is something that would enable learning and make it easier for people to acquire and develop new skills. However, there is a phenomenon called digital distraction. This is likely something that all of us are familiar with to a certain degree. In the advent of emerging technologies, it's not too farfetched to assume that people are prone to becoming more and more distracted. However, technology has evolved to a point where it has become a distraction. It used to be that people gradually adopted technology into their lives. But nowadays, human beings are born into technologically-dominated societies. They are essentially influenced by technology in their formative years, and it is now becoming a very integral aspect in the lives of many.

But how does digital distraction factor into one's capacity to learn?

Well, you need to be able to take a look at how human beings perceive survival and existence nowadays as opposed to how they used to in the early ages. Back in the infant stages of civilization, human beings were primarily concerned with the hunting and gathering of essentials like food, water, shelter, and clothing. Nothing else mattered much other than those basic necessities.

The world is no longer like that today. Society has evolved to become much more complex. The new age of civilization has brought about a species that still does prioritize the gathering of food, water, shelter, and clothing, but there is a whole new component that governs people's lives as well: information.

People are no longer just concerning themselves with the gathering of food anymore. People are prioritizing the gathering of information because they understand the importance of knowledge in this day and age. However, the acquisition of information has also been made a lot more complex due to the complications that are brought about by digital distractions. Even though technology primarily serves as a tool for human beings to be more productive and get work done more efficiently, it has also become one of the many potential distractions that keep us from focusing on what we need to be doing.

That is why in this age of information, it is very important that we can continually reassess the way that we approach learning and knowledge acquisition. It's not enough that we have the tools that we need to gather valuable information. It's essential that we are able to optimize the way that we process, retain, and apply everything we learn.

This eBook is going to be a contribution to that effort. There are indeed plenty of ways in which people can optimize the way they learn and sharpen the processes in which they acquire information. However, ironically enough, not a lot of people are going to be aware of these techniques. This is quite a shame especially in this day and age. A common concept that people have these days is that in the age of information, ignorance is a choice - and it's true. It's easy to pull up information with just a few taps and swipes of your fingertip. Yet, there are many people who choose to remain ignorant and unaware of the things that they could be up to speed on. In the modern era, you are going to need every competitive advantage that you can get. If you can further optimize how you acquire and process valuable information, then you are equipping yourself with skills that help improve you as a person.

Even though learning is truly a lifelong process, it shouldn't take you a lifetime to grasp and learn complex concepts. It would be an awful waste of time and energy if you devote your whole lifetime trying to master one particular discipline and disregard all the rest. It's like having the whole world out there available for you to see, and yet, you choose to lock yourself in your room your whole life. You shouldn't be afraid to pursue the study and mastery of different disciplines and topics. Time shouldn't be a hindrance or a limitation to your learning capacity. There are ways in which you can speed up the learning process so that you can make the most of your time. You can only dedicate so much time to learning after all. That is why you are going to want to capitalize on any methods that would help make that process easier and faster. Consider this your introduction to Accelerated Learning.

Chapter 1: What Is Accelerated Learning

Accelerated Learning (AL) is an emerging methodology that offers an innovative and comprehensive approach to increase one's capacity to absorb information, assess problems, and think of creative solutions. It is essentially a learning pedagogy that employs "brain-friendly" methods and techniques that further streamline and optimize the learning process as a whole. In order to gain a better understanding of what this theoretical framework is all about, it might be a good idea to first delve into its history and how this learning methodology came to be. From there, we can branch on to common techniques and tactics that fall under the Accelerated Learning pedagogy.

Accelerated Learning: A History

It all started with what was originally coined as Suggestopedia, a concept that was developed by respected Bulgarian professor and psychotherapist, Dr. Georgi Lozanov, back in the early 1970s. The famed professor founded the Suggestology Research Institute back in Bulgaria in 1966. It was through his work in the field wherein he was able to develop a groundbreaking teaching pedagogy that made the entire learning process easy and pleasurable. Various innovative tools were employed under his new framework in order to create a more interactive learning environment that included music, art, role-playing setups, and games. He was always someone who emphasized the importance of cultivating a learning environment that was optimized for the seamless transfer of knowledge. It was also of Lozanov's opinion that it was the responsibility of the teacher to create a learning environment that is safe and stimulating and would inspire and motivate learners in order to maximize one's capacity to learn and absorb new ideas.

He stressed the point that the physical learning environment should always be one that invites learners to engage and interact with learning materials, facilitators, moderators, and fellow learners as well. It should be a learning space that not only takes into consideration a learner's mental state but emotional state as well, so as to offer a more holistic approach to tailored learning.

Dr. Lozanov truly advocated a renewed approach to learning and knowledge acquisition in order to keep modern society at the same pace as the rapid rate of technological advancement. He saw that society was evolving quickly and saw a need for the everyday human being to adapt in order for them to stay relevant and remain competitive. He also saw the potential risks involved with enforcing inefficient and ineffective learning pedagogies. He envisioned a learning methodology that would allow for a stress-free learning environment that would alleviate pressure brought about by contemporary learning institutions and education frameworks.

The term Suggestopedia is derived from the words "suggestion" and "pedagogy". It all centers around how a teacher or facilitator's words and actions might come across to the learner. Ultimately, the goal is for the teacher to suggest that learning and understanding a new idea is fun and easy. In addition, the idea of "suggestion" offers a sense of inclusivity on the part of the learner, allowing them to offer their insights on how they might be able to learn more efficiently and effectively.

It was 1976 in the United States when the name Suggestopedia was changed to Accelerated Learning. The name change was indicative of the cultural preferences of the time, and a desire to build upon adaptations that stemmed from Dr. Lozanov's original ideas that were developed over the years. At the same time, various leaps in the field of neuroscience and education psychology offered society a lot more insight into how to better approach the dynamics of teaching and learning. Numerous techniques and approaches to teaching and learning were curated over the years and were eventually collectively identified as methods of Accelerated Learning.

Accelerated Learning as We Know It Today

The Accelerated Learning philosophy can distinguish itself from other pedagogies purely from its foundations as a learning mechanism. It takes into consideration the suggestive factors that help influence a person's capacity to learn and absorb vital yet unfamiliar information. It is a pedagogy that heavily emphasizes the importance of the teacher and the facilitator in determining the ideal learning process of a student or learner.

Accelerated Learning can provide a real structure and system for teachers and facilitators to craft learning modules that would guarantee a learner's eventual success. It can also provide a learner an emphasis on student-centered learning. There is a lot of flexibility within the learning methodology itself to minimize the necessity for a student to make adjustments. The entire Accelerated Learning process has been further enriched and substantiated due to the scientific community's developed understanding of cognitive psychology, constructivism, multiple intelligences, neuro-linguistic programming, and more. There are all sorts of learning modules and activities that are implemented and experimented on throughout various class settings, and this is continually pushing the Accelerated Learning principles forward.

The whole idea behind Accelerated Learning is to offer every single individual an opportunity to learn any concept at their own preferred pace and with their preferred methodology. It is a learner-centric learning style that is more results-oriented than process-oriented. It does away with the whole notion of having one right way to go about learning a particular topic. Ultimately, it is a learning paradigm that is driven and motivated by the success of the learner.

How Do You Apply Accelerated Learning in Your Life?

If you happen to be someone who is as invested in learning as some people are, then this book is going to help you out in your endeavors. The very fact that you read books like this is evidence of your curiosity and your thirst for knowledge. We aren't always going to be given the set of tools that we want. That is why it's always best for us to make the most out of what we have. You can only do so much in this life if your capacity to learn is limited. You should always be making an effort to open your mind and free yourself from any intellectual or mental constraints that might be holding you back from acquiring new knowledge.

Studying more about accelerated learning techniques isn't just be designed to benefit you. If you are a manager, a CEO, a father, a mother, a teacher, a mentor, or whichever kind of influential figure that exists, you can greatly benefit from gaining a better understanding of how the human mind works and how you can most effectively initiate that transfer of knowledge from your brain into someone else's. Numerous organizations and big businesses all over the world are making use of accelerated learning techniques to train their employees to ensure seamless integration into the company's system. Transformative teachers in various academic fields make use of accelerated learning modules to further sharpen the intellect and knowledge of their students. There is a place for accelerated learning in anyone's life regardless if it's for personal use or to benefit someone else.

As human beings, we are all going to have our personal limitations. However, that shouldn't serve as a deterrent for our will and desire to pursue knowledge. So as long as you hold on to that desire, you are always going to have the potential to be an intellectual powerhouse. It all boils down to you being able to find the right approach to learning new things and acquiring new knowledge. That is exactly what this book is going to be able to provide you.

Some of the tips and techniques that will be listed in this book might be right up your alley and will be of great help to you, and some of it might not be. But that is the whole point of learning and education in the first place. It's about putting yourself out there with an open mind and a readied disposition towards learning. If one method works, then that's great. Stick with it. If it doesn't work, then learn from experience and continue pursuing new avenues for learning. Accelerated Learning isn't designed to be foolproof. It's still going to ultimately depend on the kind of personality that you have and your patience in finding what Accelerated Learning technique works best for you. Learning and self-education is a journey that only you can embark on by yourself. You can have mentors and resource materials, but the will to learn should still ultimately come from within. So, you've taken that first step. Now, it's time to move on to the next level.

Chapter 2: Speed Reading

First, you need to understand what speed reading is all about before you begin to learn the methods and strategies that will enable you to become a proficient speed reader. Unlike detailed reading or active reading, speed reading is a method of reading that strives to acquire the most important information without getting bogged down in the word by word details of a piece of written material or a particular document.

If you stop to consider how many words per sentence you read actually contain the crucial information you will realize that half or more of the words used are largely unnecessary. This means that almost half of the time you spend reading is spent on empty or extraneous words.

Another concept of speed reading that is critical to understand is that it removes the editorial element of reading. All too often we can read a written document with a critical eye, one that picks up spelling or grammatical errors. Speed reading isn't just about helping you to read the same words in less time. Instead, speed reading is about helping you to reinvent the way you read altogether. Instead of seeing the written word as the information that requires only visual recognition.

Speed-reading offers you a variety of benefits, including:

- You read faster

- Save time

- Find information quickly

- Get the gist of the book quickly

- You get the detail as well as the gist

- Synthesizing information from a variety of sources

- Organize information so you can apply it

- Better recall ability

- Building up your expertise on a subject quickly

- Improving your concentration and focus

- Ignoring information you don't need

- Increase your vocabulary

- Passing tests

- Enjoying the process

Evaluate yourself

Before you start applying speed-reading techniques, you need to know what your current reading speed is.

You need:

- A timer/alarm clock

- A book you haven't read

- A calculator and post-it notes

Now you are ready to figure out how much you want to improve your reading speed. The words you read and the time it took will serve as the foundational benchmark for you to beat with repeated practice. Rushing will only lessen your accuracy, so you should always begin reading at a comfortable and normal seed. Reading the same paragraph won't be as revealing. So, select paragraphs throughout the book, on different pages, in order to accurately record your reading speed. The results of these tests can serve as your performance measure, and you can work to improve the speed at which you read using various methods.

Reading and the Brain

A thought is conjured up when a firing of a neuron associated with that thought occurs by conscious stimulation. Or in simpler terms when you know something must be remembered and you tell you're self to do so! A memory is when that neuron causes a neighboring neuron to spark simply by proximity this causes the receptor which normally lies deep within that cell to reach the outer surface of the cell. This occurs so that if the thought is conjured up again with in a relatively short time within a few hours the connection between the 2 neurons will be a lot easier. The more times this 'thought' occurs the stronger will be the bond or the stronger the memory will be until it becomes permanently etched in your mind. This is why when you learn something new you should re-enforce it within a short time frame otherwise it will be a lot harder to recall. Everyone has heard this before.

What memory is not encouraged or committed are mere words on a page. The reason why you don't forget that the Eiffel Town is in Paris or why people will never forget an old friend who has died many years ago is because of Associated EMOTIONS! Combining some words or something you heard with excitement will cause the memory to stick in your mind.

Exciting emotions increase the intensity of perception. Positive emotions also boost the long term potential, so events that happen in such a state are much more likely to be remembered

Things can be viewed a lot easier as step by step or in 'chunks' rather than by one whole mess of knowledge which has to be instilled permanently in your mind just before an exam.

Other techniques include listening to music reciting main points of whatever topic you are focusing on which empowers you. For example the Rocky movie theme or any of your favorites which would instill excitement, perseverance, courage, joy and any other motivating and empowering emotions. What many students do is focus on what they don't know, and what resources they don't have!

Positive emotions or pleasure associated with learning will remain a much longer period of time rather than negative emotions and feelings.

Five-Step Speed Reading Technique

The various techniques and methods, listed here, may ostensibly seem to be the crux of the book however, you may find that you have no success with any of them. As has already been discussed, there are both proponents and opponents of speed reading techniques. It is the above advice, in the **General Tips**, section that represents a far broader consensus.

Nevertheless, for each of the techniques below, there are a great many people who swear by their efficiency. It is not the place of this chapter to discuss the benefits and viability of speed reading – it has already been done. This book simply recommends that those, looking to experiment with speed reading, do so with an open mind and consider that each, or a combination, of the following techniques may be useful.

Use the grounding you have learned so far in the book, bear the broader advice in mind and measure your progress using the methodology described in the **Measuring** section. That will be a truer indicator of your progress than any scientific or pseudo-scientific claim in its favor **or** to the contrary.

Skimming

It makes sense to begin with skimming, as the most often referred to technique in the book, and perhaps the most obvious. Skimming simply means moving through the book and looking through the pages, without reading the full text.

Reiterating what has been said previously, skimming is **not** a technique to replace regular reading. Rather, it is a useful tool when trying to get a preliminary idea of a book's contents, and isolate hot spots or key terms for further investigation. Therefore, it is largely irrelevant to measure or consider the wpm of a skim read.

There are various degrees of skimming. In its briefest form, a skim read could be nothing more than a flick through the book, simply gleaning whichever words caught your eye. Gradually increasing in thoroughness, a skim read could entail reading the first and last paragraphs of each chapter – a surprisingly effective way to get an idea of a book's content. Increasing further; the first and last sentences of each paragraph, in a well structured book, will almost certainly communicate any key information within it. At a certain point, skimming does become reading. If, at any point, you are going through a book with the aim of at least perceiving every word, you have almost certainly stopped skimming and simply started reading – the exact line of division between these two concepts isn't a necessary point for this book to explore.

So, how can you skim effectively? And how thorough should your skim read be for any given text?

Well, for short texts such as news articles and encyclopedia entries, it might not be necessary, or even particularly beneficial to skim at all. The time you spend skimming might not earn itself back as an overall decrease in the duration of a second read, nor might it offer a significant gain in comprehension.

The type of skimming you use should depend on your goals for reading the text. If you are hoping to retain as much of the information in the text as possible, consider a fairly thorough skim. After reading through the table of contents, glance, at least, at every page. If you notice what seems to be a hot spot, with key words that catch your attention, consider dipping to examine the text a little more closely, even to the point of reading full sentences.

On the other hand, if you are just looking for a specific section, use the table of contents to guide you as best you can, and then try to glide past irrelevant sections as swiftly as possible. Try to avoid distraction from any sections, apart from instances where there appears to be a relevant key word.

If you don't find what you're looking for on a first pass, increase the level of thoroughness significantly – a gradual increase might fail once again and commit you to further reads. If you fail with a thorough skim, however, you can at least be relatively sure the information is not where you were looking.

Consider information as hierarchical. In the briefer skim reads, you may be glancing at the first and last paragraphs of each chapter. As you get more thorough, and glance at the first and last sentences of each paragraph, increase the time you spend on the first and last chapter paragraphs – these are still more significant than the rest and should therefore command more attention, relative to the other paragraphs you skim through.

When skimming, try to keep your eyes at the center of the page – not the book, but each page. This will avoid a bias on either side of the text column, as your visual acuity typically worsens at an even rate in either direction outside of your foveal vision. Try to use vertical movement in your eyes, rather than horizontal. Don't try to scan across every line as this will only end up being a poor read and take more time than the skim read is worth, without the comprehension of a full read.

Limit Subvocalization

Consciously try to avoid saying the words in your head and absolutely avoid mouthing them as you read.

Do not become frustrated if you cannot eliminate the voice altogether; maintaining that internal monologue may even help your comprehension to some degree. However, if you are aiming for **speed**, avoid reading through the text as if it is a stage play.

There are several techniques many people find helpful for limiting subvocalization. You might find one that works for you, maybe a combination or perhaps none at all. The only way to establish your preference is by experimenting.

- Chewing Gum – This will occupy your mouth and should greatly mitigate any subvocalization mouth movements you are performing. It is one of the most commonly recommended techniques for freeing your reading speed from your subvocalization movements.

- Talking – It may seem counter-intuitive but actually the logic is much the same as chewing gum. By occupying your mouth, repeating a simple phrase such as "one, two, three, one, two... (etc.)," you can somewhat compartmentalize your speech function, without demanding an inordinate amount of attention that could impair your ability to comprehend the text. Some people find this **even more** effective than chewing gum and it is a technique which can improve over time, as repeating the phrase becomes second nature.

- Accelerating – Rather than trying to limit your subvocalization in order to speed up, it might be far more effective to speed up as a method of limiting your subvocalization. Above a certain rate of reading, you simply might not be able to keep up. This can apply to any of the techniques in this chapter. While subvocalization can contribute to a slower reading rate, it does not have the power to control it. By going faster with your tracker, or increasing the speed of your software, it is often possible to simply power through.

- Listening to Music – Music is a great way to help concentrate, in almost any activity. For some people, it can also have the added bonus of reducing subvocalization. Just the fact that it provides some sound as a form of distraction might be enough. In most cases, something casual and non-lyrical, like classical music, is going to strike a better balance between occupying your senses and not dominating them. But there are no hard and fast rules; if you find that listening to death metal helps you to read fast and retain more information, nobody can tell you you're wrong!

Tracking

One of the simplest, and most common, methods of speed reading is using a tracker.

Tracing a finger, or pen, along text, is an excellent way to maintain your focus, keep a steady pace and avoid regression.

Good tracking should follow a smooth and steady rate. Hold your tracker just below the line of text and allow your eye to focus on the text itself. Continue moving through the text in this fashion and you are tracking.

The method really is as simple as that. If you read earlier chapters, you may be doing so already.

To get a little more technical, it is likely that you will not be moving your eyes at the same steady rate as your tracker. You will still perceive the text in fixations, between which there will be saccades. However, you will be progressing at a steady rate on average.

There is also a potential advantage to perceiving in fixations, which allow you to capture an aperture of information with good visual acuity. Using this logic, many, many people, who speed read by tracking, do not start each line at the start, nor finish at the end. Try to start your tracker about two words into a line and finish two words from, the end. If you feel comfortable with this, and feel that you are perceiving the full line, try narrowing your tracking even further. Progress to a point at which you feel comfortable.

Naturally, to increase your reading rate with tracking, you will need to pick up the pace of your tracker. By increasing the pace of your tracker, you will increase the speed at which you read. It is an inevitability that, at a certain point, your level of comprehension will diminish. Imagine furiously swiping your pen across the page in a blur – there's not much chance of processing any of that information in any effective sense.

Despite that, you will likely find that reading at **double** your target rate, even if you don't comprehend well, is a great way to train yourself. Work out the pace you need to track, in order to reach your target reading rate, say 600 wpm, and then double that, and read for a while. When you go back to 600 wpm, you may well experience an improvement in your ability to perceive and comprehend the text. Use this method to train regularly, forcing yourself to practice.

It is recommended that you hold your tracker underneath your fingers and palm, with your hand flat to the page. Use that grip to press the tracker to the page and slide it along each line in a steady motion. You can hold your tracker like a pen, if you wish, but this can be uncomfortable during long speed reading sessions and may result in awkward angles, particularly lower down the page.

Covering

This method is similar to, but distinct from, tracking. However, it follows much the same logic.

Covering is a hard limit to your eye regression. You can either cover vertically down the page, preventing yourself from rereading previous lines, or you can cover along each line, using your cover much like a tracker, to prevent eye regression along each line.

Your cover should be something square, like a piece of card of other hard material, which you can easily manipulate. Find something tactile, which you can grip to easily slide along the page, but doesn't create friction with the page itself.

Naturally, you should completely prevent yourself from lifting or sliding the cover upwards in order to read text you have already passed. The only referee on this count is yourself, but the entire point of the method is to avoid all forms of eye regression.

Additional options for covers can include markers, on the cover itself, which have fixation points clearly indicated. This is only suitable for vertical covers. You can use these as a guide to move across the page consistently with your eyes, somewhat filling in for the lack of a tracker along the line.

Rapid Serial Visual Presentation (RSVP)

Not to be confused with "Répondez s'il vous plaît," the "RSVP" you see on invitations to parties, kindly requesting that you confirm your attendance beforehand – it literally translates to: "Please respond."

Rapid Serial Visual Presentation, or RSVP, is a software based technique. What it does is remove the saccade element of reading by only showing you one or a few words at a time, in sequence, from text when you input into the software beforehand.

RSVP offers a number of advantages. It allows you to precisely set the rate at which you want to read and offer you substantial customization. You can probably also accelerate your reading to a high speed, relatively quickly and maintain good levels of comprehension. Additionally, it allows you to passively read, rather than run through the text with a tracker and turn pages. The software keeps the pace for you.

There is a weight of evidence behind RSVP and, although higher reading rates typically **do** result in lower levels of comprehension, the **total** number of words comprehended remains higher.

Single-word RSVP also removes the issue of spaces between words, allowing you to simply view a pure flow of text. Studies indicate that the human eye can perceive text, using this method, at over 700 wpm, higher than some of the fastest reading academics.

The one significant problem with RSVP, compared to other methods, is that it is far **far** more inconvenient to pause and focus on a single word. Although the software allows you to pause at any time, you simply won't be able to react fast enough to pause the word you want to examine. While, in theory, you shouldn't be stopping in other speed reading techniques, in practice you are likely to come across words, and names, with which you are unfamiliar. Pausing to examine this more closely is much easier when you just need to stop the pen for a few seconds, rather than pause and rewind the software.

It is, therefore, far more important to prepare properly when using RSVP to properly speed read, limiting the negative effects of excessive pausing.

Furthermore, there is some evidence to suggest RSVP can be a tiring way to read and many might find it uncomfortable to read on a digital screen, compared to paper. It is up to you to determine whether or not, and how, the method works for you.

Inference Speed Reading Technique

When you are learning how to speed read you have to keep a record of your progress. When you monitor your reading speed as you are training, it will help you to observe all of your advances, and, when you don't observe any, figure out where your problem is and fix it. Hence, you have to know what your reading speed is.

Measuring Three Things

When you are measuring your reading speed, it is important that you look at three different measurements. All three of these are required to completely understand how you are progressing with your reading speed.

1. Average Speed

The first thing you need to measure is your average speed. The average speed looks at the number of works that you are able to read in a single minute, even if you don't completely understand or memorize any of the information that you just read.

In order to measure your average speed, pick a page form your favorite book and then count how many words are on the page. Then you will need to take a timer to see how long it takes for you to read the entire page. Once you get done, divide the number of words on the page with the minutes it took you to read it. This is your words per minute average speed.

2. Processing Speed

When you are figuring up your reading speed, any good measurement will take into account your comprehension of what you have read, which you measure with your processing speed. The main goal of speed reading is to be able to read fast, but you also want to be able to understand the things that you have read. Hence, you will want to read fast, but you need to try to understand what it is you are reading. In order for you to figure out how much of the text you were able to understand, you need to answer a few questions once you have measured your average speed. The main problem with this, especially if you are doing this on your own and not using a website, is that you will have to ask somebody else to write these questions for you. The number of questions that you are able to correctly answer will give you your percentage of understanding.

For example, let's say that you were able to answer seven out of 12 questions correctly. You would then figure out your processing speed by:

$7 * 100/12 = 58\%$

That means your processing speed is only 58%.

3. Memorizing Speed

The memorizing speed is how many words you are able to read and comprehend each minute. You can get this number by multiplying your average speed with your processing speed, in percentage. This means that if your average speed was 600 words per minute, and your processing speed is 75%, you would figure out your memorizing speed by:

$600 * .75 = 450$

As you can probably figure out, the main goal of speed reading to get you to a very high memorizing speed. In order to get that, you need to have a fast average speed and you also need to have a good processing speed.

After you have figured out your reading speed, you will probably want to figure out how good or bad that speed really is. I would recommend that you don't focus on the comparison. I believe that focusing on your progress is more important than comparing yourself to others. However, there are a lot of people who will still want that information. That is why I have provided you with that information in this chapter. The following table describes how all of the different reading speeds compare to one another.

- 1 – 100 words per minute

  - Children that are learning to read will be in this reading speed range. If a learner is not able to progress beyond this range, their reading ability is seen to be at the borderline literacy range. A reader that is in this range will more than likely not have a lot of understanding and memory of the things they have read. Reading takes a lot of work when the words per minute are below 100.

- 100 – 200 words per minute

  - A person that is within this range for reading speed is typically a person who has done the minimum amount of reading that they had to in order to make it through life. This type of person normally doesn't see reading as fun, entertaining, or relaxing. Within this reading speed range, it is pretty much impossible to stay up to date on technology, world events, and so on. The reader's memory and understanding is normally less than half of what their eyes actually see.

- 200 – 250 words per minute

  - This is what is considered to be the average range for reading speed. Without any help, most of these readers are going to be stuck in this range for the rest of their reading lives. These people are constantly slowed down through regressions, concentration problems, and reading sub-vocalization. Typically, they will understand around half of what they read.

- 250 – 350 words per minute

  - The speeds in this range are just a little more than average of the majority of readers.

Typically, post-high school graduates or people who are casual keen readers are in this range. These readers will normally still suffer from regressions, but they don't subvocalize as many of the words. Normally, the readers in this section end up comprehending over half of the things they read.

- 350 – 500 words per minute

  o People who score in this range for reading speed are well over the average speed. As a result, their understanding and comprehension are typically very good, around 50 to 75 percent. These people are normally avid readers and enjoy it immensely. They may still suffer from some sub-vocalization and regressions. This is mainly because their mind will still drift away.

- 500 – 800 words per minute

  o This, for speed readers, is a useful and respectable reading speed. In this area, the reader will have amazing comprehension, around 75 percent or more. They will be the types of people that enjoy reading and find it pleasurable and they have great control over their office and daily reading needs. They are the types of people who find the book better than the movie.

- 800 – 1000 words per minute

  o This is an amazingly efficient speed for reading. This is verging on what is known as power-reading. This type of reader has very little sub-vocalization and they typically don't regress at all. They are able to understand and recognize most of the words. They are normally able to understand everything that they read. They aren't pressured when they read, and they don't have reading time problems. This person is likely to be at the top of the class or a high business achiever. A person who reads at this speed is normally a person who has undergone some quality reading improvement program.

- 1000 words per minute and more

    o Now, this is an amazing feat. This person is either a tutored or natural speed reader. The readers who read at this speed are able to comprehend most everything that they read. This person has complete control over all of their needs as a reader. Reading takes up a big chunk of their life. These people normally enjoy two or more novels every week.

With this chart, we are talking only about reading and not talking about skimming. That is why reading speeds over 1300 words per minute are not possible.

Measuring with a Program

Now, I have gone through how you can measure your reading speed naturally, on your own. However, there are a lot of programs out there that can perform these calculations for you, and will already have all of the questions ready to figure out your processing speed. The following are the most popular:

- Speed Reading test online by readingsoft.com. This is a web app that will provide you with a reading test as well as comprehension questions. However, this can only be used one time because they use the same text every time.

- Free Speed Reading Test, by AceReader. This is another web app that has several different tests that come with questionnaires.

- My read speed is another web app that measures your words per minute. It has ten different tests, but it does not give you any questions to answer to get your comprehension score.

- Speed reading test, Stapes. This is one of the best web apps to find out what your reading speed is. They have several different texts to test you on, and they come with questionnaires. The fun thing about this test is that once you have finished the text it will give you some numbers for how long it would take you to make your way through some famous books based on your numbers.

There are also a lot of apps out there for tablets or smartphones that will allow you to test your reading speed. The following two are pretty good:

- Acceleread Speed Reading Trainer, by BananaBox Inc. This is the best program when you want to learn about speed reading, and to figure out your reading speed and to keep things up to date on your progress. This comes along with questionnaires for your comprehension test.

- QuickReader – eBook Reader with Speed Reading, by Inkstone Software Inc. This is a great app to speed read your books with, and it is also useful for measuring your reading speed from time to time. This app does not come with a questionnaire to test your comprehension.

When you start training yourself to speed read, it is important that you test your reading speed every two weeks so that you can observe your progress or lack thereof. If you are training properly, you should start to see an increase in your memorizing speed. If you aren't, there is probably a problem with the way that you are training and you need to make efforts to change it.

Scanning

Scanning and skimming are techniques for reading that use keywords and rapid eye movement to quickly move through text for different reasons. Each of them is used for different purposes. They aren't meant to be used at all times. They are on the fast end of the range of speed reading while studying is at the slow end. Skimming is rapidly reading so you can get a feel for the material. Scanning is rapidly reading so you can find certain facts. Skimming will give you information in a certain section, scanning will help you find a specific fact. Skimming is like snorkeling and scanning for pearls.

People who can scan and skim are considered flexible readers. They will read whichever way they need to for a certain purpose to get information without wasting time. They never read each word and this helps to increase their reading speed. They have the skill to know what certain information they need to read and which method they need to use.

You can use skimming to preview which is reading before actually reading. You can use skimming to review which is reading after you have already read. You can use skimming to determine the main idea of long material you don't want to read. You can use skimming to find certain material for research papers.

You can use scanning to research and find specific facts, to answer a question that requires support from facts, and to study materials that are fact heavy.

Skimming

Skimming is a tool you can use to read more material in less time. It can save you many hours of reading. This isn't the best way to read. It's useful to use it as a preview for more detailed reading or if you need to review a lot of content. When skimming, you might miss points that were important or overlook meanings that were obscured.

When you skim, you are only looking for main or general ideas. It works best when reading non-fiction materials. You focus on what's important for your purpose. Skimming happens when you read and lets you look for details along with the main ideas.

A lot of people think skimming is haphazard and places the eyes where they fall. In order to skim effectively, you need structure but don't read every single word. The words you read are more important than the ones you leave out. How do you determine what to read and what not to read?

If you are doing research on a website, reading the first few paragraphs will get you an idea of what information is being discussed.

When skimming, you need to prepare yourself to move quickly through all the pages. Don't read each word. Just pay attention to heading, bold or italic type, indented, numbered or bulleted lists. Stay alert for key phrases and words, words you aren't familiar with, nouns, dates, places, and names. Try to follow these guidelines:

- Read the chapter overview or table of contents to figure out the main ideas.

- Look at the headings of each chapter to see if any words pop out at you. Read the headings of any tables and charts.

- Read the whole introductory paragraph and then just the first sentence and last sentence in each paragraph. In every paragraph, read just the first few words of the sentence to get the main idea.

- Quickly read any sentence that contains keywords that are either italicized or boldface.

- If you found something you think is significant, read the whole sentence just to make sure. Then continue in the same manner. Don't let temptation get the better of you don't read any details you aren't looking for.

- If there are chapter summaries, read them.

After you realize where the material is heading, you can just read the first sentence in every paragraph. This is called topic sentences and it will give you the paragraph's main ideas. If you don't get the main idea in the first sentence or if the paragraph sucks you in, you might want to skim more.

Keep reading only the topic sentences and dropping down the rest of the paragraphs until you are close to the end. The last few paragraphs might hold a summary or conclusion. You need to stop skimming and read the rest in detail. Your comprehension is going to be lower than if you read in detail. While you are skimming, if you think you are getting the main idea, then you are doing it correctly.

Skimming helps you quickly locate information while using your time wisely. It also increases the usable material you comprehend for research.

Let's say you have a big test in a couple days. You want to review the material but don't want to reread all of it. When you skim, you will be able to locate the information you haven't mastered and can just study that.

You can ask yourself these questions while reading to help you figure out whether or not you should skim. If your answer to any is yes, then skimming would be useful:

- Can you skip any of the material?

- Do you already know a little bit about this?

- Is there a lot to read and not a lot of time?

- Is it non-fiction material?

If you have some prior knowledge or don't think it's important, then skip it. Yes, don't read it. Skipping material might be the best way to use your time. Just because somebody wrote something down doesn't mean you are obligated to read it. If you can pick and choose what you skip and skim, you will be surprised at the amount of information you will be able to get through quickly.

Good skimmers won't skim everything. They won't even give the same attention to everything. Skimming is faster than normal reading. You need to slow down in these situations:

- When skimming concluding and introductory paragraphs.

- When skimming topic sentences.

- If you find a word you don't understand.

- If the material is complicated.

Scanning for Research

Scanning is another tool to help you increase your reading speed. It is different than skimming because you just look of a certain fact or piece of information without completely reading all words.

Scanning also uses organizational cues and keywords. When you skim, you just get a bird's eye view of materials. When scanning, you are trying to find then hold onto certain facts.

You probably scan more than you think you do. You are scanning when looking for your favorite television shows on the cable guide. You scan when you are looking for a friend's number in your telephone book. You scan when you look at sports scored in the paper. In order to be successful when scanning, you have to know how the material is structured and are able to comprehend what you are reading so you will be able to find the information needed. Scanning lets you locate information and details quickly.

First, figure out what you are researching, locate the right material, and know how the structure of the information is before you begin scanning.

Facts might be buried inside a very long passage of material that doesn't have much to do with the topic you are researching. Skim this first to see if it might contain the material you need. Remember to look at typographical cues, headings, indexes, summaries, and tables of contents. In order to understand the tables and lists, skim first to see how well they are organized whether it is most to least, chronological, or alphabetical.

The information might also be arranged in a non-alphabetical order like parts in an auto parts catalog, television listings, or category. Information might be located inside paragraphs of text or textual sense like in encyclopedias.

After you have skimmed, figure out if the material is useful. If it is, proceed to scan:

- You need to know what you are looking for. Figure out some keywords or phrases to look for. You are going to be the search engine.

- Scan for just one keyword at a time. If you try to use multiples, you are just going to get confused. If there is more than one thing you are looking for, do several scans.

- Allow your eyes to go quickly down a page until you find the phrase or words you want.

- If your eye catches a keyword, read the material carefully.

Using your hands when scanning is useful when trying to find certain information. If you run your finger down a dictionary page to find a word, to locate a meeting on the calendar, to read a bus or train schedule, this helps to focus your attention and keeps your place when scanning columns of material.

Peripheral vision is also a helpful scanning tool. As your finger moves down a list, you are not only seeing the name your finger is at but the names below and above it. Allow your eyes to work for you when scanning.

Scanning for Answers

If you are looking for information to answer certain questions, the most important step has been done for you. The question gives you the keywords you need to look for. Follow these steps to help you find the answers:

- Completely read every question before you begin scanning. Choose the keywords from the question.

- Concentrate on just one question at a time. Scan for each question separately.

- Once you have located a keyword, carefully read the surrounding text to see if anything is relevant.

- Read the question again to see if the answer you found actually answers your question.

Keep your keyword in mind while you are scanning. When do you need to scan? When your goal is to locate certain information. If you are researching material for a presentation, you can scan the book's index, reference materials, and websites. You can discover if they contain the information you need and what page they are located on.

You have probably scanned without even realizing what you were doing. With this information, you should be able to use scanning more frequently and intentionally. The more you do this, the more effective your scanning will be. The best benefit of scanning is the ability to help you be a better reader. Scanning will add another gear to your reading.

Humans have been geared to read every word on a page and it might be hard to leave words out. You have to allow yourself to overlook words by skipping, scanning, and skimming material. It all depends on what you need. You have permission not to read every word on a page.

Scanning requires concentration and can be tiring. You might need to practice at keeping your attention on the material and not letting it wander. Pick a place and time that will work for you and then dive right in.

Eye Exercises

The muscles in your eyeballs and eye sockets control your eye movements, and like all other muscles in your body, you can strengthen these through different exercises. This eye strength is helpful when you want to speed read, which taxes your eyes more than a regular reading speed because it will require you to cover more space on a page. When you make your eye muscles stronger and flexible, it will improve your vision clarity and will slow down natural eyesight deterioration that happens with aging.

Before you start your speed reading training, it is important that you train your eye muscles. This will help to expand your visual field. This type of training is meant to help you to read faster and to help you make faster connections with the things you read. While things may not go all that great at first, it is important that you practice all of this over and over again until you can increase your speed.

Fun fact, humans have the weakest peripheral vision range than any other species.

Eye Training

This is probably the hardest exercise you will have to do because it is all about speed. Make sure you go at a comfortable speed at first and don't allow yourself to get dizzy. The more you do it, the faster you will be able to go.

1. Start by staring off in the distance then start to move your eyes up and down as quickly as you can. Do this for ten seconds.

2. Once the ten seconds are up, let your eyes rest for a second and then move them from left to right as quickly as you can. Again, do this for ten seconds.

3. Rest for a few seconds, and then repeat this process three more times.

This exercise works your lower and upper oblique muscles. When you do this at high speeds, you will start to sense light and colors. For example, you may start to see stars in the middle of what you are looking at. This will cause your brain's five senses to wake up. You will feel a warm sensation, different smells, and you may even feel some pain.

Through this repetition, the sensory faculties of your right brain will begin to surface. Through rhythmically training your eyes at these high speeds, you will start to evoke images of form, light, and color. This will help you with speed reading

Thumb-to-thumb glancing

This method of eye exercise works the muscles in the eye sockets that work your peripheral vision and it helps to stretch the muscles in general so that they are more flexible and healthier.

In order to get the most from this exercise, you need to try and glance at both of your thumbs without allowing your head to move.

1. Sit or stand and look straight out in front of you, stretch your arms out to the side at shoulder length and then stick your thumbs up.

2. Without allowing your head to move glance between your right and left thumb ten times.

3. Repeat this process three times.

The first few times you do this your head may hurt a bit, and you may find it hard to keep from moving your head. This will get easier the more you do it.

Infinity Loop or Figure Eight

This is a perfect exercise to strengthen your eye muscles. This helps improve your eyes' flexibility. Here is how this exercise is performed:

1. Pretend that there is a giant figure of the number eight (8) in front of you at around ten feet.

2. Now, move the figure eight so that it is on its side.

3. Now, trace this sideways figure eight with your eyes in a very slow motion.

4. Perform the in one direction for a few minutes and then trace for a few minutes in the other direction.

Eye Writing

This exercise will have you moving your eyes in ways that they don't normally move, which gives them a pretty good workout. This exercise works the extra-ocular muscles in your eye socket and it great for increasing your eye's range of motion and eyeball flexibility. This exercise could not be any easier:

1. Stare at a wall that is located on the other side of the room. Try to use the wall that is the farthest from you.

2. Pretend that you are writing out your name on that wall using only your eyes. Basically, you should move your eyes in the shape of the letters in your name. Act as if you are using a paintbrush to write your name on that wall. You can start out writing your name in block letters and then do it in cursive.

This will be hard at first, but the more you do it the easier it will get. The first time you do it, it may not even feel like you're doing anything.

Hooded Eyes

This exercise is meant to relax your eyes. This exercise should be done two to three times whenever your eyes are in need of a little timeout.

1. Shut your eyes about halfway and then focus on stopping your eyelids from shaking. While you are concentrating on what your eyelids are doing, you are allowing your eyes to relax.

2. While you still have your eyes half closes, gaze at something that is far away from you. This will make your eyes stop trembling.

Just like all of the other exercise, you will have to practice this a few times before it feels like you are doing things correctly.

Zooming

This is a perfect exercise when you want to work on the way your eyes focus. With this exercise, you will be constantly adjusting your focus length. This will strengthen up the muscles in your eyes. Here is how to perform zooming:

1. **Sit up in a comfortable position with your feet flat on the floor.**

2. **Stretch your arms out in front of you with your thumbs up in a hitchhiking position.**

3. **Now, focus your eyes on your thumbs with your arms outstretched.**

4. **Now slowly move your thumbs closer to you and keep your focus on your thumbs until they are almost three inches in front of your face.**

5. **You will then move your thumbs backward again, still focusing your eyes on your thumbs, until they are fully outstretched.**

6. **Repeat this for a few minutes at different times during the day.**

Eye Squeezes

These eye squeezes will also help to relax your eyes, will make the muscles more flexible, and it helps to increase the blood and oxygen flow to your faces and eyes. This should take you around three minutes to do.

1. **While you inhale slowly and deeply, open your mouth and eyes as wide as you possibly can and let all of the muscles in your face stretch out.**

2. **While you exhale, close and squeeze your eyes as tight as you can as you are squeezing the other muscles in your head, face, and neck and clenching your jaw shut.**

3. **Hold in your breath as you are squeezing everything for 30 seconds.**

4. **Repeat this process four more times. After that, take a short break and then repeat this five more times.**

This is a really fun exercise to do. If you are feeling rather tense, this is a great way to release it, plus you get to make a funny face. Although, if you are in an office setting or in public, you may want to find a private spot so that you don't freak anybody out.

Around the World

Not only is this great for getting your eyes ready to speed read, but this exercise can help prevent presbyopia, which will happen when the elasticity of your eyes start to deteriorate because of the lack of eye movement. When this happens, you will find it harder to focus on things at different distances. This is how to perform around the world:

1. Make sure you are sitting comfortably or standing in an area that is generally traffic-free.

2. Close both of your eyes, or you can leave them open, but make sure that your head doesn't move at all while you are doing the following movements with your eyes.

3. Roll your eyes up, as if you are looking up, and leave them there for three seconds, and then roll your eyes down and hold that for three seconds. If you have chosen to keep your eyes open, wait until your eyes have focused on a certain object before you move your eyes to the next exercise.

4. Now, look to the far right and hold this for three seconds and then look as far left as you can and hold this for three seconds.

5. Now look up to the top left and hold this for three seconds and then look to the top right and hold for three seconds.

6. Lastly, rotate your eyes clockwise two times and the counterclockwise for two rotations.

Change Focus

This one will help strength how your eyes focus on the object. You will be alternating between close and far away objects in this exercise, so you may notice that your head starts to hurt the first few times you do this.

1. Look up from what you are currently looking at and focus on something in the distance.

2. Then look at something close up again.

3. Repeat this a few times, or until your eyes start to feel refreshed.

This is also sometimes called 20/20/20. This is because that you need to take a break every 20 minutes to look at something that is 20 feet away for 20 seconds. This is supposed to help prevent eye strain.

Palm Your Eyes

This is the easiest exercise there is, and it is exactly as it sounds.

1. Rub the palms of your hands together briskly to help warm them up a bit.

2. Put the palms of your hands over your closed eyes and then gently rub the bony spots around your eyes. Make sure you don't rub directly on your eyeballs. Do this for about 30 seconds.

3. With your palms still covering your eyes, open up your eyes and create a seal around your eyes. You should be looking into complete darkness. Stay here for a moment or two.

Clock Gazing

1. Sit in a comfortable position with a straight spine and both of your feet on the floor.

2. Picture a giant clock face about a foot in front of you.

3. Keeping your head completely still, look at where the 12 would be, then you will look down at where the six would be. You will continue in this manner:

   1. One to seven.

   2. Two to eight.

   3. Three to nine.

   4. Four to 10.

   5. Five to 11.

4. After you finish, close your eyes and let them rest for about 30 seconds.

When you close your eyes, this would be a good time to palm your eyes if you would like.

Chapter 3: What Is Memory

We've already talked a great deal about memory and the brain, but we've only just begun to scratch the surface of how your memory actually works. Even the act of recalling the simplest of details involves the stimulation of complex neural networks throughout the brain.

Interestingly enough, our memory is not some static function that happens inside the brain but is an active process that is never-ending. It is important to understand that memory is a necessary element of the learning process, but it is not the same. There are actually three important components to memory that you should understand.

•   Encoding: the process the brain uses to change data learned into a form that can be held in the memory.

•   Storage: the brain's ability to hold the data.

•   Retrieval: the brain's ability to re-access the learned data from whatever region it has been stored in.

We'll begin by knowing first the encoding process. Your ability to learn something depends heavily on encoding. When you learn, the brain goes through a selective process that categorizes information into several different areas. First, it looks at the data to see if it is related to the type of material that has already been encoded. In this regard, the content of the data could include quantity of information (the more data you have, the more complex the encoding process can be), how the information is organized, and how familiar you might already be with the information.

All of these factors and more are processed through the brain at phenomenal speeds. In fact, it happens so quickly, you aren't even aware that your brain has done it.

When it comes to encoding, environmental factors also play a role. While they are not always considered to be important, this does factor into how well you remember things. Think back on how unreliable your memory was when the temperature was extremely high, or there was a lot of distracting noise in your environment. While each person is different, these environmental factors could be a very important element that could either inhibit or stimulate your memory and how well you learn.

Other factors that could also affect the encoding process of your memory could be your physical condition. Factors such as fatigue, health, and motivation can contribute significantly to how much of the information is actually imprinted in the brain. This is why you see so many courses that address the issue of "What's in it for me?" as part of their training programs. If you do not have proper motivation, your chances of recalling the data later on will be drastically reduced.

The second phase of memory is storage. Your brain analyzes the information it receives to determine if it is related to certain conditions under which it can be encoded. Once the information is encoded, it must be stored in the brain. If it cannot be stored, no matter what you learn, it will be of no demonstrable use to you.

Our brains' memory storage has two primary types: short - or long-term memory. Both will act as filters that are put in place to ensure and protect the brain from an information overload. We are not aware of just how much data our brain picks up every day. Most of it is naturally disregarded and sifted out so that it doesn't all go into the memory banks.

Information that is considered important is retained while information that is not relevant or does not carry a significant amount of weight is tossed. For example, information that is repeated regularly will be viewed as important and will go into our memory banks but the chill you felt when the wind blew your hat off your head last winter won't. The brain sees it as having no significant relevance to the learning process so it will not be stored (unless you view it as a memorable experience related to something else). The more experience or a piece of data is repeated, the more likely the knowledge will end up in your long-term memory banks.

Finally, there is the process of retrieval or the ability to re-access the stored information, recalling it to mind again. There are many different types of retrieval. Recognition is when the mind associates an event or an object with previous experience. You can recognize a face, the answers to questions on a test, or the sound of a particular song. Recall, on the other hand, involves remembering a specific fact, or a set event, or object. You might recognize a face, but you will recall the name.

The Forgetting Curve

It is important that when you consider memory, you also factor in your forgetting curve. The two actually work together. Whatever your brain chooses not to remember, you will forget. Therefore, it becomes necessary for you to understand that forgetting also changes as you age. After many studies carried out over several years, there has been only one sure fire way to prevent forgetfulness, and that is through repetition, but we'll discuss more of this later in this book.

Suffice to say, without memory your ability to learn is rendered moot. You can't have one without the other. Your memory is the single element that makes it possible for you to link your new knowledge to past experiences. As you start working on your Accelerated Learning Program, it is extremely essential to protect this relationship between learning and memory so you can have the most efficient learning process.

Memory Retention

Because details of a particular event are not stored in exactly the same place in the brain, recalling them requires many parts to work together to assemble previously acquired knowledge. To make this happen there is a tiny little part of the brain that has to be functioning properly - the hippocampus. This straddles both hemispheres and is responsible for collecting new information, sorting it out and turning that information into a real memory before sending it to other areas of the brain to be stored. Without this tool, learning would be possible but memory would not.

In essence, it not only makes it possible to remember, but it also works as an all-important filter in deciding what data is important to remember or what can be discarded, a critical element in the learning process. But all memory is not the same. We've already discussed short-term and long-term memory, but there is a lot more to memory that you must keep in mind.

Five Types of Memory

W-Working

I-Implicit

R-Remote

E-Episodic

S-Semantic

By using this acronym, it helps to remember the brain as a device that has been specifically wired to perform certain functions. Let's look at each of these one at a time.

Working: Our working memory is extremely short-term. It lasts for only a few seconds. It's located right in the prefrontal cortex (behind the forehead) and allows you to retain several things in your mind for a limited period of time. This is why you can recall the first words someone has said to you and hold it until you can gather their main thoughts and put them together. With this type of memory, you are also able to multi-tasks - performing several small tasks at the same time. You can have a conversation with one person and wave to someone else and even read simultaneously.

Implicit: Your implicit memory allows you to recall skills you've learned like riding a bicycle, driving, or even swimming. This is why you can learn to ride a bike when you are six and still know how to do it when you are fifty. In layman's terms, we often refer to this as muscle memory. This is also the reason why when you're driving your car, you don't have to concentrate and can lose yourself in thought on other topics and never have to worry about running through a red light or missing your turn. This type of memory is stored in the cerebellum of the brain.

Remote: Our remote memory is the biggest memory storage you can have. It holds all the data you have accumulated and stored throughout your lifetime in your cerebral cortex. It can hold massive amounts of information on a wide variety of topics and never get full. However, older people tend to have trouble during the retrieval phase as they try to access this storage facility, so they must work that much harder to get through such a large store of knowledge.

Episodic: Episodic memory is the recollection of very specific personal experiences. Of course, not all knowledge is stored here but those experiences that you definitely have a connection to: a scene from your favorite movie, the exact location where you parked your car and the result of that Super Bowl game you saw. It stores memories of experiences that gave you a significant level of emotional fulfillment.

Semantic: This type of memory focuses on words and symbols and is the one area that is never forgotten. Words and symbols that are clearly unforgettable can include religious icons, certain expressions, and the fundamentals of how the world works. For example, you may forget everything else, but you will remember what a dog or a cat looks like, the smell of bacon, or your favorite food. It is this type of memory that gives us the foundation on how the world works.

When learning new information, the best way to ensure that you will remember it is to make sure that the lesson has a powerful emotional impact. This includes incorporating the five senses in the learning process and associating it with positive emotions.

New studies are now showing that lessons can be learned, but it is not sealed into your memory banks until you are in a deeply relaxed state or asleep. So, you may be in the beta or alpha stage when you learn but to seal it in your memory your brain must be in the theta brainwave state.

There have been many studies performed on humans and other animals showing that sleep has a powerful ability to boost memory, especially during the rapid eye movement (REM) stage. Repeatedly, studies have shown that during the day the brain is flooded with all sorts of input coming through the five senses, but it is unable to absorb it all while the brain is in this receiving mode. During the REM stage, the receiving mode shuts down giving the brain time to process the events it has taken in. It is during this stage that the brain can sift through everything that make sense of it and file it away in the proper memory file.

This is the primary way we dream, our mind begins to create its own story as the brain attempts to put all the pieces together and make sense of them. Therefore, to facilitate and speed up the learning process, creating easy to visualize stories related to the lesson is a very effective tool that will help you to remember.

This is why expressions like *My Very Energetic Mother Just Served us Nine Pizzas* have been so effective in helping us to recall the planets in the solar system. You can use this technique to help you recall new vocabulary and foreign languages with plenty of visual and auditory aids.

How Emotions Play a Role

Emotion is a powerful force that when used correctly can be very effective in helping you learn. After years of research, we are just beginning to grasp how malleable our mind is when emotions are involved.

It is important, however, to understand that not all emotions are conducive to learning. When associated with negative events, the brain automatically begins to shift to the fight-or-flight response, which begins to flood our system with stress hormones. The brain then uses these chemicals to control how strong the memory storage will be.

These stress hormones make it possible for you to perform certain physical reactions in an attempt to protect yourself. It also will embed into your brain extremely vivid images that you will never forget. Think about the time you were bitten by a dog, your brain will never let you forget that experience, and every time you see a dog after that, those images will come back up triggering the same fight or flight response.

The fact is that it is literally impossible for anyone to separate emotion from the learning process. This is because of all the neural connections in the brain, the majority of them coming from or going to the limbic brain (the emotional center) of the cortex. This makes emotion a more powerful tool for learning than logic.

Although the limbic brain works in much the same way as a switchboard sending all incoming data to the thinking cortex, there is a much faster way for knowledge to get embedded and that is through emotion. Since this kind of information that we have an emotional connection to could be a warning of something that is potentially life-threatening, it does not stop to be analyzed but instead heads directly to the more primal regions of the brain, giving you a more "gut" and instinct reaction.

These areas of the brain rely more on knee-jerk reactions rather than a stage of mental processing. This is why, when you get a slight glimpse of a snake in your path, your mind doesn't go through all the knowledge you have about snakes, but it focuses on how to get away fast without getting harmed.

Use It or Lose It

For older people, memory becomes a tricky thing. While learning is still possible, many think that they are already too old to learn anything new. For many, it is the time when memory begins to fail, and they stop trying.

If you were to follow the statistics, you would think that this is true. After the age of sixty, reported cases of dementia double every five years and after the age of eighty-five, 30 or 40 percent of people will have been affected by some form of memory altering ailment.

However, after many years of study, the decline in one's memory is no longer a foregone conclusion for those of advanced years. According to one study, 25-33% of participants in their eighties scored just as high as the younger ones. Some of them had scores high enough to rank at the top of mental abilities for those of all ages.

What they have learned after such studies is that the previous theory that we begin to lose 100,000 neurons every year is not entirely true. Instead, our brain cells begin to shrink in size or become dormant as we get older, especially if we do not keep them actively engaged. According to researchers at Stanford and the Albert Einstein College of Medicine, the brain does not lose cells but still has the ability to grow new dendrites even in advanced years. The new cell growth is encouraged by stimulation, so as long as you continue to learn, the brain will continue to develop regardless of the age.

Photographic Memory

You might now be wondering about those people who have what is called a photographic memory or eidetic memory. First, let's make it clear what it really is. The general belief is that once a person sees something that memory remains with them. They will be able to readily recall it exactly as it was first seen without fail.

This, however, is a misnomer. Actually, a photographic memory can at times be as faulty as a regular memory. Many factors can have an impact on what they are able to recall; how long they observed the object or event, whether they were consciously trying to study it, or just saw it in passing.

An eidetic memory is simply someone who can observe something in such a way that it leaves a lasting impression that is so strong that the visual image remains firm in the mind's eye even after it is no longer within physical view. In essence, the person remembers it exactly as it has been seen. However, that is only if they imprinted on the image in the first place.

Just because some people can remember details better than others doesn't mean that they have a photographic memory. They have simply developed good learning skills, concentration, and making relevant connections of what may appear to be unrelated data. They may also have a better grasp on how to use mnemonic devices to help facilitate the learning process than other casual observers.

The questions then become, can you develop your own photographic memory? Those who are truly eidetic are rare and are usually born with this innate ability, so they already have a head start. As they mature, they develop it further. There are several internet sites that claim that they can teach you how to develop this skill, but they are basically only offering you general memory improvement strategies. While you can improve your ability to remember things, learning how to develop your own photographic memory will take many years of practice in applying highly effective memory techniques.

Chapter 4: What is Attention

People tend to think of focus as having tunnel vision. They believe it's the ability to ignore everything around them and zero in on the task sitting in front of them.

But focus and attention management are far more complicated than that. In reality, we manage different types of attention throughout each day. These different types dictate what we notice and don't notice, and what we ignore and choose not to ignore. They also have different uses and impose different challenges.

Confused? Rest assured, everything will become clear by the end of this section. Let's start by discussing voluntary versus involuntary attention.

Voluntary Vs. Involuntary Attention

These are the two main types of attention. Voluntary attention is what you use to consciously focus on something. For example, suppose you're reading a book in the same room in which your family is watching television. You may struggle to concentrate on the text. You have to consciously block out the noise around you in order to focus on your book.

That's voluntary attention. You control it. You decide what captures your notice and what doesn't.

Voluntary attention is like a muscle. Unfortunately, it's a muscle that has, for most of us, atrophied to the point of being useless. The good news is that voluntary attention can be strengthened through application. Like any muscle, it grows stronger with exercise. That means you can overcome distractions and develop the ability to concentrate on demand as long as you're willing to put in the work. **Fast Focus** takes you through this process.

Involuntary attention is the opposite of voluntary attention. You have no control over it. A gunshot will grab your attention regardless of how focused you are. Likewise, a blood-curdling scream will break your concentration, even if you're working in a flow state.

Involuntary attention has great value when our safety is at risk. Imagine our ancestors hunting for food. They would've been vulnerable to attacks from wild animals as well as from members of neighboring, aggressive tribes. Involuntary attention kept them alert, and thereby kept them safe (most of the time).

We're seldom in situations today that threaten our lives. We live in relative safety. We go about our days unconcerned that our lives might be put at risk at any given moment.

The problem is, our involuntary attention, an important part of our genetic makeup, is still there. It continues to work hard, drawing our attention to changes in our environment that might warrant our notice. But instead of wild animals and warring tribe members, it sounds the alarm over things that are trivial by comparison.

For example, your phone beeps, chirps, or vibrates, immediately drawing your attention and compelling you to check the reason. Or you notice that you've received a new email and immediately check to see who sent it. Or you notice a friend's Facebook updates and are unable to resist the temptation to read them.

That's your involuntary attention at work. It has less use today since our lives aren't under constant threat (most of us, anyway). But it continues to toil in the background, trying to earn its keep. Unfortunately, it only succeeds in creating an endless stream of distractions.

The takeaway is that voluntary attention and involuntary attention are different mechanisms. You control the former, but have little to no control over the latter. Note that you dampen the influence of involuntary attention by exercising more control over voluntary attention. We'll talk more about this throughout **Fast Focus**.

Let's now define the difference between broad and focused attention.

Broad Vs. Focused Attention

Broad attention allows you to evaluate circumstances from a bird's-eye view. You use it to see the forest rather than the trees.

For example, suppose you're a general in a theater of war working on military strategy. You'd use broad attention to map out strike plans, envision supply lines, and forecast the movements of large groups of troops, including those of your adversaries.

Or suppose you're the coach of your son or daughter's basketball team and you're creating a game strategy. You'd use broad attention to predict the myriad of situations your players might find themselves in, and devise appropriate responses.

The best way to think of broad attention is that it provides the big picture. Once you have a grasp of your overall situation, you can apply **focused** attention to address the details.

Focused attention allows you to appraise specific situations and come up with the most suitable approaches given your resources and goals.

Let's again suppose you're a general working on military strategy. A challenge you might face is how to overtake a particular area in a war theater given the strength and number of your adversary. You'd use focused attention to resolve this challenge.

Or let's again suppose you're the coach of your child's basketball team. It's near the end of the fourth quarter with 10 seconds on the clock, and your players are up by two points. The problem is, the opposing team has a player who excels in sinking three-pointers. You'd use focused attention to create an effective three-point defense strategy.

The good news about broad attention and focused attention is that both are in your control. Unlike involuntary attention, you decide how to best wield them to your advantage.

Keep in mind, both broad attention and focused attention pose potential pitfalls. For example, concentrating only on the big picture (broad attention) will allow important details to fall through the cracks. Zeroing in on specific situations (focused attention) to the exclusion of the big picture can lead to tunnel vision, impairing your overall awareness.

I admit, this has been a relatively long section. But having a full appreciation of the different types of attention, as well as how they work, will prove useful as you learn to develop and sharpen your focus.

In the following section, we'll take a quick look at the most common reasons we tend to lose focus.

Why We Lose Focus

You know the feeling.

You have a lot of work to get done, but you're unable to concentrate on it. You're distracted. Every noise you hear, from your phone notifications to the sound of traffic outside, pulls your attention away from the task at hand. And when you finally complete your work, you have the nagging feeling that its quality has suffered due to your lack of focus.

Sound familiar? That's the experience I went through, again and again, before I learned to master my attention. It's deeply frustrating. I know firsthand.

In order to strengthen our focus, it's important to appreciate why we lose it in the first place. It usually comes down to these five factors:

- Lack of interest

- Negative emotions

- Poor organization

- Low energy levels

- Lack of control

- Let's take a quick look at each one.

- Lack Of Interest

It's easier to concentrate when you're interested in the item you're trying to concentrate on. Focus requires feeling engaged by the task in front of you. You need to feel stimulated. When you're interested in your work, you're more likely to zero in on it and ignore the distractions around you.

Negative Emotions

A negative emotional state will erode your ability to concentrate. If you're feeling stressed, annoyed, lonely, depressed, or hostile, you'll find it impossible to focus. That's human nature. Your mind will be so preoccupied with these emotions that it'll leave few cognitive resources available for managing your attention.

Poor Organization

Show me someone who follows a structured day and I'll show you someone who's able to concentrate and successfully ignore distractions.

It's easier to manage your attention when your day follows a consistent, familiar pattern. With good organization, you'll be better able to keep chaos at bay. That in turn will help you to stay focused on whatever you're working on.

Low Energy Levels

Low energy is the attention-dampening factor that people most often overlook. Prolonged focus requires a lot of energy, which comes by way of good food, sufficient sleep, and regular exercise. The problem is, many of us neglect one or more of these elements. We eat unhealthy food, sacrifice sleep for other priorities, and spend too little time moving our bodies.

Your brain is the linchpin in developing attention mastery and maintaining focus. It can't function properly without sufficient energy.

Lack Of Control

How you control your time determines how well you're able to concentrate. If you allow people to interrupt you at their whim, you'll never achieve the flow state necessary to work unencumbered by distractions. You'll never feel fully immersed in the task at hand.

You must control your time if you hope to develop razor-sharp focus. Admittedly, it's not always feasible. Some interruptions are impossible to avoid. But most of us can take steps to improve in this area.

Is Mind Wandering Always Bad?

When you lose focus, your mind wanders. But is this always a bad thing?

Absolutely not. The key is to make it work for you.

Mind wandering allows your brain to be creative. To that end, it can help you to identify nontraditional solutions to problems that have proven difficult to resolve.

This doesn't mean you should allow your mind to wander at every opportunity. That's sure to impose a cost on your performance and productivity.

You're now familiar with the five biggest factors that cause us to lose focus during any given day. In the next section, we'll drill down to the 10 most common obstacles we face in **staying** focused.

Top 10 Obstacles To Staying Focused

There are two aspects to managing your attention: honing in on whatever you're working on and staying focused during the time you've allotted to it.

In order to stay focused, you have to be aware of the condition your mind is in. For example, it's difficult to concentrate if you're tired, stressed, or agitated.

The truth is, there are **numerous** factors that can impair your ability to stay focused. This section will cover the 10 that pose the biggest challenges.

Obstacle #1 - Mental Fatigue

If your brain is exhausted, you'll find it's almost impossible to focus. You'll be prone to distractions, one after another, which will prevent you from zeroing in on the task in front of you.

Mental exhaustion can stem from several factors, but the most common one is failing to get sufficient sleep. Even if you manage to get to bed at a decent time, you might toss and turn all night. That'll rob your brain of the restful slumber it needs to prepare itself for the following day.

Obstacle #2 - Restlessness

Restlessness is defined as a general feeling of anxiety. Something is causing you to feel ill at ease. Your brain receives signals that everything is not as it should be, and devotes cognitive resources to investigating and resolving the issue.

The problem is, it's often difficult to identify the reasons we feel restless. Consequently, the brain spins its wheels trying to resolve something it's unable to pinpoint. As you can imagine, this has a negative impact on your ability to manage your attention.

Obstacle #3 - Stress

A little stress is good for us. It keeps us alert. It can even help us to hone our focus. But many people (perhaps you?) suffer from **chronic** stress. They're in a constant state of anxiety.

This persistent stress can stem from many causes. Some people feel stressed when they lack control over their day. Others become stressed when deadlines approach and they feel unprepared to meet them. Still others undergo significant life events, such as a divorce or the passing of a loved one, that cause them stress.

Stress erodes your attention. The more you feel and the longer you feel it, the less you'll be able to concentrate.

Obstacle #4 - Interruptions

Have you ever tried to concentrate on something only to be hampered by a continuous string of interruptions (coworkers, phone calls, etc.)? It's frustrating. Not only does each interruption destroy your momentum, but it takes 20 minutes to get back on track.

That's the reason it's so difficult to focus when people interrupt you over and over.

Obstacle #5 - Lack Of Mental Clarity

Our brains are oftentimes filled with trivial thoughts and ideas that have nothing to do with the work in front of us. These thoughts and ideas constitute mental clutter.

The clutter makes it difficult to concentrate. A cluttered mind is an unfocused mind.

Obstacle #6 - Unresolved Problems

An unresolved problem is like a leaky faucet that prevents you from falling asleep at night. It's there, in the background, calling attention to itself. It refuses to go away, which causes your brain to devote attentional resources to it.

For example, suppose you and your spouse had an explosive argument last night that remains unsettled. Or suppose the investments in your retirement fund needs to be adjusted in light of how certain sectors are underperforming.

It's difficult to concentrate when such unresolved problems hang over our heads and nag us.

Obstacle #7 - Poor Planning

It's tough to focus on a task or project when you lack a clear, methodical plan to follow. Your brain will jump into action and attempt to fill in the gaps. The problem is it's unskilled at doing so.

For example, recall the last time you visited a grocery store without a grocery list. Your attention was no doubt drawn to numerous items as you walked down each aisle, some out of curiosity and others out of need. The visit, which would have taken 10 minutes had you arrived with a list, probably took much longer.

That's your brain working without a plan. It's in an unfocused state.

Obstacle #8 - Physical Clutter

Take a look at your workspace. Is it tidy or messy? Is it an example of control or chaos?

That's a fancy way of saying that a messy desk hampers your ability to concentrate.

Obstacle #9 - Social Media

Recent research purports that social media has no long-term effect on our ability to concentrate. But according to numerous **past** studies, it most certainly has a negative **short-term** effect. One study, published in the journal **Computers In Human Behavior**, demonstrated that students couldn't go more than **few minutes** without checking Facebook, Instagram, Twitter, and other social sites.

No wonder so many students pull all-nighters to get things done!

Social media sites pose a significant distraction. If you're unable to resist them, you'll find it very difficult to focus on your work.

Obstacle #10 - Your Phone

It shouldn't be a surprise that our phones hobble our focus, even when we're not looking at them. They constantly ring, chirp, and vibrate, notifying us of incoming texts, voicemails, and social media updates.

In the context of attention management, trying to focus with your phone within earshot is a recipe for failure. You know this from experience. When you hear your phone chirp or feel it vibrate, it's difficult to resist reaching for it to identify the reason. Even if you manage to ignore the notifications, they'll disrupt your momentum and cause your mind to wander.

Chapter 5: Basic Memory Training Methods

From now on, the basics of creative thinking will serve as your foundation to everything that you are going to learn. So, it would be best to make sure that you fully understand them. Although you don't have to worry about not yet being able to master them as you don't have to. Creative thinking takes a lot of practice and experience; therefore, so is advanced memorization techniques.

During the old ages, people did not have access to instant memorization aids. Writing a long script would just consume a large amount of ink. Cue cards were not yet widely used. Besides, assistance is not quite good for the image of any orator or speaker that time. There were no visual aids, no PowerPoint, and no other materials that would help them remember information better and faster. Thus, memorization was all about pure skill.

In order to remember massive information, people created several techniques that would help their brain retain multiple sets of data without the need of aiding materials. These people are also called "mnemonists" which is the term for individuals who possess exceptional ability to recall a number of details with ease. Since then, the invented techniques have been proven to provide dramatic results. In fact, majority of them are still being used today.

Rote Learning

Rote learning is the usual yet least favored technique of knowledge retention. It is similar to Akinson and Shiffrin's rehearsal wherein a person repeats a list of information over and over until retained in his memory. It is the least favored technique because it tends to skip the actual learning process and does not promote creativity. Unless rehearsed more frequent than usual, information encoded through rote learning usually does not last more than a day since it already starts fading in just a matter of hours. This is the reason it is used by students who cram or who memorize lessons few hours before their actual exam.

Mnemonics

Another usual technique used most especially in school is the mnemonic. This is normally used to memorize details that belong to a common group or list. Instead of memorizing the whole list, the initials or parts of the words are combined to form another word, phrase, or sentence which is easier to remember.

Linking

Rote learning and mnemonics may not require visualization; but linking, together with all the other proceeding techniques, requires one. Linking is the method of connecting adjacent details on a list. It's basically visualizing mental images that represent the connection of the first detail to the second one, the second detail to the third one, the third detail to the fourth one, and so on.

Using the linking method, you need to choose a visual for each of the country listed. You may start the sequence of scenarios with a picture of yourself, watching shooting stars (America's star-spangled flag) in slow motion. Next, imagine the stars that hit the ground eventually transforming into maple leaves (Canada's maple leaf). After then, the maple leaves started turning green as if they are creating a field of bermudagrass (Bermuda). Then the bermudagrass field started turning into an ice field (Iceland), and so on and so forth. Again, exaggerate the scenarios. They do not have to be realistic. And that's how simple the linking method goes. It is a good option when you want remember a list of data that follows a strict order.

Peg Systems

Peg systems are also good for data in sequence. They are one of the most effective memorization techniques as a single peg can be applied to different lists. It initially requires a preliminary list before the memorizing the actual information needed.

Emotion-based Memorization

One of the aspect that affects the storage of an information is the emotional content. In this technique, an individual applies emotion to each information on the list. The emotion to associate with each detail should, as much as possible, be distinct from that of the other. This technique requires a deeper connection to imagination since emotions during visualization should be felt by the user as if they are real.

Mind Map

Mind map or mind mapping is the use of a diagram to mentally organize information in mind. This method is fit for those individuals who can maintain focus while creating a detailed diagram inside their head; although the diagram can also be initially drawn on a piece of paper. Mind mapping is commonly used to memorize a whole set of related information such a lesson with topics and subtopics.

Visualizing Names

People often find issues when it comes to memorizing names. Fortunately, there is a certain technique that is developed to make remembering names easier.

Visualizing Numbers

Methods under this suggest a way to ease the difficulties on memorizing numbers. They are actually one of those peg systems but they are specifically developed to deal with numbers. They use representations to help the mind visualize numbers.

Memory Palace

Mnemonists label this technique as the most effective method of memorization. It is pretty much like creating a storage inside your head in the form of any physical object through which you can consciously retrieve information with ease. The size and complexity of the storage depends on your choice. You can make the memory storage look as simple as a cabinet or as complex as a maze.

Techniques to Improve Your Memory

Memory lapses may be caused by distractions, preoccupation, lack of focus and weakened memory muscle. There are numerous techniques to beef up your brain muscles:

Give your brain a workout.

By the time you are an adult, your brain has already formed millions of neural pathways necessary in processing and recalling information quickly, solving easily recognizable problems, and executing common tasks almost instantaneously. But sticking to these timeworn pathways, you are denying your brain the stimulation it needs to keep growing and developing. Your brain needs some shaking up from time to time!

The "use it or lose it" principle popular in building muscular strength also applies to memory enhancement. The more you subject your brain to intellectual activities, the better you'll be at remembering information. The best brain exercises take you out of your routine and challenge you to form new brain pathways.

Good brain-boosting activities have the following elements:

- It introduces you to something new. An activity may be considered intellectually demanding, but if it is something that you've already mastered, then it doesn't qualify as a good brain exercise. The activity needs to be something that you haven't yet tried and is out of your comfort zone. It's your exposure to learning new things and developing new skills that eventually strengthen your brain.

- It's difficult and challenging. The best brain-boosting activities should be hard enough to demand your full attention. But as soon as you've mastered the activity, it won't require as much mental effort anymore and won't challenge you as much as when you were introduced to it for the first time. For example, learning to play a challenging new piece of music on the piano counts. Playing a tough piece you've already memorized does not.

- It's a skill you can improve on. Search out activities that let you begin at an easy level and move up as your expertise progresses and your capabilities improve. When a once difficult level starts to feel comfortable, that means it's time to move on to the next level of difficulty.

- It's fulfilling. A sense of fulfillment encourages the brain's learning process. It keeps you engaged and interested. As a result, you are more likely to continue doing it and the greater the rewards you'll reap. So choose activities that, while challenging, are still enjoyable and satisfying.

Think of an activity you've always wanted to try—learning how to play a musical instrument, speaking a foreign language, playing chess, or making pottery. So long as an endeavor keeps you engaged, they are sure to help you improve your memory.

Engage in physical exercise.

Mental exercise is important for brain health especially when coupled with physical exercise. Physical activities help your brain stay sharp by increasing oxygen supply to your brain and reducing the risks for disorders that affect memory retention such as diabetes and cardiovascular diseases. Exercise also encourages secretion of helpful hormones that put stress and depression in check. Perhaps the most important benefit exercise has on the brain is in neuroplasticity, by stimulating new neuronal pathways known to improve memory formation and recall.

Physical Exercises that are Good for the Brain

Aerobic Exercises

In most cases, aerobic exercises that are good for your heart are good for your brain as well. Here's how cardio exercises benefit your brain.

- Aerobic exercises repair damaged brain cells thereby improving brain function.

- Cardio exercises encourage secretion of the happy hormone dopamine. This makes you feel relaxed and happier. Regular exercise in general alleviates symptoms of depression in people.

- Aim for 120 minutes of moderate cardio exercise each week. You may dedicate an hour swimming in the morning and another hour in the evening for dancing.

- Stick to your exercise plan. Make it a habit and a part of your daily regular routine. It would help if you do it with an exercise buddy, so you could encourage each other.

- Don't push yourself to your limits. An intense exercise wouldn't do more good in decreasing your anxiety levels than an exercise done in moderation. If you are just starting, 30 minutes of moderate exercise will already do you wonders.

Yoga

Yoga, when coupled with meditation, helps focus and calm your mind. Needless to say, it reduces stress and keeps the brain in tiptop shape.

- It's also known to extend your life by slowing down cellular aging.

- People who regularly meditate often say that they feel more positive, and that a happy disposition enables them to deal better with daily life challenges.

Walking

While walking is the simplest and probably the least costly exercise you can do, it is known to greatly improve brain performance.

- Regular walks enable different parts of your brain to communicate with each other. It has something to do with the neural pathways that are strengthened during regular walks. This enhancement of the neural connections makes you better at planning, strategizing, prioritizing, and multi-tasking.

- Also, practically everyone can enjoy a good walk, regardless of their level of fitness or age.

Jogging or Running

If you are a person with a lot of energy that needs burning, jogging or running are the best forms of exercise you can do at the start of the day.

- A 15-minute run will help reduce that extra energy to a level you need to get through your work for the rest of the day without getting distracted.

- A quick run will also help you bring on a rush of the mood-booster hormone serotonin.

Group Classes

For motivation and inspiration, consider joining group classes. You'd always look forward to working out because exercising becomes play more than a boring activity. Plus there's nothing more rewarding than making new friends.

For group activities, you may consider Aqua Zumba, Latin Hip-hop, Family Yoga, Tai Chi, or Group Cycling.

Chew gum while learning new things.

Studies correlate chewing gum with increased heart rate levels resulting to increased circulation of oxygen-bearing blood into the brain. This in turn increases activity in the hippocampus, that part of the brain mainly responsible for forming memories.

Move your eyes sideways.

Make this a part of your daily morning exercise. Move your eyes from side to side for 30 seconds. Why? In studies, it was found out that horizontal eye movements strengthen the corpus callosum, a bundle of neuronal fibers that link the brain hemispheres: the creative right brain and the logical left brain.

Clench your fists.

There was a study conducted to determine how body parts may be linked to how the brain functions. It showed that clenching the hands improves a person's ability to memorize things. Making a fist with the right hand aided in learning something, and switching to making a fist with the left helped in recall.

At first, it seems farfetched that a person's hands have something to do with memory. The explanation given was that the hand-clenching stimulates the brain in a cross-wired manner. Making a fist with your right hand activates the left side of your brain; and the reverse happens with clenching the left hand.

Use unusual fonts.

Funky fonts promote better recall. There actually was a study that backs up this observation. So if you wonder how making something hard to read makes it easier to remember, here's the explanation: Think of the time you've skimmed through text, got to the end, and then realized that you didn't quite understand what the document said. The study explained that unusual fonts act like speed bumps. Changing the font to make it harder to read will slow you down so you'd read more carefully, consequently improving your recall. A more complex explanation has something to do with confidence. When you encounter a writing that's hard to decipher, you become less confident of your ability for comprehension. As you feel nervous about not understanding the material, you concentrate harder and go through it more deeply.

Doodle.

There's nothing like a blank sheet of paper to entice the brain to doodle. Research shows that doodling helps you let loose your imagination. Moreover, creating illegible drawings and writing down random thoughts encourages the brain to improve creative thinking, to stay focused and to retain information.

Laugh.

Laughter helps lower levels of cortisol, the hormone associated with stress. When secreted in high levels, cortisol is known to affect the hippocampus, the short-term memory consolidator, consequently impairing learning and memory.

Humor should be incorporated in your total wellness plan for excellent quality of life full of memories.

Start with these basics if you are looking for ways to bring more laughter in your life:

- Take yourself less seriously. Share your embarrassing moments and learn to laugh at yourself.

- When you hear laughter, gravitate toward it. You notice that you are always happy to share something funny because sharing feeds off the humor and affords you the chance to laugh again. So if you hear laughter, you knew that you just have to seek it out and join in.

- Surround yourself with images that lighten you up. Put up a humorous poster in your office. Set a computer screensaver that never fails to make you smile. Display photos of you and your loved ones having fun.

- Learn from children. Pay attention to children and realize that they are the experts on playing, laughing, and taking life lightly.

Practice good posture.

Posture is often neglected as a conscious expression of one's self. You may not be doing it right, good news is it's possible to make improvements on how you hold yourself, how it can ideally shape your life and future accomplishments.

A straight posture generally improves memory because sitting upright encourages increased blood flow and oxygen to the brain by as much as 40 percent.

Feast on Mediterranean diet.

Researches show that a diet of fruits, vegetables, nuts, and fish (a whole range of food that is common in most Mediterranean fares) is not only good for your heart but for your brain as well. Vegetables and nuts are likely to fend off memory loss especially in late adulthood. Fruits and Omega-3 in fish are anti-oxidants that will protect you from cognitive decline.

Take caffeine-rich drinks to enhance your memory consolidation.

Whether it's a cup of tea, a can of soda, or a mug of freshly brewed coffee, consumption of caffeine is the chosen energy booster for people who want to wake up or stay up. Studies have found another use for this stimulant: memory enhancer. Although most of these studies found that caffeine has little effect in creating new memories, the substance has actually improved memory recall. Research has identified caffeine to be a major player in memory consolidation, a process where memories created were strengthened leading to deeper level of memory retention and that therefore the substance is better ingested after learning a task.

Be careful, though, to check if caffeine seems to interfere with your sleep at night. If it does, reduce intake or cut it off altogether.

Meditate to improve your working memory.

The working memory could be likened to a chalkboard, where you temporarily "write" bits of information like the location details of a place you are visiting for the first time or names and faces of people you meet in an event. You hang on to these chunks of data until you are ready to sort them into those that you let go entirely (because you have no use for them anymore) or those that you commit to long-term memory (for later recall and use).

Working memory is the same place where you do quick mental computations and hold random details when engaged in conversation.

How does meditation help strengthen the working memory? Studies show that regular meditation enhances your ability to focus. Meditation will enable you to have more control over your alpha rhythm, when your brain experiences small smooth bursts of electricity sending you into a state of complete relaxation. This not only improves your creativity but it enables you to filter out all distractions making it easy for you to store important things to memory.

Have a good night's sleep.

Sleep is an important factor in memory storage. It is during slow-wave sleep that the hippocampus replays all the events that happened during your waking moments. Working under compressed time, it sorts through your experiences as it files away those which are relevant while discarding those that won't be significant in the future.

Cultivate a good sleeping habit by doing the following:

- Commit to a regular sleep schedule by going to bed at the same time every night and getting up at the same time every morning. Don't break your routine, even on weekends and holidays.

- Avoid TVs, phones, computers, and tablets an hour before bed. The blue light emitted by these gadgets triggers wakefulness by suppressing secretion of melatonin that induces sleepiness.

If you suspect that caffeine keeps you up at bedtime, reduce your intake or cut it out entirely. There are people who are overly sensitive to caffeine that even coffee taken in the morning interferes with sleep at night.

Pay attention.

Do you remember that time when you were planning to buy a red Chevrolet and suddenly you noticed that what catches your attention during your daily commute are all the red cars plying your route. Pieces of information are committed to your memory because you are interested in them. When you develop a fascination for things around you, you automatically observe important details and get them laser-etched on your brain.

Concentrate.

There are no fast-charging shortcuts to increasing your concentration. Today's world is so full of distractions; not to mention the huge volume of information that we need to process every day. We simply just cannot sort through all the information we are bombarded with day in and day out. Then there's the challenge of determining what information to keep and how to recall them fast. The secret here is to tackle big issues first so your brain won't be pre-occupied with matters that may unnecessarily clutter available brain storage space.

Sing.

Music is not only an excellent mood enhancer but a good memory tool as well. Singing exercises the right side of the brain. Consequently, it makes you perform better at problem solving. Ever notice how you can easily rhyme words when you are singing them than when you are speaking them? This is because the song's melody has activated the pattern recognition ability of the right side of your brain.

Chapter 6: Advanced Memory Training Methods

As you now know, your memory is split into more than one type. As well as your long term memory, you also have a short term version that acts as your "working" memory and the sensory memory that absorbs information in the first place from the world around you.

To learn in an advanced manner, your end goal is of course to make sure that as much information as possible is pushed through to your long term memory, but that can only properly be achieved by strengthening your short term and sensory memory at the same time.

The first step to solidifying a memory in your long term storage banks is encoding, which is the moment when information is discovered in the first place. At that moment, your brain needs to link the data to something that is familiar and important to you in order to signal that it is worth holding on to.

The second stage is storage, which is the retention of that new memory through practice in some manner. And finally there is retrieval, which is when you bring that memory back out of your memory banks and use it in some manner.

Why is all this important? Because the best and most efficient way to improve your memory is to tackle all three of those stages properly.

In other words, you need to both encode your memory properly and then store it in an accessible manner and then be able to retrieve it quickly whenever relevant. You have limited control over the inner workings of your brain, of course, so improving these stages must be done in an indirect manner.

It's important to remember that you receive a lot more information through your senses in the space of a day than you can possibly realize. Every moment, you are taking in data through all of your senses in some manner and not all of it deserves to be stored. That's where your brain steps in – to ensure you keep hold of the memory of hugging a loved one, because it's important to you, while getting rid of the unnecessary memory of scratching the end of your nose.

The information you are deliberately trying to learn is automatically flagged as important because you are making a conscious effort to learn it. But how can you make sure that memory sticks when experts estimate we've forgotten half the information we learned just three weeks later and only keep hold of a tenth of it by the time two months have passed?

The best way to do this is to expose yourself to the same information multiple times over a long period. Do not try to learn a new topic over the space of a single weekend; instead, space out your learning so that you are looking at the information for an hour or so every day over the course of a few weeks.

During that time, your brain will start to make the connections it needs between the elements of the information and between this new data and the things already stored in your memory. It will build the infrastructure that is necessary not only to store the information, but to do so in a way that makes sense for your own mind.

Do this by, for example, reading through the information on the first day, making notes on the second day, reviewing the notes on day three, trying to recall the information without your notes on day four, reviewing your notes again on day five, recall the information again on day six and so on. None of this will take a large amount of time and the hours in between allow your brain to do its own work to help you recall it.

Also bear in mind that the process of making connections happens largely when you are asleep, so spacing out your learning gives you plenty of hours of slumber for your brain to make synaptic connections.

As you look at the information again and again, you'll notice that you are becoming more familiar with its content and you are thinking about it in different, deeper ways, automatically making connections and relating it to other things that you already know or would like to find out. This analysis is the final step to making sure that your brain pushes the information securely into your long term memory.

Of course, your memory will begin to fade after a while even when you follow this technique, and that's where your notes come in handy. Make sure to set aside some time once every six months or once per year to look through all the new learning you have done in that time, reviewing your new knowledge and consolidating it (especially if you've been focusing on a single kind of learning, such as history or candle making techniques).

Look at how all that knowledge fits together and actively ponder what it means when you look at the big picture. By doing this, you will create even more connections and strengthen your recall once again.

In the next chapter, we'll take a look at some other techniques you can make use of when absorbing new information to help you improve your encoding, retention and retrieval even more.

How Do You Make Sense of Memory

The mind does not store information in slots on a shelf like a library; it merely stores many representations of what was witnessed. Take for example viewing your aunt's face, the image is not stored in one part of the brain. So when you need to recall any type of image, it is your interpretation, a representation through your own meanings and feelings which are expelled. If your aunt was a caring, loving, funny person, the image would have associations with these emotions. A warm soft image could be drawn from your memory. If on the other hand a horrible, evil aunt graces your family you will conjure up a hard looking dark restricted face. Another interesting fact is that the face based on negative experiences will be harder to recall later on. This image does not excite the pleasure center of the brain. The part of the brain that makes it easier for you to remember things

Memory and images are associated with the emotional part of the brain so when memorizing it would be advised that you elicit an emotion for clarity and faster recall.

Studying for exams or 'storing' the information needed to excel in any subject usually begins on the wrong foot. The example of remembering your aunt's face, can be easily related to your initial reaction of any work load that needs to be totally understood in detail.

This will put you in a state where your mind will have so much pain associated to the subject that sub consciously your memory retention will be reduced by a very large amount Not to mention a major decrease in your motivation to continue learning what the subject has to offer. Many people would say that you have failed before you have even begun.

Another person cannot make you feel any emotion; they can only trigger what is already in your internal reference system. Another person cannot make you enjoy certain course material because we all have different goals, varying desires and past experiences. Even though all humans have the same needs we meet those needs in totally different ways? However the good news is having the power to control your feelings, beliefs and reasons why you like different things. How you choose to interpret the world and your surroundings is 100% totally in your control!

To begin retaining any material we need to use technology which can be turned on by us at any time to see a subject as we want to see it. This technology once you master it will assure that you enjoy the weeks, days and hours before any exam! Wow what a thought, I know. This technique is so simple that it can be used in any area of your life as well as studying. Once you master this technique then the subconscious does not control you any longer. No matter how the environment presents itself you will strengthen your resolve and use setbacks as fuel.

How to Increase Memory Constantly

If you ever tried to learn a musical instrument as a child or wanted to participate in a sport, it's unlikely you made it far without someone using the phrase that "practice makes perfect". It's one of life's most commonly used clichés, but that doesn't make it any less than true.

If the learning you are attempting is intended to help you acquire a practical skill, such as learning a language or sport or musical instrument or how to fix a car or how to cook, it's not enough to simply read about it or watch videos. Even your notes are only going to get you so far – before you can turn those notes into knowledge, you're going to need to give this new skill a try for yourself.

However, the practice you will be doing is not the same as those long-gone days when you sat in front of a piano and begrudgingly played the notes of "Chopsticks" over and over while a parent nodded in the background. There's a reason most kids resent the idea of being made to practice their skills: we're not teaching them to practice in a way that is both efficient and fulfilling.

You are not simply going to sit down and repeat the same exercise day after day, hoping you'll get better at it and feeling both bored and frustrated while you do. Instead, you're going to take a more structured approach.

Your goal, when practicing, is to focus on the small skills that make up the large one. For example, let's say that you are hoping to learn to be a public speaker. That overall skill is made up of a myriad of others, such as making eye contact, pacing words, learning scripts, bodily movements, making your voice carry and many more. The same is true for any skill, so start by considering all the different smaller goals you want to meet.

List all of the small sub skills that will be involved in mastering this new talent – spend some time doing this, to be sure you are capturing them all – and then look at each one with a critical eye. Which of them is your weakest area? Which needs the most practice for improvement?

Any machine is only as strong as its weakest part and the same goes for learning a new skill. Your goal with a practice session will, therefore, be to improve that weakest sub skill until it rises past the level of the next weakest sub skill, then switching your attention to the new weakest sub skill and so on.

As you continue to practice, take time out every so often for analysis. Look overall at your skill level and identify the areas where you are not yet confident. Refocus your practice sessions to concentrate on those areas, slowly progressing your overall talent by improving the areas that need it the most.

The second important element of a practice session for advanced learning is to set goals for yourself. These must be realistic for the space of time you are going to spend in your practice room – you are not going to learn to paint like Monet in half an hour and you're also not going to be fluent in French by the end of today.

So what would a realistic goal be? As a novice painter, perhaps your goal for this session is to learn to hold the brush correctly and to feel comfortable doing so. Tomorrow, you will continue this practice with the aim of being able to hold the brush correctly without even thinking about it, such that proper technique comes absolutely naturally.

Don't be afraid to adjust your goals. Maybe what seemed like a simple task is, in fact, something that only comes with time. Perhaps you discover that an hour session is not enough to feel completely natural with a paint brush and decide you will need to continue incorporating this into your sessions over the next week.

Breaking your skill down into its elements and setting yourself achievable goals that lead you in the right direction towards your overall desire is very different to throwing a ball repeatedly at your father's glove when you were a kid. It will enable you to progress in a logical and appropriate manner, seeing constant improvements along the way and ensuring that your weakest links get enough attention to prevent them from keeping you back. In time, you'll find that you have learned your new skill far better than you would by simply repeating the same exercise an infinite number of times.

Increase Learning Efficiency by Memory Methods

To take notes and research your topic will almost certainly involve cracking open a book at some point – so much of human knowledge is written down, whether it be on physical pages or in the recesses of the internet. An advanced learner wants to be able to absorb as much of this knowledge as possible, but time, as usual, is of the essence.

To gather as much information as you can in the limited time you have available to you, it helps to learn how to read more quickly and efficiently.

A method that has seen remarkable success was devised by Tim Feriss and tested on students at Princeton University. He called it the PX Project, a three-hour experiment that increased his subjects' reading speed to almost four times what it was when they started.

The method involves learning to not read in a straight line, but rather in a series of jumps, each of which ends with you fixating on a particular part of the text and taking a "snapshot" of it in the space of half a second. It also helps you eliminate "conscious re-reading" and skipping back in the text and uses what Ferris calls central focus without horizontal peripheral vision span during reading. Finally, mastering this technique means that you should practice at three times the speed that you ultimately want to be able to read; so, if you want to be able to read two pages every minute, you must practice reading six.

Feriss's method goes as follows:

- Find a book of at least 200 pages that will lay flat when it is open, as well as a pen and a timer. Make sure you have at least 20 minutes of free time.

- Determine your current reading speed by figuring out the average number of words per page in your book. Start your timer and read for exactly one minute.

- Now to begin the practice. Use your pen to underline every line of text as you read it, ignoring comprehension of the words and attempting to spend a maximum of one second on each line. Do this for two minutes.

- Now, increase your speed as much as possible for another three   minutes.

- For the next minute, repeat the exercise but do not underline the first and last word of each line. Now reduce this further to leave out the first two and last two words for one minute. Now, for three minutes, reduce this even further to begin three words into the line and end with three words   left   to   go.

- **Finally, test your reading speed again, just as you did when you began this exercise. Do not worry that you probably did not comprehend a lot of what you just read – by continuing to practice this technique, you will gradually increase the amount you are absorbing while you read.**

This method has worked countless times, but there are other ways in which you can supplement it – or replace this technique altogether, if it does not suit you. Some tips to increase your reading speed:

- Work to drop your habit of saying the words that you are seeing in your head. We all do it, but it isn't actually necessary. We are able to process words more quickly than we can say or hear them, so reducing this tendency will allow you to absorb the words significantly more quickly.

- Make use of the end of a pen or a similar pointer to keep your place in the text, reducing your tendency to flick your eyes backwards and forwards in the text and helping you focus entirely on the words you are currently reading.

- **Practice reading multiple words at one time. Begin by attempting to read two words at once, thinking of them as connected items, and then increase this so that you are reading three or four at a single glance.**

These techniques will help you read more quickly, but that's only one step towards your goal. As an advanced learner, you also want to be able to pick out the information that matters most to you and reject the clutter that has no bearing on the topic at hand.

The best way to do this is to examine the material before you read it, looking at the back cover, the introduction and any other summaries available. A lot of the time, you'll find that the summaries contain most of the information you were looking for, allowing you to then skim through the book to find the supporting data that will help you parse and understand that information.

Skim through by reading the beginnings of each chapter, skipping over any illustrative stories or chapters that are not relevant to your learning needs. Once you are done, you will have a good idea of which parts of the book are the most valuable to you and you can go back and read those in more depth to gather the exact information you are looking for.

As you do this final part of your task, switch your brain over into analysis mode. You are not simply reading the words and hoping they jump into your memory – now, you want to retain as much as possible as you go.

The best way to do this is to ask questions of yourself about the text while you are reading it, even if that increases the amount of time it takes to read. What does this new information mean to your overall knowledge on this topic? Why is it important? Does it go against what you have already learned or does it fit within that whole easily? How could you summarize this new information in a single sentence?

By the time you have concluded your reading with these new techniques, you should find that you have absorbed this book considerably more quickly than you could have before you improved your reading speed and that you can recall the important information much more easily – and in the right context, to boot.

Advanced Strategies for Accelerated Learning

A lot of people think they have a terrible memory and find it impossible to remember phone numbers, facts and other snippets of information when they want to. Actually, as we've just discovered, that's not really the case – they simply haven't discovered the best methods for their own individual mind to make that learning stick.

To help with that, let's review some tried and tested memory boosting techniques for you to try. They may not all suit your unique way of thinking, but it's certain you'll find at least one or two you can make use of when you are learning something new:

- **Decide to Remember:** This may sound obvious, but think back to what we discussed in the previous chapter. Your brain needs to know that information is important to you, and telling it directly that you consider it vital is a fairly obvious way of making sure it does. The next time you are told a fact that interests you, given somebody's address or come across a new piece of information while reading, pause for just a moment. Tell yourself consciously and deliberately that you want to remember that piece of information.

- **Use Your Senses:** As we've already discussed, information comes into your brain from all five of your senses and, the more senses it attracts, the better your chance of retaining it because the more places it will be stored. Involve your senses as much as you can in your learning – find ways to touch, taste, smell, hear and see the information wherever you can. Obviously not every sense will be relevant in every case, but get creative and you'll find plenty of ways to at least use your ears and eyes and mouth in your learning.

- **Use Mnemonics:** Mnemonics are memory devices in which you organize information in the form of a list, a word, a poem and so on. A good example of a musical mnemonic is the ABC song most children use to learn the alphabet, using the melody as an anchor to recall the individual letters. A name mnemonic involves reorganizing the first letter of each item in a list to create the name of a person or thing; a model mnemonic involves creating a diagram or image of the information that you can easily bring to mind.

- **Make Information Important:** When we discussed taking notes, we talked about color coding your writing and adding pictures and diagrams. This technique is also important to your memory, because it highlights clearly the pieces of information that are the most important to your conscious mind. Your subconscious will follow suit, taking the cue that you consider this data to be vital and storing it accordingly. The more you do this, the more you train your brain to look for the items you consider important and store them.

- **Make Connections:** Memories in your brain are not stored in separate boxes, completely apart from one another. There are links between those boxes, created to help you make sense of the world. For instance, when you think of a dining table, you may also think of Thanksgiving, a set of cutlery your grandparents once used and the overall idea of dinnertime. These are separate items of information, but your brain has linked them together because they are connected in some way. It's not always as obvious as the fact that cutlery is used at the table and once a year it's used for a holiday meal, but this example does illustrate how connected your knowledge can be. A great way to improve your recall is to deliberately make those connections – stop for a moment when you've absorbed a piece of information and think about how it connects to your knowledge base as a whole.

- **Tell Stories:** As we've mentioned before, human beings are great at remembering stories – we are perhaps better at recalling a good tale than anything else we encounter. If it's appropriate to the knowledge you want to recall, turn it into a story – write it down that way in your notes. If it doesn't seem appropriate, think a little harder. Perhaps you're learning the periodic table of elements as part of understanding chemistry better. Can you create a story about the relationships between those elements? It can be as whimsical as you like, such as imagining hydrogen as lots of little water fairies buzzing around the universe, while helium, a noble gas that shares its light elements, floats nearby shaking his head in disgust.

- **Organize the Data:** This is another technique you can make use of during your note taking. Reorganize your knowledge into a new pattern, one that makes more sense to you. Organize lists of items into categories or concepts into batches that fit together well according to your overall understanding of a topic. How you do this will be very personal – some people might prefer to list things by concept, others by visual similarity and so on. The advantage here is that you have given yourself a category to remember. Much like the card boxes in an old library, this means you only have to root through a small list of categories to find the right area for remembering your data, rather than trying to sort through the entire breadth of information stored in the library of your mind.

- **Test Yourself:** The only way to know if you recall a set of data is to test your memory to prove it to yourself. However, it's also a great tool for learning the information in the first place, so it's a good idea to build testing into your study sessions. For instance, you could spend one session reviewing the dates of different battles in a war and then the next session attempting to recall that information by writing it down – it can be as simple as that. Reviewing your results will also keep you up to date with the areas that still need more work to make sure your knowledge is properly stored.

Create Flashcards: These handy little tools are great as a memory aid because they combine note making with testing yourself. On one side of the card, write a prompt or question; on the other, write the answer. Test yourself frequently with the flashcards to see how well you have recalled information. Once you have it down to a fine art, set those flashcards aside and review them again after a period of time has passed, when the memory has begun to fade. Finally, to really cement that knowledge, it can help to create a new set of flashcards that presents the information in a different way or comes at the knowledge from a new angle. This will stimulate your brain to start making new connections and look at the knowledge differently, which will make sure it is encoded properly.

Image Memory Method

You might think that people who can recall a hundred images in the exact same order have magical powers, but the truth is that they have mastered the memory technique called Visualization and Association. While it does take plenty of practice before you can get to recall extensive details entirely from memory, anyone can apply this technique effectively if they try.

The Visualization and Association technique relies on the natural tendency of the brain to remember images better than information that was heard or read. The reason is that images are more concrete while ideas in the form of words are more abstract. However, by associating images with abstract thoughts, one can make the latter much easier to recall.

The following sections provide you with strategies on how to use this technique:

How to Use the Technique to Remember Abstract Information

Two skills are required to enable you to use this technique effectively, and these are your creativity and concentration. When encountering a piece of information you need to memorize, you need to visualize a creative image that best represents it. Then, you need to concentrate on that image until it becomes a part of your long-term memory.

The more unique the image is, the easier it would be for you to remember it. This image would then serve as the mental hook that will enable you to recall the more complex and abstract information you have associated it with.

Let us say you need to memorize Maslow's Hierarchy of Needs, which consists of five levels: physiological, safety, love, esteem, and self-actualization.

To commit this to memory, you can visualize a pyramid of five floors. On the first floor, you see a man eating and drinking inside a shack (physiological needs), on the second floor, you see a guard (safety), on the third floor, you see a couple (love), on the fourth you see a teacher (esteem), and on the top floor you see the pharaoh (self-actualization).

By making this visualization as vivid as possible, you can easily recall the information to which it refers.

How to Use the Technique to Remember Numbers

Throughout our lives we need to remember strings of numbers, whether they are important dates, phone numbers, mathematical formulas, bank account numbers, and so on. The trouble is that we sometimes doubt ourselves in times when we need to recall them (**was it five three nine, or five three six?**).

If you experience this more often than you should, then you can apply the Visualization and Association technique to cement the exact string of numbers into memory.

For example, if you need to remember the theorist Abraham Maslow's birthday, which is on April 1, 1908, then you can visualizehim playing an April Fools'prank (April 1) on your 19-year-old cousin and 8-year-old niece (1908). By recalling this mental image, you would then remember the string of information (April 1, 1908) with utmost certainty.

How to Use the Technique to Remember Separate Facts

It is not so hard to apply Visualization and Association to isolated pieces of facts. However, it becomes a bit more challenging when the time comes for you to memorize many different facts within the same period of time, as is common when you are preparing for an exam.

To use the technique in remembering a string of facts, what you need to do is creatively connect the different images you had visualized for each separate fact.

For instance, if we go back to the first two examples stated earlier, you can visualize everything happening in the same room: Abraham Maslow playing an April Fools'frank on your cousin and niece, with a poster of the five-level pyramid in on a wall in the room. Thus, if you have to recall any of these facts in writing an essay, all you have to do is conjure this overall image.

It is important to note that this technique requires constant practice and impenetrable focus in order for it to work. It might sound tedious and time-consuming, but when you do apply Visualization and Association, you will realize that you can save a lot more time compared to you using rote. And besides, it would make memorization a lot more interesting.

Train your Memory

Try out the Visualization and Association technique by looking at the following list of words for three minutes. Visualize the words into images and then connect the images together by associating them into one large picture. When you are ready, cover the words and write down as many of them as you can remember based purely on the images that you had created.

Are you ready? Here are the words:

Eight	Cook	Phone	Bee	Kiss
Socket	Cake	Peach	Chair	Dance
Singer	School	Water	Slap	Bird
Watch	Zebra	Robot	Woman	Shield
Book	Story	Sleep	Hand	Fish

If you were not able to recall all of the words, do not take it against yourself. It only means that you need to practice further. And the more frequently you apply this mnemonic, the better you will get at associating images and then recalling them together.

Chapter 7: Self-Motivation Tips

All of the advanced learning techniques we have learned so far in this book have something in common: they will not work for you without an element of self-motivation. If you think about the most successful businessmen, scientists, academics and experts in the world, you'll quickly notice that they all invest time and effort into thriving within their field.

There's no such thing as a free lunch, as they say, and this is especially true for mastering a new skill or embarking on a new area of learning. As you have read through these chapters, did you find yourself thinking that the techniques described seemed too time consuming or difficult?

Did you think that perhaps you could short cut your way through them or tackle this another time, when you are more free to do so? Maybe, or maybe not, but the big question is: have you begun to put any of them into practice yet?

The majority of people are content to simply let life happen around them, happy with the idea that things always get better even if we don't do anything to make them better. Unfortunately, this is a fallacy. You will not become an advanced learner without putting the effort in to achieve it.

And so, first you must visualize what it is you want to achieve and list all the reasons why it is important to you. The more you believe that this learning will enhance your life, and the more ways in which you think it will do so, the more you will feel energized to achieve it.

Next, you need to set yourself the right goals. These need to be specific so that you have a very definite end point in mind – a moment when you feel that you have achieved the learning you set out to achieve and are content with what you have done.

You should also determine how you're going to tell what progress you've made, so that you can measure it as you go along. Is it that you have learned to conjugate a certain number of verbs this week in French? That you are now able to recall a certain amount of facts? That you can play a certain song on the guitar? What are your incremental goals?

Be sure that both your end goals and the steps in between can actually be achieved. You need high standards, but also attainable ones – your willpower will only ever suffer from shooting for unreachable stars. You should also set yourself time limits and deadlines to keep your focus straight and narrow and encourage you to work towards your goals in a timely and consistent manner.

With your planning achiever, you must now consciously and deliberately make the decision you are going to do this. The commitment you make must be iron clad and unbreakable – you must be prepared and willing to change your life at least in a small manner to incorporate the work you'll need to do to achieve this goal.

The little voice in your mind may try to convince you to go against this commitment – it's perfectly natural, but it's not going to get you to your goal. Telling yourself you can do this tomorrow, that you're too busy, that you have other responsibilities, that you're too tired will not move you towards your vision. This voice must be banished and ignored.

And finally, you must build yourself a schedule, setting aside time every day to work on your learning. Recall that we discussed repetition as an important tool for memory? Setting aside small portions of time every day is vital for your learning to be as effective as possible. Once you have carved out this time and space, you must then follow through and keep up your new habits even as the initial excitement begins to wear off.

Only you can make this change in your life and become an advanced learner. Fortunately, you also possess all the tools that you need to make it happen.

Conclusion

At this stage, you have learned about and hopefully put to work a number of new methods to help you prepare yourself for learning, absorb new information and store it in your long term memory. The hard part is done – somewhere in your mind, the learning you hoped to achieve is nestling quietly, waiting to be put to use.

But that last element is just as important as the rest of your journey. Simply knowing a thing is not useful to your life; for it to truly be useful to you as an advanced learner, you need to know how to make best use of it.

How you do this will depend largely on whether your new knowledge is practical or cerebral. If it's practical, now is the time to go back out there and practice your learning in reality until it becomes second nature to you. At that time, when your skill has been honed, you will have a deeper understanding of where to go next – what additional skill or technique would complement or enhance what you can now do.

If it's cerebral – geography, history, physics and so on – then you can reflect on the knowledge and continue to make those connections to other parts of your knowledge banks, building your own mental picture of the world around you and how what you know affects what you see. Again, reviewing the information will give you a good idea of where there are gaps in your knowledge and what you would like to add to your stores to continue your path of knowledge.

Your path does not end with cementing one set of knowledge in your memory. It's about making use of your learning and continuing to seek new pieces of information and new areas to extend your attention towards. This, after all, is what sets the advanced learner apart from the rest of the world: the eagerness to increase your knowledge constantly and consistently and consciously.

With your new techniques to support you, that's exactly what you can now do. Go forth and absorb information wherever you find it, seeking out new knowledge wherever it lies and adding it to the treasure trove in your mind. Now, as an advanced learner, there is nothing in the world that a little effort and hard work won't help you learn and understand.

How to Analyze People

A Guide to Speed Reading of Body Language, Use Psychological Manipulation Techniques for Influencing People and Understand by Emotional intelligence What Every Mind is Saying

Introduction

Actions speak louder than words. I'm sure you've heard that many times throughout your life. It is a common phrase. Actions don't say all that much if you don't know how to read them correctly though. It would be like trying to have a discussion with someone in a language you don't understand.

This book is going to change that for you. It will cover non-verbal communication. It will cover how to interpret the meanings of this type of communication in all the body parts that could be involved. It will bring you insight and understanding. Then actions really will speak louder than words for you.

It will explain what the different personality types are. It will also explain how to understand yourself, and why this is important. Knowing your personality type can be a huge advantage when it comes to interacting with others. Why it is important to understand yourself will also be covered in this book.

The limbic section of the brain will be discussed. The actions and processes it is responsible for. How they influence your behaviour and how they interact with other sections of the brain. The limbic section of your brain is the section responsible for your emotions. This can be a very enlightening discovery.

Have you ever thought that someone was being dishonest with you, just had that feeling in your gut, but you weren't sure? Once we discuss the ways to detect deception, you won't have that worry anymore. You'll be able to detect the deception.

You aren't going to be taught some skills and then thrown to the wolves. The ways to become better at reading people will be discussed as well. Obviously you need to practice, you may be thinking. You're right you do need to practice, but there is a lot more to it than that.

Have you ever had the experience where you're trying to get information from someone, and no matter how many different ways you ask the information just isn't forthcoming? You may well have ended up feeling like you were interrogating them. Worse, they may have felt like that too. We will cover how to read the situation and how to ask the right question to get your information as well.

Have you ever had an interview or a meeting with someone you were intimidated by? Once you learn how to influence people with your body and your mind, you will be able to enter these situations with confidence.

You will be able to influence them with non-verbal communication. That will give you a huge boost in confidence.

Also included will be a discussion on how to perfect the ability to analyze people through practice. Not only will there be explanations, which there will be. There will also be examples and exercises that you can complete to accomplish this. You will be able to perform these exercises again and again until you are a master at analyzing people. I can't wait to get started, so go ahead and turn that page and let's get going.

Chapter 1: Non-Verbal Communication

What is non-verbal communication? When I say non-verbal communication you probably think the facial expression, or maybe stance. While you would be right that those are forms of non-verbal communication, there are a whole lot more forms of non-verbal communication than just those.

Let's go over what they are, and then we'll take a deeper look at them. Let's start with facial expressions. Different cultures can have vastly different non-verbal communication and behaviours. The facial expressions representing happy, sad, mad or fear are similar enough throughout the world to be considered universal.

How many emotions can be expressed with just facial expression? There's quite a few actually. While we've already said happy, sad, mad and afraid, there are also ones such as surprise, disgust, confused, excited, desire and contempt. That's quite the range of emotions that can be expressed with facial expressions.

And then you can add in there the varying degrees of each emotion, for example, mad can range all the way from mildly annoyed up to complete rage. Each variation will carry different expressions with it. Learning how to interpret the different expressions will make it easier to interact accordingly with people.

You may have been told growing up to maintain eye contact, or look at someone when you're talking to them. There is a good reason for that. Some things you can notice that give you indications about how a person is feeling are if they maintain eye contact or look away. Are their pupils dilated or not? How fast are they blinking? These are all clues to be considered when evaluating non-verbal communication. The shape of their eyes will tell you a lot about how they're feeling as well. When we experience different feelings, our reactions trigger different muscles in varying degrees resulting in different expressions.

If a person looks you directly in the eyes and maintains eye contact while speaking, this is most often a sign of interest. They are paying attention to the conversation. If a person won't look you in the eye, keeps looking anywhere else but at you, they may be trying to hide their true feelings. It could also mean that they are uncomfortable or even distracted though. If a person looks directly into your eyes for too long, it can feel intimidating, but perhaps that's their intention.

These are just a few examples of the different options you will need to learn to decipher to become a skilled non—verbal communication specialist. While it may seem intimidating if you look at the art of non-verbal communication as a whole, we will break it down step by step and make it easier to digest.

Blinking is a natural act of eye movement; however, the frequency of the blinking can give us clues about what a person is feeling. If a person is blinking faster than normal they may be feeling uncomfortable or distressed. On the other hand, if they are blinking slower than normal this could be a sign that they are purposely trying to control their eye movement.

You may have heard the term "bedroom eyes". It refers to pupils that are highly dilated. While the light in the environment plays a big part in controlling pupil dilation, emotions factor into this as well.

As previously stated, experiencing different emotions will trigger different chemicals which trigger varying responses. These responses will each trigger different muscles which results in changing the appearance of the eyes as well as other parts of the facial expression.

There is a wide range of emotions that can be indicated by the mouth. Some of these are distaste, disapproval, worry, stress, happy, optimistic, sad or mad. Some of these are obvious, such as a smile generally means happy or optimistic. It could also mean sarcasm or cynicism though. A frown is most often interpreted as sad, disapproving, but could also be worry, distaste or stress.

Gestures can be pretty obvious and easy to interpret; however, some of them have different meanings in different parts of the world. One example of this would be the ok symbol, made by making a circle with the thumb and forefinger while holding the other three fingers up. In some parts of Europe if you made the same symbol you would be telling the person seeing it that they are nothing. Continue on to some South American countries and the same gesture becomes a vulgar one.

Another example is the V sign. Raising your index finger and middle finger and separating them into a V. Most often this is interpreted as peace or victory. If you go to the United Kingdom or Australia, this symbol with the back of the hand facing out has an offensive meaning.

This is why it is absolutely necessary to understand that someone coming from a different culture may be giving entirely different signals than you are expecting while using the same non-verbal gestures you would be expecting to mean something entirely different.

Some of the different signals that can be conveyed with the arms and the legs are defensive, aggressive, in control, bored, anxious, angry, frustrated, impatient, uncomfortable and closed off. This is just the arms and legs, we still have the posture of our body to go.

Some of the personality characteristics that can be shown through posture are open, confident, submissive, focused, bored, indifferent, hostility, unfriendliness, and anxiety. There is still more that has to do with non-verbal communication.

If someone typically stands in a closed-off posture and tends to look anywhere than at somebody and their usual answers to questions are monosyllabic, it is quite possible that the person has low self-esteem, or perhaps they are just a very private person and like to keep to themselves.

Have you ever heard of proxemics? It is a term that refers to the distance between people that are interacting. An intimate distance is six to eighteen inches, and usually denotes familiarity or a closer relationship. One and a half to four feet is considered to be a personal distance. Typically this level is reserved for family members or close friends.

A social distance is four to twelve feet. This will largely be determined by how well you know the person you are interacting with. Someone you know well may be closer to the four-foot range, whereas someone you only know vaguely may be more comfortable at the ten to the twelve-foot range.

In public speaking situations, we typically use the public distance of twelve to twenty-five feet. This required distance to feel comfortable is also apt to change between different cultures. It is well known that people from Latin countries are comfortable with interacting at much closer distances than those from North American cultures.

If someone you have never met from a Latin country or with Latin ancestry were to approach inside of the four-foot custom we are used to, does not mean they are trying to be intimidating. This is where it helps to understand other cultures and customs. This way if you have interactions with someone of that culture, you will have a least a basic understanding of their customs and won't be offended by something that is common practice for them.

Some common gestures include waving, pointing, and using fingers to represent a numeric value. Some non-verbal signals are not allowed in courtrooms because they are too powerful, or have too much influence. Some of the common ones you can see in a courtroom are the lawyer who's not speaking glancing at his watch. This is seen to mean that the other lawyer's argument is tedious.

When a witness is testifying on the stand, sometimes the opposing counsel will roll their eyes. This is seen as an attempt to discredit their testimony or to imply that it is not credible.

Another area of non-verbal communication is paralinguistics. This is a term that is used to refer to vocal communication other than words. Such as the tone, inflection, volume and pitch of your voice. Changing any one of these characteristics can change the meaning of what you are saying. Learning how to use these characteristics can be a very powerful tool.

This can be a fun and enlightening exercise if you are inclined to play with it. Try saying something in different tones and then at different volumes. Change up your inflection and try different combinations. You can record yourself and then play it back and see how the little changes have such an impact on what you are saying.

Attitudes, as explained in psychology, are an important part of analyzing someone. The definition we will work with is a learned tendency to evaluate things in a certain way. The ABC's of attitude is explained as affective, behavioural, and cognitive components.

The affective component would be how the person, object or situation makes you feel. The behavioural component would be how the attitude influences your behaviour. The cognitive component would be your thoughts and beliefs about the subject.

Remember back to when you were a kid. Did you ever see someone being bullied on the schoolyard? Maybe you have even bullied yourself. How did that make you feel? That is a perfect example of the affective component of a situation.

Using the same example, if you witnessed someone being bullied on the schoolyard and avoided the situation, or if you proceeded to intervene. This decision would be based on your beliefs of what is the right thing to do. This becomes an example of the behavioral component of a situation. Your attitude towards bullying influenced your decision on whether to intervene or not.

And of course, the cognitive component was showcased when you were deciding whether to intervene or do nothing. The act of weighing your beliefs with possible outcomes, and making a decision is the cognitive component at work.

These are important because depending on the attitudes you have developed your interpretation of non-verbal communication may be different than the person standing next to you. This is because of we all filter information in a different manner.

There are two types of attitudes as well. These are explicit and implicit. Explicit ones are ones that we are consciously aware of and that have a huge impact on our behaviour. While Implicit ones are ones that operate in the unconscious sphere but still affect our behaviour.

An example of an explicit attitude would be if you watch crime shows at all, when the police are questioning people in the vicinity of a crime scene, and even though people saw what happened they choose to say nothing. This is an explicit attitude that helping the police is unhealthy for them.

An example of an implicit attitude would be the family who lives on the corner and have reiterated daily that helping the police is a civic duty. The child from this household coming forward to tell police officers what happened is an example of an implicit attitude. The belief that this is the right thing to do has so been set in their mind, that it is a subconscious attitude that causes the behavior even though subconsciously.

Touch is another form of non-verbal communication that needs to be considered. Touch can be used to communicate affection, familiarity, sympathy, care, concern or nurturance.

It has been seen that people of high-status tend to invade other peoples space more often and in a much more intense manner than their counterparts. Sex differences make a difference as to how touch is used as well. Women tend to be the comforting, caring type use of touch whereas men tend to use touch more for asserting power or control over others.

Touch can have either a very comforting effect, an intimidating effect, or even a mildly uncomfortable effect. It depends on the situation. Different types of personalities employ different types of touch depending on the outcome they are seeking to gain.

There are numerous ways our body language speaks on our behalf. From slouching to looking down. Or maybe it's the handshake you use when greeting someone. Is it weak or firm? Faking a smile or angling your body away from the person you're speaking with.

Avoiding eye contact or folding your arms in front of you. Blocking someone by placing something between you as you're talking whether it be a book, your computer, or maybe even a desk. Don't check emails or focus on your phone while you're talking with someone. Being distracted tells them you're not interested.

Did you know your appearance is also part of your non-verbal communication? From your choice of color, clothing and even your hairstyle are just a few of the ways your appearance speaks for you. This is why first impressions are so important.

Studies have shown that appearance can change a person income by up to 15% in some cases. Culture factors into how appearance is judged too. In western culture, thin people tend to be placed above everyone else, while in some African cultures full-bodied people are considered healthier and placed above the rest.

How you stand conveys a message to anyone interacting with you. Whether it's with your hands on your hips, or maybe your hands clasped behind your back. Crossed arms, fidgeting or crossed legs all relay information in non-verbal communication. We will look more closely at how to interpret the different aspects of non-verbal communication in a later chapter.

Now I will explain how to understand yourself and identify your personality type. This is important because it allows you to set your goals and live your life in line with your personality and your passions. This greatly increases your chance of success.

It's a lot easier to get up in the morning if you're heading out to go fishing or some other activity you enjoy than if you're getting up to head into work, isn't it? Some people have that level of enjoyment in their work, but it is not a very common occurrence.

The first step is to identify your morals. Everybody has their own internal set of morals that guide them. This is often referred to as your inner voice. That little voice that says what are you doing or what were you thinking when you stray from your morals.

Cartoons would depict this as the little angel sitting on your shoulder. Telling you that what you're doing or thinking of doing is wrong. This can be closely related to your conscience but is not the same thing.

The next step is to recognize what your values are. Values are the things that are important to you. Some people might value being close to family, while others might value financial security. Your values help you to set goals that are going to align with your personality. For example, if you value financial security, you may set a goal of having a certain amount set aside in a bank account.

If you value being close to family, it could manifest in different ways from living in close proximity to family. Perhaps it is the catalyst for the Sunday family dinners that seem to be declining in modern society.

Now you need to learn what you are passionate about. If something holds your interest for long periods of time or captures it repeatedly without much effort, this is probably something you're passionate about. While your values motivate you to set your goals, your passions are what will give you the drive to reach them. If you build a job or hobby around your passions you will be much happier than if you ignore them completely.

Let's face it, most of the goals we will strive to reach will involve some level of resistance. The difficult times when it may seem the best thing is to give up. When your goals are in line with your passions it can provide the needed motivation to keep going even when the going gets rough.

Next, you need to determine if you are an extrovert, or an introvert. This is determined by how you interact socially. After a long hard week at work, do you go out with friends to recharge your batteries, or do you need alone time at home to recharge? Extroverts tend to be spontaneous, and like to be with other people. Introverts on the other hand enjoy alone time and like planning out their days.

Now track your rhythms, when you feel tired, or when you feel wide awake. When you feel like exercising, and when you are hungry. Keeping track of these things will help keep your mind and body in sync. If you're a night owl, you likely don't want a job with an early morning start.

We all have strengths and weaknesses, that's a natural fact. Keep track of what your strengths are, and what people tell you that you did well. Keep track of when you feel like you're succeeding at a task, or when you feel like you're struggling. You can use this information for two purposes. You can use it to improve your weaknesses or you can use it to play to your strengths.

The time has come to see how right you are about yourself. Ask some family members or close friends to give you their opinion of your personality traits. The things that they see you do regularly. Compare these to what you thought about yourself. If it's a match, you're probably right about your personality. If your friends and family consistently have a different view of your personality than you did, you may need to think about your behaviour and make sure you're looking at what you do, and not what you want to be doing in the future.

Chapter 2: Different Personality Types

In this chapter, we will examine the different personality types. Then we will look at how to identify your personality type, and why it is important to understand yourself. So let's get right into it. Just let me say I was able to find sixteen different personality types.

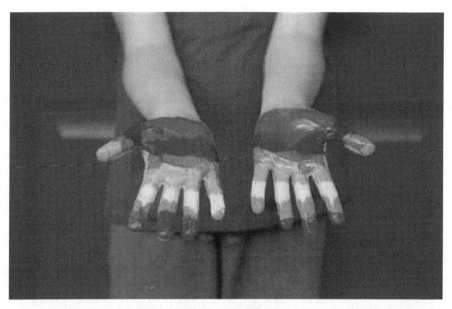

First I will start with ISTJ. This one is known as the Duty Fulfiller. This personality type is generally referred to as introverted sensing with extroverted thinking. That means that their main way of interacting with the world around them is by focusing internally. This is where they take things in through their five senses.

Their second method is external. This is where the logic comes into play and they can deal with things rationally. This personality type is generally quiet and reserved with their main concern being security and peaceful living. Their sense of duty is felt internally and it is strong. It is responsible for the serious air that most ISTJ personality types are known for. It also provides their motivation which allows them to succeed at most tasks they undertake.

Honesty and Integrity are of paramount importance to this personality type, and as such they are dependable, faithful and extremely loyal. Although they are generally known to take things seriously, they also have a humorous side that is known to be fairly off-beat. This can be quite entertaining, especially at family gatherings or work-related functions.

This personality type is not made up of your lawbreakers. They are quite comfortable with laws and tradition, and will not normally step outside of the societal boundaries they are familiar with unless there is sufficient reason. Sometimes if someone of this personality type had an intuitive side that was underdeveloped, they could become obsessed with structure. This is where you get the ones that insist on doing everything by the book.

People of this personality type are quite often taken advantage of in an unintentional manner. This is because they have such a strong sense of duty that it is difficult for them to say no. This tends to result in them having way more work assigned to them than they can reasonably do. This is why many people of this personality type end up working super long hours.

This personality type believes wholeheartedly in being accountable for their actions and thrives in positions of authority. They will expend massive amounts of energy in the pursuit of a task they deem necessary to reach a goal, but will strongly resist anything that doesn't make sense to them, or that they can't see a practical application for. This personality type usually prefers working alone but can work quite well in a team when it is required.

The people in this personality type are not the rock the boat types. They are more inclined to go with the flow and stick with what is familiar to them.

ISTJ's have tremendous respect for facts, but they tend to have a difficult time accepting an idea that differs from their own perspective. In this situation, if they are shown the relevance of the idea by someone they respect or care about the idea will become fact, which they will then internalize and support.

These are the type of people that will assume you're wrong just because you don't agree with them. Unless they greatly respect you, convincing them of the merit of your argument is nearly impossible.

This personality type is generally very traditional and very family oriented. They make great parents and tend to be excellent providers; however, they have a tendency to express their love in actions rather than in words. Under stress, this personality type tends to lose sight of anything besides what could go wrong. This will tend to make them depressed by their loss of ability to see things calmly and reasonably.

The next personality type is ISTP. They are known as the mechanic. They are typically quiet and reserved and are compelled to find out how things work. They have excellent skills with mechanical things. They are good at logical analysis and typically have excellent powers of reasoning.

People with this personality type are the ones that enjoy logic puzzles and will often argue the opposing side of something they believe just because they can. Their beliefs are not easily swayed, but they enjoy playing devils advocate to a large degree.

People of this personality type are fiercely independent and very adventurous. They tend to be attracted to things like motorcycles, airplanes, skydiving, surfing. They thrive on action and are usually fearless. They believe in doing their own thing not following rules and regulations. However, they do follow self-imposed rules relentlessly. They believe in the equal and fair treatment of others.

This personality type typically craves alone time. This is because this alone time is when they can sort through all the facts they have externally absorbed in their interactions with the world around them. They need to sort through them and make decisions and they do that best when alone.

This personality type is an action-oriented person. They prefer to be doing something. They are good at following through with whatever they start and tend to be very athletic. They have good hand-eye coordination and are good at tying up the loose ends.

The people who have this personality type tend to be very simple in what they desire, and are typically very optimistic, trusting, loyal and receptive to people. They tend to turn away from any commitments that will constrict their behaviors though.

The next personality type is the ISFJ which is known as the nurturer. People of this personality type are truly warm and kindhearted. They believe the best about other people and tend to keep negative feelings inside. The problem with this is after a while those negative feelings about people become firm judgments against people. Now they are very difficult to dislodge or disprove.

The people that make up this personality type have exceptional memories. It is not uncommon for them to remember something in such detail that they can recall a conversation including facial expressions years after it initially took place. The information they store away is typically very accurate.

This personality type has a clear idea of how they think things should be. They respect tradition and rules. They tend to believe in the systems around them and rarely challenge them as they believe they are there because they work. Unless you can show them undeniably why a new method is better than the method that is already in place, you can forget about swaying their opinion.

People of this personality type learn better by doing than by reading about something in a book. They are a hands-on type of person. They tend to be really good at interior decorating and tend to have beautifully furnished homes. They are often the best gift givers because they can choose a gift that will truly be appreciated by the receiver.

This personality type has a strong sense of responsibility and duty. People tend to rely on them regularly. They also have the tendency to become overloaded with responsibilities because they have a hard time saying no. They are sensitive and as such tend to get depressed when criticized regularly.

The next personality type is the ISFP, commonly referred to as the artist. These people are extremely in tune with their senses and quite commonly create or compose things that strongly influence those senses.

People of this personality type are difficult to get to know well because they are quiet and reserved. They will share their ideas and opinions with people they are close to however. They tend to be found in rolls that allow them to contribute to peoples sense of well being and happiness.

This personality type is usually animal lovers with a profound appreciation for the beauty of nature. Very original and independent they don't tend to conform to what others think they should be. They do value people that understand and support them.

People who don't understand them may misinterpret their unique way of doing things as being carefree and light-hearted, but this personality type actually takes life very seriously.

People with this personality type are extremely perceptive and aware of others around them. They are startlingly accurate in their perceptions of others. Warm and sympathetic, they genuinely care about others and tend to show their love in actions rather than with words.

The next personality type is the INFJ, known as the protector. People with this personality type are warm and caring, gentle and highly intuitive. They also make up only one percent of the population. This makes them the rarest personality type.

Having things orderly and systematic in the world around them is very important to someone with this personality type. They tend to regularly evaluate and re-evaluate their priorities. They operate on an intuitive basis and are entirely spontaneous.

People with this personality type know things intuitively without knowing why and with no knowledge of the situation at hand. They are typically right and usually know it. Their inner and outer worlds may conflict resulting in some disarray such as a consistently messy desk.

This personality type is typically deep and complex people. They tend to be private and share what they want when they want. They are typically difficult to understand and can be quite secretive. They are very sensitive to conflict and do not tolerate it well. They tend to internalize it resulting in health problems.

One downside of this personality type is that they never achieve complete peace with themselves. They have strong value systems and are very stubborn. They don't believe in compromising their ideals. In some ways, this personality type is gentle and easy going, while in other ways they are hard-nosed and stubborn.

They are capable of great depth of feeling and personal achievement, but life is not easy for this personality type. They tend to have high expectations of themselves and their families.

The next personality type is the INFP, known as the idealist. This group of people is focused on making the world a better place. They are constantly searching for value in life. They have a tendency to be perfectionists as well as idealists. Their end goal typically remains the same, to make the world a better place for others.

The people in this personality type are typically thoughtful and considerate. They tend to be good listeners and are a natural at putting people at ease. While they may be reserved in expressing emotions, they are a valued friend and confidante due to their genuine interest in understanding people.

People with this personality type do not like conflict and will go to extreme lengths to avoid it. When it is forced upon them, they will approach it from the perspective of their feelings. This can make them appear to be irrational or illogical.

Surprisingly they make excellent mediators because they so easily understand peoples feelings and truly want to help them. It is easy for them to solve other peoples problems. With any conflict, even one they are personally involved in, they don't focus on who was right and who was wrong. They focus instead on how the conflict makes them feel. They don't want to feel bad, so they need to resolve the conflict to relieve these feelings.

This personality style does not deal well with logic and facts. They are a more feeling oriented person and dealing with logic is difficult at the very least for them. In the heat of anger, they may use logic, throwing out fact after fact in an emotional outburst. However, most of the facts thrown out will be wrong.

People with this personality type may find it difficult to work on projects in a group. Their standards are so much higher than everybody else that it makes it difficult to be in a group. The person of this personality type may have control issues, simply because of their high standards.

Expressing themselves vocally is extremely difficult for this group. They are exceptional writers however. They often find work as counselors and teachers. Some may even end up in other social service positions.

The next personality type is the INTJ, they are known as the scientist. This group will place a high value on intelligence, knowledge, and competence. As a result of this, they most often place extremely high standards on themselves, and continuously strive to achieve them.

People of this personality type are natural born leaders, however many of them will choose to remain in the background until they see a need to take over the leadership. Once in leadership roles, the people in this personality type excel because of their ability to see the reality of a situation objectively and they are adaptable enough to change things that may not be working effectively or efficiently.

This group of people is supreme strategists, and typically have a plan for every possible contingency. They spend a lot of time inside their own heads, and if they don't ensure that their feeling side is well developed, they may have difficulty giving people the level of intimacy that is required.

The people in this personality type are typically seen as very judgmental. They are quick to offer judgments that are based on their intuition. Unless they have a well-developed ability to express themselves they may well be misunderstood. They tend to dismiss input from other people quickly and as such are often arrogant or elitist.

If the people in this group do not have well developed conversational skills, they typically become abrupt with people. It is not uncommon for people of this personality type to become isolationists when they lack sufficient communicational skills to express themselves effectively.

The next personality type is INTP, and they are often referred to as the thinker. This is the group where the absent-minded professors come from. They tend to be focused inside their own head more than outside. They are constantly pursuing knowledge, and continuously proving or disproving current theories and coming up with new ones.

They are typically very enthusiastic and skeptical when approaching problems. They tend to disregard and established methods of confronting the problem in favor of developing their own strategy to do so.

This personality type does not like to be in a leadership role. They are quite flexible unless it concerns their firmly held beliefs. They are most commonly very shy when meeting new people; however they may be quite self-confident and gregarious around people they know well, or when discussing a subject they know well.

The people in this personality type are typically independent, unconventional and very original. They won't place much value on traditional goals like security and popularity. They may also appear to be restless and temperamental.

Next, we will look at the personality type ESTP, this one is known as the doer. Enthusiastic, excitable, outgoing and straight shooting, these people are doers and their world is action. Blunt, straight forward risk takers, they are willing to just plunge in and get their hands dirty.

This group is very perceptive about peoples attitudes and motivations. They tend to pick up on little clues that most other types don't even register. They are most often a couple of steps ahead of whoever they're dealing with. Rules and laws are seen as guidelines instead of mandates.

Gamblers and spendthrifts are common in people with this personality type. They are typically good at storytelling and improvising. They tend to fly by the seat of their pants as opposed to making a plan. They rely more on their ability to adjust to occurring situations than the ability to plan for those possible outcomes.

They don't see any use for theory and as such have difficulty in school. Even though they may be brilliantly intelligent school will be a chore because they get bored in classes where they don't think they are gaining any useful information.

This group needs to keep moving, and as such, they make exceptional salespeople. Their natural overabundance of energy and enthusiasm make them natural choices for entrepreneurs. They are fun to be with and are great at getting things started. However, they are severely lacking when it comes to the matter of following through on things that have been started.

The next personality type is ESTJ, they are known as the guardian. They live in the present and keep their eyes scanning their personal environment to ensure everything is as it should be. Their beliefs and standards are very precise and set in stone. They don't understand when someone disagrees with their beliefs.

They take charge of people and as such naturally find themselves in leadership roles. They tend to be self-confident and aggressive and can be very demanding and critical. This is because of their strongly held beliefs. They are known, however, for being extremely straight forward and honest.

They are generally model citizens but have a tendency to become too rigid. They also tend to ignore peoples input and opinions, because they value their own so highly. This group is often defined as conscientious, practical, realistic and dependable.

The next personality type is ESFP, known as the performer. If people use words like lively, fun, center of attention to describing you and you relish excitement and drama in your life, this is your personality type.

With strong interpersonal skills, they land in the role of peacemaker quite often. Their personal values greatly influence their decision making, in the process increasing their sympathy and concern for the well being of others.

With their inherent dislike of theory and future-planning, they are not recommended for advice giving; however, they excel at providing practical care. While the people in this personality type tend to not look at long term consequences of their actions, immediate sensations and gratification are assigned more importance than responsibilities and duties.

This personality type also has an appreciation of the finer things in life. Good food, good wine, etc. They also appreciate the aesthetic beauty around them and usually have many beautiful possessions.

The people who make up this personality type are typically very practical even though they detest structure and routine. They prefer to go with the flow, improvising when necessary, and learning from hands-on experience.

This personality type provides people that are great team players. They typically like to feel strongly bonded with others. They enjoy a connection with animals and small children than most other types lack. They also appreciate the beauty of nature.

Now we will turn to ESFJ, otherwise referred to as the caregiver. This personality type is typically people persons. They love people and are extremely efficient at reading others and understanding them. They also have a skill for bringing out the best in a person.

These people need approval from others to feel good about themselves. This could be why they take their responsibilities so seriously and are so dependable. Security and stability are very important to them, and when they see something that needs to be done, they do whatever it takes to ensure that it is done.

The people with this personality type will compare their values and morals with the world around them. Their morals will be determined by their community as opposed to internal values.

At their best, the people in this group are warm, helpful, energetic, sympathetic, consistent and enthusiastic. They believe in tradition and laws. They tend to accept laws without question, and this could be greatly influenced by their desire for security and acceptance.

People of this type who don't have the benefit of growing up with a healthy set of values to learn from can develop questionable values. With no internal value system to straighten them out, they totally believe in the values they are following even if they are skewed.

The next personality type is ENFP, the inspirer. The people in this category are typically very warm and enthusiastic. They possess the ability to talk their way into or out of anything. They can also motivate people to action quite well.

This group will typically place great value on interpersonal relationships and may be overly emphatic and gushy about it when they are young. They have a strong set of values and are continually striving to obtain or maintain inner peace.

The people of this personality type have a great need for independence. They rebel against being controlled or labeled. If they lack proper guidance as they grow up, or if they veer off later in life, this personality type can be very manipulative, and very good at it. They have the gift of gab, and this makes it very easy for them to get almost anything they want.

The next personality type is ENFJ, the giver. This type is more of a people person group than any other type. They gain their greatest joy from accomplishing things to benefit other people.

They can typically make people do anything they want because they have such exceptional people skills. For the most part, people in this personality type will have unselfish motives. However, with less than ideal development, they have been known to use these exceptional people skills to manipulate people.

These types of people have strong values, but because their main interest is to bring about change in others, they tend to interact with others on their own level. Kind of like a chameleon, rather than as an individual. The people in this type have a strong need for close, intimate relationships. They are loyal and trustworthy once in a relationship. They will expend much energy creating and maintaining these relationships.

The next personality type is ENTP, the visionary. This type has a distinct advantage in life. They can instinctively understand things at a much deeper level than most of us reach any other way. This group is typically very mentally quick. This makes them great conversationalists, and they tend to enjoy verbal sparring as well.

This personality type is often referred to as the lawyer type. They base their actions and decisions on an objective list of rules and laws. The guilt or innocence of a client wouldn't enter into the equation. The people of this type are typically creative, clever and curious.

They tend to struggle with following through on things they have started. They are upbeat visionaries, who greatly value knowledge. They will typically spend their lives seeking a higher understanding.

The final personality type is ENTJ, the executive. They are natural born leaders with a strong drive for leadership. They fit quite naturally in the corporate setting. They are very career driven.

The people in this personality type are not typically tuned in to the feelings of others. They tend to desire a congenial, devoted relationship with their spouse. However seeing as they are so career oriented and driven, they tend to be away from home lots, physically or mentally, and this can take a toll on their relationships.

This personality type is best suited to someone who has a strong self-image and is also a thinking type. They have many gifts which enables them to have much power. They need to remember to pay attention to the balance in their lives, as they tend to forget about it and become unbalanced.

Chapter 3: Components of the Limbic Brain

In this chapter, I will cover the limbic brain system. Where it is, What the parts are that comprise it, and how it functions. Basically the limbic system is a bunch of separate parts that are connected together, and the whole is used for processing emotions.

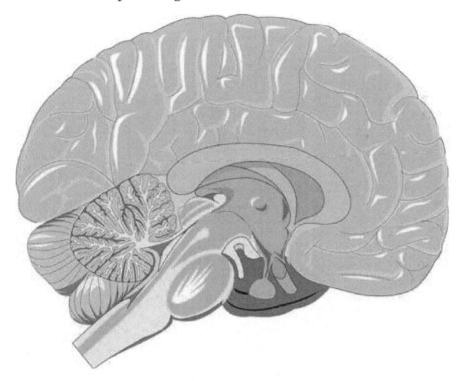

Many parts of the limbic system are buried inside our brain. These are referred to as subcortical structures. This means that they are located beneath the cerebral cortex. There are actually some areas of the limbic system that are part of the cerebral cortex. The orbitofrontal cortex is one, but it is often referred to as the hippocampus.

The purpose of the limbic system is to control the emotional responses, level of activation, motivation, and even some types of memory. These emotions are what control the self-preservation and preservation of the species. Such as the fight or flight concept.

The first area of the limbic system I will talk about is the Limbic bark. It is a transition zone allowing the neocortex and the subcortical structures to exchange information. This is the area where things that happen to us is processed and classified. They are associated with good, bad, painful, etc.

Found below the hippocampus the main function is the storage and retrieval of memories. This is known as the parahippocampal gyrus. Cingulate gyration is another area also wrapped in the limbic bark. It is in charge of processing and controlling the release of emotions.

This brings us to the hippocampus, which is located in the middle of the temporal lobe. It has multiple connections to other sections including the hypothalamus, septal area, cerebral cortex, and amygdala. It is in charge of storing long term memories. It also has to coordinate between learning and memory.

The hypothalamus is really an impressive section. It is located in the optical tracts, in the inferior part of the thalamus. It has many connections with many different parts of the brain, the frontal lobe, spinal cord, brainstem, and hippocampus to name a few. It is in charge of maintaining a balance in the functioning of our organism.

It is in charge of monitoring temperature, glucose and sodium levels as well as hormone levels. This gives it reign over stress, emotional reactions, appetite, sexual reactions, and sleep. Just to name a few. There are much more technical names and descriptions for many of these functions; however, that is not the scope of this book.

The amygdala is an almond-shaped structure that has two nuclei, each of which resides in a temporal lobe. It has long been understood that memories that have emotional importance attached to them are stronger and more deeply embedded than others. This is controlled by the amygdala.

It is also in charge of regulating emotional facial expressions. This task is done in an automatic way, that we are not really aware of. It is a very important task that is needed to allow for proper social interaction.

Another important thing that the amygdala is tasked with, is the processing of fear as it relates to behavioral conditioning. This is where we learn that a certain thing or place is associated with some form of danger. It builds an alarm system so to speak that when this thing or place is encountered the body arms itself for defense.

So basically we have two different types of memories. The unconscious ones which are referred to as implicit memories of fear. The amygdala is responsible for learning and storing these. The other type is the conscious ones which are called declarative memories. The hippocampus is responsible for cataloging these. These ones are ones that can be consciously evoked.

The septal area is located just above the anterior commissure. It has numerous connections to the hippocampus, the hypothalamus, and other areas. It is responsible for regulating the limbic system and alert levels to prevent triggering from an overactivated false alarm.

This allows us to maintain memory and attention to be prepared to react to our environment appropriately. Septal nuclei also have integrated functions in emotional, motivational and pleasurable sensations.

The Tegmental Ventral Area is found in the brainstem. This area is responsible for our pleasant feelings. It accomplishes this by releasing dopamine into our systems. If injured it impairs a persons ability to feel pleasure, and this tends to lead to them seeking that feeling through other means, such as drugs, food, etc.

In the fissure of Silvio, you will find The island crust also known as the Insula. Its function is to process and interpret. Primarily it focuses on pain. However, it does also process primary emotions like love, joy, hate, anger, sadness and even fear. Actually it processes the subjective aspects of these emotions. It is also the area that lets you know you are hungry or if you want to reuse a drug.

The orbitofrontal cortex connects to the amygdala. It participates in our being able to determine someone's intention by assessing their looks, gestures, and speech. Injuries in this area have been known to cause issues such as inability to empathize with others, disinhibition as hypersexuality, lack of impulse control with drugs, addictions and talking dirty.

The Basal ganglia are made up of a nucleus of accumbens, pale globe, putamen, and black substance. Their role is to control motor functions. The nucleus of accumbens is an important part that is strongly involved in addictive behaviors. It also contains the reward circuits as well as sensations of pleasure. In addition to these, it also does aggression, anger, and fear.

There are conditions which affect the limbic system, and I will cover them here. The first one is Autism. It appears that areas such as the amygdala, cingulate gyrus, orbitofrontal cortex have reduced functioning capabilities in individuals with this condition.

Kluver-Bucy syndrome arises from the amygdala and part of the temporal cortex being bilaterally extracted. People with this condition typically explore everything with their mouth and experience a loss of fear as well as indiscriminate feeding.

Limbic encephalitis causes people to develop dementia, memory loss, and involuntary movements. The parts of the limbic system it affects are the amygdala, hippocampus, cingulate gyrus, insula, and orbitofrontal cortex.

Certain forms of dementia can produce symptoms of emotional uncontrol. It accomplishes this by affecting the limbic system, or the parts associated with it. The area that is associated with disinhibition symptoms is the frontal-temporal cortex.

Anxiety disorders could arise from a failure in the control function of the hippocampus and the cortical structures. These areas normally exert control in the modulation of the amygdala.

When you have smaller, disorganized hippocampal neurons, the anterior cingulate cortex and thalamus contain fewer inhibitory cells. These cells are usually referred to as GABAergic cells. The volume of the limbic areas is reduced. All these points to schizophrenia.

Limbic epilepsy affects a person's ability to learn new things. It increases the chances of the person suffering from anxiety or depression. It is also referred to as (MLT) which stands for Temporal Lobe Medial Epilepsy. It causes these issues by creating lesions in areas like the hippocampus and amygdala.

It is believed that ADHD Attention deficit disorder and hyperactivity may be caused by a failure in the limbic system. These patients tend to have a larger hippocampus. The amygdala and the orbitofrontal cortex have lost all effective connections between them. This results in the uninhibited behavior typically associated with ADHD.

Studies of patients with Affective disorders, which is also known as depression, have shown variations in the volumes of the basal ganglia, amygdala, hippocampus and frontal lobes. Some areas of the limbic system have also shown less activation.

Chapter 4: How to Interpret Non-verbal Communication in Different Parts of the Body

Now I will look closer at the different methods of non-verbal communication that I discussed earlier. I will explain how to interpret non-verbal communication in different parts of the body. Non-verbal communication is an integral part of our communication. It is primarily used and interpreted in an unconscious manner. Knowledge of non-verbal communication signs can improve interaction resulting in a greater shared understanding.

It is important in trying to interpret non-verbal communication to consider the context. The context that non-verbal communication was performed can greatly influence the meaning of non-verbal communication.

One of the most important parts of reading non-verbal communication is your mindset. You need to emphasize four attributes when preparing your mindset to analyze people. These are first of all to be open. Then you need to add being inquisitive. Follow that up with some creativity, and top it all off with being slow to judge. This is the mindset you need to analyze people.

Reading non-verbal communication is best done when you read many signs in a cluster as opposed to just one single action or movement. For example, this will be from a male perspective, but it fits any gender, it's just an example. If you got the impression from a woman you liked that she was interested in you, how do you know for sure? Without looking like a fool.

Suppose the action that gave you the impression that she likes you is that she was playing with her hair. While you may have read that this is a sign for attraction, and it is, it can also be applied to playfulness. You need other signs to add to your interpretation. Other things you can look for would be, how is she standing? Is she leaning forward? Are you getting a sideways glance? Is her head tilted?

It is important in reading people if you want to be good at it, to base your interpretation on more than just one sign. After all, you want to be sure your interpretation is correct before going all in, don't you? No one wants to walk into a situation expecting success only to crash and burn.

One thing you don't want to do while you're trying to learn to interpret non-verbal communication is to focus on every little sign and try to interpret them while you're trying to maintain a conversation.

There is just too much information to process and you'll lose where you are in a conversation and have a sudden silence. Not to mention how awkward this sudden silence will be. Just try to enhance the signs you can pick up on, and for now, you can interpret them later.

This is why typically we focus on the conversation and our subconscious interprets the non-verbal communication for us. The key to being good at reading people isn't to shift your focus from verbal conversation to non-verbal conversation. It is to expand your awareness and be present in the moment.

If you know what to look for you'll see it, and if you know the meaning you'll interpret it immediately. If you don't, or you miss it, don't worry, you'll get better with practice. It's like riding a bike, you might scrape your knees a few times, but you'll get the hang of it.

An excellent way to practice reading people is to do it when you're doing nothing else. For example, if you're sitting at the park, watch the people around that are having conversations and even some that aren't. What is their body language telling you?

Another good way is to watch tv with the volume muted. Interpret what is happening by the actions of the actors. With this method, you have the ability to turn the sound on every couple minutes to see if you're right about what is going on. It makes for good practice because you can authenticate your interpretations.

The main thing to watch for when communicating with someone is doing the words they're saying line up with the body language they're using. If they don't line up, you'll know it. You have to go with your gut, and later when you're more proficient you'll have the skills to look at your observations and know what it was that tipped you off.

As mentioned previously you need to consider the context when reading non-verbal communication. This can extend to location, who is talking, and you must remember that culture plays a part here as well. Just because non-verbal signs mean one thing in your culture, doesn't mean they mean the same thing in someone else's culture. Don't be afraid to ask someone if you don't know. Most people are happy to talk about their culture.

Facial expressions are a common form of non-verbal communication. Our face tells those around us what is going on inside. When you're happy to do you consciously decide to smile, or does it just happen? What about when you're sad? Do you consciously decide to frown? Nobody taught you how to do these actions, did they?

The one thing that you need to consider when interpreting facial expressions is that people can mask their true feelings, so facial expressions aren't always a good indicator of truth. It's possible to tell though if a smile is being faked. Is the jaw relaxed or clenched? Are their eyes sparkling? These are a few things to look for when trying to determine if a smile is real or not.

The good thing about facial expressions is you can practice them in a mirror, trying to convey the emotion you're after. This does two things for you, first of all, you gain better control over your facial expressions. Secondly, you gain more familiarity with the facial muscles used to make different facial expressions.

The smile is an interesting expression. There are dozens of different varieties of smiles. While we are taught to believe a smile means happy, it often means so much more than that. If you are a female and you smile at someone, it quite often means connection or empathy. Trust and joy are also displayed through a smile. Affection, attraction, sarcasm, contempt, recognition and even fear can all be displayed with a smile, as well as many more.

If you abuse the act of smiling, it will lose its effect. Nobody will believe anybody who smiles all the time. Kind of like the little boy who cried wolf. A big plastered on smile doesn't fool anyone. Especially when you overuse it. A genuine smile can be immeasurably useful in putting people at ease, whereas an insincere one is easily recognizable.

One use of the smile that comes with advantages and pitfalls, is the woman's use of the smile to get a man's attention. If you're sitting at a bar and a female comes and sits down, makes eye contact with you and smiles at you, you're going to pay attention to her, aren't you?

The pitfall to this is that men interpret this as a sexual invitation, whether that's the way it was intended or not. This can result in unwanted attention and uncomfortable encounters on both sides.

For males, the smile almost works in reverse. While some smiling is good, it has been shown that men who smile too much lose masculinity points with a woman. They prefer a man who is tough or masculine as opposed to one who tries to appease them.

As far as spotting the phony smile, the first thing to look for is to look at the person's eyes. Are they smiling as well? It has been scientifically proven that a genuine smile squints the eyes making them crescent shaped. This is also what gives the crows feet around the eyes, and the crinkles around the nose.

Other things to watch for in trying to determine if a smile is genuine or being fake, is how fast it appears. A genuine smile doesn't appear instantly on demand. Real smiles are a gradual thing and last longer. They don't stay frozen on your face. The size and symmetry is another thing to look for. Real smiles aren't all that big, and they're not always symmetrical. When we fake a smile we want to sell it so we overstretch it.

This is not to say that all fake smiles are a bad thing. Sure the stewardess who gave you the million-watt smile when you boarded may well be frustrated and can't wait for anything more than this trip to be over with, but she's being polite. Sometimes the fake smile simply means I'm trying.

A huge part of facial expressions in non-verbal communication that is often associated with sexuality and other stronger emotions are the lips. Their shape color and size easily create attraction. They can look very kissable, and seem to be saying "taste me". Or they can be very unapproachable. If they are drawn thin and the jaw is clenched, there isn't much attraction or desire to approach.

The tense mouth, which pretty much speaks for itself, is when the lips are pressed together to make a thin line. This is commonly over a clenched jaw, which gives a tense, solid image. Sometimes the lips may even be sucked in making them appear even thinner.

Think of it like a dam, being used to contain emotions. British people refer to this as a stiff upper lip. The ability to remain strong even in the face of negative happenings. It is seen as a strength as opposed to the negative connotations associated with it by others.

Slightly parted lips, on the other hand, are typically seen in more exciting occasions, such as courtship. A common sign that someone wants a kiss is that they keep their lips slightly loose and keep glancing at the other person lips. It is often a preliminary step in a kiss.

Pursuing the lips is when the lips are drawn in to create a tight round shape. There are two common interpretations of this expression. Typically it is seen when someone is trying to suppress their anger. It could also be that they are trying to relay disagreement. The other interpretation for this expression is indecision. In this instance, it is when someone is weighing the options between two choices.

Perking the lips is commonly referred to as either the duck face or the kissing face. Blowing air kisses to someone is cute, but overusing it quickly detracts from its cuteness. Keep this in mind when taking pictures. It is typically a playful expression.

Pouting is a facial expression that is most commonly found in kids who are showing their displeasure with a situation. Adults do it as well, but for the most part, it tends to be a lot more subtle. Except in the case of a woman using it to manipulate a man and get him to do what she wants. In this case, it may well be blatant and very over dramatized to be effective.

Licking the lips is a facial expression with two possible interpretations. This one is really important to understand the context so you don't get the wrong interpretation. The first type of this is the sexual lick, which is where the tongue starts in one corner of the mouth and slowly moves across the upper lip, and then back across the bottom lip. Done slowly and properly this is a very sensual move. Typically it is a flirtatious move and often considered a bold one.

The other form of lip licking is a quick almost pulling off the lip with the tongue. Often done in a subtle form, it is done to release nervous tension. Many times it is thought to be associated with telling a lie, but that is where context is needed, as that's not always the case. It could just be an uncomfortable situation.

This is why you need to have context when interpreting non-verbal signals. You don't want to create unduly stressful situations because you jumped to conclusions based on one single non-verbal signal. Even if you receive the signals that interpret to say someone is lying, it's not necessary to call them on it. This will be a case by case thing as well.

Perhaps sometimes it is necessary to call them on it. However sometimes if you know they're lying, that is all that matters.

Biting the lips is typically a stronger form of licking them. It is often a sign of an insecure or shy person as well. Context makes it pretty easy to tell if it's being done as a sexual gesture or out of nervousness. Sticking out the tongue is pretty straight forward, so I won't even go there. Context is important with that one too though, as it could be playful or not.

Head tilting is pretty straight forward but I will quickly mention it here just for completeness sake. Basically head tilting tells us if someone is in agreement with what we're saying, or if they disagree. Aggressive head tilting such as thrusting the jaw forward is a sign of aggression and disagreement. Retreating is a sign of fear and defensiveness but is also used when a person feels negative about what they are hearing.

Tilting the head to the side can have different meanings in different settings, in a job interview this combined with a nod will probably mean they find what you're saying interesting. In a courtship setting this combined with a half smile or a sideways glance typically means interested and teasing.

Head nods typically mean yes while shaking your head means no. The speed and duration of each can offer an idea of how much the person agrees or disagrees with you. Another thing that can factor into their degree of agreement or non-agreement, is the intensity of it. For example, is it a slight head nod, or a more fully engaged head nod. Is the person lightly shaking their head or emphatically shaking it.

Body gestures concerning the torso are simple to understand. Just remember that someone is either opening up their front or protecting and shielding it. If someone stands with something between you or holds a book in front of them, they are uncomfortable and closing off. This can be seen with many situations, a good example would be when you walk into your boss' office, does he or she retreat behind the desk, or do they come around to your side of the desk? These things really do happen on a regular basis.

If the same person lowers the book when you start talking and keeps their arms at their side, they feel comfortable with you. Most likely they agree with what you are saying as well. We tend to cross our arms or perform some other form of closing off or shielding our front when we don't agree with something someone is saying. This is our protective stance.

When it comes to the body and how we stand, there are three options. Leaning forward, leaning backward or standing straight up. Leaning forward is an open response which indicates being engaged, which tends to happen more with agreement than disagreement. Leaning backward is like putting the brakes on. If you were a salesman and you're giving your spiel and your customer is leaning back with their arms crossed, it's time to switch tactics, you're losing them.

This is something good salespeople have learned to realize, and when they spot these signals, they switch tactics, there's no point flogging a dead horse, and try a different approach to get them leaning back in again. This is how some of the good ones as they are often referred to can save a sale that seems like it's lost.

Staying upright in the middle is kind of like neutral. You're not leaning forward in agreement or engagement but you're not leaning back and putting the brakes on yet either. To stick with the salesperson example, at this point you haven't lost them, but they're not very committed either. You can continue your pitch but watch for very slight, very subtle shifts in any direction. If the switch is forward, keep going, whereas if they subtly shift slightly away from you, try something different. It may make the difference between success and failure.

Obviously, with the leaning back, putting the brakes on, you need to switch tactics immediately, or you may lose them. In these scenarios, as with most interactions, you need to pay attention not only to their non-verbal signals but to the non-verbal signals you are giving them. If you lean in slightly, do they respond? If they move away, what happens if you slightly move away? Especially when you practice this in situations that have no serious repercussions, you can have fun playing with it.

Standing with your hands on your hips is a sign of authority. It is typically considered a sign of action or readiness for action. Some common places to see it is someone waiting for a bus, a parent waiting for a child to answer them. Maybe a school principal waiting for a misbehaving student to explain themselves.

When you attend social functions, pay attention to the people in the room. Are any of them standing with their hands on their hips? If so are they the ones people approach for direction, or information? These are good ways to get familiar with some non-verbal signals and see them at work first hand.

Our genital area is another area that is used for communication, although not regularly. It is also more common in males than females, but it is not male exclusive. Covering the genital area with the hands tends to indicate insecurity or shyness. It most often occurs during times of distress and vulnerability. Like when we're being reprimanded.

Combined with a shoulder shrug, this gesture is used to send a strong message of innocence. Performing body movements that expose the genital area while most common in young males trying to display their sexual interest, it is seen sometimes in women. When seen in women, it indicates a non-conforming woman who doesn't much care what society thinks and will do what she wants and get what she wants.

Chapter 5: The Ability to Detect Deception

This chapter will be about knowing how to tell if and when someone is lying to you. Firstly, I will say that this is possible because lying is harder than being honest. It requires more mental effort, which creates more stress and anxiety. It is people's emotions that blow the whistle on them when they lie.

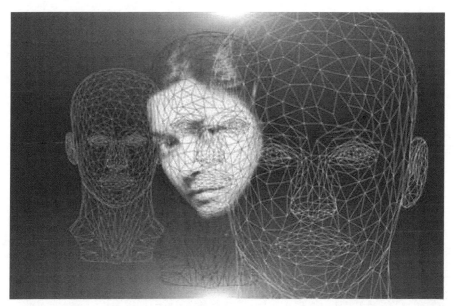

Many people find it a simple matter to lie verbally. It is like second nature to some of them. It is an entirely different concept when it comes to hiding a lie and keeping unconscious gestures or facial expressions from exposing it. It is difficult to catch lying even with non-verbal communication on a regular basis. Even some of the experts miss sometimes.

I will give you some tips on things to watch for that give away that someone may be lying. They are what gamblers would call a tell. With practice, you should be able to improve not only your deception detection but your understanding of non-verbal communication as a whole.

Non-verbal communication is used to portray emotions ranging from attraction to deception. The eyes are often referred to as the window to the soul, and that is because they are very expressive of your emotions. They are probably the hardest part of non-verbal communication for many people to learn to control. Facial features can be quite expressive as well.

It's easy for someone to plaster a smile on their face, and if they know the signs, they can probably even make it look fairly genuine. Their eyes will tell the truth though. If you're sad, it is almost impossible to get your eyes to show anything else.

Pacifying behaviour is one action that you need to learn to watch for. The most common methods of this are touching the face, biting the lip, and when seated running the palms of their hands down their legs. The reason they do these things is because the brain is uncomfortable for some reason. Stimulating nerve endings will pacify the brain.

Now before assuming that everyone that performs one of these actions must be lying, you need to remember that there are numerous reasons why their brain might not be comfortable. They could be talking about a subject that is disturbing to them. You don't want to assume too quickly that one gesture means for certain they're lying.

This is why I have said over and over again, that non-verbal gestures and signals need to be read in context. It is also why you need to have the full picture, not just one single action. I don't feel this issue can be stressed enough. There are enough people in the world already that are prepared to jump to conclusions, we don't need to add to their number.

That is also why it is important to establish a baseline for the person in question. You need to know if there are certain situations that always result in them performing these gestures. Sometimes if you haven't had time to watch this person prior to this incident, you could if you needed proof to establish the baseline after the incident you believe to be them lying.

This would mean though, that you need to postpone any act of calling them on their lying until you have had time to establish the baseline. Typically you would want to establish the baseline first, and if that's not possible, you may need to rely on only the contextual information you observe.

Performing one of the gestures associated with pacifying behaviour does not in itself prove deception. You can't base this on one act alone. You need to know a baseline so that you can know if the gesture is a deviation from the baseline. That is when it is likely to be indicating deception.

An important part of understanding non-verbal communication is to not jump to conclusions too quickly. When you are watching someone and notice an unexpected non-verbal gesture, take time to think about it and ask yourself what it might have been a reaction to.

If the unexpected non-verbal gesture can be recognized as being a reaction to something that took place immediately preceding the gesture, it is better to know it now than after you have drawn your conclusion and possibly shared it.

When you are talking to someone and you see them make an obvious non-verbal gesture, you need to remember not to overreact. Don't start saying I knew you were lying to me, or some such thing. Remember that the subconscious gesture that represents stress is the same gesture that represents deceit.

It is impossible to tell the difference between the two reasons for the same gesture. What you can do however is to ask more questions without alerting them to the fact that you know they're lying to find out how they're feeling. Try and come up with questions that show why what you believe to be a lie doesn't make sense, but keep it relevant to the conversation.

The baseline allows us to establish a new normal for each person. The interpretations we learn for non-verbal gestures are generalized, and not every person is the same. Because one person does a non-verbal gesture out of discomfort or as a means of protecting themselves, doesn't mean that this is the case for everyone. The baseline gives us something to compare the person's behaviour to their own typical behavior as opposed to a generalized view of what it should be.

It is important to obtain a baseline because some people regularly do something during a conversation that unless you have a baseline to compare to might make you think they're lying. For example, some people like to stand with their arms crossed over their chest while they're talking. Most commonly this would be interpreted as a defensive closed off position. While it can be a closed off defensive position, it is also a comfortable stance for some people when they are absorbing and thinking about the conversation.

There are some people who have unconscious reactions to being questioned that may make them seem like they're lying unless you have a baseline to compare it to. I knew a guy who every time you asked if he was looking at a woman he would blush even if he wasn't. I'm not sure why, but I know his wife used to love teasing him and making him blush. If you didn't have a baseline, it may seem like there was something happening to cause it when in fact it was caused simply by the suggestion of something happening.

This can often be evidenced when the same behavior occurs even when the situation being questioned changes. This is what a baseline can do for us. It is beneficial not only to us in obtaining accurate information, but also to the people we are reading in order to give them a fair reading as opposed to one steeped in generalization.

One place where non-verbal communication is used regularly is when investigators are interviewing someone. This could be a suspect or a witness or even a character witness. In this setting preparing the room properly can either add to or detract from the interpretation of non-verbal communication.

While it is not essential, the investigator should keep in mind when setting up the room that it should at the very least accomplish two things. Those two things are that firstly the room should be arranged in a way that the interviewee will be comfortable. Secondly, the room should be arranged so that the investigator has a clear view of the interviewee at all times. This makes it possible for the investigator to see non-verbal communication as well as focus on the verbal.

The alternative reason for maintaining a clear view of the interviewee is psychological. When you are trying to close someone out, what do you do? Place something between you. Placing a table or other object between you is aiding the interviewee in closing off communication. The exact opposite of what you're looking for.

If the interview room is a comfortable place, the interviewee will be more relaxed, and this will make signs of stress and unease easier to be spotted. It also makes it easier to spot things that the behaviour could be in response to. This can help to eliminate false positives. Making it easier to determine what is useful information and what is not.

Illustrators refer to the general hand motions people make when carrying on a conversation. It is not really important what motions they are making, what is important is the speed they are making them at, and the amount they are using them.

While it is quite common for people to use illustrators to help get their point across when the stress level increases their use of illustrators may increase or decrease. Any change in their illustrator usage could be a sign of deception. It is not only an increase that may show deception.

Manipulators are another thing to watch for. Like Illustrators they are also handed movements; however, these ones are not used to help get a point across. The sole purpose of these hand motions is to release nervous energy by doing something.

Common ones are clasping and releasing their hands, or perhaps fiddling with jewelry such as a ring or something. It could be as simple as picking lint off their clothes. Picking at their fingers or fingernails. Those are some of the more common manipulators.

It should also be mentioned that just because these are common manipulators, does not mean that they can't also just be habits. It is essential to remember that these are general occurrences and that people can and do deviate from the norm.

Another non-verbal gesture that can indicate truth or deception is what is referred to as full-body positioning. As you would expect it involves the positioning of the whole body. During a conversation, as the questions become more serious, an honest person will have a tendency to lean towards the person they're talking to.

The flip side of that, of course, is the person that is being less than completely honest may do one of a couple of things. They may lean back away from the person they are talking too. This is emotionally putting the brakes on, trying to discourage the conversation. The other thing they might do is to totally change their posture.

If a person is being made really uncomfortable by the conversation, and are being dishonest, they may do what is called fleeing the room. That doesn't mean getting up and leaving. It is an emotional fleeing. Their upper body may continue to face the person they are in conversation with, but they may shift so that their legs are facing the door. This is typically interpreted as the unconscious mind trying to get the person to leave. It is also a common non-verbal cue for the other person to end the conversation.

This next one you have probably heard of and dismissed it as being too easy or too obvious. That is covering the mouth. That's right, just like when we were kids they may cover their mouth with either their fingers or their hands. A lot of people tend to interpret this as a subconscious effort to keep dishonest words from coming out.

You should remember that non-verbal clues by themselves are unreliable. They can be interpreted and used for direction to ask more questions and dig out the truth, but they should not be used as proof of deception. Especially when it is a single gesture. It is important to look at the context, the person state of mind, and their baseline.

Some people exhibit gestures on a regular basis that would typically be expected of a person that is stressed or being deceptive. There are also people who are continuously stressed, so it should be no surprise for these people to be executing stress indicating non-verbal gestures.

If you ever talk to a scientist about the reasons that non-verbal gestures will give away someone who is lying, they will typically suggest one of three reasons. They may also suggest a combination of the three reasons.

The first one I'll explain is the affective approach. A lot of people refer to this one as the emotional approach. It suggests that there are three emotions that are typically experienced by someone involved in being deceptive. They are excitement, fear, and guilt.

The guilt would be because of the act of deceiving someone. The excitement is because some people experience what is known as "duping delight" which is a euphoric feeling at getting away with something. The other emotion typically experienced is fear. This could be a fear of being caught in their deception. The belief is that because of those emotions their non-verbal gestures would not be normal and therefore would reveal their deception.

Just as there are some people who live in a constant state of stress, I'm sure there are those who live in a constant state of deceit. As it becomes their norm, there is no sure way to say that they would indeed portray the non-verbal clues that we would expect of them. This is another instance where having a baseline for the person helps.

Another reason most scientists may offer is referred to as the working memory model. Often it is also referred to as the cognitive load approach. This approach works on the belief that persons non-verbal communication will give them away because it is easier to be honest than deceptive.

The dishonest person has to tell a lie that fits with the situation in order for it to be believed. They have to avoid contradicting themselves, and they have to remember exactly what they said. The simpler it is the easier it is to repeat it correctly if asked. It needs to be complex enough to be believable though.

That is a lot of extra things to be thinking about all while trying to tell your lie and appear like you're not lying. Hesitation could be considered to be part of this, as perhaps they are running checks on their story before committing themselves to it. They don't want to be caught in their lie. If it didn't matter if they were caught, they probably wouldn't bother to lie about it.

The last one is the attempted control method. This one works off the assumption that the deceiver may be concerned with their non-verbal gestures giving them away, and may, therefore, try to control those actions. The downfall of this method is that the deceiver may end up overcontrolling their behaviours and may, as a result, end up executing behaviours that appear fake. They may suppress body movements so much in order to prevent their non-verbal clues from giving them away from that they become rigid which then gives them away.

It is possible for all three things to happen at the same time. There will typically be one more prevalent than the others, and this will depend on the particular situation as well as the person involved. High stakes lie tend to elicit nervous responses, while non-verbal cues that indicate increased cognitive load are more typical in situations involving complicated lies.

Motivated liars are the aptest to try to control their voices and actions to prevent their non-verbal cues from giving them away. It is still necessary to understand that while these behaviours can represent deceitfulness, they don't necessarily do so. An honest person, nervous because they are being questioned could also exhibit any of these non-verbal cues. It is important to consider the context and to be willing to question deeper to find the truth.

It is always better to ask more questions to try to verify your suspicions than to just take the first non-verbal clue as proof of your suspicions. It is better to err on the side of caution, or as you may have heard it said, innocent until proven guilty.

Chapter 6: Becoming Better at Reading People

Now that you have an understanding of non-verbal communication, you need to practice in order to get better at analyzing people. You want to start small and work your way up. I mean, after all, Leonardo da Vinci didn't paint the Mona Lisa the very first time he picked up a paintbrush. Don't put too much pressure on yourself. It's ok to take time to get good at a new skill.

A good place to start is to practice understanding other peoples emotions. Typically these present more of a struggle and therefore require more effort to mask than feelings. For this reason, many people tend to have emotional leakage even if they're trying not to show you how they feel.

These little leakages of emotions are most commonly referred to as micro-expressions. They show up briefly before we are able to mask them over. Sometimes they are present because the person you're talking to doesn't think you're looking at them. Sometimes they just can't be helped. They are a subconscious gesture more often than not.

Let's take a look at some of the emotions we express. If you can recognize the base emotions you will progress much quicker at becoming effective at reading other people. You will still need to practice, but you'll have a good foundation to start from. The foundation is the most important part when building anything, so don't be afraid to spend time solidifying your foundation. You'll reap the rewards later.

The look of fear on somebody's face is quite often confused with a surprised look. There are a few details that can tell the difference for you. To start with on a fearful face, the eyes won't be open as wide as they would be on a surprised face.

When you're expressing fear your mouth is pulled wider as your lips tend to move back as opposed to the slack-jawed open mouth look of surprise. The eyebrows can also help you differentiate between the two emotions. When expressing fear the eyebrows are a lot flatter than they are with surprise.

The eyebrows tend to arch when showing surprise. While all these differences are distinctive, they are also pretty minuscule, and as you practice you'll get better at spotting the differences, but don't worry if you don't catch it every time at the start.

When somebody is expressing happiness, the most likely expression is a true smile. If you look at the corner of the lips, they should be pulled up if it's a true smile. The other feature that says it's a real smile is the crow feet at the corner of the eyes. You can also look at the lower eyelid and see if it appears pouchy. These things all grouped together to say it is a real smile.

Context is important in this situation as well. If someone is extremely tired but are giving you a genuine smile, it may not appear as vibrant and substantial as it would if they were not so tired. Factors like this need to be taken into consideration when interpreting the non-verbal signals you are receiving.

There are three things to look for to determine if someone is showing anger. Start with the brow. Is it furled? Good now move onto the eyes, the lower eyelids should appear tight and the upper eyelids should be raised. The lips should be tight and pressed together. Disgust and anger are commonly confused, however, disgust will also include a raised upper lip and the nose will have a wrinkle. Neither of those is present in an angry expression.

In identifying the expression for embarrassment, the neck should be exposed. This is because the head will typically move down and to the side. The embarrassed smile is different as well. The lips press tightly together but raise slightly at the edge. Kind of more like a grin than a smile.

Don't confuse this one with shame. When looking at an expression of shame the head will typically move straight down as opposed to down and to the side. There also will not be a smile. It is easy to confuse these two, and especially when you're first starting, you may need to pay specific attention to the smaller details to interpret it correctly.

When trying to identify a prideful look, look for the head to be tilted back and the jaw will be thrust out. Very common expressions of power, that go hand in hand with pride. They should also have a slight smile with just the corners of the lips raised to indicate their happiness.

Don't confuse this look with contempt. While the two are close, when you see contempt the head tilt will be there, but there won't be a smile. Instead, you will find an asymmetrical movement of the mouth. One side will be tightened while the other side won't be.

With a look of surprise that was mentioned when we talked about anger, there will be the slack-jawed open mouth look. As well if you look at the eyes, the difference you will find with surprise is that the eyebrows will be arched. Also, the upper eyelids should be raised.

Identifying an expression of contempt will involve ensuring that the head is tilted to the side. The corner of the mouth should tighten only on one side. Sounds an awful lot like disgust doesn't it? With disgust though you have the wrinkled nose and raised upper lip, whereas with contempt the eyes will be looking to the side. There will be no raised upper lip and no wrinkling of the nose.

We have previously mentioned disgust in connection with both anger and contempt. Another point to look for in identifying disgust is the mouth to open and the tongue to stick out. This is believed to be in case there is the necessity of vomiting. It makes it easier to distinguish between disgust and anger or contempt though.

A flirting expression typically consists of the head is turned away, but the narrowed eyes making contact at the same time. As well as the corners of the lips being pulled up, the cheeks should also rise slightly. If you need another item to distinguish a flirtatious smile, the eyes should be slightly narrower than a neutral face.

A painful expression is typically fairly easy to distinguish. Typically in a painful expression, the eyes will be tightly closed and the eyebrows are usually lowered. At the same time the bottom half of the face the lips will tighten and press upwards. More like a grimace than a smile. This is quite often seen when somebody is being empathetic to another person's pain. There are a few variations of the painful expression, based on whether it is an empathetic pain, physical pain and even an emotional pain may be slightly different.

A compassionate expression typically involves the pulling in and raising of the eyebrows. Along with this, the lips will be compressed. Most often compassion is mixed up with the look for sadness. The eye movement is the same, but with sadness, the lips don't compress. Instead, they pull down. As you can see mixing these two up would not be very difficult.

With amusement, the signs you look for are the head being thrown back and the mouth is open. The eyes should be narrowed and, just as with a legitimate smile, you should see the crows feet appear at the corners of the eyes. If you really need to make sure, the open mouth should be surrounded by relaxed muscles. A lot of times people say the eyes will sparkle, but this has not been scientifically proven.

When we're expressing interest, the eyebrows will typically raise straight up. As opposed to with happiness where the muscles around the eyes won't be so contracted. The corners of the lips will tend to be raised in a slight smile. The smile won't be nearly as exaggerated as the smile of happiness.

A look of sadness is typically identified by the eyebrows. The eyebrows will pull in and slightly up. This will result in the skin of the forehead above the nose having the appearance of a pouch. The corners of the lips will be pulled straight down. This expression is commonly confused with shame. The movement of the eyebrows is actually shared with compassion.

To correctly diagnose desire you need to look at the mouth. Licking the lips, or possibly puckering them, maybe even biting them signals desire. The mouth is typically opened with the tongue slightly sticking out. Although it is somewhat related to love, desire won't typically include the head tilt or warm smile associated with love. The eyes may look quite similar though.

Shame is primarily about gaze aversion. The head typically tilts down, and the chin is pulled in towards the neck. The eyes are lowered. This is a very submissive look as well. Commonly confused with sadness, shame doesn't involve the eyebrow movements or pulling down of the lips that are found in a look of sadness.

To tell when someone is being polite, look for a slight smile. It will be missing the signs of true happiness though. There will be no crows feet visible around the corners of the eyes. The cheeks will remain normal, not be raised like in a smile of genuine happiness. This again needs to be considered in context, as there are variations in the level of happiness and as such there are variations in the non-verbal signs that accompany the expression of the emotion.

Embarrassment is typically accompanied by at least one hand touching the face. This is often thought to be a defensive reaction. The head will be moved down and to the side, and the mouth will have the lips pulled together and raised in a slight smile. It is often thought that a reddish tinge to the neck and cheeks is a sign of embarrassment. This seems to be true in some people, but it's not that reliable in diagnosing embarrassment. Embarrassment is sometimes confused with humiliation, but the two are very different.

Love is very similar to happiness in its expression. The bottom eyelids will be tightened changing the shape of the eyes. There won't typically be crows feet, but the lips will rise in a slight smile. Not quite as exaggerated as a smile of happiness though. These features will be combined with a head tilt to the side. This shows the intimacy and connection that is not associated with happiness alone. This expression is commonly referred to as having a look of dopiness.

An important part of being able to read people is learning to trust yourself. More specifically you need to learn to trust your gut. Your intuition, It is your internal truth meter that doesn't work on logic, but gives you a primal response based on non-verbal signals before you have a chance to think. It lets you know if you're comfortable with someone, and if you can trust them or not.

Another thing you need to do to improve your ability to read people is to get in tune with yourself. Your body comes equipped with many systems to aid you in reading people. The one I'm referring to now is goosebumps. That's right goosebumps. Goosebumps are actually pretty impressive when you understand them. While typically thought to signal to be cold, goosebumps actually have a part in signalling many more things than that.

You have probably heard of having goosebumps being referred to as a goose walking over your grave, or maybe you've been told it means you're cold. While you do get goosebumps when you're cold, that is not their only and definitely not their primary purpose.

Have you ever experienced deja-vu? That feeling when you realize you've known someone before, yet you just met them? That connection seems as if you've known them forever. Similarly, there is an experience where you have lived through a situation before. Now you are living it and it's exactly like it was before, right down to the words being said. Have you ever noticed that during experiences of deja-vu you have goosebumps? This is not a coincidence.

Goosebumps are a very intuitive tool, and we need to learn to trust them if we're ever going to be really good at reading people. They are designed to alert us when we connect with someone on a deep internal level. Maybe we were moved or inspired by something they said. Perhaps it's more of a feeling connected to them.

Quite often people will refer to the nudging they get from their goosebumps as a tingle. So you could say they are the silent alarm system that gives us an intuitive tingle when we are experiencing either deja-vu or a connection with someone that we're unaware of. Being tuned in to our own bodies enough to recognize these tingles will allow us to act on the notifications as opposed to passing over them unaware.

Have you ever been in a conversation with someone and all the sudden you had this quick little "ah-ha" thought about the person you were talking to. Then just as quickly as it came you were on to the next thought and it was gone again. Well, those little flashes or "ah-ha" moments are critical insights, and if you're not paying attention to them, you'll miss them. These are your subconscious trying to reveal something to your conscious mind. The more we work at it, the stronger this link between subconscious and conscious can be strengthened.

Another thing you may have noticed, or maybe you haven't noticed it yet is experiencing physical symptoms intuitively. Have you ever been talking to someone, and all of a sudden your back hurts when it had felt perfectly fine a few minutes before. Or have you ever left an event that was pretty uneventful yet you felt depressed?

These can all be signs of intuitive empathy. This can be very useful sometimes, but not everybody engages empathy to this level. Another area to look at is our emotional energy. Some people say we have an aura around us that can be seen and depending on our energy the color will change. It is also believed that we have an energy around us that can be felt. This may be the same energy realized on different levels, or perhaps they are two separate and distinctive things.

The Chinese refer to this energy as Chi. Regardless of what you call this subtle energy, it is the reason some people make you feel more alive like you could do anything when you're around them. While others will make you feel like you're being dragged down. When you instinctively want to avoid someone or leave their presence as soon as possible, this is your subconscious mind reacting to the unseen energy. This is often referred to as giving off a vibe.

Reading peoples emotional energy doesn't need to be difficult. It can greatly increase your accuracy in reading someone. It's typically done subconsciously, but everybody we interact with will typically either entice us to get closer or repel us away making us want to get away from them. If their emotional energy is attractive, it will make us want to get closer to them because their emotional energy is attracting us.

Others will make us want to run away from them, and we may even feel like we're being pushed away from them. This is their emotional energy repelling us. It's what brings like people together. It could also be why opposites attract. The one who has less appealing energy may be attracted to the one who has positive energy because they make them feel better. Typically the one with the positive energy will be much more in tune to these things, and will feel the other persons negative energy but will want to help them.

The eyes are referred to as the window to the soul because they reveal so much about us. If you take time to notice peoples eyes, you will see that they will tell you if someone is guarded or hiding or if they're home, which will tell you if they're emotionally available for intimacy or not. Also even when people can learn to control their facial expressions, put on a mask so to speak, it is very difficult to conceal what is shown in our eyes.

Physical touch is a huge indicator of a person's emotional energy. The most common is the handshake. If a person is timid, or not wanting to commit their handshake will be limp. Where a confident person or one willing to commit will have a firm handshake. If someone has clammy hands it typically indicates that the person is anxious for one reason or another. An exceptionally firm handshake sometimes referred to as a bone-crushing handshake is not a sign of a more confident person, this is typically someone trying to intimidate the other person. Unless in the odd case it is someone who just doesn't realize their own strength.

A hug is the next most common form of physical touch that we use to evaluate somebody's emotional energy. When we hug somebody we tend to notice on a subconscious level if the hug feels warm and secure. If it does it will typically give a feeling of being safe, and draws us closer to the other person. On the other hand, if the hug makes us want to cut it short and put distance between us, it is typically referred to as being cold or closed off. It gives us the feeling of being shut out or abandoned.

The tone of someone's voice is another form of non-verbal communication. It can tell us much more about a person than the words they are saying. Some common feelings that can be relayed in the tone of someone's voice are a feeling of abrasiveness. This is like sandpaper, often referred to as they grate on you. Maybe you will get the feeling the person is whiny or snippy. You could even get a soothing feeling. It's not hard to imagine which of these energies will attract other people.

You can have some fun experimenting with this one if you like. Get a video recorder or use your cell phone and record yourself saying the same phrase, but alter your tone of voice each time and notice the difference. Does the meaning of what you're saying change with the different tones and inflections in your voice. You can also try changing the volume as well.

The reason behind these feelings we get when interacting with other people, especially when it comes to tone of voice, is that sound frequencies cause vibrations. These vibrations are picked up by our senses mostly on a subconscious level and then relayed to our conscious minds as a feeling. A big part of learning to analyze people is to tune in to

304

yourself. Learn to listen to your subconscious and how to recognize what it is telling you.

Chapter 7: Read the Situation and Ask the Right Question

I have stated earlier that when somebody's non-verbal signals make you think they may be lying that you should ask more questions to find evidence of your suspicion. That's all great but if we don't know how to ask the right questions we're still not going to get the information we are looking for.

So how do you know what to ask? Open-ended questions are a good place to start. This is why these are commonly used in surveys. The reason is that an open-ended question entices the respondent to answer in a thoughtful honest manner. If you ask leading questions, you may get the answer you're looking for, but it won't necessarily be an honest answer. It will most likely be the answer the respondent thought you were looking for.

If you look at any survey the one thing you will notice is they have the same types of questions. The importance is the phrasing of the question as much as the actual question itself. Some examples of questions you will find on surveys are What did you think of our service? How can we improve our service to you? What did you think of a certain product? How did you feel while using this product? What could we do to improve your experience of using this product? How could we improve your overall experience of using our service?

The list is endless of the questions you will find on surveys. The important part is how the questions are asked. What do you notice about the examples I gave you? How did they make you feel? Unless I'm mistaken they should have made you feel like your opinion was valuable. Perhaps even like you were providing a service or doing a favor in return.

I'm not sure if you noticed, but they all start with How or What. You may even remember some uses of these open-ended type of questions from your childhood. What were you thinking? How come you did that? Interesting isn't it. If you ask a question that is a yes or no question you aren't going to gain much information. However, if you ask open-ended questions such as any of the above you will hopefully get a much broader range of information.

An important part of asking the right question is to be purposeful. By that I mean to make sure that your question serves a purpose. Obviously the purpose is to gain information, but if you have a tendency to ask the same thing three or four different ways the only possible purpose of this would be confirmation of the answer. It runs the risk of annoying the person being questioned though. Perhaps that is your purpose.

If you think, for example, that your teenager lied to you about their whereabouts last night, you may want to make your questions about what they said happened or where they said they were. This will allow them the opportunity to give away the fact that they weren't actually there. If you have a good idea of where they actually were, you can ask a few questions about their story, and then sneak one in about what you believe actually happened without sounding accusatory.

A good rule of thumb for asking the right question is to keep it simple. The more complex you make your questions the more you reduce the likelihood that you will get honest answers. The person hearing the question is going to interpret it in a manner that may give it a different meaning than what you were asking for. Simplicity helps to reduce the chances of this.

If someone is unsure of what you are asking, they may ask for clarification or they may just push ahead with what they think you're asking. In the latter situation, they will be at least half focused on if they interpreted your question correctly. Do you see how that could lead to less informative answers?

There is a saying that the quality of the solutions you arrive at is directly influenced by the quality of the questions you ask. There is a lot of truth to this saying. Computer programmers refer to this as GIGO. Any idea what that stands for? It stands for Garbage in, Garbage out. In other words, if you put garbage in you are going to get garbage out. If you ask quality thought-provoking questions, you will get quality thought-inspired answers.

In this day and age, everybody must have at least heard of Google even if you haven't used it yourself. Did you know that Google is about more than just finding whatever information you're looking for. It's also about learning that if you don't ask the right question you don't get the right results. The more focused your query becomes the more relevant your results are. Try it out. Start with something vague and then keep getting more and more focused on the core request.

Have you heard of Socrates, the Greek philosopher? He developed a method of disciplined questioning that is aptly called Socratic questioning. It can be used for many purposes some of which include to get to the truth of things, to uncover assumptions, and to analyze concepts. All three of those are useful in learning to read people.

These Socratic principles were first used in a method called Socratic solitaire by Charlie Munger. You start by asking a series of questions, and then you answer those questions. You continue back and forth, and this will not only show the width and breadth of your mind but will increase the multidisciplinary aspects of your mind as well.

This is an awesome tool for self analyzation. The only thing that can impede you is if you get stuck in a series of wrong questions. You need to ask the right questions to get the information you're after. There is a limit to what you can learn from self-discovery, reading books and even searching Google. At some point, you need to add another human being.

You've probably heard that there's no such thing as a stupid question, and while that's a cute little saying, that's all it is. It's wrong. While the questions may not of themselves be stupid, if the person asking the question isn't going to learn anything from it being answered, then it's useless. That's pretty close to stupid in my opinion.

Let's look at some examples of these type of questions. The first type is the one that I refer to as sponge questions. People that ask sponge questions are lazy. They don't want to put in the effort to learn themselves. They want to know the answer, and soak it up and don't care how it was arrived at. They are intellectually dishonest.

Then there are the wrong questions. These are the ones that are based on incorrect assumptions. When not knowing comes from incorrect assumptions, it can be forgiven, but not so much when the asker is closed-minded regarding their incorrect assumptions. If the asker is not willing to entertain new ideas or the fact that their assumptions could be wrong, then answering their question also becomes useless.

Then you have the ugly questions. Yes, I said ugly questions. How can a question be ugly you might be thinking. Well, I'll tell you. When a question isn't really a question but a statement that has been disguised as a question. You might be wondering what I'm talking about. Let me be clearer.

What I mean is the person who is asking a question even though they don't have a question. They need to ask something to draw attention to the fact that they're there, and in the process are trying to impress others with how much they know. Not only are these a waste of time, but they are also only meant to make the asker feel better about themselves. They are intellectually bankrupt.

Any question that is precluded with "Don't you think..." is not a real question. You will not find a question starting this way that is not fueled by bias. This makes them dangerous no matter where they are voiced. These are some examples of bad questions.

Now that we know what bad questions look like, we know what kind of questions to avoid, and we can look at what good questions look like. A good question doesn't necessarily bring you to an answer. How can that be a good question, you're wondering. Easily, it can make you look more closely at your ideas and in the process defines a new question.

Another thing a good question does, is it highlights the fact that the person asking the question is actively participating in finding the solution. They are actively applying their intelligence to the task rather than passively waiting for someone else to provide the answer.

So how do you design a good question? It starts with humility. A good question doesn't presume to assume any entitlement to the solution. The attitude makes the question. Being aware, paying attention and willingly participating in finding the answer. These are the things that count.

These are the things that lead to the development of thought-provoking questions. The person asking the question becomes entitled to the answer because they're competent and have the right attitude.

Be willing to put time into the development of your question. And don't worry bad questions pave the way to good questions. If you spend time in self analyzation utilizing lots of bad questions, don't worry, with practice you will become adept at eliminating the bad ones and you will find the good questions.

What do you do if you don't understand the answer? Just like a farmer prepares the soil before planting, you need to prepare your mind before asking the question. If you sufficiently wrestle with the question prior to asking it, this prepares your mental soil to receive the answer and let it germinate. Socratic solitaire is a good exercise for this.

Don't be a sloppy thinker, write down your thoughts. This is the best way to organize your thoughts and decide what needs to be in the question, and what doesn't. It is important that your question be clear and well expressed. It doesn't need to be flawless but should be precise. It should show that you've put thought into it.

Good questions are where developing deeper understanding is founded. Good questions fuel thought. They exercise the mind. They also reveal issues that may otherwise not be uncovered. In short, a good question is one of the best gifts you can give.

Essential questions are what provokes us to focus on substantive and significant thoughts. Questions are what drive us to think, therefore the quality of our questions determines the quality of our thoughts. The quality of our thoughts directly influences the quality of life we experience.

When we apply our intellect through discipline to determine what lies at the center of an issue, our thinking becomes grounded, and we are able to ask the necessary questions to deal with the issues that are relevant to the current situation. There are many areas in life where it is necessary to ask the appropriate questions in order to be successful.

Asking the right question is rarely addressed in school, and a lot of people don't even pause to think about it. There are different categories of appropriate questions as well. Some are for academical issues, some for our thoughts. Our feelings and desires will have their own as well. Some will be analytical in nature while others will be evaluative.

I will try to outline the power that is contained in asking essential questions without sounding too scholarly. When the answer to a question creates another question in itself, though is driven forward as inquiry. If you have no questions originating in your mind, you are not participating in learning anything substantive.

If you look at any of the fields of study that exist such as biology, or physics even biochemistry, none of them would exist if the people who laid the foundation for them had not asked the basic questions that started them thinking in that direction. If no one ever wondered how chemical processes interact and if they change within living things, biochemistry wouldn't exist.

If you want to be skilled at thinking, you need to become skilled at questioning. An indispensable tool of the intellectual variety is the essential question. Achieving a state of mine that produces essential questions as second nature is an achievable and desirable goal.

Effective questions are powerful, open-ended and thought-provoking. They do not lead the person being questioned and they are not "why" questions. While there are situations that require the use of "why" questions, these are more suited to gaining information; however, they also carry the possibility of making people defensive. This makes it necessary to use them sparingly and carefully.

"What" and "How" questions tend to be effective questions, especially when combined with the patience to wait for the answer and not provide it. Effective questioning contains not only the ability to listen for the answer but also the ability to not judge while you're hearing the answer.

When we judge what the person we're talking to tells us, we place our opinions over what they are saying. This can effectively block us from learning new ideas. It also makes the person we're talking to feel like they're being judged which makes them close off and be less willing to communicate. When we suspend judgment they feel like they're being listened to and understood. You don't have to agree with someone to understand their position.

Chapter 8: How to Influence People with Your Body and Your Mind

Human beings are constantly telling those we meet about our status, who we are and how we feel. The way we carry ourselves naturally without conscious thought makes these things instinctively understandable to those that we meet. This can either have a positive or negative impact on how people see us and thus on how they interact with us.

When you choose to make those signals a conscious effort, you then have the power to decide how you come across to people. How they perceive you and how they will interact with you. This allows you to have better connections, communication, and influence over those you interact with.

If your body language portrays that you are confident, assertive and powerful other people will be more likely to be influenced by you. You need to balance this with body language that invites people to connect with you. Otherwise, they won't trust you and will be more apt to feel dominated than connected.

It is a fact that people listen to people they trust. If you learn to use your body language appropriately you will be able to become trustworthy. This will allow you to become more influential and persuasive.

While it sounds simple, a smile is one of the most powerful tools there are for connecting with people. When people see you smiling they will think of you as approachable, confident and warm. These are all characteristics that instill trust as well. If people like you they will be more willing to listen to what you have to say. A smile is the first step in building this trusting relationship.

This is why it is important to smile whenever you meet anyone. It needs to be a genuine smile though. Use your eyes as well as your mouth to smile. If you're having a bad day or are in a bad mood, thinking of happy occasions or someone you love can make it easier to form a true smile. If the person you are interacting with is in a bad mood, you may want to start by being sympathetic and understanding and work up to a smile. In this way, you may elevate them from their bad mood and strengthen your bond with them.

The rapport we have with other people has an enormous effect on how easy it will be to get them to listen to you. It also profoundly increases the chance of them supporting you. How do you build rapport with someone?

Rapport is built when you find something in common. The easiest way to find something in common with someone is to use your body. If you subtly copy their movements, they will feel a connection to you and won't even know why. If they cross their legs, do the same. If they rest a hand on the table, rest yours there too. When they start to copy the movements you are doing you are in a good position to be able to influence them.

So how do you get people to say yes to you? Obviously you have to make them want to say yes to you. An excellent way to do this is to get them nodding their head before even asking anything. When you nod at someone, they feel subconscious like they should nod back.

When they are talking start nodding slightly as if you agree with their statements. When it's your turn to talk nod slightly and watch them return the motion. Once someone is nodding their head, their inclination is to agree with you as long as your proposal is reasonable.

Height differential is a great way to gain the advantage. What I mean is if you stand up while the person you're talking to is sitting down, you automatically gain the upper hand. When you do this, they feel that you are more dominant and powerful. This will make their instinct to give in to you. As long as you don't lean in to close and make them feel bullied.

This also works when making phone calls even though the other person can't see you. It makes you feel more powerful and dominant and this will come through in your voice. This will make it easier for you to have those assertive conversations when you need to.

People love to be flattered. Flattery is a tricky art to pull off without sounding like you're sucking up. When you use your body to make them feel flattered it is less so. To show an interest in them simply tilt your head or body towards them. It is much more common for them to agree with you when they feel important and listened to. When they unconsciously mimic your leaning in, you have established a good rapport.

Don't overdo it when you lean in towards someone. If they move back you have definitely shown that you're in charge, but you could come off as intimidating or threatening. You want people to like you and not to be scared of you.

Your feet are a tool of great subconscious influence when used properly. If you point them at someone it indicates interest. This will help to build trust. Also if you are asking someone to make a choice, if you subtly point your feet in the direction of what you want them to choose, subconsciously they will be led to choose in that direction. They also work for getting someone to end a conversation without you having to say anything. If you point your feet and subtly angle your body toward the exit, they will subconsciously realize it's time to leave.

When you want to show someone you're in charge, standing in a pose similar to superman's with your hands on your hips and your feet wide apart will make you appear dominant. Not only will it make you appear dominant, but it will also make you feel dominant. This is due to the release of testosterone that this pose elicits.

Sometimes you need the feeling without the appearance, and you can accomplish this by assuming the pose for a few moments before meeting with the person. When you meet with the person you can assume a more welcoming open pose and still feel the effects of the testosterone.

I'm sure you've all heard of first impressions and how important they are. It's true they are. From the first time people meet you they are constantly analyzing you to see if you're someone, they should have dealings with. If you learn to control your body movements, you can learn to gain trust, stand out and win credibility every time you speak.

Struggling with how to get someone to like you. It's not as tricky as it seems. Ask them to do you a favor. As crazy as it sounds, if someone does you a favor, their subconscious will say that you must have been worthy of receiving whatever the favor was. Therefore they must like you. It has been proven that someone who has done a favor for you will be more likely to do another than someone that you have done a favor for.

Another technique that has proven successful is often referred to as the door in the face technique. Start off by asking someone for something much more than you actually want. Something ridiculous that they will refuse to do. After they refuse the request, return a little while later and ask for something reasonable. The thing you originally wanted. They will feel bad for having refused you the first time, and when you present them with a reasonable request they will feel compelled to grant your request.

Using a persons name or title depending on the situation can have very positive effects. You should know that this technique can seem very corny though. It has been proven that a person name is the best sound for them in any language. Their name is a core part of who they are. When you use their name, you give them validation. They then subconsciously are influenced to have a positive opinion of you, because you validated them. Similarly using someone's title, for example, if you want an acquaintance to be a friend, referring to them as such is a method of self-fulfilling prophecy. Or if you refer to someone as a boss who you want to work for. Their subconscious will tell them that's who they are in relation to you.

Flattery works well, and in contradiction to the saying flattery will get you nowhere, it will actually get you everywhere. It has been shown though that people have a habit of looking for cognitive balance.

What this means is that if you flatter someone of high self-esteem, they will probably look on you favorably because you have just reinforced how they feel about themselves. If you flatter someone with low self-esteem they may have a less positive reaction because what you're saying is in opposition to how they feel about themselves.

Mirroring someone's behaviour can have positive effects, not only for you but also for others not even involved in the situation. Researchers have discovered that if someone is mimicked, they tend to behave positively with the person that mimicked them. This is thought to be because they felt validated by the person mimicking them.

They discovered that not only do the people that were mimicked have positive interactions with the person that mimicked them, but with other people who had nothing to do with the situation. This is believed to be because the validation the person who was mimicked feels increases their self worth in their eyes, and the higher self-esteem will make them feel more confident and this will radiate positively to everybody around.

Another trick is to ask for a favor when someone is tired. Most often when the person is tired, they will put it off or may say I'll do it tomorrow. This is because not only are they physically tired, but their emotional energy level will be low. However the next day they will likely do it because people tend to keep their word.

Another technique that has proven successful is the opposite of the door in the face technique. In this case, you want to start out with something small, and preferably easily done. Studied in a marketing sense, it has been proven that once you get someone to commit to supporting something if you wait a couple of days to ask for another commitment, or for them to buy something, they tend to comply.

Another method of endearing someone to you is to not correct them when they're wrong. Instead of objecting and stating your opinion which tends to lead only to arguments, listen to them. When they're done point out the areas where you have common ground, and build from there. This will promote dialogue more than arguing, and they will be more inclined to listen when you present your point of view. This also allows them the option of being corrected without losing face.

When you're talking to someone a simple technique to endear yourself to them is to listen to what they are saying and then paraphrase it and repeat it back to them as a question. This will show that you understand them and that you listened to them. This will strengthen your friendship with them, and they will be inclined to listen to you when you are talking.

Pupil dilation is a subconscious way of showing interest. In studies, it has been shown that people with dilated pupils are seen as more attractive than those without. This is something primarily controlled subconsciously, but if you can learn to consciously control it, it gives you another tool to add to your arsenal to influence people with body language.

When you quickly raise your eyebrows typically seen when greeting someone familiar, often referred to as eyebrow flashing, it creates a cognitive reaction in the person you flashed. They wonder if they know you, or may subconsciously return the eyebrow flash establishing a connection even if there wasn't one previously.

Burst their bubble. By that, I mean their bubble of personal space. When someone intrudes in our personal space we are aroused. Depending on who it is how we deal with that arousal will be different. If it is a stranger entering our bubble, we typically tend to back away. If a loved one it is usually a much more positive response. This is why crowded elevators are arousing.

How long you maintain eye contact when you gaze at someone can show interest, unless it's a stranger, then it will be processed in connection with other signals from you and could be perceived as a threat. This is common in the wild as well as with people. If monkeys hold eye contact too long the receiving one will become agitated.

Touch can cause many different reactions. When it is a touch or a hug from somebody we are attracted to or a love interest, it causes the release of the love hormone, oxytocin, which produces feelings of sexual attraction and bonding. If it's from a stranger, it can have different effects. A study performed with waitresses in a restaurant resulted in the ones who touched their customer's arm when bringing their bill receiving higher tips than the non-touches.

A sigh will gain someone's attention. Think back to the last time a friend or loved one sighed when they were with you. What was your immediate reaction? Something along the lines of What's wrong? This is quite common as there are a number of reasons a person might sigh, and thus the sigh gains our attention and a desire to know what caused it.

It has been suggested that a shrug disarms people who are confronting someone. There is no research proving this, to my knowledge, but it has been suggested further that if you watch president Trump you will see this in action.

Chapter 9: Perfecting the Skill of Analyzing People Through the Practice

One of the best things you can do if you want to improve your ability to analyze people is to read more often. This doesn't mean the skimming through a book while your thoughts run in a million different directions, but rather to think about the plot, each of the characters and other options of what could happen.

This will stimulate your thinking. It also provides an excellent opportunity for you to check your logic skills. Furthermore, it will expand your imagination. These things will, in turn, increase your ability to analyze people.

If you don't have time to read or the inclination but spend significant amounts of time driving every day, whether commuting or driving for work or for whatever reason, find some thought-provoking podcasts to listen to. These can also stimulate your thinking.

Most of them will offer useful tips on how to stimulate your creativity and challenging ideas and thoughts. This all works together to increase your mental capacity which you've guessed it increases your ability to analyze people.

You may not believe this, but it has been shown that regular exercise of moderate intensity has been shown to be directly related to increased mental capacity. There are all different types of exercise that you can choose from, but if you choose something like tai chi that you have to learn and memorize moves as well as execute them fluidly, you may increase your mental capacity and your physical stamina as well.

Playing brain games is a great way to increase your mental capacity as well as your analytical skills. You can turn off the tv and play a game with your family and track your progress over time. Perhaps your family is not interested in playing brain games, but no worry, there are many brain games out there that you can play by yourself.

Expand your circle of acquaintances. There is nothing wrong with having a close group you generally associate with, but conversations will most likely follow similar paths. Socializing with people you don't normally interact with can offer you different ideas, perspectives, and stimulating conversation.

If you're not sure where to begin, you can begin by attending a networking gathering and interact with each person there. You may be surprised at how much interacting with new people will stimulate your thinking and get new ideas flowing.

Keeping a journal is a good way to improve your logical abilities as well. We tend to get caught up in things and it is easy to feel overwhelmed, but when you write things down it tends to remove the emotion from it and let you look at it in a logical way. It also makes it easier to look back on things and track your progress.

An essential yet often overlooked task is to learn something new every day. It's not relevant so much what you learn as the fact that you need to learn new things every day. It can be a new recipe you try or a new hobby you develop. Often once schooling is finished and the day to day of work takes over many people forget all about learning. Learning new things keeps your mind active and just like any muscle the more it's exercised the better shape it will be in.

If you do have time that you could devote to education, you might want to look at some online courses. The key is to pick something you have no experience in. After all, we want to learn new things not just improve on the skills we already have. There is a wide range of topics that are available in online courses now. It shouldn't be too hard to find something that you have no previous experience in.

If you're struggling in any area of your life, it is quite likely that you will be able to find an app to help you analyze your habits and pick out and correct any bad habits you have developed. The more well rounded you are as a person, the better able you will be to read someone else. Self-improvement is a commonly overlooked method of improving any skill. Balance is key to success, so to be successful at learning to read people, you need to read yourself and find balance.

I already mentioned previously that reading is a great way to improve your cognitive abilities, but there is a way to improve on even that. You could look at joining a book club. Some of the benefits that will provide, are that you will read books you otherwise probably wouldn't even look at.

Not only will you read those books you wouldn't normally look at, but you will have to analyze those books. Then when you discuss them with the other group members, you will gain different perspectives and challenge your thinking. Plus in the process, you'll most likely make some new friends with some common ground.

Get curious about something. Curiosity inspires our motivation, which in turn inspires our creativity and intelligence. Curiosity causes us to question ourselves and those questions encourage us to consider alternate methods and possible outlets. This causes us to compare what we previously knew, or thought we knew, with what we have learned. This leads to logical solutions. So when the curiosity bug bites you, embrace it and ask questions. After all the more you learn the better your analytical skills will become.

Practice being observant. It is all too common nowadays for people to be engaged in rushing around trying to get things done as quickly as they can and not focusing so much on how well they can get them done. Take the time to slow down and focus on the details. Pay attention to your surroundings and see what is going on around you.

Watching how somebody does something might spark an idea for you or give you insights as to how to solve an issue you were dealing with. A key element of improving your analytical skills is to challenge yourself to constantly learn more. If you're open while you do this, you will increase your ability to appreciate and comprehend different concepts. This will, in turn, assist in streamlining your process of finding solutions.

Math problems are an excellent way of improving your analytical skills. They are structured in such a way that you are provided information and then forced to use that information to find the solution. The more complicated math problems you solve, the more your logic and reasoning skills will develop. This, in turn, means the more your analytical ability will increase.

Some things you can do is identify math problems in everyday life, and then take the time to solve them. Or if you have the ability and access, you could enroll in a college level math course. Many of these courses will help you develop your analytical skills.

Some of you may be pleased to know that there are a number of video-games available now that help to improve analytical skills. The ones that focus on strategy and other games that require solving problems to achieve big goals.

Debate clubs are excellent ways of increasing your analytical abilities. Your point of view and theories will constantly be challenged by people who are also trying to improve their own analytical abilities. Your analytical skills will develop with participation in almost any social group providing it promotes seeking knowledge and exchanging of ideas.

There are a number of ways to improve your analytical ability, and these can be broken down into many more categories I'm sure, but one thing that can have a profound impact on your ability to analyze things, people or problems, is to expand your knowledge base. The more you have in your knowledge base, the more tools you will have to choose from when it comes to understanding and interpreting information. Also, there are many ways to increase your knowledge base.

When it is recommended to read lots, it does not mean pick a topic or genre that you enjoy and read lots about it. The best method of improving your knowledge base is to read lots over a wide range of genres or topics. Subscribe to informative magazines, attend lectures or other academical talks. You could consider going back to college or taking other educational classes in your community.

Learn to take the time to think about things. This applies to everything in your life, the more time you take to think about things before making decisions the more your analytical skills will improve. This doesn't mean to dawdle in making decisions, but the important part is to look at the situation from different perspectives and to visualize alternate scenarios.

Don't immediately choose the easiest solution, but think about it and consider all options and outcomes. Don't discard the easiest solution either though. It could prove to be the best one after all, but it is best to consider all options before making a decision.

An excellent example of this would be a chess game. Before you make a move figure out what your opponents most likely response will be. Then continue to think about all the other options of responses he or she could make. In this way not only will your chess game improve, but your analytical abilities will increase as well.

Expanding your world view is one of the best ways to improve your analytical abilities. While this may sound simple, it is not a quick fix and is not easily done. The results are fabulous though. Travel is a great way to expand your world view, but that is not always feasible in every situation.

Other ways to expand your world views is to set aside your religious, political and cultural beliefs about truth. Think of different ways of viewing the world. Different perspectives to look at it from.

Pick a position or idea you would normally dismiss immediately, and work to understand it. How would you defend this position to someone like you that would normally dismiss it without really even considering it?

You can also go out of your way to meet people and interact with people who are very different from yourself, this will help you to learn to accept and learn to understand ideas that are different from what you would normally associate yourself with.

Teach yourself to find the connections in things. Many things that we encounter on a daily basis are connected and those connections are most often overlooked. This can be exercised on a walk in the bush, what animals do you see? What connections do they have with other animals, seasons, pollution, the list is almost never-ending.

Learn to look at things in a cause and effect method. With your walk in the bush, and the animals you're seeing, what would happen to their water supply if there was a severe drought? Where would the repercussions of that stop, or would they?

Think also about the similarities between things. Are all living things the same? Do spiders require any of the same things as humans do to survive? Historical connections are another area to look at. What cycles, patterns, and trends do you notice? What about the difference before and after the war?

Paying attention to detail is extremely important. There is a saying that says the devil is in the details. If you don't know or don't understand the ins and outs of a problem, or all the details of something you're trying to find a solution for, you are a lot less likely to come up with a workable solution that will actually address the areas of concern.

Another way of honing your analytical and observational skills that is extremely helpful is to contemplate the natural order of things. Instead of just accepting that things are the way they are, try to figure out why they are that way. This will give you a new and improved understanding of the world, and you will be motivated to think about complex issues. Keep questioning instead of just accepting the easy answer. The easy answer will come quickly and many people stop there. Don't fall into this trap. Keep questioning until you get an answer that is more thorough and complete.

Conclusion

Once you've spent some time working on improving your analytical abilities, it is time to put those skills to work. This can be done by taking on more responsibilities. Whether it be at work or applying for a new more challenging job, or doing something on a volunteer basis. Taking on new responsibilities will allow you to make use of the skills you have honed, and allow you ways to keep improving them in the process.

In order for your analytical skills to have any benefit to you, they need to be used daily. A conscious effort to use them on small things every day will keep them sharp and ensure your performance is top notch.

Try to avoid taking the easiest simplest route to solve a problem. Instead of using a calculator, solve that math problem in your head, or on paper. Look for the harder way to solve things as opposed to taking the quick and easy way out. Invest the time, it will pay off in your skills.

Now that you're comfortable with your analytical skills, it's time to pay it forward and start helping others improve their skills. There are many ways to do this, from working with your kids, family or friends that may have educational or professional struggles. You could start a blog to share what you've learned, or perhaps someone at work could use a mentor.

Overthinking

Be yourself and fast improving self-esteem using success habits & meditation.
Build mental toughness, bet in slow thinking and declutter & unfu*k your mind from stress eating & drinking

Introduction

You are on the verge of learning fundamental functions of the mind that will eliminate the oppressive stress and anxiety of overthinking, overanalyzing, and ruminating or obsessing over moments of the past or future. Not only will you learn to overcome overthinking, but you'll also learn how to use significant tools, tips, and exercises that professionals use all the time with overanalyzes in therapeutic work and coaching.

You should know that you are not alone and there is nothing wrong with you if you find you often are stuck on negative thoughts and machinations. A great many individuals around the world also face the challenge of learning to untrained yourself from the negative thought patterns and behavior patterns you have developed over time.

As you move through the following chapters, you will become familiar with what overthinking is and why we do it, especially in the morning and at night. You will gain clarity on what positive thinking really is. You will see how positive and deliberate thinking can be used together to reduce the frequency and degree of overthinking. These processes will also help you to eliminate old negative thinking patterns and negative behaviors, and replace them with positive and beneficial patterns of thought and behavior.

As you learn to use these tools, you will be introduced to over a dozen techniques and exercises you can practice, to train your mind to think and act deliberately in your benefit. The practices of mindfulness, minimalism, and meditation play an important role in the techniques and exercises you will learn. With this information, you will gain understanding about the origins of these practices and how to apply them to your own goals.

By the time you are done with this book, you will have gained confidence and control over your own thought processes, and you will be prepared for what to do next to maintain positive momentum.

Chapter 1: Understanding

Overthinking

In a lesson to do with eliminating overthinking, it is a smart idea, to begin with understanding what overthinking really is. How do we do it? Why? There are benefits to analyzing a situation, and even for imagining a worst-case scenario, but go too far and you are creating a volatile and dangerous mix. Overthinking can be fatal.

In this chapter, you will become familiar with what causes overthinking, what defines overthinking, why we overthink at night and experience insomnia, and what the harsh results of overthinking can look like.

First, look at what being an over-thinker is like and if you might be an individual who overthinks, too. There are natural reasons that trigger you to overthink, but there are harmful learned behaviors that cause you to grind yourself down with worry and anxiety. Get a sense for whether or not you overthink, and why.

Determine If You Overthink
Imagine you are waking up in the morning. Maybe it's Wednesday. Maybe you did not get much sleep to begin with because your mind was racing with thoughts all night. Your eyes open. You recall what day this is, and what that means in terms of obligations. Then, suddenly, that trickling thought of today's obligations turns into a raging torrent of thoughts. Everything you were thinking about last night; additional

thoughts and worries, and soon it feels in your chest as if you might be drowning.

It is a paralyzing feeling. The lack of taking action compounds your feelings and now you experience guilt for not taking action. You feel doubt in the choices you might make. You become critical and even cruel to yourself. This vicious little whirlpool gains momentum as you put more thought, worry; energy toward it. It spins in one place moving fast but going nowhere except deeper into the waters. It is exhausting and even frightening, and you have not even risen from your bed yet.

As you go through the motions of your morning routine, your mind is somewhere else. In the shower, you move through step 1: wash step 2: rinse, step 3: repeat, but your mind is focusing acutely on what was said to you last night. What does it mean? What does it really mean? What you should have said in response. What might have happened if you said what you should have? What might have happened if you did not say anything at all?

Your mind is not acutely focused now. Perhaps you have washed with soap; used shampoo, but you have not enjoyed the smell of the soap. You have not enjoyed the hot water in your muscles. You have not appreciated the refreshing clean of your hair.

The same happens as you continue your morning routines, getting coffee or breakfast, but not observing it; not appreciating it, not even disliking it and desiring something else. This continues through the day. The momentum of overthinking every scenario fills your mind and dictates your actions. Alternatively, really, your lack of action. You therefore consistently find yourself in the past or the future mentally and emotionally, and never in the present moment of life.

Why?

In many cases, an individual may feel a fear of living in the moment. This is often because the individual has worked himself or herself into a thought-place where they feel an overwhelming obligation to make sure the "now" goes perfectly. The individual may feel a fear of, essentially, messing up life or doing it wrong.

The individual has learned through one experience or another (or maybe several) that there is a great negative consequence if the moment does not go according to plan. A parent, a teacher, a sibling or a friend may have taught this lesson; even oneself. An important and memorable moment did not go according to plan, causing a feeling of loss, negativity, or discomfort for the individual and likely others around them. The individual remembers this event, and with it, the negative feelings associated. The next time a similarly important situation arises, the individual (either consciously or subconsciously) refers to the previous experience for help. The weight of making the right decisions is coupled with the negative feelings of the time it went wrong, and this is when the individual begins to overthink.

What initially starts as a thought process to help the individual safeguard against a situation going wrong, eventually deteriorates into a compulsive thought-behavior that is no longer serving or helping. In fact, it is very likely harmful or debilitating. Thoughts of doubt and second-guessing begin to occupy the individual. In an attempt to control and safeguard the situation as much as possible, the individual analyzes, then super-analyzes, every angle and direction.

Examining a situation to make the best decision is a beneficial thing- it has kept us alive, but here is the critical difference. An individual who analyzes a situation and then takes an action based on that critical thinking is practicing a healthy process. An individual who analyzes a situation but stays spinning in analyzation without taking action is not practicing a healthy process. In a sense, the individual has been rendered paralyzed by their indecision. The indecision is a result of staying stuck in the overthinking pattern. Does this sound like you?

Causes of Overthinking
It is important to understand at this point, that the subconscious mind works diligently to construct an internal map of reality. When something crosses our path, the mind analyzes the conditions and makes determinations; is this safe, is this beneficial, and so forth. The mind records this bit of data onto the internal map of reality. Then, the next time a similar assessment need be made, the mind reviews the data on the internal map of reality in order to make a faster, safer, more beneficial decision now. Our minds are collecting and recording data for our individual internal maps of reality all the time. For example, let us say you are getting a loan for a new car. You skim the contracts and agreements for the loan and the vehicle and sign all the documents. Months later, you realize you have been paying, and will continue to pay, additional fees you did not anticipate because you only skimmed the agreements. Your mind records data about this experience and plants it on your internal map of reality. The next time you are signing for a loan, chances are your mind will quickly recall this experience on the map and you will not make the same mistake again. Instead, you will be safe and read everything thoroughly. In this case, the subconscious mind and your internal map of reality have served you well and protected you. That too is now recorded on your map, reinforcing what you know about reading contracts carefully. The more this situation occurs, the stronger the reinforcement becomes. This becomes your internal map; what you know and believe about your reality.

We can simplify this further with another example. Most of us have never experienced non-gravity. In fact, every day we have been alive, we have experienced and observed gravity; its effect on us and the world around us. The idea that we will experience gravity's effects has been practiced for us, greatly. Each of us has a very prominent marking for gravity on our maps. The idea that we would be able to move through our day without gravity seems preposterous. The map tells us that is not going to happen.

However, here is the crazy thing: we are reacting to, and living by, the information on our maps, and not by the actual real world. Most of us have not gone through our day with zero gravity, yet some of us have. Some of us are dedicated members of various space programs and astronautics. These individuals have really experienced enough non-gravity in their days to have a much different mark on their maps about gravity. Our map says, no you cannot experience non-gravity. However, in truth, it is that you do not experience it, not that you cannot.

The mental map of reality is a mental function we have adapted over hundreds of thousands of years as a means of survival. Think of one of our Neanderthal ancestors. He is catching fish in a stream and a panther approaches. Our ancestor is unsure of this creature and suddenly experiences a great deal of danger, fear, and stress, but luckily comes away mostly unharmed. This experience is marked on his mental map. The next time our ancestor spots a creature like that, he can make the decision faster to move to safety, knowing what he now knows. I hope that this mark on his map keeps him alive longer because he knows the dangers of the situation.

However, millennia later, in the midst of the Roman Empire, another of our ancestors challenges his map. Even with everything, he has ever observed or experienced about the dangers of giant wild cats, he declares, "I think I can take this creature." The map is challenged; the belief on the map is challenged. Lion tamers are born into the world and have continued for centuries. The internal map of reality for a lion tamer has a little bit different a mark than perhaps the average person. A first-time encounter with a wild animal does not generally make us think we can take it. Our map is much more heavily marked with the survival etch. However, we do know that some people are able to dominate a wild animal to drive it away, and we know some people make careers of taming wild animals. Therefore, that possibility is more real on our map than say, zero gravity.

Our observations and our experiences change our maps. Most importantly, it is challenging our individual map; challenging the belief on the map that expands our map. The mind naturally wants to expand the map and gather as much information as possible. You can give your mind the healthy activity it wants, by replacing habits of overthinking with positive and deliberate thinking.

So what caused you to develop this unhealthy thought process? What causes us to overthink and overanalyze the data on our maps?

There was a time when you did not feel this way, even if it was as a child. Try to recall a moment when you were thought-free and just enjoying the moment. A concert, a nap, a walk through a spring garden, watching animals or children at play, reading, watching a favorite movie, driving with the music up loud, spending time by the water, spending time with someone; just living in the moment. Free from critical and analytical thought. Your senses focused acutely on the present experience; the smell of the air, the perfection of the scenery, the pleasure of the company, the wind in your hair. You are capable of being worry-free and in the moment. You just need more practice.

You have been practicing a particular pattern of negative thought for so long, that you are well versed at performing it. It may have served you once, but it no longer does. In fact, that well-practiced path is likely harming you in ways you may not even realize, both emotionally and physiologically.

As responsibilities begin to build on us, and we are weighed down with financial stress, family worries, and emotional trauma, our mind develops the habit of analyzing the situation for the best possible outcomes and worst-case scenarios. These are practically infinite and as the imagination entertains each new river of possibility, tributaries; subtopics, side-questions arise, and more of those. The mind, in a way, can become addicted to following these little story-scenarios. In fact, following them so much, that it keeps the individual from making a decision or moving forward. The lack of decision-making and general activity now allows time for the mind to again follow dangerously hypnotic tributaries. Why is it some of us don't get distracted by the tributaries?

We have practiced thoughts repeatedly that reflect self-doubt, worry and anxiety, self-critical beliefs, and a lack of self-confidence. We panic and freeze because of a fear that we are going to do something wrong, make the wrong choice, or say the wrong thing. The fear of this causes us to again follow the negative tributaries. The fantasy scenarios we concoct keep us repeating the story in our mind. This practiced thought we keep thinking becomes a belief, and soon, the mind believes the story that we will fail, more than the story of us winning, simply because the fear of it kept us repeating the dreadful fantasy repeatedly. It is not uncommon for those who overthink, to develop a fear of the now moment and doing it wrong, so rather than confront the now moment, they hide from it in their minds and busy themselves with overanalyzing, under the guise of taking action. The choice to retreat to one's inner mind rather than face the circumstance is the comfortable choice because it is the well-practiced choice. Rather than risk the consequence and reward of the situation, the over-thinker creates a pseudo-moment in the mind; many of them, as a distraction from making an ultimate decision or taking decisive action.

As overthinkers, we have essentially trained ourselves to think this way and to believe this way. These are the well-tread paths on our maps. However, if the internal map of reality can be expanded and changed, it is true that our thought-patterns and behaviors are also adjustable. If we have trained ourselves to think this way, we can untrain it, too. Our self-doubt grows, as we remain stagnant. It requires progress in some direction -any direction- to grow and gain positive and healthy momentum.

Defining Overthinking

In order to understand how we can correct the thought-behavior pattern that is no longer serving us as it is, let us take a closer look at what overthinking entail. You will generally find that the description of overthinking is to think about something too much or for too long; to worry and ruminate over a person, event, or thing. What is "too long"? When you come to the point that you know a decision must be made but you delay and dwell in worry or rumination instead.

The two major expressions of overthinking are worry and rumination. When you worry, you are obsessing over the outcome of a future event. When you ruminate, you obsess over the outcome of a past event.

This is you, driving in your car, thinking in your shower, lying awake in bed, thinking about what you might have said...what would have been the perfect response...what would have been the perfect last word...the perfect decision. What might have happened if you did it this way? The other way? Unable to let go of the past event and move on. Again, the avoidance of moving on by focusing on the past may manifest because of a fear of making another perceived "wrong decision" and suffering the perceived consequences of it, in the now. Alternatively, if you are obsessing over a future event, you are still avoiding the responsibility of the now moment, and the required decision that can only come from you.

There are common thought-patterns and behaviors that are often shared amongst over thinkers. Do any of these examples sound like patterns you practice?

- Reliving high-pressure, or embarrassing moments
- Asking a great deal of "What If" questions to yourself

- Spending a great deal of time considering the hidden meaning in words, posts, text messages, responses, email
- Rehashing conversations
- Reliving mistakes
- Losing track of surroundings because your mind is elsewhere
- Spending a great deal of time thinking about circumstances you cannot control
- Trying to not think of the thing makes you think of the thing more

In a clinical sense, the disorder of overthinking is noted by the extreme stress, anxiety, and fear of making a decision. Again, this is essentially a fear of making the wrong decision. Making no decision at all may have, at one time, been the better solution for you; it allowed you to avoid the consequence. However, you have likely come to a point now, when opting to make no decision is more detrimental and frightening than making the wrong choice. You realize you cannot continue with this pattern and achieve the goals and desires you harbor.

Though anxiety, fear, and doubt are often the side effects of overthinking, they can also be the cause of it. It is common for individuals with anxiety disorders and acute fears to resort to overthinking in an attempt to protect oneself. Of course, as we see, this behavior does not serve the individual but actually cuts him or her off from further progress.

Overthinkers seeking to overcome these negative thought behaviors eventually, confront the idea of control, and of controlling one's environment and circumstances. The over-thinker wants as much control as possible over the scenario to ensure nothing goes wrong, but therein lies the problem, and perhaps the solution. We each, ultimately, have little to no control over the circumstances that arise, but we have full control over the ways we react to and manage them. Dealing with the idea of control, and thus the lack of control, allows us to face this realization and move us closer to the idea of letting go of control over a situation. Instead, we learn to trust ourselves to make smart and lucrative decisions for ourselves. Instead, we develop confidence in the moves we make, regardless of the result.

An over-thinker may perplex themselves with the idea that infinite scenarios could play out about this one thing. While in a sense this is true, in a grander sense, there are only one of two results that can happen, and both are beneficial. You will either win and the scenario plays out in the best possible way, or you lose and you still gain a great deal of knowledge and experience for next time. Therefore, it is still a win, though perhaps not the win you had in mind. However, perhaps, the one you needed. Essentially, you cannot make the wrong choice. Unless you stay still.

Overthinking at Night

One of the most common problems, and side effects, for overthinkers, is insomnia or the inability to get a restful sleep. For the overly critical mind, the best time to practice indecision seems to come when the individual craves rest. The mind, experiencing (conscious or subconscious) guilt, believes it should be using the time for rest to work out dilemmas instead. If there is time to sleep, there is time to work out a problem. Except rarely is it worked out.

Instead, the individual ruminates or obsesses on it, and in the meantime, suffers the side effects of sleeplessness on top of overthinking. If the individual felt a lack of confidence in making a decision before, a lack of sleep will only compound issues like second-guessing and self-doubt. The perceived consequence for "messing up" a decision will be exaggerated and seem more dramatic. Without sleep, the individual loses grip on overthinking. Negative thoughts and worries that would have been more easily dismissed wrack the brain. Meanwhile, the clock keeps ticking away, approaching the alarm to wake you from the rest you did not receive.

Think of the most recent time you have been lying in bed, thirsty for sleep, but unable to stop your mind. Instead, it follows all the little tributaries that lure you into insomnia with obsessive, ruminating thoughts.

You want to sleep but there are so many angles and possibilities to examine and practice repeatedly in your mind. There are so many worries and traumas to think about. These thoughts and scenarios keep you awake well into the morning so that even if you are able to catch a brief amount of sleep, it is nominal and unrefreshing. When your alarm goes off, your thoughts begin to spin with the obsessions and worries, and ruminations of the problems that existed yesterday and the day before.

However, there are methods and techniques that you can learn and practice that will help you to resolve the negative behavior of overthinking at night, and the negative pattern of sleep deprivation.

Often, when an individual suffers from overthinking when trying to sleep, they also suffer the same or similar fate upon waking. It is as if a train of worries has been rushing through your mind keeping you awake all night. Alternatively, if you do fall asleep, when you wake, that train is right there roaring through. It can feel like the train never stops; as if you have no control over its momentum. Worries and fears race through you when you try to sleep and they are still racing when you try to wake. Even the moments of life that are supposed to deliver relief, like sleep, are exhausting and unsatisfying.

As you move through these chapters, you will learn several techniques and exercises that work particularly well for overthinkers at night. These practices will encourage you to recognize and acknowledge the unwanted thoughts that come into focus but to dismiss them promptly and without giving them your full attention. There are several ways you can do this including through sorting and assigning ideas and utilizing positive distraction, which gives you are analytical, mind something more productive to focus upon.

At night and in the morning can seem the time your negative thoughts and worries flood in the fastest and with the most pain and fear. For this reason, engaging in a nightly practice that deliberately slows the thought process and prompts you to put worrisome scenarios into proper perspective. By putting negative worries and doubts into perspective, and by engaging your critical, analytical mind with tasks for distraction, the body is able to achieve rest.

Overthinking at night can be a persistent and debilitating pattern, but by learning and practicing the techniques and exercises herein, you will be able to manage anxiety throughout the day, before bed, and when you wake.

Results of Overthinking
The damage done by overthinking is deep and harsh. In both a figurative and literal way, the act of overthinking to brace for impact is similar to bracing for impact in a vehicle accident. Bracing oneself for impact is a natural response, but it often does far more damage. There are plenty of examples about injuries from accidents that be worse with bracing, and better without. When we overthink to brace for impact, it is similar; it is more dangerous and more damage is done.

Overthinking can actually kill you. Though it is not overthinking that is directly responsible for the death, the results of overthinking can and do often lead to death. In fact, stress is arguably the most pervasive killer among us today, surpassing any other illness.

If overthinking has not been fatal for you yet, dwelling on perceived shortcomings, inadequacies, and mistakes increase the chance of developing various mental, emotional, and even physical disorders:

- Anxiety
- Depression

- Insomnia
- Paralysis, mental or physical
- Headaches
- Stiff joints and muscles
- Fatigue
- Inability to stay present at the moment

These are only a few of the illnesses that overthinking can bring you. Overthinking is often linked with other disorders like PTSD, bipolar disorder, dissociative disorder, and many others. The aspects of one irritate the other and the disorders go back and forth, compounding the stress, anxiety, and fear the individual experiences.

If we cast our glance just a bit further, we can see that the results of overthinking truly reach everywhere. This kind of stress and pressure will clearly do damage to your emotional and mental self. We have even seen that it can be responsible for physical health. However, just how far does it reach?

Overthinking can ruin your personal life. It is not hard to imagine that the individual with an overthinking habit can become worse with time. If the negative patterns are allowed to continue, imagine what they could infect. Friendships and romantic interests all may suffer due to the over thinker's tendency to worry, ruminate and criticize. As the negative thinking patterns take over, it becomes more and more challenging for the over thinker to enjoy the company of others, or the splendid events and opportunities available.

The same can happen with a career. Overthinking can paralyze the leaders of a business, and then, inevitably, the business itself. Decisions become too hard to make, or too risky. When risks are taken, it is with a lack of confidence and finesse. Others lose confidence in the authority and value the business once delivered. It does not take much to collapse a business empire. A few little negative words.

If overthinking has overtaken your personal life and your career, it is a safe bet that these negative habits have infected your fun time, too. Why even schedule a vacation anymore if every little thing is bound to go wrong? Why try if you know you will fail? Why dance if you know you will look silly? Soon, worries have driven out the opportunity for enjoyment in any form.

These results do not need to be yours. Continue reading for a thorough breakdown of overcoming overthinking with a new set of efficient and effective tools for success.

Overcoming Overthinking

Your priority is no longer to follow any thought wherever it wants to take you. This will only continue to lead you down the tributaries of yesterday and tomorrow and leave you with negative emotions.

When these unwanted thoughts rise up and demand your attention, your priority is now to acknowledge it and dismiss it. Acknowledge it and dismiss it. Acknowledge it and dismiss it. This is one of your most important new positive thought patterns.

It does not mean the idea has to stay gone forever. At some point, it will feel good or productive to think about that thought again perhaps. You can work with it then. For now, it does not need to be given your attention.

There are exercises throughout this book that will help you to acknowledge the unwanted thoughts when they creep in, to dismiss the unwanted thoughts when it's not convenient for you, and to bring them back into focus when it feels good to do so.

The mind may, naturally or artificially, manufacture another negative idea or story for you to focus on and chase. A naturally occurring thought might stem from an immediate need, such as safety or shelter. Whether it is natural or artificial, it matters little because you will be equipped to handle it. If an idea comes, to you that is unwanted, you can determine whether it needs your immediate attention or not; chances are it does not. In all the cases it does not, you will now be equipped to acknowledge them properly and dismiss them promptly, in order to make room for positive thought patterns that benefit you.

Overthinkers have a tendency to focus on only the negative details of a situation and filter out the other pieces of information. It is a magnification of all that is wrong and a dismissal of all that might be right. Overthinkers often, look at a scenario as black or white; right or wrong, one or the other. There is no middle ground or grey area. This is an unrealistic view of the world. There is white, black, and a wealth of options in between.

If these traits sound like your own, you may also be the type of thinker that makes an overgeneralized and sweeping statement based on one shred of evidence. An example of this is when you might text your friend, but he or she does not text back. Your mindsets to ruminating on why and negative little tributaries tell you it is because your friend is mad at you. Soon you are sure your friend hates you and is never going to respond to you again. This is a sign of jumping to conclusions and exaggerating and expecting disaster.

However, these thoughts are distorted. The overly analytical mind (deliberately or in deliberately) convinces the subconscious mind that the story is true and you begin to act in accordance with this idea. These inaccurate thoughts and ruminations reinforce negative thoughts and emotions and only cause us to keep repeating the story and living it.

How can you beat your mind at its own game?

It will not be magic. Overcoming the negative pattern of overthinking will take your desire. If you do not really want to change, you really will not. However, if you are tired of your negative thought patterns and your negative behaviors, you can change with thought modification, positive thinking, and deliberate thinking. If you are willing to dedicate your effort, especially at the moment, and if you are willing to dedicate a little time, these issues can be reduced and eliminated.

In addition, it will feel like magic. The freedom, self-confidence, and creativity that you will experience because of getting control over your thoughts and emotions will be incomparable. Personally, your self-worth will soar. Mentally, you will experience clarity and relief from frustration and stress. Emotionally you will feel less frequent unwanted emotions of doubt and sadness.

You cannot always choose the circumstances that happen to you, but you can always choose the way you react to them. So will this information work for you and teach you to stop overthinking and negative behavior? The answer is yes, and no. In addition, how you react to that is your choice. If you make it through these chapters having learned a great deal that works for you and your process, you will have won; you will have learned to stop overthinking. If you make it through this book and you find you have absorbed nothing of value, you have still learned that these methods and practices are not the ones that resonate with you right now and that is okay. In fact, it is excellent to know that, so that it might help you to find the techniques that do help you. Your reaction, and thus, your reality, are ultimately your choice.

In the following sections, you will begin to learn how to sort and organize the negative thought and behavior patterns that are no longer working for you. Soon, you will be ready to make clear and confident, practical, choices regularly and without overthinking.

Chapter 2: Understanding Positive and

Deliberate Thinking

In order for us to overcome the habits of overthinking, it is important that we first understand two of our biggest allies on this front: the power of positive thought and the power of deliberate thought. Both of these concepts play a very large part in the successful replacement of negative thoughts with thoughts that serve and benefit you. By understanding what positive and deliberate thinking is, and how your mind and body reacts to them, you are able to use these tools to slow the negative momentum you currently have and build momentum in a desirable direction instead.

Positive Thinking
It can represent different things to different people, but the best way to understand positive thinking is to think of it as an attitude. The individual who uses positive thinking carries this attitude and conducts their thoughts and actions according to it. It is the individual's goal to feel good as often as possible, and he or she uses any tool possible to accomplish it. This often means that when circumstances seem undesirable, it is the positive thinker who finds the positive aspect, but not because they are deluded about the truth. Simply because the priority to feel good is higher. The individual seeks to make the experience as pleasant as possible.

It is often the case that positive thinkers once were over thinkers. It is not uncommon for a healthy mind to think critically and practically, and to analyze circumstances and scenarios. However, sometimes that healthy critical-thinking turns to rumination or worry and the individual breaks off into a tangent about anything. The mind and body have learned the habit of analyzing every situation, no matter how significant, and even to over-analyze it. The mind and body have learned from previous experiences that analyzing, planning, and preparing creates the safest circumstances for you when there is a negative impact.

To guard against damage from negative impact, the mind and body continue to follow the pattern it has been taught; to overthink. However, at some point, the thought-pattern; the behavior, fails as a guard against the impacts of life and instead, only damage has been done to the individual through worry and obsession.

The individuals started as critical, analytical, thinkers and they continue to be. Many of these over thinkers recognize that they cannot continue to repeat the same thoughts and habits and achieve different results. For different results, there must be different thoughts and actions. Even one of the most widely referenced scientists of our time, Albert Einstein, reminds us that scientifically, we cannot repeat the same actions and get different results. Scientifically, philosophically, this is the case. Rather than fight this law, the critical thinker applies it, and changes from the old, negative thought patterns to the positive replacement thoughts that feel good to focus on and spin tangents around. By doing this, the critical thinker does not struggle with the mind's tendency to wander. Essentially meaning if you want to spin tangents and daydreams, spin them around ideas that feel good to think about.

Positive thinking is not just the practice of good-feeling thoughts and ideas; it is also very much the observation and recognition of the thought-patterns and behaviors you currently repeat now. It takes bravery to be a positive thinker; you cannot fudge the truth and lie to yourself so easily. You have to be brave enough to see yourself where you are in an objective way. When you can make this observation with an objective lens, it becomes much easier to excel at making these positive changes to your patterns of thought and behavior.

There is not just one way to practice positive thinking. There are many different ways to apply this practice to your life. You need not master them all; just find a few you like, that really feels good for you and use those. Add a new technique here and there for fun.

Without the practice of positive thinking, it can become a tricky pursuit to stop negative thoughts and behaviors. Often what will happen without a positive pattern to replace a negative one is that one negative habit will be replaced with another negative and harmful behavior? For example, if an individual practices binge smoking to cope with anxiety, and he or she stops smoking, this might be replaced with binge-eating, or another negative behavior or thought-obsession where the smoking once was. This occurs because we tend to learn more negative coping skills than positive ones.

When you first begin positive thinking, it can feel as if you have no momentum going in that direction. That is okay. This path may not have been used much and it will take some treading to gain momentum. That is okay. The more you hone it, the more effortless it becomes.

Recognize Negative Thinking
One of the first steps in making a change to add more positive thinking to your routine is to recognize negative thinking when and where it happens. There are often times we can be harder on ourselves than others are and in some cases, this can be caused by purely physiological reasons and have little to do with our emotions.

Consider times when you are exhausted from physical exertion or a time when you are sick with a cold or flu or even allergies. The physical stress that the body experiences while it tries to repair itself can cause you to focus on the other topics in your periphery that echo those feelings of exhaustion or sickness. This focus on the negative begets more negative thoughts and very often this can come in the form of self-criticism, especially if you're lying in bed sick with nothing much to do but ruminate in your own head and stew in your own thoughts. Ask yourself: is the stew full of nutrients or toxins.

The same can happen if you are experiencing trouble sleeping or if you have not eaten well or at all. The phrase "hangry" is a recent representation of this occurrence made known by Snickers ads. Hangry, of course, is a combination word made from "hungry" and "angry" and meaning that if one does not eat; he or she will become moody and angry with others until sustenance has been eaten. In the same way, that being overtired or hungry can make you angry, it can also play a role in how much negative thought and behavior you resort to, out of habit and as a coping mechanism.

Though some negative thinking comes because of physical sickness and exhaustion, much negative thinking is the result of the mental and emotional stress of some kind. This stress could be expressed as any number of mental or emotional disorders such as PTSD or clinical depression. In some cases, there is actually a physiological response triggering in the individual that may put them into a period of deeper anxiety or depression, and for this reason, it could be said that is yet another physical cause of negative thinking, though the physical mechanism occurs in the nervous system. During these periods, an individual may practice heightened self-criticism and negative thought.

Similar circumstances arise when an individual is put into a situation of high stress or pressure, or when there is a high level of obligation or expectation from the individual. These circumstances can easily trigger an individual to think and act in a more negative and self-critical way. The body and mind react this way out of habit to plan and protect the individual. Nevertheless, as we have seen, this negative behavior is mistaken for a healthy beneficial process simply because the mind thinks it helps to guard against impact from the world.

Regardless of what triggers the individual for negative thinking, like attracts like and soon the individual is drowning in only thoughts that represent negativity, doubt, and worry. It works very much like a train on the tracks. Let us say your train is pulling out of the station. It is heading in one direction and slowly picks up speed. Slow at first and the wheels start pumping, but soon the train is headed in one direction with great momentum. Thinking gains momentum in the same way. When you start to build momentum in the direction of negative thoughts and ideas, the more you repeat and dwell in those negative ideas, the faster your momentum builds in that direction. But good news: positive thinking can build the same powerful momentum.

When the train is moving in one direction with great momentum that is a bad time to step in front of it or pull the emergency brake. Braking fast and bringing the train to a full and sudden stop is going to be harsh on the train and its contents. It is going to send cargo flying and jostling about. It is ill-advised. So what do you do instead of stopping that negative train on a dime? Gently, slowly, ease up on the momentum. Bring the train to a slow roll. Eventually, to a gentle stop. When you are ready, you can let your train rest in neutral for as long as it feels good to be there. Finally, when it feels right, you can point the train in a new direction and slowly pull away, gaining steady momentum, naturally, safely, and comfortably.

To accomplish this with the momentum of thought, you must first recognize the direction you are going and do not chastise yourself for it. In fact, you should congratulate yourself for being brave enough to take an objective look at your own thought patterns. Once you recognize the train is headed in a direction that feels less than good and looks less than productive, you can practice thought exercises that will slow the momentum on the negative thoughts by getting general and going neutral.

Slowing Down a Fast-Moving Train

Let us look at an example of how it is possible to slow down a thought-train headed in the wrong direction with strong momentum.

This will give us a better overall understanding of how positive thinking works and how we can use it to benefit our own healthy development. We will take the example of an average individual waiting for a job offer they have been hoping for. In a moment of doubt, the individual gives attention to the following idea:

- I won't get this job

The subconscious mind begins to imagine what that will be like. It spins a little tangent about the moment the individual finds out he or she didn't get the job...how much time and effort it will be to keep looking for another job...what it feels like to be defeated again. The train has left the station and it is heading in a negative direction. Soon, other thoughts join that first one:

- *I won't get this job*
- My interview could have gone better
- Other applicants are better than me
- I never get the jobs I want
- I should have tried harder
- I should have dressed differently
- I should have answered differently
- I always sabotage myself

In less than 60 seconds of thought, the momentum has built steadily in the negative direction. As these thoughts continue to gain momentum in the wrong direction, the subconscious mind is listening and believing the story, it is being told. The subconscious mind believes the story so much that it starts to generate emotions based on that story. The individual begins to feel sad, cheated, doubtful and used.

Now that the subconscious mind believes the story, it shares this information with other parts of the mind that control what the body is physically feeling. As these negative ideas and stories are repeated to the subconscious mind, the body begins to act in accordance with these stories, too. If the individual repeats thoughts and stories that reiterate feelings of exhaustion, anxiety, and fear, the body physiologically begins to experience these symptoms. The individual may begin to feel fatigued in the body. Muscles and joints may become stiff and sore or tight where stress is held in the body. Feelings of anxiety can cause the body to start feeling panicked, even leading to an actual panic attack just from thinking negative thoughts.

With all this momentum behind the train, how is the individual supposed to stop it safely? The idea is to take the first offending statement and make it more neutral and less negative, but still something the individual actually believes. That is to say, it is rather impossible for the individual to lie to him or herself. The individual cannot just change the sentence from, *"I won't get this job"*; to *"I know I've got the job!"* Chances are the individual will not readily believe they will have the job, so the positive phrase is only more of an antagonizer and sarcastic reminder of *not* getting the job. Instead of antagonizing oneself, the individual can practice a less specific, more neutral, but still believable statement.

The individual may change the thought: *I will not get this job*

To the thought: *I do not know if I am going to get this job*

Already, there is less stress and pain in the statement. It is true, the individual does not yet know whether they were chosen for the job, so logically, this statement is sound; it is believable. It is also not as negative and hurtful; it is not so final.

Now the individual may go forward from that statement and propose another general, neutral, better-feeling idea. Alternatively, the momentum of the negative train might be so strong that the individual is pulled back in that direction. That too is okay. When it happens, the individual can simply acknowledge it has happened, and get general and neutral again.

Let us see some more examples of how the individual can use this positive thinking tactically to slow down negative thoughts and bring the train into neutral:

- I won't get this job → I don't know if I'm going to get this job
- My interview could have gone better → Some parts of that interview went really well
- Other applicants are better than me → I have the experience and the desire for this job
- I never get the jobs I want → I've really liked a couple of the jobs I've had
- I should've tried harder → I did what I could do and that's enough
- I should've dressed differently → I dressed respectfully and professionally
- I should've answered differently → That one answer I gave was a big hit
- I always sabotage myself → If I get the job good and if not, good

343

The adjusted thoughts are still true for the individual, but they also feel better to think and they do not give the negative thought-train more power to sustain its momentum. When the individual replaces negative thoughts with those that feel less resistant; less stressful, less painful, the momentum of the negative train slows down. It is as if the individual stops shoveling coal into that train's fire. It has not given the fuel it needs to run, so the train begins to slow down. If you continue to practice positive and deliberate thinking, then the momentum of this negative thought-train will eventually roll to a neutral. A thought-train can be brought to a neutral place by practicing the shifting of ideas from non-serving, to serving; from negative to neutral (or positive). Watch our same trigger phrase move up the scale, from feeling bad to feeling good for the individual to think about and repeat.

- I will not get this job.
- I never get the jobs I want.
- I do not know if I will get this job.
- At least once or twice, I have landed the job I wanted.
- It is possible I could get this job.
- I would not have made it to the interview round if I were not qualified.
- I would be very good at this job.
- I can see myself at this job.
- I can see myself liking this job.
- I have many ideas to bring to this job.
- I have the experience or the drive for this job.
- It is a good thing if I get this job.
- It is a good thing if I do not get this job because the perfect job is coming.
- Even if I do not get this job, I have already learned so much.
- The next time I interview, I will be even better.
- I would be happy with this job or not.
- I am so proud of myself for applying to this job.
- I am a perfect fit for this job.
- This job would fit really well with my other goals and cares.
- This job, or a job like it, is meant for me.
- I will get this job.

With a short amount of words and time, the individual has softened him or herself on the subject of the job. No statement went harshly against the individual's core beliefs, and each neutralizing thought brings the individual's thought-train to a slow.

When you first begin to practice this technique of shifting ideas and internal stories in order to slow the train, it can feel a bit rusty. This may especially be the case if your wheels have been practicing turning one way for a long while. When you start to turn the wheels the other way, it is a mostly unused motion. It will take a few minutes to knock the dust off it and get it going. However, if your mind is capable of sending ideas speeding down a track in one direction, it can do the same in another direction. A positive and deliberate direction.

Be easy on yourself when practicing this and remember there is no such truth as doing it wrong. If you find yourself back to the familiar old negative thought patterns, it is ok. It is even natural for that to happen. Acknowledge it, put yourself facing the positive direction again, and return to building that momentum. Eventually, the train that is given the most attention and energy is the train with the stronger momentum.

There is a simple way to tell if a thought is serving you, or tormenting you: how it feels.

- "I hate everyone"... feels pretty bad
- "I love everyone"...feels untrue and mocking, so still feels bad
- "There is one person I don't hate in the world"...less friction in that statement
- "There may even be two people in the world I don't hate"... less friction in that statement
- "I don't hate everyone"... less friction in that statement
- "Some people are ok"... less friction in that statement
- "That one guy a particular time was good"...feeling better
- "That person from history did some stuff I like"...less friction
- "This person alive now does stuff like that, too"... feeling better
- "It's nice to know at least a couple of good people"...feeling better
- "I hate that person who made me mad still"... more friction in that statement
- "But at least I know this good person over here"... less friction
- "I have respect for this person"... feeling better
- "But I still hate that one person"... more friction again
- "But at least I don't have to see that person anymore"...less friction

And so on, you go; fine-tuning your thoughts deliberately.

Deliberate Thinking
To do something deliberately is to do it with intention. Deliberate thinking, then, is quite simply the act of thinking thoughts with deliberate intent. Very often, individuals can feel as if they have no control over plaguing thoughts. It is as if these thoughts come into your line of focus and demand your time and energy like bullies or authorities that are out of one's power to control. This is not necessarily an exaggeration. If we do not practice keeping our thoughts in check, they will start to bully us and it can feel futile to try to cast those thoughts aside. They are so loud and so aggressive that we feel it is necessary to focus on the thought now and until it is resolved.

345

In reality, this is a choice.

The average individual is capable of navigating and managing thoughts of their own accord, but it is the lack of practice doing so that makes it feel useless. If you have never driven a car before, it does not mean you are incapable of driving; it means you have not been taught to drive. If your intention is to truly get a grip on overthinking, then you can do this with the practice of deliberate thinking. When you notice thoughts beginning to demand more of your time and attention than feels good to give it now that is the perfect time to practice deliberate thinking, rather than allowing your thoughts to run wild and unchecked. This is an opportunity to reclaim more power and influence over the outcomes and results you see in your daily life.

When you practice deliberate thinking, it means taking responsibility for what happens in your life; for what will happen in your future. You cannot ask for your power back only to relinquish it when something undesirable happens to you. You cannot take responsibility for the goodness that is coming to you, and leave the responsibility of the discomfort. You are responsible for it all, or you are under the control of external elements of which you surely have no control.

If you accept this responsibility, it means you no longer blame other people and other circumstances for your position. You have, in one way or another, brought the position to yourself. It may feel uncomfortable to accept that you are primarily the cause of your own discomfort. However, if you are brave enough to accept this, it comes with incomparable freedom. If you are responsible for all that has come, then you are responsible for all that will come. If you learn to effectively use tools like the power of positive thinking and the power of deliberate thinking, and then you are free to sculpt whatever future you desire.

Deliberate thinking, like positive thinking, is more about a change in attitude than anything else is. It is about the deliberate intent to train yourself for better thinking, and better-feeling thoughts. When something happens that is not in alignment with that goal, it is your job as a positive, deliberate thinker, to change your perspective on the subject, or to acknowledge its presence and dismiss it from your attention promptly. This doesn't mean ignoring the issue altogether, it means dismissing it until it feels good to work with it, think about it, and figure it out.

There may be a subject that feels big, scary, and uncomfortable. It has been buzzing around you for a while now. It calls on your attention and demands your focus even when you do not intend to be thinking about it. The thought creeps in as you are working or as you are attempting to enjoy the company of a friend. It stomps and shouts at you and demands your attention, growing louder and more unruly by the minute. It is ok to dismiss that thought for now, even if the subject is something you certainly must confront. However, chances are you do not have to give your attention to it at this very moment. Practice dismissing those unruly thoughts and send them back to the waiting room. Eventually, you will regain a reasonable degree of confidence and power over your habits of thought, and it will, at some point, actually feel good to deal with and resolve the tormenting issue. Rather than fight with oneself, the deliberate thinker practices control and dominance over thought; dismissing the situation from focus, for the time being.

In addition to an adjustment of attitude, deliberate thinking requires self-assessment and observation. In the same way, you must become more aware of when you are practicing negative thoughts, you must become more aware of when your thoughts are directionless and unintentional.

Pay attention to when you are thinking becomes chaotic and unintentional. Pay attention to how you are thinking; what thought patterns and behavioral patterns do you automatically resort to just because it is a habit? If you have often played the part of a victim or a martyr, for example, do you automatically take up this role when a similar situation occurs, regardless of how you actually feel, or what you could actually do? Do not punish yourself for an automatic behavior; just recognize it and replace it. It once may have served you well to play the part of a victim or a martyr, but now it no longer serves as it used it, and in fact, is a hindrance to your progress and evolution.

By paying attention to the thought-habits you have formed, you can more easily recognize when you are about to fall into a pattern of habit, as opposed to a pattern of new thinking and new behavior that will benefit you. With this recognition, you can more easily and more quickly practice taking control of your thoughts and re-route your train before it gains too much momentum in the wrong direction. Deliberate thinking requires that you assess when you think, how you think, and especially what you think, and then, make deliberate improvements to those. What you think about most should be chosen deliberately by you and it should be based primarily on how good it feels right now to focus on it. You practice these thoughts and actions deliberately because they are more satisfying for you and more beneficial to you.

How to Use Deliberate Thinking with Positive Thinking
The combination of positive thinking and deliberate thinking is unbeatable and this is a major factor for the insight and focus on this book. These are your two most powerful weapons and there is nothing you cannot confront without them. These tools remind you that you have the power and you are in control. Not necessarily control of all worldly circumstances, but rather, how you react to them.

If deliberate thinking is to think with intent, this could, in theory, mean the intention of dwelling in uncomfortable, bad-feeling thoughts. Deliberate means intentional; not necessarily good. To practice intentionally, but without the benefit of positive thought, could land you in a similar or worse nightmare of overthinking.

Positive thinking without deliberate thinking is a pattern with no goal or destination; no sense of accomplishment. It can be easy to float through the day enjoying every butterfly and rainbow, but without intention behind your patterns of thought and behavior, there is little to be gained. Overthinkers generally want to regain control over their thoughts in order to accomplish something; a series of things. Happy thoughts without direction may feel good, but your train will be headed to an unknown destination. If that is your intention, so be it, but many of us have other intentions in mind and this will be most easily accomplished by a combination of deliberate and positive thinking.

An example of using these tools in conjunction might be the coworker who just handed in a report that could make or break their promotion. The coworker is a deliberate thinker so rather than fret and focus on all that could go wrong with the report, he or she deliberately chooses to look at the experience in a good light (regardless of the outcome) and chooses to stay focused on the topics that feel good. The coworker recognizes that by doing this, his or her additional work is of a higher quality and he or she can contribute greater suggestions at subsequent meetings. If the coworker had not practiced deliberate thinking, the negative worries and anxieties of submitting the report would hassle him or her for at least the rest of the day. Focusing on other work would be difficult and the coworker would have little to no value to add at meetings.

Positive thinking is your train's fuel and your intention is the track. With both, your train will quickly gain momentum in the direction you have chosen. With one but not the other, your train will build momentum but beheaded in an unknown direction, or it will be pointed in an intentional direction with no fuel to get it there.

Pros and Cons of Positive and Deliberate Thinking
Let's be honest; there are plenty of benefits and advantages to practicing positive and deliberate thought, but like any tool, it can be misused. If you would like to make the change from Overthinkers to the intentional thinker, it is important for you to be aware of the pros and cons of this practice. Identifying the advantages and disadvantages of positive and deliberate thought will ensure that your practice is effective and your attitude is benefitting you.

It is possible for someone to fall into positive thinking but end up misunderstanding it and misusing it. These individuals can dig themselves even deeper into discomfort. Therefore, it is highly recommended that you familiarize yourself with some of the most common advantages and disadvantages of employing this method of positive thought modification. Let us assess the following list so you know what to watch out for and what to look forward to.

Disadvantages of Positive and Deliberate Thinking

1. Only Positive Thoughts - Eradicating all "negative" thought can be detrimental to the individual. Some of the thought processes referred to as negative actually helpful and beneficial to us. Considering a worst-case scenario can help us to plan and prepare for an outcome so that the impact is not felt so harshly. Emotions like fear and worry can, in some cases, protect us from dangerous circumstances. It is important to accept this as part of your repertoire and rather than see this as a negative, consider it a positive thought-behavior. However, do not let this thinking spiral out of control. There is a difference between mitigating damages by considering worst-case scenarios and stewing over worst-case scenarios for an excessive amount of time, or in a way, that exhausts you. Too much focus on a problem will not protect you or mitigate damage; at some point, not even all the thinking in the world can change the outcome of a scenario. Find your balance with each.

2. Ignore Real Life - It is possible to become so enamored with the idea of positive thinking that the individual may begin to ignore primary concerns. While it should be your priority to think about that, which feels good, it does not mean you should neglect important aspects of day-to-day life. Neglecting that which needs your attention does not actually feel good anyway. It may be a delay in dealing with those uncomfortable feelings, but you still know in your mind and in your heart, those issues are there and they need your attention. If you find yourself having to confront an uncomfortable circumstance, as a positive thinker, you do not mindlessly ignore it. Instead, you acknowledge its existence and make a deliberate decision to confront the issue now, or at a better time in the near future. This is not ignoring; it is prioritizing. It is not pretending the problem is not there, it is choosing to look at the circumstance as more than just a problem.

3. Positive Thinking as Your Only Tool - While positive and deliberate thinking can be a powerful tool for thinkers, it is important to recognize that is not the only tool you have. Becoming overly reliant on this one method of thinking and behavior actually creates another automatic response for your mind and body to follow whether or not it is actually the best course of thought and action. You end up in a spot much as you started in, where your actions and thoughts are rote, mechanical, and not deliberate. This actually morphs a once-positive pattern into another detrimental habit that is not actually serving you, but just acts as another coping mechanism that does not serve you well.

4. Judgment from Others - Just because you're at a point in your life where making positive and deliberate changes to your thought- and behavior-patterns feels good, doesn't mean everyone around you is ready for it. Be as gentle with others as you are with yourself and do not expect others to fall in line and think positively along with you. Often times, this journey is one you make on your own. It is unfair to expect someone else to adapt so quickly. They can achieve this on their own, and from their own experience, but you cannot force someone to ride your train. Instead, accept that there are people and ideas in the world you will not always agree with and that is ok. It is not your job to eliminate that from your experience. It is your job to manage how you react to those circumstances.

5. Removing yourself from the Fuss - This can be a difficult step to cross over because we are, largely, social creatures. We want to express and share. However, a brief look around you will demonstrate that a great many conversations taking place are neither positive nor deliberate. Spending 45 minutes arguing politics online with another person is likely not part of your deliberate goal. By giving your attention to this debate, you are likely slowing down your train by conjuring feelings of frustration, helplessness, and even anger. This can send your train jolting the wrong direction down a negative path. If you are to remain as much as possible in good-feeling thoughts and deliberate action, you will probably have to forego these kinds of conversations, at least for a while until you are able to approach them as an objective, positive, thinker. If you really miss this kind of interaction, consider creating your own dialogue about the topic but set some deliberate parameters first.

6. Self-Punishment - It can be a natural reaction for many Overthinkers to punish themselves mentally, emotionally, even physically, when they find themselves slipping up and letting the negative train build momentum again. Do not punish yourself. You have not done anything wrong. Allowing the mind to naturally swing back to uncomfortable thoughts is absolutely part of the process. To be mad at yourself for slipping back is equivalent to the carpenter who hammers one nail into the wood and becomes mad that not all nails were hammered into the wood at that moment. You will always have new nails to hammer; it is okay. It is natural for the mind to do this. Your job is to be gentle on yourself when this happens, recognize it, and redirect your thoughts. That is all.

Advantages of Positive and Deliberate Thinking

The advantages of positive and deliberate thinking are more obvious and easier to see than perhaps the disadvantages are. By now, you should have some idea that positive and deliberate thinking yields highly beneficial results, especially when employed by Overthinkers. Here are some of the most beneficial rewards:

- A sense of clarity and clear thought
- The power to acknowledge and dismiss thoughts without guilt or delay
- The decrease in stress, which plays an enormous part in how the body physically feels and reacts
- Lower rates of depression
- Greater resistance to immune-system illnesses
- Greater self-worth
- Higher levels of confidence
- Self-accomplishment and self-actualization
- A better general mood and attitude
- A sense of well-being and everything in its place
- A certainty that you can handle life's circumstances in a healthy way
- Your healthy practice becomes a model for others to follow
- Gained control over thought-patterns
- Removal of automatic responses that are no longer serving you
- Removal of harmful behaviors that are no longer in alignment with your deliberate goal to feel good

Through this chapter, you have learned what it means to be a positive thinker and you have uncovered some of the misconceptions about this process. Similarly, you have discovered what it means to be a deliberate thinker, and what can happen for you when you combine these two tools for your success. Now that you have a solid understanding of what overthinking consists of, and what positive thinking consists of, let us look at how to put these concepts into action. In this next section, we learn about thought modification and how to introduce this practice safely into your day.

Chapter 3: Thought Modification

This chapter will focus on understanding thought modification. You will learn what thought modification is and how it relates to overthinking and positive thinking. You will get a look at how this therapeutic technique can be applied in your daily life in order to decrease the frequency of negative behavior or thought-pattern, and how to increase the frequency of positive behaviors or thought-patterns. This approach is often used in clinical cases as a supplement to other therapies and personal coaches and certified hypnotists to help an individual replace negative habits with positive ones often use it.

As you move through this chapter, you will become familiar with three primary examples of replacing negative habits. Three of the most common negative behaviors individuals wish to replace are drinking, smoking, and overeating. It is no surprise that these three behaviors are frequently the focus for those wanting to end bad habits. Drinking, smoking, and overeating are classic coping mechanisms widely shared across the globe.

In order to cope with stress and anxiety, often brought on by overthinking, the individual resorts to stress relief. Through past experience, the individual has learned that at least one of these coping mechanisms makes he or she feel better, at least temporarily. When another stressful circumstance occurs, the individual's mind automatically recalls the last action it took to feel relief from stress and that was to practice the negative habit of drinking, smoking, or overeating. As the individual experiences more stressful situations, the automatic response to engage in a negative behavior to feel better is recalled and practiced.

At some point, however, that negative behavior will not deliver the same relief that it used to. The disadvantages begin to outweigh the benefits. The automatic response that began for a positive reason (to cope) has become harm and hindrance. It is then that the critical, practical, thinker acknowledges the need to replace this negative behavior.

A Brief History of Thought and Behavior Modification
In order to not overthink it, the history of thought modification will be kept simple and fundamental to our practical application here is this book. Thought modification and behavior modification are different, but they are really the same. To modify thoughts is obviously focused on the thought, and to modify behaviors is focused on the actions an individual takes, but we can also understand this as the same for our purposes. While there are of course unique differences between each study, we can focus on the similarity. Ultimately, the behavior is not carried out without a preceding thought. To get action; behavior, we must first have thought. It is thought about a thing that leads us to a certain behavior. We take these actions and engage in these behaviors in the hopes of creating a certain outcome or result. To rid yourself of the habit of overthinking, you will modify your thoughts, and to replace negative behaviors, you will modify your thoughts (first), so we can consider it all thought modification, which in some cases includes an action or behavior as well.

The roots of thought modification begin in the early 1900s when psychology, in general, was experiencing a burst of study and interest. Edward Thorndike takes an interest and focus on a new field of study then referred to as "instrumental learning". This study focused on what we largely refer to as classical conditioning, wherein a certain stimulus elicits a certain response. Thorndike is well known for contributing "the law of effect" which states that when satisfying stimuli are given at the completion of a behavior, the behavior is more likely to be repeated, and if unpleasant stimuli are given at the completion of a behavior, the behavior is less likely to be repeated.

Where have we heard this before? Are any bells going off for you? We most classically know a similar study of this from Russian physiologist, Ivan Pavlov, around the same time with something called conditioning. Pavlov famously studied conditioning in a well-known experiment with salivating dogs.

In his experiment, Pavlov was able to link a previously unlinked stimulus with the response of the dogs to salivate. Initially, dogs would have no reason to react to the sound of a bell with salivation in anticipation of food. However, Pavlov noticed that his dogs would begin to salivate when they would hear the approach of the lab assistant. This is because the dogs had learned that when the lab assistant would enter, they would be fed. Pavlov expanded on this and created a scenario in which the dogs would hear a bell just before the lab assistant would enter. Eventually, the dogs linked the sound of the bell with the event of being fed. In the end, whether the dogs were visited by the lab assistant or not, whether they were fed or not, the dogs would begin to salivate at the sound of the bell.

What does this have to do with overcoming overthinking? It is important to understand conditioning (the result of a response from an environmental stimulus) because conditioning is how you have developed your negative behaviors, and re-conditioning, or thought modification, is how you will replace them.

Into the 1930s, Harvard's Pierce Professor of Psychology, B.F. Skinner, took this study further, developing the study of "operant conditioning". Skinner's ideas were based largely in the works of Pavlov and Thorndike, but his primary deviation was in the stimuli. Skinner felt the previously constructed idea of stimulus and response was not complex enough to express the human experience. Instead, Skinner suggested that the response was deliberate and intentional and not just an automatic response, at least in the case of humans. This distinct difference makes Skinner the father of "operant conditioning". Operant conditioning thought modification is largely based upon.

Skinner's operant conditioning is saying that you are capable of making a deliberate choice for one thought or another; one behavior or another. Human beings are self-aware enough that this is part of the decision-making process. This is why some individuals seem to take the path of least self-preservation, despite knowing the consequences. It is saying you are not a simple creature with only the capacity for rote response.

Examples of Thought Modification
Below, you will find three distinct examples of individuals applying thought modification to replace negative behaviors with positive ones. You will notice that even though the exact details are different from case to case, the formula stays the same. The individuals in each example all experience an unhealthy habit of overthinking and this leads them to seek relief in unhealthy behaviors like drinking, smoking, and overeating.

Pay attention to how each example applies aspects of positive thinking, deliberate thinking, and behavior modification and see if you can identify each. Note whether any of these applications spark ideas about how you might apply positive and deliberate thought as you aim to reduce overthinking and perhaps other behaviors that are no longer serving you.

Example #1: The Individual Who Replaces Drinking

In this case, the individual has acknowledged he has a tendency to overthink and this leads to drinking as a way of coping with the stress and anxiety he feels. This individual experiences some degree of paranoia and self-doubt; often worried that others are thinking the worst of him and do not want him around. Sometimes, he will focus on the thoughts that tell him his friends love him and no one is judging him, but other times, he finds himself obsessing over made-up fantasies that others are talking behind his back about how much they hate him and all the stupid things he does.

The individual realizes that both versions of the story exist in his mind. He has a story in his mind about his friends who love him for being himself, as much as he has a story about how they hate him. Sometimes the majority of his concentration is on one version of the story and other times he is giving his attention to the other.

The issue for this individual is that when his mind is already focused on thoughts and feelings of self-doubt, self-criticism, and fear, other ideas like it join them. It is so much easier to be pulled into the emotional distress of a story about how everybody hates him when he has been subjecting himself to self-criticism and self-cruelty for the last 30 minutes. This individual's train is headed the wrong way with a great deal of momentum.

As these negative thoughts join one another, they compound the stress, doubt, and fear experienced by the individual. When the individual craves relief from these painful thoughts, he begins to drink. Nothing too drastic has ever happened, but the individual notices he does not like the way alcohol makes his body feel in the morning. He does not like the lack of focus and concentration he has after a night of overdrinking. He does not like relying on a substance for relief. Most of all, he does not like the initial overthinking that causes him to start spinning out of control with negative ideas and imaginings.

The hardest part is done. The individual has recognized this behavior pattern is no longer a help to him; it is actually harmed and an inconvenience. The individual recognizes that if most of his issues have arisen because of unhealthy thinking habits, this must be the place to start the healing and rejuvenation. He starts the improvement process with his thoughts; where all action and reality begins.

In order to reduce the frequency of drinking and replace it with something positive, the individual considers and selects a replacement behavior. The act of drinking has been a way to feel a release from stress and to get free from oppressive thoughts for a while. Therefore, the individual selects a replacement behavior that will also deliver relief and momentary escape. This individual loves to make music and loves to play the drums. Lately, he has not had the focus or energy to play because of the drinking pattern he has formed.

When he does play though, he feels like he is in his own world; the problems of reality and all the paranoid and oppressive thoughts disappear. Banging out a few of his favorites on the drums helps him to release even more stress than the drinking. When he has done playing drums, he feels energized and excited. He is thinking about making music and he spends more time in his music studio in the basement. He wants to replace drinking with drums. When he comes home at night, he adjusts his routine a bit. Instead of pouring a drink while he is still in his work clothes, he will put on some comfortable clothes and go straight to his music studio. Instead of the first whiskey of the night, he lets loose all the day's frustrations on the drums, pounding out what feels best and what he wants to play.

The individual has organized a few techniques and mental exercises that work well for him in controlling and dismissing unnecessary thoughts that feel bad. He has also selected a replacement behavior. Now, he adds another key piece for conditioning, the punishment, and reward. The punishment and reward, in this case, will be financial.

The individual decides to change his typical routine only slightly, but with big results. He will come the same way home each night. He will even continue to stop at the same store where he buys whiskey. Instead of making a whiskey purchase though, he will transfer $25 into his savings account from his phone or from the ATM at the store. Every day, he takes the time to stop and watch the numbers in his savings account increase. He is attentive to how it feels. He takes time to enjoy that feeling, and then runs into the store for anything else he might need, and heads home to put on comfortable clothes and get to his studio.

At the end of the week, if he has transferred the $25 a day instead of spending it on whiskey, he treats himself to a shopping trip to the music store with that money. If he slips up and buys whiskey, then he must transfer $50 to a charity he is selected via the app, which helps kids afford instruments and music lessons. He feels he will be less apt to slip up as the whiskey would end up costing him 3x the amount. He also feels that a shopping splurge is a strong incentive because there is a list of equipment he would like to get.

All of these actions are conscious or subconscious affirmations to himself that he does not have to focus on the negative exaggerations, and that he does have control over these thoughts and his behaviors. He is proud of himself for learning to replace negative behavior and in the meantime, experiences all sorts of benefits and advantages to having done so. Soon, the individual's train has changed direction and has built up such positive momentum, that life is enjoyable and a weak coping mechanism like drinking is not desired anymore.

Example #2: The Individual Who Replaces Smoking

In this case, the individual has fallen into a recent pattern of overthinking, overanalyzing, and self-criticizing because of stress from work. She has recently been challenged at work to prove she has what it takes for the position she wants. Others in the company want this position, too.

The competition has become fierce and she feels that everything she does is being scrutinized under a microscope, so she must do it perfectly. She loves the challenge and wants the job; she does not mind the hard work, but she keeps over-worrying herself into exhaustion and self-doubt, and all of her creative progress and excitement are drained. That energy ends up being used to worry or imagine negative scenarios repeatedly.

She tries to recall when she has been this stressed and anxious before, and when she finds the moment in her memory, she recalls she was smoking a cigarette then as a way to cope with her stress and pain. This sends her to the store for a pack of smokes. She has one on the way home. It is familiar. It does actually somewhat lessen the stress she currently feels; she feels a relaxation from this experience.

Before long, she has a smoke on the way home from the office. She starts to have them on the way into the office. It is not long before she is in the smoke-pit outside with all the other smokers on smoke-break. It is not long before she buys a carton of smokes, which she said she would never do again.

Now though, this individual is noticing health concerns. She cannot breathe as well and she occasionally has shortness of breath when she should not. She is coughing more. Her throat is irritated. Worse still, the relaxation she initially gained back has faded. Now she is left mostly with an expensive, unhealthy habit that does not even deliver a satisfying result anymore. It really only gives her a few minutes extra to stew over negative ideas in her own mind while she's on a smoke break.

This individual has recognized that over-analyzing and overthinking recent work challenges to a negative and obsessive degree is holding her back from success and it is causing her to develop negative behaviors as coping mechanisms. She has decided to change this pattern of thought; to modify it, and to replace the negative behavior to smoke.

In order to replace the negative smoking behavior, this individual makes more changes that are significant to her routine. She decides she does not necessarily need a direct replacement for smoking; that is to say, she does not need a replacement habit to do every hour. She had not smoked for years and did not need to do something every hour to feel better, and that is what she would like to return to. Instead, she plans to reward herself with the massage units at the gym. Her gym membership includes access to the hydro massage bed and massage chairs, but she never makes time to do it. She goes to the gym every other day and she plans to treat herself to 10 minutes of massage every time she has not smoked in-between visits.

This is not her only plan for removing this negative smoking behavior. This individual has also paid a visit to a certified hypnotist for extra help. The hypnotist has performed a version of operant conditioning that adds an instant and unwanted stimulus to the smoking experience if she chooses to smoke. When this individual needs extra reinforcements in the moments she may feel like smoking a cigarette, this operant conditioning will do the work.

The stimulus that the hypnotist has added to the smoking experience is an unwanted taste in the mouth. The hypnotist brings the individual into a trance-state and guides her through the experience of having a cigarette, but in this imagined scenario, the individual is prompted to notice the already unpleasant flavor of smoking. The hypnotist expands on and exaggerates that experience, convincing the individual that it is the most wretched flavor she has ever tasted. He relates a number of highly unpleasant sensory cues to this experience, making the individual think of the smell of truck stop portable bathrooms when she lights up.

All these unpleasant sensory perceptions are linked with the behavior of smoking, and soon enough, this individual finds herself unable to even smell an unlit cigarette without her stomach turning. It is only a matter of days before she is in the massage chairs and has not smoked since. Because she has stopped smoking, she feels more involved at work and she does not feel people are talking about her behind her back as she did when she would go out for a smoke break. She regularly treats herself to the massage equipment at the gym and uses that time to deliberately practice healthy and positive thinking exercises. She considers it a full-coverage gym membership where she can exercise her body and her mind.

Example #3: The Individual Who Replaces Overeating

In this case, the individual has just recently started living on her own, alone. As a result, she has adapted some poor eating habits lately. There is no one else eating with her, so she is less apt to take the time to ensure her meals are balanced and sensible. In addition, after the stressful days, she has been having, she feels she deserves the foods she craves.

Little confrontations will set her into a pattern of overthinking. Some small interaction in traffic on the way home, and it is the only thing she can think about. She focuses on the scene repeatedly. Was she in the wrong? Should she have said something different? How dare those other drivers blame her! She creates a great comeback that is 20 minutes too late. She wonders what that driver's problem was. She stews over it. She creates all kinds of little stories of injustice and wrongdoing and gets herself all worked up.

By the time she gets home, she is hungry, tired, and stressed from all the overthinking she has been engaged in. She orders delivery, or goes through the drive-thru and gets something comforting and fast. She justifies this by thinking she should not have to cook if she is tired, and she deserves the indulgence to take the edge off from the day.

However, after a few weeks of this pattern, she has gained weight and she feels unhealthy. These experiences add to her overthinking and cause more stress. Reaching for pleasurable food indulgences have become the thing that is causing her stress.

Instead of continuing this unhealthy pattern, the individual commits to practicing an assessment activity in place of every time she would normally give in to the unhealthy craving. For as long as it would take to drive to McDonald's and back, and as long as it would take to finish eating, this individual commits to using that time to understand her impulses and thought patterns better. She understands that her poor habits are the result of poor thinking.

To do this, she will sit and write in a journal, answering a series of pre-designed questions to help her better understand her impulse to eat junk food and dismiss it. At the end of this time, the individual hopes to have dismissed the craving, and to have even replaced that craving with one for a nutritious home-cooked, well-balanced meal.

This individual has included an extra incentive as a reward. If she can stay on track with healthy home-cooked meals, she will treat herself to an upgrade around her new space. Maybe it is curtains, or new furniture or appliances; she has a list of lots of things she would like in her new home. She decides for every month she eats out only one time, she will treat herself to the latest upgrade she has had her eye on. Six months into the future, this individual has developed quick, fast, and delicious eating habits and her new space is looking better than ever.

In the previous three examples, each individual had their own set of challenges and goals, but the formula was very similar in each case. The individuals recognized that current habits were no longer working for them. They each applied attention and objection analysis to their current thought-patterns, and implemented mental exercises to deal with internal confusion and stress in a different way. They all replaced negative behaviors with positive ones, though there was variance on the technique and intervals of practice and reward (or punishment). In the next section, we will focus on two more key concepts to make you a better positive thinker.

The Subconscious Mind and the Movie
We have mentioned briefly the role of the subconscious mind in terms of overthinking and positive thinking, but now we look closer and spend a little more time understanding how the subconscious mind works and how we can use this information to develop positive thinking behaviors.

The subconscious mind is a frame of mind and not necessarily a place in the brain. The subconscious mind is a reference to a frame of mind between conscious aware thought and unconsciousness. The subconscious mind, most notably, is where your imagination lives.

The subconscious mind believes what it is told. It does not know the difference between fantasy and reality; it just believes the story it is told and acts in accordance. What this means for you, the positive thinker is that if you keep feeding yourself negative stories about losing and staying down, your subconscious mind believes this. It acts in accordance with this, looking for every piece of evidence of this in your reality and shouting for your attention when it is found: "Yes, you were right, look at this awful thing! Yes, you were right to look at this terrible person! Yes, you were right, look at this political mess!" What's more, it is not only your subconscious that acts in accordance; your body begins to act in accordance with these thoughts as well. Soon, mentally and physically, you are living the same story you have been repeating. However, here is the magic: if the mind believes what it is told, then you can tell it positive and beneficial stories that you are subconscious mind and your body will begin to respond to and act in accordance with.

Here is an example of how the subconscious mind believes what it is told and acts in accordance. Think of a book or a movie you have experienced that has such a sad or touching scene that you actually end up crying and feeling emotion. Your logical, conscious mind knows this is only a movie. This is why you do not actually run and hide at the scary parts, and this is why you do not actually call for help when a character gets hurt. Your logical mind can determine that this experience is only a movie; it is not real.

The subconscious mind is different. It cannot tell that this is only a movie. All the subconscious mind cares for is the story; the emotion, the characters. Therefore, when you get to the part in the story that brings you to tears, it is the doing of the subconscious mind. The subconscious mind believes the story being told and therefore it starts to feel the emotions of the story. Your subconscious mind, the great imaginary genius, become so engaged in the story and the emotions that it causes your body to physiologically react to the emotions you think you are feeling. The body literally begins to cry because the subconscious mind is experiencing sadness, despite it not being real.

If the subconscious mind is so ready to believe the stories it is told, consider taking 10 minutes to sit in a quiet and comfortable spot to experiment with this. Set aside a few minutes to spend daydreaming and making up the details of a positive story. Make it a story about how you get the thing you're wanting and how good it feels to have it...what you do with it... let the imagination wander and encourage yourself to feel emotion about the story. The more you repeat this positive story to yourself, the stronger it becomes and the more your mind and body subconsciously believe it. If you practice this enough, your mind will be scouring your experience for every shred of evidence to support your story about everything going right. Your body will physiologically act in accordance with the idea that you are doing well and things are always working out for you.

The Mental Map and the Plastic Mind
You are familiar with the concept of the "internal map of reality" from earlier. This is the map of reality we form in our own mind based on experiences. We develop this map so that we can make more valuable, faster, safer decisions in the future. However, as we have seen, building this map can limit us sometimes as much as it can help. We react to our map of reality, and not actual reality, so that means when your map says something is impossible, you tend to believe it is impossible even if, in real life, there is a possibility.

However, the good news is your mind was molded that way, and it can be just as easily molded to fit a newer, more productive and beneficial, shape. With every new piece of information and experience, neuro-pathways are forming or repeating in the mind. When a thought is repeated enough, the neural pathway becomes well-practiced and well-rehearsed. It happens even faster than you may realize.

However, what happens when there is a significant interruption to those pathways, like a stroke or an aneurysm? Is everything learned, lost? In some respects, yes. In another way, no. The neural pathways that existed previously in the damaged part of the brain may be lost, or at the very least, they may be hard to repave. On the other hand, the brain's ability to develop new neural pathways in undamaged areas is remarkable. It is not that this remarkable development only happens when the brain experiences trauma; neuroplasticity is at work in you all the time. In its simplest form, neuroplasticity is occurring when you change a previously held belief, for example. It is thanks to neuroplasticity that we are able to modify our patterns of thought and behavior.

Chapter 4: Techniques to Prepare for Change

So far, you have familiarized yourself with some of the key causes of overthinking and negative thinking. You have gained knowledge of primary traits and side effects that result from overthinking and repeating negative and fearful stories to yourself. Similarly, you have become familiar with what it means to be a positive thinker and what it takes to begin changing the negative patterns you have established.

With a solid understanding of both positive and negative thinking, it was easy for you to build upon to develop an understanding of thought modification. Now you are familiar with the origins of behavioral conditioning and how this study has grown into thought modification and cognitive behavioral therapy.

You are beginning to see how all of this information comes together in a plan and process to reduce and remove negative thinking from your behavior and replace negative habits with positive ones. You are gaining clarity on how these tools can be an effective part of your thought rehabilitation.

There are three more foundational tools to add to your toolbox. The three techniques in this chapter are some of the most widely studied and commonly applied techniques to help individuals and patients to shift the way they think and develop positive patterns instead. These techniques are known as "the 3 Ms"; mindfulness, minimalism, and meditation. We will look at the origins of each and how to apply these concepts to your own shift in thought-patterns.

In addition, you will see examples of each of these as they apply to thought modification, and what you can expect to see because of implementing these tools in your daily life. These concepts will help the overthinker keep his or her mind from wandering, and it will help bring the wandering mind back to home base when the thinker says to return. Use these approaches below to defeat overthinking, end negative automatic behaviors, and declutter your environment and your mind.

Minimalism

Origin

The idea of minimalism has existed in various forms and practices for many years and through many generations, and maybe better known as the idea of "simple living". History's Mahatma Gandhi, for example, was a proponent of simple living at the turn of the century. Gandhi believed that the individual had become too commercial; in addition, consumerist, too enamored with material possession, and because of this, the individual had become spiritually, morally, and creatively bankrupt. In order to reignite our spirit, creativity, and ethics, we must return to a simpler lifestyle. He frequently practiced this way of thinking and living; rejecting extravagance and indulgence, and making his own food, clothing, and shelter.

The minimalism we typically know of and refer to is a version of these ideas, though often not so extreme. In the 1960s, the United States latched onto a trend in art and fashion known as "minimalism" and coming from Europe and Japan. In the world of art and fashion, the idea of minimalism detoured from the ideas of Gandhi, but at the root, they had not. The idea was still to accomplish greatness with the least possible means. In art, this resulted in strikingly stark abstract paintings and sculptures; absence of color paired with a solitary bold color, sweeping minimal lines and movements, little to no fine detail. These ideas were inspiring and groundbreaking and indeed set the stage for minimalist architecture in the U.S. through the 60s and 70s. Homes and buildings were designed to capture natural light. Materials were organic aesthetics such as wood and stone. Lines were simple; nothing ornate. Flat, clean surfaces, everywhere. Again, though quite different in some respects from the teachings of Gandhi, the architectural designs still echo the ideas of simple living by using natural materials, open-concept space, and natural lighting.

Minimalism has since evolved into a mindset and a lifestyle practiced by many in order to feel a sense of peace and order in daily life. This mindset still consists of the echoes of Gandhi and minimalist art: less is more. What is meant by that ultimately is that the less you have to be distracted by, the more you learn to grow, love, and learn; the more you develop spiritually and creatively.

Application

For overthinkers, we can take this same concept and apply it to thought modification.

Less is more. When you have fewer thoughts vying for your attention and focus, you can give a higher quality of attention to the most important thoughts. When you downsize your possessions, you can find and use the possessions you do have, more easily. You can use and store these items properly. You can enjoy them more thoroughly. This can bring a very calming peace to your environment, but doing the same with your thoughts can bring that peace to your mind.

Sift through and toss the junk. It is okay to sort through
the thoughts, wonders, and worries of your mind and scrap the stuff that is no longer working or that no longer fits. The beliefs from high school that you have been carrying around and acting on, are they still what you really believe or are you just holding onto them? As situations arise and you call on your thoughts and beliefs to guide you, ask yourself whether the information you are operating with is actually the information you still believe - or need. Toss what is not serving you and making decisions will suddenly become much easier.

Set clear and measurable goals. Prepare yourself for
the success of your goal. This means that when you set a goal, picking what you want is the first step, but not the last. Pick the goal you want, but then, make sure to set a clear deadline. Make sure to set clear parameters. This will help you to measure the success and speed of your goal. You will have a benchmark of what you expect and if you start to veer off course, you will be able to notice it quicker and adapt to it better. A goal without a deadline is a daydream.

Simplify your environment. Whether this means getting rid of some old furniture you have been meaning to sell at a yard sale, or it means painting the room you have been meaning to finish painting, simplify it.

Especially if you have one spot in the home that you can call your own, start there. Clear it and organize it. Get rid of items you no longer use or want. File paperwork. Clear items out of drawers and cupboards. Declutter your space. Then, simplify it further by bringing in one or two solid, muted colors that are calming to you and conducive to your space. Add natural elements like plants or pictures of plants and nature. Keep materials natural and basic. Keep up with your space and give it a little TLC once a week to ensure it stays a peaceful environment for you to relax in.

Minimize worry.
When you begin to panic about an idea and your mind races looking for the answers, minimize the millions of tributaries and stories about the idea down to one idea. You have the question, and you have the answer. The answer is hard to hear when all the other thoughts are yelling at you. Eradicate the other stories with one story. You have the answer. You are listening to it. It is coming.

Reuse positive thoughts.
When you find a set of thoughts that feel good, even just one or two, reuse them. Stick to them for a while. Enjoy them. Expand on ways to enjoy them. Repeat them. If a particular idea or phrase puts everything into perspective for you, use it often. Repeating the ideas and beliefs you do truly hold in your life now, helps them to become stronger in your subconscious mind and on your internal map of reality. It also allows the older beliefs you no longer agree with to dissolve away.

Forgive and forget.
For an overthinker, it can be helpful to practice minimalism when things go wrong. If you have done something to let yourself down, or someone else has, consider letting it go. Do not be so hard on yourself. Holding onto that guilt is reminiscent of hoarding and that is not a minimalist approach. Let bygones be bygones. Forgive and forget, and start anew.

Expectations
By implementing minimalism in your mind and in your environment, you will be adding calm and clarity to your lifestyle. When you keep the fundamental pieces and let the rest fall away, you are suddenly able to see and enjoy the fundamental pieces at full value. This can serve us well in our thought processes and in our physical environment.

It is not uncommon for overthinkers to have trouble cleaning and organizing the home. This occurs because the individual overthinks the cleanup process; stopping to assess each item, where it should go, how it will be used when it will be needed... It becomes too overwhelming and the things around the individual build-up. A minimalistic approach helps the overthinker to declutter the surrounding environment and the internal thought-house.

Mindfulness

Origin

Mindfulness, like simple living, is a concept that goes very far back through history but comes to the U.S. through relatively recently means. In the 1960s, the United States grew more familiar with Vietnamese Buddhist monk and activist, Thich Nhat Hanh. Hanh studied, practiced, taught mindfulness, and in fact taught at Princeton and Columbia University in the 60s. It is primarily through the teachings of Thich Nhat Hanh that mindfulness has found its way into Western culture.

Thich Nhat Hanh taught in mindfulness to regularly take notice of where you are in your mental process. He also taught the importance of slowing down to live in the moment and practice the small daily pieces of life with extra-sensory focus.

American medical professor and society founder of the University of Massachusetts Medical School, Jon Kabat-Zinn, recognized the teachings of Hanh. For a time, Kabat-Zinn was a student of Hanh's and eventually went on to develop the study of mindfulness, as we know it today.

Many of the techniques and practices used today in coaching and therapy, as well as personal practice, are rooted in the same two concepts:

Bring yourself back. Refocus, recollect your thinking. When your mind begins to wander from the one thing you are doing, gently bring it back.

Savor the moment you are in right now. Rather than wanting to rush through one thing to get to another, appreciate the step you are at in this very moment. If you are washing the dishes, your mind should stay on the one dish you are washing. You pay extra close attention to the experience of washing this one particular plate in this one particular moment. If your mind starts to slip and think about the next plate you will wash, you gently bring it back to the plate you are holding and focus on, quite literally, the task.

Application

Practicing mindfulness is a wonderful complement to practicing minimalism. Both remind the individual that simple is better. If it feels too complicated, you can probably simplify it, whether it is a physical space or a mental attitude. Here are a few mindfulness techniques commonly used by practitioners and therapists, as well as self-practicing individuals. Keep in mind they are all to do with a focus on the small and simple pieces of everyday life. They may seem mundane at first glance, but that is the point here. Something we might normally rush through is something we should fully observe and appreciate. That includes the moments that are not so enjoyable.

Sit in a chair, only. Find a chair and sit in it. Do not do anything else. Sit in the chair only. Sit in that chair for about 5 minutes and when your mind starts to wander, bring it back to the observation of the chair. How does it feel? How does it smell? What does it feel like? Hard or soft? Silky or leathery? What does your skin feel like on the chair? What does it sound like when you move in the chair? In addition, when your mind begins to wander, gently bring it back to focus on the experience of sitting in a chair, and nothing else.

Eat mindfully. When you are eating, alone or in a group, at home or at the office, in any situation you find yourself eating practice mindfulness. Move your utensils more slowly than you normally might. Take a bite on your fork or spoon that will easily fit into your mouth without a struggle. Chew that piece of food more slowly than you normally might. Pay closer attention to the textures and flavors. Put your utensil down while you chew. Take a sip of water after swallowing your food.

Engage the senses. This can be something as simple as enjoying the smell of the soap or shampoo you use in the shower, or something as extreme as skydiving. There is a wide range of activities from one to the other and you are sure to find comfort somewhere between them. Give your senses a new thrill. Visit a new city or town. Listen to new music. Rent a car just to switch it up. Try a food you have never had. Find ways of igniting the senses.

Listen and nothing else. When someone is talking, give your full attention to him or her. Be attentive to the language they use to express themselves. Pay attention to their body language and what they do not say. If you are on the phone with someone, sit down and talk to them as if they were in front of you. Avoid talking on the phone while you are doing 10 other things around your house.

Do not multitask. Get it yet? It is about doing one thing and one thing only, and dedicating your focus and attention to that one thing until it is complete. As often as you can, practice giving your full attention to one process at a time and watch how much faster you, excel at the activity.

Learn from pain. It is part of life, there is bound to be some discomfort. If you want flowers, you have to have showers. Mindfulness says to be patient and kind with yourself about that, too. In the moments of life that don't necessarily feel good subjectively, you can still experience calm and happiness in knowing that you will learn and grow from this painful experience.

Expectations

The primary benefit of practicing mindfulness is giving the analytical mind something to do and focus on; observe the moment, savor the moment. The busy analytical mind has an activity to engage in which keeps the mind from otherwise following the negative streams of thought to a sad conclusion.

The secondary benefit of practicing mindfulness is the natural increase in positivity. By practicing mindfulness, individuals often gain satisfaction from the realization that they could enjoy doing things much more when the goal is simply to enjoy doing anything that comes to them.

In addition to these rather abstract benefits, the practice of mindfulness can benefit in physical, measurable ways, too. Mindfulness often helps to lower heart rate and blood pressure, increase circulation, release tense muscles and joints, and assists in helping sick individuals to recover faster.

Meditation

Origins

Meditation is an ancient practice that dates back as early as 5000BC and perhaps even further. Thus, it is difficult to say with any accuracy when and where meditation began. What is easily known is that meditation began to make its way into the United States at the end of the 1800s, as the western world became familiar with India through Great Britain. At a time in society when the paranormal and the occult were all the rage, meditation, and any exotic alternative that broke norms and challenged taboos, fit right in.

Meditation on a large scale can represent a religious devotion. Meditation on a smaller scale can offer a decrease in perceptual stress and anxiety, and improved health, especially of the heart and circulatory system. It is recommended that you meditate for as little as 10 minutes each day. Meditating for a longer period can be beneficial too, but for many, it creates too much resistance and only 10-20 minutes is achievable. A routine practice of 10 minutes or more, at least once a day, can have a significant impact on you physically and mentally.

Many people think meditation does not work for them or they cannot do it. This is an unfortunate misconception. In almost every case of this, the individual has been misinformed about what meditation is, and what has to be expected. When the individual is freed from the restrictive thoughts of what meditation must be, they are able to enjoy its benefits without resistance.

Application

There are many different types of meditation, but in one form or another, most forms of meditation focus on creating a silence in the mind. In whichever form of meditation you practice, this usually means that you become quiet, still, and focus on an external stimulus like the sound of your breathing or the sound of the wind or water. When your mind begins to wander, you bring it back to the moment and refocus on the sound of your breath, or the wind, or the water.

Let us take a look at several types of meditation that can be easily practiced almost anywhere, by almost anyone. Pay attention to which forms of meditation sound comfortable to you and test one out today.

Kindness Meditation: In this meditation, exercise you sit in a peaceful and quiet location for about 10 minutes with your eyes closed. During this time, you keep your mind on only one thought. The thought is usually a message of loving-kindness you want to send to someone.

For example, let us say a friend has a broken leg and you are hoping for them to recover soon. To perform a kindness meditation, prepare a short basic sentence that expresses your love for your friend and your desire to see them well again. As you meditate, repeat this phrase as a sort of mantra, all the while trying to elicit the positive feelings of seeing your friend well again. When the mind wanders, bring it back to this mantra.

Progressive Relaxation: In this meditation exercise, you sit in a calm and quiet environment and become still and soft. Typically, you would begin by slowing the breath and listening to it; concentrating on the sound of it. After about a minute or so, you focus on one small aspect of your being with the goal of relaxing it. For example, let us say it is time to relax your jaw. Wiggle your jaw and stretch it out for a moment. Imagine the tiny muscles and nerves in your chin relaxing. Imagine your tongue relaxing. Move your tongue around in your mouth and feel it relax. As you relax each part, you move to another, slowly relaxing pieces of yourself from head to toe. If you intend to practice meditation for longer than 10 minutes, this is an excellent one to start with. It keeps the analytical mind focused on the task, and the extra relaxation makes it easy to stay in this meditation for upwards of 20 minutes.

Breathing Exercises: There are many different breathing exercises that work effectively and the key is to find one or two that you really like to use. In a breathing meditation, the main objective is to only focus on the sounds and feelings of your own breath. When the mind wanders to other thoughts, it returns to the breath. One very common breathing exercise is to close your eyes and breathe in and out slowly and comfortably. As you inhale, count to 3. Hold your breath in your lungs for a moment and then exhale and count to 5 so that your exhale is slightly longer. Focus on this practice only for 10 minutes. Another popular breathing exercise is to breathe slow and deep and when you do, imagine that breath going into a sore or uncomfortable area of the body; a sore back perhaps. You imagine that breathe stretching out the sore area and giving it a good massage, and as you exhale, you imagine the soreness leaving with your breath.

Kundalini Yoga: This yoga practice doubles as a meditation practice and the individual experiences peace of mind through focus, and physical health benefits as well. To practice Kundalini, you would learn a set of poses or movements that you would blend. Each time you restart the movements, you focus on making them as perfect as you can. When the mind wanders, you bring it back to your form. The set of movements usually includes 4 - 8 poses that start over at the completion of each set.

There are of course many other forms of meditation and if none of these sound as if they will suit you, do not give up on meditation. Consider what it is you are looking for in an effective meditative exercise and then use other resources to find the form of meditation that will best suit you.

Expectations

By adding as little as 10 minutes of meditation to your day, you are reducing stress and anxiety. You're quieting the mind and training it to know that obsessive negative thought patterns are not the only thought patterns you have at your disposal. Giving yourself the opportunity to rest the body and mind simultaneously for just 10 minutes a day promotes emotional health and enhances self-worth and self-actualization.

Meditation is an excellent tool for lengthening the attention span and improving the memory and it can actually reduce memory loss for seniors as they age. You can look forward to more control over your thoughts and emotions with 10 minutes to realign and focus.

In this chapter, you've prepared for making positive changes to your thought and behavior process by equipping yourself with the 3 Ms; mindfulness, minimalism, and meditation. You are more than ready to move to the next step and establish new thoughts and behaviors.

Chapter 5: Practice Makes Perfect

You have approached the ending of this book and now you have the opportunity to put everything you have learned into motion. This chapter functions as a workbook set of exercises and assignments for living life through your new lens. It is recommended that you try each of these exercises at least once. It can often be the exercise you initially think is too simple or too silly that brings the best insights.

By trying all of these exercises at least once, you will be able to find a few that you really enjoy, or that offer you the greatest benefit of practice. Again, if you find you do not like even one of these exercises, do not give up on overcoming overthinking with the power of positive and deliberate thought. Many other techniques and practices have been designed to bring results. Take time to consider what you are looking for in an exercise or practice, and do some research. You will find one or two processes that work well for you.

Take a few minutes now to review all the information you have learned through the first chapters. Then review the collection of exercises and find one you can practice for 10 minutes today.

Now You Know...
Here is a reminder of all you have learned in the previous chapters. As you scroll through this list, be cognizant of how this new information is already positively influencing your thoughts and behaviors. Keep in

mind how this new information will help you through the exercises to follow.

- Definitions and examples of overthinking, traits of overthinkers
- What causes overthinking
- Why we're such an analytical pack of thinkers
- Why nighttime is the worst time for overthinking
- The mental, emotional, and physical results of overthinking
- Definitions and examples of positive thinking
- Definitions and examples of deliberate thinking
- How to recognize negative thought patterns
- How to slow down thought momentum
- How to use deliberate thinking to accomplish goals
- The pros and cons of living a positive and deliberate lifestyle
- What is thought modification, conditioning, and cognitive behavior therapy
- The history of thought modification and its development and involvement with positive thinking
- Examples of thought modification through drinking, smoking, and overeating
- The Internal Map of Reality
- The plastic mind and how neuroplasticity can help overcome overthinking
- The role of the subconscious mind that believes what it's told
- Minimalism and its origins, applications, and expectations
- Mindfulness and its origins, applications, and expectations
- Meditation and its origins, applications, and expectations

Exercises for Positive Thinking and Thought Modification
As you look over these exercises and find the ones that suit you best, keep in mind that we are, generally speaking, creatures of habit. As such, it would be a smart idea to repeat the exercises you do like, daily. These do not have to take up too much of your time, but the more frequently you practice them, the stronger they become in the mind, and the faster they deliver results. In addition to practicing them daily, it is also a good idea to try to practice them at the same time each day. The body and the mind become accustomed to this and behave in accordance. This is similar to the body craving a cigarette around 4 pm but in a positive way.

The following exercises are designed with you in mind. These practices are used regularly to help overthinkers and worriers get a grip on thought patterns and behaviors that are no longer serving them. Use these techniques to practice positive thinking habits and to dismiss negative thoughts that compete for your attention and focus.

The One for One Technique

This technique is best used to combat negative thinking habits by encouraging the individual to practice positive thinking, thereby strengthening the neural pathways associated with positive thoughts. Implement this action anywhere, anytime, with no preparation needed. The exercise can be done in silence in your own mind, or aloud. This works in the shower, in the car, in the grocery line, in the office, and before bed. Application is instant and takes only seconds to complete.

The key to using the One for One technique is paying attention to the internal dialogue going on in your mind through the day, in the shower, in the car, in the grocery line, at the office, or in bed. This encourages the individual to pay closer attention to the negative thoughts that cause stress through the day, which often rise to attention automatically and from the previously learned behavior to do so. The negative thought comes as a matter of routine, and this method conforms to the routine but alters it.

By using this technique immediately when negative thought patterns are recognized, the counteractive positive thinking becomes associated. This means that when a negative thought pops into your mind demanding your attention, your mind and body will begin to utilize the positive counteraction as part of the entire process. Rather than continuously repeat and inflate the negative thoughts, your newly trained mind will know that the negative process ends with a positive twist, instead of repetitive negativity. Your mind will become practiced in this after only a few practices. Instead of a thought pattern that says: Negative thought → negative repetition, the thought pattern says negative thought → positive thought.

To practice this exercise:

1.   Take notice of a negative thought that is plaguing you in the current moment.
2.   Isolate the one thought.
3.   Repeat the negative thought to yourself once more, but very slowly, pausing between each word, and breaking its flow and cadence.
4.   Replace this negative idea with a positive one. This can be on the same topic or an altogether different topic. The positive idea should be something accurate that you easily believe.
a.   Example 1: I am too fat to wear this → I am making better eating decisions.
b.   Example 2: I am too fat to wear → these clothes are so comfortable.
c.   Example 3: I am too fat to wear this → My dog loves me.
5.   Repeat the new positive idea, very slowly, pausing between each word.
6.   Repeat the positive idea again, very slowly, but this time taking care to imagine the positive emotions or senses of the statement.

a.   Example 1: "I'm making better eating decisions" IMAGINES a delicious meal that satisfies cravings and fills you with nutrients and pride for making a healthy decision.
b.   Example 2: "These clothes are so comfortable" IMAGINES the soft and easy sensations of wearing comfortable clothes and feeling comfortable and happy in them all day.
c.   Example 3: "My dog loves me" IMAGINES the emotion of happy times playing with the dog and sharing a special friendship.
7.   Now allow the idea to repeat 2 or 3 more times in your mind, but at your thoughts' natural and ungoverned pace.

As you continue to become more aware of the automatic and obsessive thoughts in your mind, notice if this negative idea returns. If it returns, repeat the positive replacement sentence. If you would prefer to update or change your positive statement, do so. This exercise is a practice in deliberately creating a positive thought for each negative one you notice. It is less about the words you use in this case, and more about the feelings you are replacing. Essentially, for every time your mind causes you to feel a negative emotional feeling from overthinking, you will deliberately match it with positive emotion. Creating more emotions that are positive deliberately strengthens the neuro-pathways in your mind to experience happiness on your own, naturally.

3x5 Breathing

This is a common breathing technique used in meditation and in the practice of mindfulness. Like most breathing exercises, this is designed to guide the individual into a slower frame of mind that most often includes a slowing and calming of the body, as well. The individual is encouraged to listen to, and focus on, his or her own breath. When the mind wanders, gently guide it back to the breathing exercise.

This exercise can be practiced almost anywhere and at most times, but it does require the individual to block out the rest of the world for a solid 5-10 minutes for maximum benefit. There is no preparation necessary, and while it is nice to practice this exercise in a comfortable and relaxing space, it is possible to implement this in a space that is not perfect. Doing so will actually only strengthen your resilience to block out distractions and concentrate deliberately for 5-10 minutes.

The primary function of this exercise is to regulate a slow and steady breathing pattern of 3-count inhales, and 5-count exhales. It is also suggested than when breathing in, you breathe deeply through your nose, and when exhaling, you do so through the mouth as if you are blowing air out from your lips.
By adding this breathing exercise to your repertoire, you will improve focus and memory and decrease stress chemicals in the body. This

exercise also decreases the overall sense of anxiety, lowers heart rate and blood pressure, relieves muscle tension, and improves eyesight.

To practice this exercise:
1.   Get as comfortable and quiet as possible where you can sit undisturbed for 5-10 minutes.
2.   Sit comfortably and close your eyes.
3.   Breathe in deeply as you normally would and exhale.
4.   Hold your breathing for a moment on the exhale.
5.   Inhale again, but this time, breathe in slowly and steadily for a count of 3 in your head.
6.   Hold your breath for a count of 3 in your head.
7.   Exhale, but this time, exhale in a slowly and steadily for a count of 5 in your head.
8.   Inhale again, slowly and steadily for a 3-count.
9.   Exhale again, slowly and steadily for a 5-count.
10.   Continue this pattern of slow and steady inhales and exhales at a 3-count, and 5-count, respectively.

You may opt to continue to hold your breath in between inhaling and exhaling as part of your pattern, but it is not mandatory. Do that which is most comfortable. If the mind begins to wander, gently bring it back to the observation of the breathing process. Your analytical mind should be listening closely to your breathing for any sign of faster or unsteady flow. The analytical mind can also remain focused on the evenness of your counts, trying to maintain the slow and steady flow. After a 5- or 10-minute period, you can slowly open your eyes and readjust to your immediate surroundings. With regular practice of this breathing exercise, you will teach your mind and body that you have the power to bring yourself to this peaceful moment whenever you want. This is a personal micro-vacation you can use any time in your day it feels good.

Relief in, Pain Out
This breathing exercise is commonly used in meditation and as a supplement to pain therapy. This exercise is designed to guide the individual into a slow and steady breathing pattern and into a feeling of physical relief in sore or tight spots in the body. The individual should listen to his or her own breathing and focus on a sore or tight spot in the body that would benefit from attention. Your analytical mind should be paying acute attention to every little feeling in that sore spot as you move through the activity. The analytical mind can also busy itself with the task of observing the breath to keep it slow and steady. When the mind wanders, gently guide it back to focus on the feeling of the sore spot throughout the exercise.

This exercise can be practiced almost anywhere and at most times, but for maximum benefit, it will require the individual to sit undisturbed for a solid 5-10 minutes. There is no preparation necessary, and while it is nice to practice this exercise in a comfortable and relaxing space, it is possible to implement as a commuter passenger, at the office, in the shower, at bedtime, or anywhere you can secure 5-10 minutes uninterrupted.

The primary function of this exercise is to regulate a slow and steady breathing pattern that is used to soothe a part of the body that would benefit from attention. When breathing in, breathe deeply through your nose, and when exhaling, do so through the mouth as if you are blowing air out from your lips.

By practicing this breathing exercise regularly, you improve focus, memory, decrease stress, and anxiety. This exercise also lowers heart rate and blood pressure and does a particularly effective job of releasing muscle tension.

To practice this exercise:

1.   Get as comfortable and quiet as possible where you can sit undisturbed for 5-10 minutes.
2.   Sit comfortably and close your eyes.
3.   Breathe in deeply as you normally would and exhale.
4.   Hold your breathing for a moment on the exhale.
5.   Inhale again, but this time, breathe in slowly and steadily for a count of 3 in your head.
6.   Hold your breath for a count of 3 in your head.
7.   Exhale, but this time, exhale in a slowly and steadily for a count of 5 in your head.
8.   Continue a pattern of slow and steady inhaling and exhaling.
9.   Bring your attention to a place in your body where you may be experiencing soreness or tightness. Consider muscles, joints, bones, tendons, and appendages. Hips and shoulders often hold a lot of stress tension and can make a good choice for focus.
10.   Continue to breathe slowly and steadily, and focus your attention on the sore area of your body and how it feels.
11.   On your next inhale, imagine all the air you are inhaling is traveling to the sore spot in the body. As the air arrives at the spot, imagine the spot being wrapped and enveloped by this air. The air gently and warmly massages the spot in the body and gives it a gentle stretch.
12.   As you exhale, imagine all the soreness of that spot releasing and coming out through your breath.
13.   Continue this pattern of steady and slow breathing, while imagining the breath is massaging the soreness out of the body.
14.   Repeat the pattern several times, focusing on any feelings of relief in the area of the body.

If the mind begins to wander, gently bring it back to the observation of the area of the body, and the steadiness of the breath. After a 5- or 10-minute period, you can slowly open your eyes and readjust to your immediate surroundings. With regular practice of this breathing exercise, you will reiterate to your subconscious mind that you have the power to ease pain in your own body and mind.

Worry Window

This exercise is helpful for those who tend to overthink and worry or ruminate on perceived problems. Because of the nature of this exercise, it is particularly useful at the start or at the end of each day. This activity requires a full 30 minutes, and can end up taking less time, but not more. This activity also requires that the individual sit in a quiet space and have a notebook and a writing utensil.

It is highly recommended that you do not use a computer, tablet, or phone to perform this activity. All of these devices invite too much distraction from the activity. Furthermore, the cognitive functions that take place when we write with our hands are different from those when we type. For this exercise, the cognitive functions that occur with physical writing will be most suitable.

The primary objective of this exercise is to encourage the individual to unload all of the worries and concerns in their mind, but within a 30-minute window, and no more. The idea is that once you have given attention to each of the concerns by identifying them in the notebook, you can set them aside for the rest of the day, or night. You are not ignoring the issues, and you will give them each the attention you should, but at this specific moment, you cannot do anything about them, so you let them simmer on the lists you make in your notebook until you are ready to come back to them later.

If worries and concerns come to mind after you have done the process that is okay. You know you will have 30 minutes tomorrow to dedicate to the issue if it still needs your attention by then. Even the most professional of businesses and organizations typically operate with a 24-hour timeframe. 24-hour response time is a reasonable request that you would likely extend to others, so you should allow yourself the same professional courtesy. Acknowledge the worry that has arrived late, and check it into the waiting room until your 30 minutes tomorrow. Obviously not every concern can wait and some issues may demand your immediate response. This exercise is designed for the worries and concerns that do not need your immediate attention but demand and steal it from you anyway.

Use this 30-minute window of time to get out all of your concerns or worries for the day. When you are done with the activity for the day, you must commit to sending all other worries to the waiting room until the next 30-minute activity. 30 minutes a day is more than enough time to spend worrying, so get it all out in the 30-minute window of time.

To practice this exercise:
1.   Sit in a relatively quiet and comfortable space where you can have 30 minutes without interruption.
2.   Set a timer, watch the time, or regulate the measurement of time in some way that you can give yourself 30 minutes, but not more than that. You may not need the full 30 minutes.
3.   Open your notebook and add the date to the top of an entry.
4.   Scribble out: "The regard that has a question for my thought today is:"
5.   Create a list by adding each worry or concern to the notebook page under that statement.
6.   Be as detailed as you want to be; including details helps to create the feeling of giving the issue fair time to be heard. You can repeat items as much as you need on the same list or different lists.
7.   At 30 minutes, stop hard on the list.
8.   Scribble out: "That's the only time I have at the moment. I'll be reachable for 30 minutes tomorrow."
9.   Close the notebook.

Remember that if additional worries creep into your mind after you have finished for the day, to send them to the waiting room until your 30-minute window tomorrow. After several weeks of practice, you will notice your lists getting shorter and the time was taken getting shorter. This is due in part to your subconscious mind and your body learning through this activity that to worry in such a way is a tedious waste of time. Your mind will be making this connection for all the time you are writing, and your body will be making a connection as you sit in the chair and your arm becomes tired and stiff from writing. It will literally feel like a relief to stop worrying when you stop writing. As a pro-tip: keep your Worry Window notebooks. When it feels like a good time, look back through them and see how you are thought patterns have evolved.

Rephrasing
This exercise is an excellent way to train the mind to think in a positive and deliberate way while decreasing the automatic response to think negatively. This is another exercise that requires no preparation or special setting, and it can be done anytime, anywhere in seconds.

The main function of this exercise is to prompt the individual to be more aware of the way they speak. Often times, we phrase ideas in a negative way, talking about what we do not want instead of being clear about what we do want. The subconscious mind hears what you say, but it does not distinguish between whether you want the thing or do not want it, it just

380

acts in accordance to the story it is told. For example, if you keep repeating: "I don't want to fall...I don't want to fall...I don't want to fall..." the subconscious mind reacts to: "fall...fall...fall..." This exercise encourages the individual to alter the sentence, and therefore tell the subconscious mind a positive version of the story. The sentence could be altered to "I want to keep my balance...I want to keep my balance...I want to keep my balance...", and the subconscious would act in accordance with "balance". This exercise challenges the individual to recognize this negative pattern and to augment the statement when it occurs.

By implementing this practice in your daily life, you train your mind to automatically think in a positive and deliberate way. The negative thought habits will decrease as they are rehearsed less and less frequently. This activity also serves as an excellent mechanism for repeating positive ideas and stories to your subconscious mind so that the mind and bodywork in accordance with the story.

To practice this exercise:

1.   Bring your awareness to the language you are using aloud to express yourself.
2.   Identify a negative sentence that suggests something you do not want.
a.   Example 1: I do not want children to go hungry at school.
b.   Example 2: I do not want to get upset in traffic.
c.   Example 3: I do not want to go to the event.
3.   Play around with your vocabulary and augment the negative statement from what you do not want, to what you do want.
a.   Example 1: I do not want children to go hungry at school →; I want children to be well fed at school.
b.   Example 2: I do not want to get upset in traffic → I want to be calm and cool in traffic.
c.   Example 3: I do not want to go to the event → I want to stay home and relax.

The statement can be about something significant or not. The idea is to become more familiar with, and practiced in, forming positive thoughts in place of negative ones. By implementing this process in your daily life, you will bring more self-awareness to the way you talk and repeat ideas. It will increase your ability to speak clearly on the things you do want. After a matter of weeks, your language will have adapted to automatically think of ideas in the positive rather than negative, and to express them this way.

Reframing

The reframing exercise is very similar to the rephrasing exercise but differs in that it is a bit more complex. In reframing, the individual is encouraged to take a situation he or she feels negatively about, and put it in a new light; paint a different picture about it. This can be done anywhere, at any time, and takes only seconds or minutes. It can be done silently in your own mind, or aloud. Reframing aloud has the added benefit of strengthening the story, and the emotion of the story, to the subconscious mind with an additional auditory version of the story.

This exercise works well for individuals who regularly overthink, and form exaggerated and dramatic stories based on one small piece of evidence, often taken out of context. Examples of situations that reframing can work well on might be someone standing you up for a date, someone taking the seat you saved, someone cutting you off in the grocery aisle, a stranger giving you a nasty look, and so on. These situations often put us on the defensive quickly, as we feel we are being wrongly judged or mistreated. It is easy to imagine a personal injustice or that the situation was done against you, personally.

In order to reduce this pattern of negative thoughts, and to practice positive thoughts, this exercise forces the individual to look at the situation objectively as if no personal emotion was involved. Through this lens, the individual can often slow the pattern of negative thought and put the situation into a more realistic perspective.

There is no systematic instruction for this practice. When you notice a situation, you feel personally offended by, stop. Take a moment to analyze what is really going on from an objective point of view. Ask yourself if you could be seeing some of these details wrong and if something else, which is not a personal attack on you, could actually be going on. Imagine a scenario in your mind, where the same situation plays out, but it has nothing to do with you. For example, the person who stood you up could have had an emergency. The person who took your seat probably did not realize they did it. The person who cut you off in the grocery aisle could have been in an important rush to get somewhere. The stranger with the nasty look could have made that face because of a thought of their own, and they just happened to be facing your direction.

For a clear idea of reframing, consider this example:
You are driving in your vehicle. Traffic is heavy and slow. You approach the intersection where traffic is heaviest and slowest. You get ready for your turn to go, but there is oncoming traffic still. As you wait and watch for your turn, a truck a few vehicles behind you honks its horn loudly. You immediately take this to mean the truck driver thinks you are taking too long to turn, and it makes you defensive. This is immediately

followed by a sense of injustice. If you had been taking too long, ok, but with this traffic, you clearly have no way of going yet.

Now you feel that the other drivers around you probably feel the same as the truck driver; you are taking too long...you are in the way...you are an inconvenience...you should not be driving... Before you know it, your imagination has already proposed several worst-case scenarios and you have felt the emotions from them- and you have not even made your turn yet.

A small and meaningless scenario like this can cause an immense amount of stress for an overthinker. Furthermore, long after you have made the turn, completed the drive, and had dinner, the scenario remains on your mind. Not only on your mind but also in your body, have caused tension and high blood pressure among other things.

Time to reframe the situation. Imagine yourself back in the car, in the traffic. Everything is as it was, the truck is behind you. You approach the intersection and wait. Now imagine behind you, in the truck, the driver is in a rush to get to where he is going. He is fidgeting and he is impatient in his car. You can imagine him tapping on his steering wheel or dashboard in a futile attempt to make traffic faster. He is mumbling to himself and cursing. The driver's problem is that he has to go to the bathroom very badly but he is stuck in this awful traffic. Finally, he cannot take it and in his frustration, the driver lets out a honk. This is the honk you hear that you mistook for being directed at you. The truck driver did not mean to honk directly at you; he is merely honking at the frustration of the traffic in general. Rather than being angry and defensive with the truck driver, you laugh and feel bad for him. The entire situation feels differently now and elicits a much different set of emotions.

Ultimate Pool

Ultimate Pool is an ultimate exercise for the overthinker. This practice does not follow a set of systematic instructions and is a bit more of an abstract practice. This can be done anytime, and almost anywhere, but it will require the individual to have about 5-10 minutes of uninterrupted time. Because of the nature of this exercise, it makes an excellent practice before bed or when you wake up. Here is what you need to know:

No concerns spinning around you that feel good. Did you know you could knock them back aways? It is ok to do that. Like a cue sending a pool ball gliding.

If you get good at pool, you can knock back many of those concerns so that you are only looking at a few that feel good to think about. When you find those other pool balls gliding back into your zone, it is cool. It is okay. You have the cue. Knock them out aways again. However, you cannot knock those concerns away without replacing them. Moreover, obviously, you need to replace them with the ones that feel good to think about. So return to those.

If you find those other ones keep returning to you too often; demanding priority of your focus, then you change your priority. Your priority is now, above all else, to feel good. Every second. This is unachievable for mere humans. So then, as many seconds as possible. Practice focusing on only the ideas that feel good. When you slip, it is cool. It is okay. Acknowledge it and return your focus to the ones that feel good. This is how you get good at ultimate pool.

If you think that will not work because it is ignoring the other thoughts, you are wrong. You are not ignoring them. You are concentrating your focus on others. Eventually, some of those concerns you sent gliding out will come back into your zone at a time it actually feels good to think about them. You will resolve them then. So be easy on yourself.

Tune your focus. The further you seek it, the better you get. Can you do it for 10 seconds? 20? Eventually 60 seconds; a full 5 minutes? You can make yourself feel better for 60 more seconds than you could before.

Practice sending a few pool balls gliding. Find a few that feel good to give your attention to. Chalk your stick. Focus.

Tips for Effective Practice
Some exercises may sound too simple or silly for you, but you are encouraged to give each exercise and technique a chance. It is not unusual to find that the simplest concepts are actually the trickiest; the silliest seeming practices may be the most revealing.

Some of these exercises will resonate with you more strongly than others. Stick to the ones you like and do not force yourself to engage in exercises that feel uncomfortable or stressful, as these may only increase a feeling of self-doubt or wrongdoing.

Humans are creatures of habit. Rather than try to break that, your aim is to use it. Set a time to meditate each day. Make it approximately the same time each day, in addition, so that that body physiologically learns the new and healthy patterns you are implementing.

Take time now. Some of these exercises will require you to be in the midst of an unhealthy or negative idea forming before you can use the techniques. In addition to setting aside specific times to practice, include spontaneous practice. Use a few exercises or techniques that require no preparation, special location, or specific materials for your spontaneous practice.

Be patient with yourself. You have been trained very well to overthink, overanalyze, and self-criticize, so it will take a little practice before you start to dissolve those patterns and establish new ones. Being patient, gentle, and forgiving with yourself in this process, will teach you to be the same way with yourself in future endeavors.

Be patient with others. Not everyone is ready to understand the information you are working with. Many of these ideas are confusing and challenging to understand. In many cases, these ideas can challenge others at their core beliefs. Others may not be as ready and as open as you may to understanding this and making positive changes. That is okay. It is not your job to make them ready, and it is not your job to teach them. Your focus is on your behaviors and your practice and improvement. If others are interested in the positive changes, you are making, it may feel comfortable and nice to share this information with them and listen to the information they have about these ideas. When others are not interested or are made uncomfortable, do not force it.

Do not stop here. This is only the beginning. This information has primed you to go into the world and discover the world of positive and deliberate thinking that awaits you. Listen to TedTalks, read books and articles, stay up-to-date on the fascinating field of neuroplasticity. Keep the positive momentum and keep your train rolling.

Conclusion

Highest compliments, the dear thinker! You have made it to the end of *Overthinking: End Negative Habits, Develop Healthy Patterns and Unf*ck Your Mind.* Even better, you have completed the initial, crucial, steps to better your life and manage overbearing thoughts.

As you have worked through these chapters, you have expanded your knowledge on the patterns of both negative and positive thoughts, how to identify them, and how to manage them. I hope that you have gained insight, confidence, and practical application from the information in this book.

Overthinking is now a topic that you can make sense of, and you no longer need to feel alienated or broken. You understand what positive thinking really means, and how to use it in conjunction with deliberate thinking to modify the negative patterns you have established over time, in your thoughts and in your actions. You have also learned what to watch out for in terms of the advantages and disadvantages of using positive thinking to make changes in your life.

Not only have you become familiar with the practices it takes to overcome overthinking, but you have also learned that positive and deliberate thinking can help you to modify negative behavior patterns you have picked up along the way, like drinking, smoking, and overeating. As you aim to replace those negative behaviors with positive ones, you will be able to use your internal map of reality and the subconscious mind to help you achieve these goals.

When your life feels disorganized and cluttered, you can clean the slate with minimalism. When the moments of the past or the future have hypnotized you, mindfulness will bring you back to center focus. When it is time to rest the mind from the world, meditation will take you there. These are now your tools.

When you slip up or forget what to do, the exercises in this book will set you back on point and help you to get down to the nitty-gritty positive work once again. You are encouraged to continue practicing regularly with the wealth of knowledge you now have, and to expand your knowledge and evolve yet again.

Practical positive thinking and deliberate behavior will take you a long way. Your mind is not ill. It has never been ill. Your mind wants to think, analyze, discover, and form patterns and stories with the information of the world. It is only that the focus is askew. With this information in this book, you are ready to stop fueling your mind with negative and empty thoughts and instead fuel it with healthy content to digest.

At this point, you have put your brain in a wonderful direction. The momentum you have going is impressive. Pull the whistle; it is full steam ahead.

The Art of Manipulation

Powerful Dark Psychology Techniques on How to Influence Human Behavior, Effectively Deal with People and Get the Results You Want with Persuasion, NLP and Mind Control

Introduction

Do you often find it hard to convince your friends to do something you want? Is it difficult for you to explain your viewpoint to your boss and positively influence him/her so he/she agrees to put you as the team leader? Do you experience a tough time making your spouse/partner understand and accept your opinion and have those on board to pursue an idea? Do people see you as more annoying than influential? Do you wish to have a superpower that makes you come off as an influential and charismatic individual whom everybody loves and is always ready to listen to?

If you answered yes to these questions, it is likely you currently have poor communication and manipulative skills and are yet to learn the art of convincing and inspiring people. This important skill is crucial if you wish to be successful in your personal relationships, career, professional life, social circle and any aspect of life that involves dealing with people.

It can be quite tricky to effectively deal with people, help them come on the same page as you and convince them to do what you wish, but it is nonetheless doable and if you committedly work towards the fulfillment of this goal, you can achieve it.

Influencing, inspiring and persuading people are an art, which needs to be treated like one. Instead of wanting to control everyone as if they are your puppets so they dance to your tune, your goal needs to be to positively influence and lead them. Yes, you can have ulterior motives that you wish to have fulfilled, but if they are positive and you do not intend to harm anyone, you are on the right track and there is nothing wrong with making others agree with you. However, how can you achieve that?

The answers to that question are locked within this book. This book is a handy guide that provides you with detailed insight into the importance of influencing people while providing you with actionable, helpful and effective techniques to effectively deal with them and get your desired results every time.

In order to live happily in our world, we need to start to become more aware of manipulation. When you can recognize that someone is trying to control you, it will be much easier to stay out of their controlling grasp. This book will take you through the process of getting back to a place of independent individuality where you are able to consistently make your own decisions.

When you start to better identify manipulation, how it develops, and how it has affected your life, then it will only become easier to navigate without it. Interacting with others can include doing your best to avoid it healthily. However, stopping ourselves from being manipulated isn't the only important thing we will be discussing.

We will pay significant attention to how you can become a persuasive person yourself. Though you might have been hurt in the past by manipulation, or even damaged your mental health by being the manipulator yourself, there is hope, now that we can work towards a better future for ourselves. This is done by becoming an inspirational and potentially influential person.

Manipulation is dangerous, but when it is put in a more positive light, it can become healthy influence. If you are able to be a persuasive individual and not only get what you want, but fulfill the needs of others as well, then it will become easier for you to be able to get the things that you desire the most in life.

Rather than always doing things you don't enjoy, being the "yes man," or letting people take advantage of your good nature, you can become just as influential as the people who have tried to control you previously.

You might even be at a point where you fear manipulation altogether. Why would you want to do something to others that has actually caused you grief in the past? This kind of thinking is because we have only been aware of the negative types of manipulation. In order to live a harmonious life, it is essential that we are becoming persuasive individuals who know what we want. Not only that, but it is important to ensure we have the tools to understand how to get these things.

The first important step in this process is to investigate the personality types of manipulators, as well as the people whom they commonly go after. You may have heard of the common personality type, "Narcissist," a person who is only concerned with himself and getting the things he wants. Narcissists might take advantage of empathy, or highly sensitive people who are more concerned with the wellbeing of others.

After that, we will further explore positive manipulative personalities and the way that you can adopt some of these helpful practices in your own relationships. When you can do this, you will be able to better see the way that positive influence can change your life for the better.

Aside from that, we will also be discovering how our bodies communicate, the signals and responses that we give off, and what others might be taking away from our body language. The better you can understand influence through ways besides our verbal communication, the easier it will be to avoid becoming influenced yourself and to better persuade those around you.

After we understand what all of this means, it will be easier to learn and practice the rest of the influential tips that we will be sharing throughout the book. At the end of the day, remember that you should only be positively influencing others. Though it might seem easier to negatively manipulate those from whom you want something, the person whom you would be hurting most in this process is going to be yourself. Always look for ways of positive influence so that you can mutually benefit both parties.

Chapter 1: What is Manipulation?

Manipulation is fundamentally the art of getting others to do exactly what you want them to not necessarily by paying attention to their desires or in extreme cases even harming them. It comprises a series of techniques such as charm, charisma, hypnotism, persuasion, trickery, coaxing, misinformation and much more.

The underlying objective of manipulation often is "I need to trick people to lead them to give me precisely what I require or desire." However, not all forms of manipulation are bad. At times, they can be used positively to turn the game around and help you get what is rightfully yours or what you're being deprived. For instance, a stingy boss refuses to give you a promotion or pay raise that's been due for long. No forms of logical or meaningful persuasion work with him or her. In such circumstances, manipulation can be used in a positive manner to help you get what is rightfully yours.

Manipulation generally stems from a fundamental belief that your needs or desires are above everyone else's. You place yourself at the epicenter of the universe and believe everything revolves around your desires. It can be given a more positive twist when you realize that connect with other people and work towards aligning their desires with yours. In such a situation you will end up positively manipulating people into doing what is good for them and you. This way you are likely to end up on their side and they'll not feel like they are being fooled.

For instance if you think there's no one who can keep your date or partner happier than you, you try and align their desires with yours. You know you will keep them happy when they get married to you and vice-versa. There is a positive manipulation and persuasion, where he or she does not get the feeling that they are being tricked. You are in fact doing what is good for both him or her and you. As a person in love, you are trying to lead them into a powerful bond that you truly believe in. Is manipulation wrong here? Well, maybe not!

Unlike persuasion, manipulation occurs at a deeper and subconscious level. It is carried out by attempting to change to the fundamental beliefs and experiences of people to get them to do what we want. This can be done by using a variety of raw and sophisticated methods ranging from hypnotism to seduction or top-notch verbal skills. It is sometimes performed by distorting someone's idea of reality to get them to think and do what we want them to. People will then start behaving and thinking about reality precisely as the manipulator wants them to.

Have you seen Shakespeare's tragedies such as Macbeth or Othello?

He understood manipulation in human relationships, leadership and political ambitions before the term became popular.

Lady Macbeth absolutely manipulated her husband through a series of psychological techniques to kill King Duncan and take over the Scottish throne as its powerful ruler. He then launches into killing spree to guard him against suspicion, doubt, and enmity, which leads him to become an example of tyranny. The bloodbath that follows and the ultimate civil war lead to the downfall and death of Macbeth and Lady Macbeth.

Lady Macbeth as well the witch sister's resort to major manipulation through the tale. They trick, goad, instigate and encourage Macbeth into performing horrific acts that ultimately seals his fate. They manipulate him into believing that he alone will be the king of the land, thus sowing a seed of ambition and hatred for Duncan, which eventually leads Macbeth to kill Duncan.

Another Shakespearean classic, Othello thrives on the plot of manipulation. The villain, an ambitious trickster, called Iago creates the most vicious, deceptive and sophisticatedly manipulated plot for sowing the seeds of doubt in the mind of Othello against his love Desdemona.

He tricks Othello into believing that Desdemona is being unfaithful to him (Othello) through a series of carefully planned and manipulated scenarios. Iago is believed to have had a fantastic insight into human psychology that he craftily used to have his way into power. He orchestrated a complicated plot to eliminate his arch-nemesis by leading Othello to believe that Casssio (Othello's favorite and most trusted lieutenant) is involved with Desdemona and thus being disloyal to his master. Iago hopes to take Cassio's place as Othello's chief lieutenant.

This pretty much sums up the idea of manipulation. However, like I explained above, even though it has negative connotations, not all forms of manipulation are evil. If channelizing positively, they can be used to bring about change in a constructive manner.

Whether you realize it or no, you are being constantly manipulated in your daily lives. The tool of manipulation is used almost by every marketer or business that is getting you to buy their stuff and live in a specific way as suitable for their profits. "Buying xyz brand of sports shoes makes you look like a professional and cool athlete" or "vote for abc political party if you really want to witness change and people's welfare." It is in your face, all-pervasive and everywhere – there's just no escaping manipulation in your personal, social and professional life.

Chapter 2: Types of Manipulation

Many of us are aware that manipulation is a form of deceit. Manipulators are the people who use deceptive tactics to achieve what they want, but this is regardless of the consequences to those around them, particularly to the victims of their tactics.

Manipulators are not worried about how their manipulation will affect you personally or psychological damage that they inflict; all they care about is getting the results that they want. These results could be anything from getting to pick the restaurant to getting access to the funds or gifts needed to perpetuate a particular social standing.

Knowing the warning signs is a start, but knowing the type of emotional manipulator you are dealing with can also help you in defending yourself against them and their deceptive tactics. So let's talk about the various types of manipulators out in the world, thus gaining a more complete understanding of how they operate to achieve their ends.

Indifferent

First up is the indifferent manipulator, which is the one that acts like they don't care. These manipulators often seem indifferent towards anything you are doing or saying. This indifference is not just toward your actions, but any circumstances in your life, including difficulties or even celebrations.

In acting indifferent, these individuals have actually caught your attention. You spend time and energy attempting to achieve that breakthrough to capture their attention, thus hoping to achieve a deeper connection. However, they have already singled you out for some specific reason, so they will provide just enough interest to keep you hooked without really breaking out of the indifferent cycle.

In fact, the more indifferent they act, the more questions you are going to ask because you genuinely care. However, when you start asking questions that is when the manipulation starts in an earnest fashion, because now a manipulator can use that they have information provided through those conversations to dig their hooks in ever deeper. Without them having to do or say anything directly, they have begun to play on your heart strings, thus achieving the goal of your personal emotional investment into their lives.

As the victim, you are now in a position that allows them to use your sympathy to "make them feel better", but in reality, the manipulator is now just starting their sting to take from their victims whatever they want, from the emotional to the material. But when the victim has nothing left, then the manipulator moves on to their next victim, typically without any real remorse.

Still at this moment, you are still a goose to be fleeced, so the indifferent manipulator may also take advantage of another type of manipulator, which is the one that is always in distress or poor me.

Poor Me

This particular type of manipulator may be the easiest to spot, but in combination with other traits, makes them easy to fall for over and over again. So what do the poor me manipulators do so effectively when dealing with their victims?

The poor me manipulators use sympathy and guilt, appealing to their victims need to try to help another human being in trouble or assist someone out of a sense of charity or faith. Appealing to their victim's better nature is one consistent way that a manipulator will attempt to get into someone's head. Often it is this goodness that a manipulator can turn on their victim.

It is simply part of our human nature to feel for people who are struggling through something or who are facing various challenges different from the ones that we are facing. We react by doing what we can to help them out, so we tend to cater to their demands without realizing we are being manipulated.

The demands can at first appear reasonable, but over time, will simply grow in complexity. These requests quickly turn into commands and ones that often prove to be real time suckers. Thus, your whole world suddenly becomes completely focused on the manipulator. So the isolation can begin, making it harder for you or loved ones to observe the manipulation and point it out to you.

Critic

As with other manipulators, this particular type is a bit more aggressive than the first two types. They will actively focus on their victim's habits and emotional cues. After finding areas of sensitivity or weakness, the manipulator will begin to focus on them, subtlety at first, and then gradually growing bolder over time.

While it might be easy to spot what a manipulator is doing, many of us who fall victim to manipulators are helpless to stop it, unless we work on improving our mindset. Other ways to help avoid being a victim or getting out of a manipulative situation involve using anti-manipulation techniques.

The critic uses criticism as a way to get what they want because the victim is trying to please, although the critical manipulator will set a bar for their standards, which the victim will find impossible to meet. The constant criticism for their victim contributes to neither making them feel like they are not good enough nor will they ever be good enough. Through manipulation the critic makes you feel like you are worthless and they are better than you.

Thus, to achieve a better sense of your own self-worth, the victim will attempt to be more like the critic or to do things just the way the critic prefers them. Personality changes may also occur, because the victim just wants to gain the affection and praise of the critic. However, the victim does not know this goal is simply unachievable. With the tactics we discussed earlier, the critic is able to use a carrot versus stick approach to keep their victim within their grasp and easily influenced.

Still as bad as these types of manipulators can prove to be, there is one that can be far worse. Why? Because they are willing to go much further than any of the others to achieve their goals, including using fear and violence.

Intimidators

When this particular manipulator comes into play, the victim can be in a very dangerous place. These manipulators are the worst of the worst; they are even more aggressive than the critic. In fact, the intimidator is not just critical, but they use fear and violence to make their victims cower.

These manipulators are more familiar with the stick, than using a more carrot like approach. Once their victim is afraid, these manipulators can easily have their demands met. In abusive relationships with intimidators, the tactic of using anger comes out frequently, along with the need to punish. Both of these tactics play into the fear aspect of the intimidator.

Let's face it, when we are afraid of someone, as individuals we tend to give in much quicker than if we felt in a position of power or a defendable position. These manipulators are all about stripping away any sense of being able to defend yourself, physically or psychologically.

Nobody dares stand up to a person who uses fear to manipulate them because they are literally afraid of what that person might physically do. This is where the manipulator uses violence or the threat of violence to complete their hold on the victim. Abusive spousal relationships often demonstrate this type of intimidation manipulation with a mix of violence all too well.

So now that we have a greater understanding of the manipulator, their types and tactics, it's time to get a better understanding of the victim. If you have recognized a loved one in the information just discussed, you might recognize some of the traits in the following chapter as well. However, you might be the one displaying those traits. Let's see how those traits play into a manipulator's hands and then later on, we will explore ways that you can defend against a manipulator or make the right moves to remove yourself from their grasp.

So what specifically about your personality or way of carrying yourself is sending up flags for a manipulator to zero in on?

Chapter 3: Manipulating the Mind Through NLP

Everybody's conceived with a similar essential neurology. Our capacity to do anything in life, whether it's swimming the length of a pool, cooking a feast, or writing a book relies upon how we control our sensory system. Along these lines, quite a bit of Neuro-Linguistic Programming (NLP) is dedicated to figuring out how to think more effectively and communicate more adequately with yourself as well as other people. But what does NLP really mean?

"Neuro" is about your neurological framework. NLP depends on the fact that we encounter the world through our five basic senses and interpret that sensory data (sight, sound, taste, touch, and smell) into manners of thinking, both conscious and unconscious. Perspectives trigger the neurological framework, which influences physiology, feelings, and conduct.

"Linguistic" alludes to the way individuals utilize language to understand the world, and then convey that experience to others. In NLP, linguistics is the investigation of how the words you speak impact your experience.

"Programming" draws intensely from learning hypotheses and determines how we code, or rationally perceive and understand, our experience. Your own programming comprises the inner procedures and methodologies (thinking designs) that you use to make decisions, fix problems, learn, analyze, and achieve desired outcomes. NLP demonstrates to individuals generally accepted methods to recode their encounters and rearrange their inward programming to get the results they need.

How to Manipulate Using NLP

One method that has shown success in relieving the physical effects of anxiety and insomnia is to follow the feeling. Using this technique the patient begins by relaxing deeply. Then the patient is instructed to name where the feeling is placed in the body. This will be uncomfortable but it is necessary for the patient to know exactly where the feeling is and to acknowledge its presence. The patient is told to just feel it but not interact with it. Then the patient is told to ask questions of the feeling. Ask the feeling what it needs to help it leave the body. Take note of the first thought that comes into the mind. Check to see if the feeling is still present. If it is, then ask the feeling the question again. Keep accepting the feeling while questioning it. Keep asking the same question until no more answers come and the feeling is gone.

NLP may seem to have its basis in something dark and mysterious, but it really does not. NLP is nothing more than a method to use to teach the mind how to release the control that negative events have on the physical well-being and emotional state of the person. Think of the mind as a series of pathways. Every habit a person indulges in has its own pathway in the brain. When a stimulus occurs—something seen, heard, smelled, or remembered—a message is sent to a particular spot in the brain along a particular pathway. This is the spot that holds the memory for the reaction the mind has decided is appropriate for this stimulus. If a person sees their favorite cake they experience hunger. This is the mind's response to the stimulus the body received. So pathways can be created from good and bad experiences. The purpose of NLP is to reroute the pathways of negative stimuli and change the reaction to something pleasant and not something harmful or negative. In this way, NLP can be used for great benefits to people.

Mind perception

Impressions from signals in our surroundings unintentionally impact our thoughts to a specific degree. Up to 99% of our subjective actions might be unconscious.

Along these lines, it is possible to influence someone's psyche by priming the environment—putting a specific object or message near the subject that sidesteps the conscious personality, but is picked up instead by the subconscious personality. Most traps of the mentalists work exactly in this way, as they may wear a red tie that will be overlooked by the conscious personality as though unimportant, but registered by the unconscious personality of the observer without even knowing it. Presumably, it's done by using the word READ as a part of the discussion, for example, which will trigger the shading RED in the observer's brain.

These ideas are validated in the onlooker with deliberate behaviors that are utilized by very talented NLP experts. The truth of the matter is that the simpler the recommendations, the more the unconscious personality get affected.

Mind control procedures

There are a few personality control procedures utilized by NLP experts to control others' minds. For example, closely consider the subtle signals of people like eye movements, pupil dilation, apprehensive tics, body flush, non-verbal communication, speed of breathing, and so forth as they can be associated with the feelings of the individual. For example, eye movements can be tracked to decide how one acknowledges and processes data. Let's say you ask someone about the color of his car, which is not nearby. When he answered, his eyes moved toward the upper right corner before his answer was spoken aloud. Essentially, the eyes moving to the upper right corner would be visual recognition that he's attempting to recall the shade of the car.

Real experts have even conveyed their words following the rhythm of the human heart, i.e. 45 to 72 beats per minute, so that they could create a condition of suggestibility in the listener.

They often give you an anchor, which makes it simple for them to place you in a specific state just by tapping or touching you. For example, imagine that you're talking about love and you're listening to the personal experiences that an individual is sharing with you. He's recalling them, living those feelings a second time. If you can tap your fingers on the table, or touch him in a certain spot (for example, a strong touch on the left shoulder), you can associate those positive love feelings with your physical anchor. If you need the individual to recall those feelings another time, you can tap your fingers or touch the left shoulder again. You will control their feelings without them knowing it.

NLP experts even use a particular set of words that appears typical, but are more suggestive. These "hot" words are more suggestive for being more closely associated with the five basic senses. Words and phrases like "hear this, see, feel free, in the end, implies, now, as, in light of the fact that," and so on can conjure a specific perspective like emotional, confrontational, imaginative, and observational in the brain. When you use these certain words, you can gain control over the content of your thoughts, and with practice those of others.

The interspersal hypnotic technique, a form of behavioral momentum, is largely used in NLP. Basically, science has proven that when tasks include easy responses it increases the probability that less preferred and/or more challenging tasks will be performed. This incognito hypnosis strategy can have an impact on an individual's psyche to a more prominent degree. However, it does not force them to perform an action they are already against: this may require a significant programming of the brain.

You don't want anyone to be able to do the same to you without your full consent. Therefore, here are some ways in which you can protect yourself and your loved ones. A wide range of individuals have attempted to use NLP to talk me into buying something, or making decisions to their advantage. The following is a list of defensive strategies you can apply to defend yourself.

1. Be aware of, and careful about, individuals replicating your non-verbal communication.

If you're conversing with an individual, who may or may not be into NLP, and you see that they're mimicking your body language, the way you're sitting or standing, or reflecting the way you're holding your hands, test them by making a couple of specific movements and checking whether they try to emulate you or not. Gifted NLPers will have practiced veiling this, however, novice NLPers will be more likely to duplicate your intended movement.

2. Move your eyes in irregular and unpredictable directions.

Particularly in the initial phases of establishing affinity, a NLP client will give careful consideration to your eyes. You may believe this is because they're seriously inspired by what you're saying. They're watching your eye movements to discover how you store and then retrieve data. In no time flat, they won't just have the capacity to tell when you're lying or making something up, but they'll also have the capacity to determine what parts of your mind you're utilizing while you're talking. This can help them tune into what you're thinking, and how you're thinking it, so that they appear to have some sort of psychic knowledge into your deepest thoughts. Weird, right? Well, if you've read my other books on persuasion, you should know by now how the eye accessing cues work. An astute hack for this is just too haphazardly shoot your eyes around— admire the walls, to one side, side to side, down—makes it appear to be natural, without a precise pattern. This will drive a NLP individual completely nuts because you'll be diverting from their assessment.

3. Try not to give anyone a chance to touch you.

This is quite clear, although, a bit difficult to apply in everyday life. In any case, suppose you're having a discussion with some person you know practices NLP, and the conversation puts you in an emotional state—you could be laughing real hard, become furious, or start uncontrollably weeping—then the individual touches you. For example, patting you on the back or tapping you on the shoulder. This will "anchor" that emotion with that physical interaction. Then, on the off chance that they need to put you back in the exact same emotional state, they can touch you in the same way, on the same spot.

4. Listen for dubious language.

An essential strategy NLP borrowed from Milton Erickson is the use of dubious language to initiate trance or hypnosis. Erickson found that indirect language is capable of leading individuals into a trance state, because that indirect language can tap into an individual's unconscious response patterns. On the other hand, using more direct language could prevent an individual from entering hypnosis because it may not connect at the unconscious level. Former President Obama used this particular strategy in the "Change" campaign. It's an ambiguous word, and every audience will read their own agenda in it.

5. Listen for "make you an offer" language.

Have you ever heard (or used) phrases like: "Don't hesitate to unwind." or "The pleasure is all mines for you to sample this food or test drive this car, etc..." or "Make yourself at home."? Watch out for this! This is noteworthy knowledge from pre-NLP therapeutic specialists like Erickson: an ideal approach to inspire a person to accomplish something is by asking them to give you authorization. That's the reason gifted specialists will, by and large, NEVER direct you to a specific act: "Go into a stupor." Instead, they will use phrases like "Please, take all the time you need."

6. Listen for nonsense.

"Nonsense" can be summed up in garbage phrases like "The more you release this emotion, you can move confidently into any situation with the force of your increasing prosperity." The specialist isn't really making a clear statement. Simply, they're attempting to program your internal reactions and shift your thoughts toward the feeling or reaction they prefer. Thwart these attempts by asking things like "Would you be more straight-forward?" or "What precisely do you mean by that?" Two things will happen: it disrupts the strategy and shifts the discussion into clear, concise language, breaking the "hypnotic" strength of the "dubious language" examined earlier.

7. Find the hidden meaning.

Individuals practicing NLP rely on language with subtle and/or layered implications. With the statement, "Healthy nourishment and regular sleep for me are far more critical than anything else, wouldn't you say?" It appears to be undeniable, and you could likely concur with little question or thought. Beyond any doubt, nourishment and rest are vital, but that isn't the only vital thing happening in that statement. You might be wondering, what's the subtle or layered message? "Healthy nourishment and regular sleep for me are far more critical..." Even though the speaker emphasized themselves and their opinion, the structure of the closing question, "Wouldn't you say," asks you to consent to it. That's the first step toward the "make you an offer" language discussed earlier.

8. be aware of your attention.

Exercise extreme caution when daydreaming around people who practice NLP. Even looking off into the distance is enough to welcome a word or touch that might trigger your unconscious. Here's an illustration: A NLP client wanted to motivate me to provide unpaid work for some brand marketing. For a second, I wasn't paying complete attention, basically staring off into space. And, without letting a single second pass by, she began with the not-so-subtle attempt to practice the power of suggestion (see point 7). She started by discussing how she almost never uses her marketing budget, because outlets and business vendors send her samples and review copies of products and media for no cost. "No upfront costs," she murmured. "Everything I need, anything, I just get it for free." She'd simply made it too easy to catch on.

9. Remember you are in control.

When you are being presented with a choice, give yourself a chance to think it over and avoid making large or small decisions off the cuff. Try to give yourself at least 24 hours before settling on a choice. Especially, if you think, or realize, you're being controlled. Remember you are in control, and simply remove yourself. NLP systems are most used by sales and retail employees to trigger hasty purchases. When you recognize this, simply leave; you don't have to accept just because something is offered.

10. Follow your instincts.

Most essential to this list: when your gut reacts first, you wonder if this person is messing with you, something feels "too good to be true," or you just feel uncomfortable, don't ignore it. Especially if you work regularly with NLP individuals; quite often, they can appear to be shady. If you feel confident enough, or that it won't endanger your safety, call them out on using NLP methods and leave the situation or ask that they stop.

Chapter 4: Dark Psychology

Dark Psychology is the art of manipulation and the control of one's mind. Personality scholars agree that there is a personality profile, the dark triad, that determines certain behaviors socially or extremely selfish that involve suffering from others and skip social norms, thinking only of their benefits over anything or person.

The dark triad (or the Dark triad) is a personality profile based on a combination of the following three factors:

Psychopathy (Psychopathy): is a person with a tough personality, "callous," cruelty behaviors, and a very limited empathy. They are people who have no remorse, moral, or ethical standards are indifferent, and are often cynical and insensitive.

Machiavellianism (Machiavellianism): people with superficial charm and very manipulative. For example, they are people who can use other people to get what they want; they lie, they take advantage of who they can cheat and cheat.

Narcissism (Narcissism) consists of belief of superiority, grandiosity and vanity, and high emotional explosiveness. They are people who want everyone to admire them and pay attention to them, who believe they deserve a higher status or a social prestige and who expect special and favorable treatment and who, if they are not treated as they think they deserve, can react with anger, rage or aggressiveness.

Also, they are usually people with an unpleasant treatment (even being superficially charming), with very limited self-control (they can be very nice and suddenly have a fit of anger); they are usually aggressive, not very responsible and are not honest.

There is a great difference between the sexes, because it is much more frequent to find this personality profile in men than in women, unlike other personality profiles (such as an anxious profile).

What is manipulative behavior?

Deception is central to manipulative behavior. Very manipulative people are experts in the game of deception and in combination with the general coldness that they (often) have, they are merciless.

People who manipulate a lot often do not see people as living beings, but rather as a means to reach a goal.

That often means that once they have arrived at their 'destination,' they will certainly not think twice about leaving you on the side of the road.

The worst part is that they sometimes want to play it so that you are the guilty one and they are the victim. That is the tricky thing with people with manipulative behavior.

From small things about insisting that you come to their office or take you by surprise and immediately make a choice that is also part of the manipulation. This is also in line with one of the other important parts of manipulative behavior: intimidation.

Manipulators like to intimidate and belittle because it puts them in their position of power and puts them above others.

People also manipulate for power and money, but also status and vanity. So manipulation is often the improvement of one's situation (at the expense of others!)

Causes of manipulative behavior

Unfortunately, the cliché that people who show manipulative behavior during their youth have been mistreated or have suffered trauma is true.

Being physically abused by parents or emotionally by, for example, narcissistic parents can have a huge effect on a child who can express himself in terribly nasty ways.

Another reason that people behave manipulatively is when there is a lot at stake, such as in politics.

A certain type of people will do everything to stay in power once they have experienced it, with all the consequences that entail.

Many narcissistic people, such as managers and politicians, do everything to maintain their power and status.

This is often also why a 'ladder' is created at schools and universities with a group of people who will do everything to stay 'at the top.'

The parties, luxury houses and cars, expensive watches, and designer clothing, everything is about them to convey a sense of authority. Often these people are also narcissists.

However, there are also people who naturally have the impulse to behave manipulatively, and they are often found in the situations mentioned above. These people are also called psychopaths.

Examples of manipulative behavior

Although this may all sound a bit far away and perhaps even unrealistic, manipulative behavior is more than enough in everyday life:

You wrote an important file yesterday afternoon and gave it to a colleague so that they could look at it again and then send it.

When you came to work this morning, your boss was at your desk and started screaming angrily that you never wrote that file.

So after the boss was finished, you went on high legs to your colleague, and something very strange happened: your colleague claimed that you never gave him that file, but he did it in such a convincing way that you started your memory to doubt!

This is gas lighting and is a textbook example of manipulative behavior.

Manipulative people will also not accept guilt under any circumstances:

You and a friend fought this week, and after thinking about it for a while, you also concluded that you might have reacted a bit exaggerated.

You determine to go to your friend's house to make it up, and after you apologize and get accepted, you notice that your friend did not apologize.

If you ask for it subtly, the answer is short: "No, of course, I don't have to apologize! If you hadn't done that stupid, I wouldn't have gotten angry. "

This is, of course, strange reasoning and is almost iconic for manipulative behavior.

There is one good example of manipulative behavior:

You were ill this week, and that is why you were sick at home all week. It was so bad that even walking from the bed to the couch was too much trouble.

Fortunately, one week later you feel a little better, and if you are down the line later that week to encourage your son to play football, you tell one of the parents along the line about it who took your son last week because was sick.

The answer was not what you expected:

"Is that all? That's nothing, man! Last year I was so sick that I bruised my lungs, I coughed so hard! And yet I stood along the line! Because you should be there for your children, you just don't have to put yourself up like that and just come along. You are a good parent, aren't you? "

Not only was this a bad answer (because you were sick last week and you really couldn't), it was also a manipulative answer.

The parent has not only minimized your problems and put them in the spotlight, but they have also belittled you.

Chapter 5: The Power of Persuasion

When we lead another person to do something or make a certain decision of our own choosing, what is it that we are actually doing in order for this to happen? Are we actually sending out brainwaves or signals into the Universe that tell the other person what he or she will do? Of course, guiding another is possible with direct communication. You ask someone to do something and that person does it. Yes, this is a form of controlling someone, but it's with that person's willingness to carry out whatever it is that you have requested. You can even make someone else do a particular thing by using blackmail or threats. There is a multitude of possibilities when causing another person to perform something of your choosing which are both positive and negative. How about when you are able to do this and that person does not even know that it's being done?

The vast majority of everything that we do and every action that we take is a result of some form of conglomeration with others. This is excluding small decisions that we make daily and the routine tasks we do during our daily lives. Things as what to watch on television and when to turn that television on are not included in this topic. What is included are most of the major decisions that you, and everyone else, will make each day. These decisions are dealing with both work and outside of the workplace. We conglomerate more often than we realize. This is primarily because we, as human beings, are social creatures by our very nature. We tend to generally work together so that we all are satisfied and fulfilled.

Let's look at an example of how we allow our decision making to include others. The best example to use would be those who have families. This should include most everyone, but there are exceptions to every rule. When there are partners involved, most decisions made are done so with you working with your significant other. Deciding on a house to buy, without consulting your spouse about it, wouldn't go over too well. The same can be said with benign things such as what to make for dinner that night. The list of decisions can go on forever. Most of the time, your spouse probably is able to make his or her own decision without much guidance, but there may be times when you would like to help sway a particular decision in one way or another.

If you were about to purchase a new family car, and you wanted a certain color and model, but your wife didn't like the same, you would try to come up with reasons as to why she should change her mind and agree with you. This would be a form of direct communication, but you are still attempting to control her through a form of manipulation. You are already aware that she isn't agreeable with you on the specifications for the new car, but you are going to try to sway her anyway. You are trying to change her mind though, what is known as, persuasion. Persuading someone simply means that you are causing, by several methods, someone to do or believe something that they otherwise wouldn't. If you are able to convince your wife that the vehicle you like is better because it has all wheel drive, which is good for the winter, and she changes her mind because of this, you have persuaded her in that way.

Another way in which to look at the art of persuasion is what we do as parents. For those with children, you are most likely well acquainted with the ins and outs of persuasion. Parenting would be a horrible experience if we were to simply demand that our children do certain things. Imagine what kind of feedback you would get if you were to simply tell your child everything; he or she must do without ever giving any kind of explanation or reasoning behind your thought processes. You wouldn't do this long before you were met with a great amount of resistance. Therefore, parents need to develop a means of persuasion which best suits our particular child based on his or her characteristics and understanding.

What about decisions made by those who are not in large families or that have children? Excluding the workplace, would there be times in which that person's decisions were due to the opinions and ideas of others? How about what that person wears each day? Even if you are not in a relationship and you have no children, there are still considerations in which partially lie with others. When you go to the store to buy clothes for work, what factors come to play with your purchase? Of course, things such as comfort and price are factors. What about style? A man isn't going to buy a lady's shirt and wear it to work. That isn't because it's more expensive or less comfortable. It's probably because he does not want others to see him wearing ladies clothing while working. With this, he has allowed the thoughts and opinion of others to dictate, in some fashion, what he will wear to work.

In the previous examples and scenarios, each person is aware of what is going on. The wife who does not like the all-wheel-drive car knows that her husband does like it. She is aware that he is trying to cause her to change her mind about the purchase. Even being aware of this, she is receptive to his attempt at persuading her and he ends up being successful. The kid knows that the parent is trying to lead him to make a specific decision that he may have initially been against, but he knows that his parent believes it to be in his best interest. The clothes that the gentleman purchased at work were purchased by those standards which have been set by society in general.

Now, let's look at persuasion in the workplace. It's here where your ability for persuasion and to manipulate has the best chance of paying off in a positive way. Why do we go to work in the first place? In order to best know how to use manipulation at work, it's a good idea to understand why it is that people go to work. There are only a few possible reasons. First, and most common, people work in order to get paid. Everyone needs money to live. Most believe that the more money, the better. Therefore, many workers will gladly come to decisions they believe will increase their pay or advance their career. Another reason for working is to actually provide a service to others or provide some sort of goods. However, going back to the basics, it all leads to the dollar. Keep this in mind.

In the workplace, when is there a need for persuasion or even manipulation to begin with? A good guess would be if someone at work wants to manipulate another, it's likely because such decision or action will benefit him by advancement or by more money. If you are interested in learning how to manipulate or how to persuade while at work, why do you want this? I'm sure it's for advancement or a raise. Remember, everyone at work is there for the same reasons. If you want to manipulate a coworker, find a way to make that person believe that he or she will also benefit from whatever it is that you want. They are there for the same reason as you. Use that knowledge to your advantage.

The other side to this is somewhere I wouldn't recommend going, but it's worth mentioning. The best method is to identify what the other person wants and make them believe that to be a result. Likewise, you could also identify things the other person fears. This is totally within the scope of manipulation and not with persuasion. If someone isn't given a good reason or something to gain from an action, that person may fall to the thought of losing something valuable. This happens with bad management often. Threaten to take someone's job and they will do a lot for you.

Here is something to remember. If you manipulate someone by using negative tactics, you have forever destroyed any possibility of a positive relationship with that person. You will be an enemy. Yes, you may be feared and through this gain some control over that person but the outcome will always be negative. If you choose to carry out your plan using positive tactics, you not only can have the same outcome but can also gain other things for future use. Things such as having a friend in certain positions can go a long way. This is where the patience, mindfulness, and sight of the big picture come into play.

Another fact that needs to be remembered is that we don't cause any other person to do anything at all. We are each responsible for our own decisions and, at the end of the day, we are the ones making those choices. No matter how skilled someone may be at manipulation, that person will never actually make another person's decision for them. The best we, as manipulators, can do is lead those people to their decisions. Remember this key point also. In order to manipulate anyone, you must make that person believe they need what they are choosing and it's that person who is making the decision. This is the most important part of learning to manipulate others.

The last key factor, which is especially relevant in the workplace, is there is a difference between manipulation and persuasion. The two different terms are commonly used interchangeably but are different. A manipulator tends to be more aggressive and requires less of the person in which he or she is trying to control. Also, when it comes to negative or malicious intent, manipulation is much more common than techniques of persuasion. Manipulation will often include things such as threats and blackmail. Results from this are commonly negative and harm is usually caused. Persuasion is more of a fluid, give and take, technique and usually has better outcomes. Those who use persuasion count on participation, and common knowledge of what's happening, from those who are the target. This is much like a teacher and student relationship. The defining difference between persuasion and manipulation is simply whether or not the person doing it intends for the result to be best for all involved.

Just like with every other ability that isn't possessed by everyone, there are principles associated with persuasion. Principality is very important and parallels with character. A lack of principles leads to someone who is trifling and harmful to others. Let's look at some of these and how they apply. The first, and most basic, principle has already been mentioned in this chapter. Its persuasion is not manipulation. It's important to remember this because there is a big difference between the two and most people want no part of manipulation. This is referring to those practicing it and not the victims. Another principal will be mentioned again several times throughout this book. That is persuading the persuadable. This means you need to select your subject, person to persuade, correctly and make sure the timing is correct as well. Context is important as well. Now, keep this in mind. For someone to be persuaded, he or she needs to be interested. If they are not interested, there isn't going to be a way of persuading them. Think of a child in school who does not pay attention. That child isn't retaining any of the information from class. The teacher is attempting, or should be attempting, to pass on information to the student but, because of disinterest, that student isn't learning.

There is a principle that states, "reciprocity compels." Humans inherently want to return favors. This is where reciprocity comes into play. This will be further discussed later in this book, but payback is a great tool for persuasion and even manipulation. Another is persistence pays. This should be good common sense. I once heard a story of a fish that was in a fisherman's bucket. The fish kept leaping out of the bucket and onto the ground. After doing this several times, the fisherman finally put that fish back into the pond. Another principle is to be sincere when complimenting and never lie. Don't assume anything either. Always try to build a rapport with the other person. This will prove extremely beneficial. It's almost impossible to persuade someone at all without some kind of rapport. It's possible to manipulate but not persuade.

Some other principles are to create scarcity. "Hurry and come because there are only a few left in supply!" This is something you will see on television commercials for automobiles. Along with this, set expectations this is dealing with others and not yourself. You need to understand their reasoning behind their expectations. There is a need for behavioral flexibility and the transfer of energy. You need to motivate and excite others and not drain them of all their energy. Not go too far and become spastic. Be sure to clearly communicate and learn to properly articulate your words. This gives the appearance of intelligence, professionalism, and know-how. Along with this, learn to be confident and never appear timid or to be second-guessing you.

Now, let's look at the primary skills one need possess in order to become a master manipulator or someone of great persuasion. Each requires a skill set which is unique. Both require a good deal of intelligence. If you are not intelligent enough to understand your target and circumstances, you may as well hang it up. Mindfulness, or the knowledge of your surroundings, is key to success. Another form of needed intelligence is what is known as, emotional intelligence. The person of persuasion needs to be skilled with this type of intelligence.

Assertiveness is also a good trait to possess. Those who tend to be shy or non-controversial are not usually good at guiding others. If you have a hard time leading yourself, you can't lead others. This is just good common sense. In addition, there is also a need for patience and the ability to stand back and just watch. Impatient people are not good at persuasion or manipulation. This is due to the process, more often than not, requiring some time and attention. Unless you are planning on taking a firearm and pointing it at the person you want to do something, then telling them what to do, you will need some time to get it done. Remember, you are not making the decision. The other person makes it and you are just trying to lead that person there.

Charisma is important too. You need to come off as a likable person. We tend to go along with and agree with those whom we like. Take politicians for example. One of the first characteristics a politician tries to portray is likeability. "I'm a nice guy. Yes, I'm trustworthy and hardworking, but I'm really nice. Vote for me because you will like me." That probably sounds like a familiar statement does not it? That politician is beginning the task of persuasion. He or she is trying to make you decide to vote for him or her.

The few traits mentioned, are the basic building blocks with the techniques of manipulation and persuasion. As with all other rules, there are exceptions, but more often than not, a good manipulator needs to be intelligent, charismatic, and assertive. Then he or she needs to combine all three and then apply them with diligence and patience. A manipulator must know his or her subject well in order to really manipulate. Again, that person is actually making his or her own decision. You, as the manipulator, must make that person think that it's in his or her best interest. This is unless you are going to use trifling techniques, such as blackmail, but then you don't really need the first three traits anyway. A person who blackmails need only have one thing. That is what information, or ammunition, he or she plans on using. This takes no skill. It only takes the ability to not care about others.

In order to really lead a person to some decision, you must look at all aspects of the situation. First, be sure that you know what it is that you want from the situation. Be sure of it. Then you need to find a few positives for the other person too. You need to make your target feel like you are not leading him or her on in any way. Make them feel like they are in control and are making the decision alone without your intervention. This is the best method because it allows for no ill-will to develop and all bridges will remain intact. Also, some people resent others leading them to make decisions, also known as persuasion, and they will be less likely to go with the program. So, make them think they are wearing the "big boy" pants.

Before you really begin to work toward your goal of persuasion, make sure that you have everything lined up. You have thought of many possible scenarios and setbacks along with how to handle them. Don't start with having only one or two benefits to lead your target into believing they are going to receive. Think of as many as possible. Also, think of negatives that are likely if they don't come to a certain decision you are planning. You make them see it like this; to make the decision leads to the land of milk and honey and to not make that decision can be threatening in some way. This isn't blackmail and don't take it to a dark place. Tread lightly with this and tailor it according to the situation and those involved.

Chapter 6: Defining Desired Outcomes

The idea behind being a persuasive person, the main objective of persuasion, is to get something in return. There is no sense in practicing the art of persuasion if there is nothing desired in return. Persuasion means to cause someone to do something specific. Therefore, some sort of gain is desired, some sort of end result.

In order to know the intended end result of the persuasive effort, there must be a defined desired outcome. The person doing the persuading wants something tangible, something definable. But what do they want? Well, that is completely up to them to decide. But they must decide, before engaging in any form of persuasion, exactly what they hope to achieve at the end of the conversation.

This is what is meant as defining desired outcomes. The thing that is desired must be decided before any kind of persuasive tactics begin so that the person doing the persuading understands the desired outcome.

Pretend the office is holding a meeting to decide the location of a new office. The old office is small and cramped. The business is growing and needs more room to be able to continue to grow. So an office meeting will take place where, hopefully, the new location will be decided upon. This is the first step in defining the desired outcome, knowing what the proposed outcome is. In this case, it is the location of the new office.

So the meeting has been set for a particular time and place. Finished, right? Wrong. Without some sort of order and organization, the meeting will be unproductive and the desired outcome probably will not happen. The meeting is crucial to the desired outcome. Without some sort of specific plan then the meeting is nothing more than people in an office meeting in one room to make conversation.

So now it is necessary to set up the meeting; to have a plan as to how the meeting will proceed. Since this is a meeting of the entire office, there is no need to decide who to invite since everyone will be in attendance. So the next step is to create the agenda for the meeting. Will there be time for questions? Will certain people be invited to participate by offering specific recommendations for the new location? How will the ultimate decision be reached? All these factors need to be decided before the meeting begins.

When beginning the meeting be sure to mention the desired outcome. Let everyone know exactly what they are there to discuss. Make sure everyone involved knows and understand the desired outcome. Set a specific time for discussion and a time when the decision will be made. Then when the meeting is reaching the end of its prescribed time restate the objective and determine if a decision can be made or if more research is needed.

An outcome is nothing more than an end result that can be seen and measures. It is the consequence of the action. It is the conclusion that comes from persuading someone to do something. In any desired outcome there are four things that will need to be decided before the desired outcome can be decided upon. Those four things are: is something specific desired, is something already owned needing to be kept, who should be connected with and how, and what skills are needed to achieve the desired outcome.

It is important to decide these things because the underlying objectives will definitely affect the way the outcome is to be gained. It is similar to a football game where there is a defensive team and an offensive team. One group attacks the opposing team and one group defends against the attacks from the opposing teams. Each team will have a different set of priorities and procedures. Their desired outcomes will be quite different from one another. Each team will need to decide what it is they want to learn, defend, or acquire. The goal will determine the game plan.

The goal is the desired outcome. Behind any goal and its desired outcome is the need for change. Some sort of change needed has been identified and will be achieved. The path to achievement begins with setting a goal. The end of this journey is the desired outcome. It is necessary to understand that these are two separate entities that work together to achieve a result.

A goal is a destination. An outcome is a specific thing; it can be seen and measured. While setting the goal is vital to receiving the outcome, they are two quite different things and should be treated as such.

Goals always have reasons behind them. Something that is thought of as being necessary to happiness, to wealth, to health, or just because it is truly desired, is just not there. Whatever the reason is, it is that exact reason that drives forward progress toward the desired outcome. In order to be able to progress, to go forward to the goal, that goal and the idea of achieving it must be firmly entrenched in your mind. Without a steady focus on the goal, there is no possibility that the goal will ever be reached.

Imagine going to work every day for fifteen years, doing the same job every day. Imagine this is a job that needed college courses, so it was a chosen job. During the past fifteen years, doing the same job every day has been rewarding and profitable. There have been several promotions, the last of which came with a private secretary and a lovely large office. Several other people, who have not been working here quite as long, are now the team that directly reports every Monday in this large new office.

But going to work has become somewhat boring. The job just does not bring the amount of satisfaction it once did. The problem is not in the job itself but in the person doing the job. What seemed so right all those years ago now feels so wrong. What is really desired is more interaction with people. In managing other people, a new skill has emerged: the ability to take raw recruits and mold them into productive team members with a bright future. That is the job that brings happiness and satisfaction.

But while this thought has been firmly entrenched in the mind for months now, no changes have been made to get closer to the goal of that type of occupation. And so every Monday morning is filled with team meetings, every day is filled with spreadsheets, and every Friday is filled with boundless joy that another work week has passed. Why?

The answer to **why?** Is procrastination. Whether intentional or unintentional, procrastination has ruined many good intentions. Unintentional procrastination does happen sometimes. Everyone has that moment of "oops, I meant to take care of that today I'll get to it first thing in the morning." That is unintentional; something was forgotten. Intentional procrastination means knowing something needs to be done but putting it off until whenever. Many people do this with dreams and desires, especially those that will require extra work to accomplish or simply just a big leap of faith. Changing careers when one is firmly established is a scary thing. But what someone wants at twenty is not necessarily what they want at forty. People change. Their hearts change. They must be willing to follow their dreams and make them a reality. But people procrastinate out of fear.

So ask these three questions:

1. What exactly am I afraid of? Do I fear to lose a great job that will pay for my kid's college and not being able to find one that pays as well? What if I have to take a pay cut and can no longer pay the mortgage? What happens if I lose my health insurance? These are all valid question that must be addressed when considering a large change in employment.

2. What will I gain if I am able to conquer this fear? What great gain will be realized? Will it be a new job, a new career that is more in line with current life goals? Maybe the real dream is the chance to help other people.

3. What do I do to fight this fear? Accept the fear as real. Acknowledge its existence. Then make a plan to reach the new goal and proceed without waiting. Go forward without procrastination.

Now, it is time to set a goal to make this dream a reality. Identify the goal as specifically as possible. The more specific the goal, the better the chance is to realize that goal. Vague goals are nothing more than wishes. It is as simple as the difference between "I want to lose weight" and "I want to lose twenty pounds." The second statement is a specific goal that can be measured as work toward it progresses.

Know exactly what is desired as a reward when the goal is achieved. If the goal is weight loss, perhaps the reward is being able to wear that dress featured in the store window. If the goal is learning how to swim, then maybe the goal is to swim in the ocean for the first time ever. Plan how this goal will be achieved. Think about the senses that will be used along the way and how they will make this progress easier or more difficult.

Visualize the plan and try to imagine any possible obstacles. That does not mean putting the obstacles in the path, but in being aware of the possibility that they might crop up and having a plan to defeat them. If the intended goal involves weight loss, what will be the plan for coping with the buffet during the holiday season? If the goal is to complete classes online then what happens if the internet goes out or the computer crashes? It is necessary to have a back-up plan to deal with life's little emergencies.

What will be used for markers along the way to track progress toward the goal? If the goal is weight loss, then perhaps a wall chart with every five pounds lost marked in red. Perhaps a drawing of a thermometer, with the goal being the mercury bulb at the top, and the thermometer is filled in gradually with every pound lost. Have a system in place to track these milestones.

Be aware that working toward any goal might come with negatives attached. Changing careers will most certainly mean a change in income. What if the career change means moving to another state? Is that a viable option? An extreme amount of weight loss will mean constantly refreshing the wardrobe. It is important to be aware of anything that might be seen as a negative effect of reaching the goal. These must be acceptable or the goal will need to be changed.

And when little distractions occur along the way, do not let them cancel out any progress that has already been made. Life happens. All roads have bumps in them. Even Shakespeare knew that no matter how good the plan was, it might not work. So acknowledge the fact that little bumps in the road will happen and have a plan to overcome them. Maybe it was a temporary lapse in judgment. Maybe it is a sign that the current path needs to take a bit of a different direction. The choice is solely up to the person who set the goal and created the path. And when the goal is reached, so will be the desired outcome.

Chapter 7: Mind Control Techniques

Some synonymous terms of mind control are brainwashing, thought reform, manipulation, exploitive persuasion, sociopsychological manipulation, behavioral change technology, and a few others. As previously mentioned, there are both good and bad reasons for mind control, but we tend to only see things which are negative.

There are a few different types of manipulation. Here, we are going to discuss 2 of those types. First, there is the sociopsychological manipulator. This is someone who attempts to use social influence in order to lead someone into a change in behavior or a decision. This can be indirect and deceptive in nature. It's also possible for this to be direct. With this form of manipulation, there is often great pressure put on the target individuals. An example of this is peer-pressure, but there are much bigger examples that we rarely notice.

One of the best and most common uses of psychological manipulation is marketing. We don't think of marketing as being this and it isn't usually negative in nature. One exception to this is with negative political ads. However, marketing is simply persuasion on a large scale. Let's look at television commercials. What are they exactly? Years ago, there were ads for cigarettes. Most of those who have a few years under the belt will probably remember the Marlboro Man. He was a healthy cowboy who portrayed a tough image. He was usually on horseback and sucking down a cigarette. We never saw anyone with cancer or being unable to breathe on those commercials. There were also numerous tobacco ads with very physically attractive people, both ladies and men, who were holding lit cigarettes in the ad. In reality, those who smoked for a long time usually looked anything but like the people portrayed on television and in the printed ads.

What about the commercials that attempt to lead us to believe that if we buy a certain product, our lives will somehow instantly become great? "Buy this drink and you will forever be ecstatic!" I like the pharmaceutical ads. "Are you feeling sad and depressed? Talk to your doctor about blah medication and kiss the sadness goodbye." There is no mention of what the possibilities for the cause of this sadness may be and how the best treatment is to stop what may be causing the problem, if possible, and not simply medicating it. They may even use pictures of cute little puppies or laughing children. They have associated something joyful and peaceful with their product leading you to subconsciously form the same connection. This is manipulation at its best. How about fast-food ads? It's a well-known fact that most people need to eat healthy in order to be physically fit. Eating this which are proven bad for you may not be a terrible thing if done in moderation but only in moderation. Have you ever seen an out-of-shape person on a fast-food ad?

When we are teenagers, in high-school, we are bombarded by psychological manipulation from all angles. We had to deal with the advertising seen on television and in magazines. We had to deal with growing up and listening to our parents. Then there was the, ever so dreaded, bombardment of peer-pressure. I am sure that everyone remembers this. Peer-pressure is simply the culmination of several kinds of social manipulation. This happens when outside ideas are placed in one person's head and then that individual passes them on. One child is made to believe that a brand of clothing is the best thing since sliced bread. Then he or she tells others that leading them to believe the same and to run to the store to buy them. This goes on and on. As time goes on, and we progress in technology, the pressure, and the manipulating, of teens is increasing at an exponential rate. Now, not only are kids pressured at school but due to social media, this is a never-ending cycle. It's worth mentioning that this all takes place without commonly being noticed and recognized for what it truly is. We call it "life" or "growing up" but what it is it really? It's mass manipulation.

Previously mentioned in this book, there is the beautiful art of political persuasion. We are constantly subjected to political ads and campaigns. Most of the time, important issues are thrown out of the window and candidate's pasts or mistakes, or transgressions, are brought to the forefront. A particular person may actually have the answers needed for positive change, but that does not matter when the political ads come out. We are led to forget that a certain candidate has an impeccable record of public service and good deeds and led to only think about one night that individual had too much to drink while back in college 20 years ago. This is becoming ever more prominent. Candidates don't even need to do this kind of advertising or manipulating, themselves. Anyone who can afford it can take it upon themselves and begin a smear campaign against someone and because of the way our brains work, if we see an ad enough times, we will begin to believe what we are being told.

Here, let us look at what we have learned, and are learning, about manipulation from another perspective. Let's look at it in a way that we can protect ourselves from it. Yes, you may be reading this book in order to learn how to do it, but you can also learn how to recognize that it's being done to you and how to block it. It begins with knowledge and mindfulness. If you are aware of these tactics and why they are being done, you are able to protect yourself from them. If you see a cute puppy on a tire commercial, know that puppies have nothing to do with car tires and that the commercial is only trying to manipulate your thinking and attempting to lead you into associating the two.

The examples for psychological manipulation are so numerous there could be an entire series of books written on this topic alone. However, for our purposes, we will move on to the other form of manipulation. Now, we are going to discuss a much darker method utilized to manipulate others. With this particular tactic, there is usually never a positive outcome for the target. This tactic is harmful to others and is not recommended for you to try in this book. Personally, I would rather you stay far away from this form of manipulation.

Now let's look at an emotional manipulator. Unlike with psychological manipulation, emotional manipulation is almost always negative and does harm to others. With this technique, the manipulator preys on the emotions of those in which he or she is targeting. An example of this is when a child is able to manipulate parents into making decisions based on their feelings of guilt. Whatever the cause of this guilt, the manipulator will use it to his or her advantage. For instance, if a parent needed to cancel out on some outing with a child. Then the child brings that up at a later date as a reason for why that parent should or shouldn't do something. "Dad, you didn't take me to the record store last Friday. So, the least that you can do today is taking me to the clothing store." The child is playing on the fact that his or her father feels bad about not being able to take the child to the record store and is using that to persuade or manipulate him into going to buy some clothes.

One area where this manipulation often creeps up is with those suffering from addiction. It may seem odd to bring up something like addiction in a book about manipulation and persuasion, but that is actually a big part of the world of addiction. Anyone who has been touched by this disease can relate. This isn't simply referring to addicts. It includes their family, friends, and support network too. Actually, the ones who are not actually addicted are most likely to be the targets of emotional manipulation; Not the other way around. Why is this case?

Most addicts need to be rather intelligent and able to manipulate others. Otherwise, they probably wouldn't be able to be addicts. They wouldn't usually have the necessary resources. Addicts need those who are known as enablers. These are those who, with or without their knowledge, enable addicts to continue their use of whatever substance they desire. This can be with money or can be something like babysitting an addict's child so that the addict can go out and use. Most people wouldn't help with things like this, but they are put in positions where they see it best to go along with the program of helping that addict. One common method an addict will use here is emotional manipulation.

I have personally been part of the life of an addict and I will use some of what I experienced as an example. A very good friend of mine, due to things beyond his direct control, became an addict in his adulthood. Although he was an adult at the time, his addiction led him to regress back to his teenage years. What is meant by that is he began to live his life as if he were still a teenager. He moved back in with his parents and began to look to them for financial support. Its here were my example of how addicts will manipulate falls into place.

As we have seen, guilt is one method where an emotional manipulator will use in order to successfully get what that manipulator is trying for. With my friend, he was trying to get money in order to feed his addiction. I'm not talking about a few dollars here and there. He was spending somewhere in the area of $100 to $250 per day on drugs. Although he did have an income, it wasn't sufficient enough for these expenditures. So, he went to his mother for money. At first, she was able to tell him no. Then he began the guilt tactics in his manipulation. He used mistakes that his parents had made against them. He was able to identify those things from his past which bothered his mother the most. It didn't take long before he had turned his mom into a total enabler and this began her emotional downfall.

It wasn't his intention to harm his mother. Addicts think differently than everyone else. He just wanted the drugs he felt that he needed. Although it wasn't his intention to hurt her, that's exactly what he did. He would remind her of some time back when he was a kid where things were not especially rosy. His father hadn't been the best dad and that is what he brought up. His mother, on the other hand, was a great mom but she felt partially responsible and guilty for what he had to endure from his dad. He didn't hesitate to bring those things up with her. She would jump at his every word. He played the emotional manipulation card well and, because of this, created an enabler that helped him drag out his addiction for years.

One of the best things that an emotional manipulator can use to lead another is love. This is just as, if not more, powerful than fear. This form of manipulation is probably the most damaging. It towers over blackmail and other trifling techniques. Love is a powerful motivator and this can be tweaked to be very unhealthy. Eventually, he regained his life, dropped the drugs, and is now spending what life he and his mother have in order to make amends to her and his entire family.

Other relationships are also subject to emotional manipulation. Unhealthy marriages are one example. In these relationships, usually one of the two will be the manipulator and the other his or her target. This is a very one-sided relationship that commonly is one person living only to please the other. The other will continuously take and take until there is nothing left. He or she will use whatever tactics are necessary to keep this going. Of course, there is almost always severe and irrefutable damage done to one of the two. This not only leads to divorce but can lead to much worse. It can lead to one of them being destroyed for the remainder of their life.

Now, let's look at one area where both psychological and emotional manipulation can occur simultaneously. We have all heard of cults but what do we actually know about them and those in which are affected. Cults, and those harmed by them, are widely misunderstood. There are many myths associated with cults and unfair stereotyping of those who are former members of them. Nevertheless, cults, and cult leaders, are prime examples of manipulators who use all of the available tactics in order to control their subjects.

What are some of the myths that are associated with cults? Here are a few. People can just leave if they are in a cult and wish not to be. Only stupid or non-assertive people join cults. Cults are based on religion. Cults are strange and their members are anti-social and usually outcasts. These are just a few. Now, let's look at the truth and how manipulation plays a key role in the cult leader's abilities in controlling members.

I remember learning about the cult leader Jim Jones and how he led over 900 followers, a third of them children, to commit mass suicide. In truth, not all of them drank the poison. Some were shot. They were the people who refused to drink poison because they wanted to live. How did they wind up in that situation, to begin with? It's complicated and is another topic that an entire series of books could be written. Here is a short summary.

Jones was very charismatic and intelligent. He was able to identify, or be mindful, of the wants and needs of people specific to that time and location. He was able to identify with those people who would follow him and he made them truly believe that he would be the one to lead them to better lives. He did this through manipulation and persuasion. He was both honest in some things and dishonest in others. In the beginning, the cult wasn't the way it had become at the end. As with all successful manipulators, he had to slowly progress in his power and he had to demonstrate extreme patience. After making them believe he was best for their lives and it was in their best interest to follow him, he began to place more control over them. The members were virtually prisoners by the end. They had invested all of their financial, emotional, and psychological resources into the cult and now we're trapped. Then Jones became dark and his mental health drastically declined. He was able to take them all down with him. We say to each other that there is no way we could harm a child, especially our own child, or anyone else for that matter. However, by the time the mass suicide took place, they had no choice. It was poison or a bullet. A horrible truth but a real example of the power that a manipulator can gain and the destruction that can come as a result.

Now that we have taken a look down that dark path, let's come back to the lighter side of persuasion. Here is something to think about. Reviewing some previous information in this book, what is the first step in persuasion and manipulation? First, you need to find out what it is that you are wanting. Then you need to find a way to make your target feel as if he or she needs or wants the same. If not the same, a way for your target to think that he or she will somehow benefit from what you are trying to get them to do. You need to make it enticing. This does not have to be a lie. This is especially relevant to the workplace. There is probably nothing that will benefit you, while at work, that will not also benefit someone else. Use this to your advantage.

If you are truly intelligent and able to read and understand others, you will probably be able to identify reasons for that person to go along with your wishes and those reasons are genuine. You won't need to go to the dark place of manipulation. You will be able to simply persuade someone else based on joint benefits. A good word to remember is conglomeration. This means to bring together. If you have the ability to cause someone else to make a decision and you have done this without lying, harming another, and with integrity, you have proven yourself to be a true master of persuasion without gaining the stigma of being a trifling manipulator.

Chapter 8: Mind Control with NLP for Love and Relationships

In this chapter, we will discuss how NLP can be beneficial to healthy relationships. We will learn what truly good and fulfilling relationships are based on and built upon. We are going to explore techniques that can be used to strengthen relationships as well as those which can help us in establishing healthy relationships. There are many factors that play a role in good relationships. We are going to discuss the importance of our mental health and readiness prior to entering into any partnership, or relationship, and possible outcomes associated with having and not having these factors.

We all want and need certain things. There are basic needs for all of us and one of the most crucial ways in which we can have our basic emotional needs met is with healthy relationships. We all want to be loved. He all wants to be desired and needed. We all long for compassion and understanding. All of these can be acquired in good and healthy partnerships. Likewise, a bad relationship can be devastating. Most of us carry around baggage, such as negative emotions, fear, and anxiety from previous unhealthy relationships and this can actually place barriers between us and others when we find ourselves in new relationships. True fulfillment usually can only be found in the emotional qualities within our personal relationships.

Every good relationship begins with a clear and comfortable frame and state of mind. Maturity of both parties is a factor as well as timing. Your goals and wants need to be compatible with the person which you want as a partner. Your values and beliefs need to match. These ideas and characteristics are tangible and very important in the overall health of any relationship. If you find yourself in a great relationship, the benefits are numerous. You will gain confidence and feeling of self-worth that can't be matched. Just as important, you must remember to also transmit this to your partner. You should always treat your partner in the exact ways in which you wish for them to treat you. In doing this, and having this knowledge, you are able to know what it is that your partner wants. You just need to see what it is that your partner is doing and take it from there.

Before we are able to be the kind of partner we should, we must first be good within ourselves. If you enter into a relationship, while you have self-doubt or internal difficulties, you are entering a partnership that is doomed from the start. A perfect couple consists of two people who are able to function well as individuals but function as a partner just as well, if not better. This is the first step in entering any relationship. You must be good with yourself. This is a must and shouldn't ever be compromised. The second important point that needs to be addressed is you must establish what, or who, it is that you desire. This is your own personal decision based on your personality, desires, ideologies, and belief system. It does not matter what others believe you need or what you think you should have. At the end of the day, what matters is what you actually want.

The next part of entering into a good relationship is timing. This isn't just important to you, but it's also important with your partner. Are you looking for "Mr. Right" or "Mr. Right Now?" Are there things going on currently in your life that may prohibit your success in the relationship? Are these things, not only able to hinder you, but are they able to hinder your partner as well? Timing is important and crucial to the longevity of the relationship. If you are a point in your life where there are other priorities that take precedence with you, you should wait until those priorities shift and you are able to become capable of making your partner the priority that he or she deserves.

Once you have decided what it is that you want, have concluded that now is the time for you to enter into a relationship, and have covered all of your predetermining factors, now you can begin to open up to the possibilities of finding the right person. Here is when rapport becomes important. What is rapport? It's basically your similarities and likeness with someone with whom you are interested in entering a relationship with. It's also the establishment of trust with that person. With rapport, there are many individual factors that can be used for determining compatibility. Some of these are personality types, values, beliefs, culture, political ideologies, interests, religious beliefs, and so on. Of course, there are also physical characteristics, such as gender and body types, that need to be taken into account. However, some characteristics can't be over accentuated because it will lead to mimicking the other and can actually cause a loss of rapport.

It's crucial that the rapport which is established in the beginning, and the reasons for your attraction to your partner, and his or her attraction to you, be kept at the forefront of each partner's minds throughout the relationship. It all too common for people to enter into relationships with guns blazing, meaning being the perfect partner, only to begin to relax and change once the relationship has been established. One partner, or both, will use all available techniques to get the other to enter into a relationship but, once they are in that relationship, the other partner believes he or she can tone down what it was they were doing in the beginning. This is one of the most common reasons for relationships ending. Keep in mind; the reasons for someone falling for you are the same reasons that will make them want to stay with you. If you remove the reasons for their attraction, they have no reasons to stay with you. Often, we see children born of relationships used as new reasons, but this does not work. This leads the partnership to morph into, what can be seen as, a business relationship. There will be no real emotional connection in the relationship and, even though that couple may remain together, they will lack the comforts and fulfillment of needs in which they desire.

Now you have identified what you want, making sure the timing is right, and have met that special someone. Now, what do you do? You need to make sure that your partner feels the same about you. There are several ways in which a person can see that he or she is loved by the other. These ways should be identified at the relationships beginning. A few methods are by what the other person buys and places him or she takes you. There are also things such as the way in which they touch you, the looks they give, or what they say. Identification of these is important as they can be used to gauge the continuance of love throughout the relationship.

The best way to determine how you can best assure your partner that you love him or her is by doing for them what they tend to do for you. For instance, most likely if your partner puts her arm around you at times to assure you of her love and affection, you can bet that if you do the same, she will believe that you do love and appreciate her. We don't tend to do things to or for others, especially those whom we care about the most, that we wouldn't want to be done to us. Although this is commons sense, it's also a great method to gauge or determine how your significant other is feeling about you. As the relationship progresses, this will come naturally and will take much less conscious effort. Just be sure to not allow these things to stop just because the relationship is no longer new.

NLP has devised a few strategies to determine areas in relationships. Areas such as attraction, love, and desire are all strategized with NLP techniques. First, you must know your partner. This means that you should know what those subtle gestures and tones of voice your partner will display depending on how he or she is feeling. Know what your partner fears and what he or she wants. You will pick up ideas as to how to carry these things out simply by learning your partner. Be sure to never use this knowledge for manipulation. There isn't a positive outcome in relationships where manipulation takes place.

One technique you can use to ensure that your partner is in love with you and wants you is to temporarily remove yourself from his or her presence. This does not mean that you can tell your wife that you are going to the store for a lottery ticket only to not return for a week. However, in short time frames, absence can signal want or lack thereof. Just like the cliché, absence makes the heart grow fonder; this is built on the same premise. When using these kinds of tactics, please never overuse them. Here is some advice. If you are an insecure person needing constant approval and reassurance that you are loved, you should take care of that issue prior to ever entering into a serious relationship. If not, you are not going to be a good partner and, if your shortcoming does not end the relationship, it could lead it to become a codependent partnership or, at the very least, a very unhealthy relationship. Again, you must first make sure that you are a good candidate for entering into a relationship prior to taking that next step.

Previously, we discussed those who are in sales and tactics which they can use in order to lead someone into a particular purchase. With relationships, you are not simply selling yourself to another and then the job is over. It's a continuing process forever. Never relax and believe that you have your partner and him or she isn't going anywhere no matter what you may or may not do. This mistake has been made countless times by many divorcees. You should always be selling yourself, your worth, your compassion, and your desire for your partner.

Now, we are going to look at the real world and all it gives us. As much as most of us wish it were, life isn't perfect. Regardless of what good we may do or how good of a person we may be, life will often provide us with the short end of the stick. When we would like milk and honey, sometimes we get vinegar and stale bread. That's just the way it is. It isn't going to change. So, the best that we can do is better preparing ourselves so that we can handle the difficult situations as they come. With relationships, there is no difference. We may be a great person, but things happen. We can know our partner perfectly, be the most affectionate and caring person, and have the utmost consideration for our significant other but that may fall short if given the right elements.

The most common reason given for divorce is what is known as "irreconcilable differences." What is this exactly? Webster defines it as "inability to agree on most things or on important things." It isn't suggesting that one or the other partners are inadequate or bad. It's simply that, for whatever reason, they find themselves disagreeing. First, did they have these disagreements when they first entered into the relationship? Hopefully, they didn't. If the relationship was established properly, there must be another reason for these differences. Both partners were independently ready for a relationship. They each chose their partner carefully and paid attention to every detail, no matter how benign. Both did their very best at pleasing the other and showed a great deal of compassion and love. So, what's the issue here? Many of us have witnessed relationships just like this. Both people are independently great as individuals. Both are loving and compassionate. Both appeared to be perfect fits for the other and they seemed to get along great and really loved one another. So, what happened to them and their relationship? I've seen couples divorce and it made me think that, if they didn't make it, the rest of society is doomed.

Think of this; you meet someone at the beach or any spot you can imagine. You are both at that exact place at that exact time. You may both have everything in common too. However, both you and the other person took different routes to that spot and lived through different circumstances while on the way. Even though you both find yourselves to be at the same point, and with the same characteristics, you took different paths there. This means that it's likely that you are not both going to react or respond to every event the same and those events may lead you to go in different directions. Another way to look at this; you may both like the same sports team. The difference is why each of you has this opinion of that team. One of you may be a graduate from that particular university, while the other just picked last season's champions. This probably means that the alumnus of the school is less likely to decide that he or she no longer favors that team. There are infinite ways to look at this. Regardless of the possible ways, the ending remains the same. What does this mean? Are we all just simply at life's mercy and subject to emotional trauma at the drop of a hat? Not exactly. Although we may not be able to change the situation when finding ourselves here but we can at least know why. First, don't give up. Do whatever you are able to in order to carry both you and your partner through the tough spot in your relationship and you may find that you both were able to beat the odds and remain together?

Let's look at what it means to have taken different routes. Obviously, the previously mentioned scenarios were only metaphors. The location isn't an actual place but a specific state of mind and life situation. Regardless of the spectrum of commonalities you and your partner may or may not have, you both will respond, and react, to things differently. One of you may be able to brush something, such as a traumatic event, off but the other isn't able to do that. Let's look at this. Both you and your wife have a particular religious faith. This is one of the main commonalities you found of yourselves that led to your relationship. Later down the road, your wife either endures a traumatic event, or meets a really influential person, either causing a dramatic shift in her religious ideologies. Now, what was once the main glue that kept you together has deteriorated to where there is no more left. Not only does she no longer agree with your religious faith, her new found beliefs totally contradict what you believe. What do you do when faced with this situation? Both of you are strongly holding to your individual beliefs and not willing to waiver. Both accuse the other of being naïve. Neither of you are bad people, but you are no longer finding the same rapport you once had.

You both joined into the relationship only after taking the proper steps and exercised due caution in choosing the other as a mate. Even though this was done, life didn't care about that. Circumstances led to the separation of you and your partners beliefs and both of you are much too committed to your independent ideas to compromise them. Therefore, you now are at constant odds and the negativity within the relationship grows stronger each day. One day, it will lead to resentment and even hate. You have taken the necessary steps in attempting to salvage the relationship to no avail. So, as the very last resort, you decide to part ways. This happens every day.

Just like the baggage we carry due to prior bad relationships; we carry lessons learned and individual ways of dealing with certain issues which are based on these lessons. It's one of the ways in which we are individual but is also a way in which we can find ourselves at odds with another. The best thing to do is know what and how things are going and this can give you a good idea as to what is about to come.

To conclude this chapter, NLP is extremely important and beneficial in the relationship. This isn't just with the beginning of the union but throughout its entirety. You have to first know yourself and then using NLP you can learn your partner. Knowing your partner can prove invaluable in maintaining a healthy and long relationship. Also, the relationship will be much more fulfilling to both parties. Remember that serious and personal relationships prove beneficial in many areas in life and isn't limited to just the partnership. It's beneficial for both of you as a couple, as individuals, and as part of society as a whole.

Chapter 9: The Most Powerful Mind-Power Tool

Humans spend countless hours seeking new ways to work just about anything. Through endless hours of research, they pour over books and journals looking for the message that will tell them the secret to harnessing mind power. Many never realize that the most powerful mind power tool is already on board and just aching to be used. It is the human brain, the mind itself.

Every time a person practices a new habit or thinks a new thought, they make a new pathway in the brain. Every time the habit is used, or the idea is thought, the nerve pathway becomes even stronger. The human brain is wired at birth to be an efficient machine and it is ready, from birth, to make an ever increasing amount of nerve pathways and to strengthen the pathways that are used the most.

Sometimes thoughts and habits need to be changed for the improvement of the person. When people decide that they would like to make a change in their lives, there will be a period of adjustment. This is true whether the change is mental, emotional, or physical. During this period of adjustment, there will be some level of discomfort. When a habit or a thought is already formed, it has made its own path in the brain. When a stimulus is seen or heard, the message travels along the preset nerve pathway to the spot in the brain that controls that thought or habit. In order to change a thought or a habit, it is necessary for the nerve path to be changed. Until the nerve path is changed, the old nerve path will remain in the brain. The discomfort comes from the brain trying to automatically access the old pathway and the new pathway at the same time. This is painful for the brain to do.

It is easy to become frustrated when the brain goes back to its old patterns of thought and habit. Never fall into the habit of placing blame on a lack of willpower. Willpower has nothing to do with it. It is a very difficult thing to override preset pathways in the brain. The brain is a very powerful tool. When will power fails and mistakes happen, remember to use kindness and compassion in dealing with the failure. The brain is very efficient at doing what it does. The only way to change the pathways in the brain is to keep working on new pathways that will eventually obliterate the old, undesirable ones.

The brain needs a clear understanding that changes are about to take place and new pathways are about to be laid down. Remind the brain that new habits and new thoughts will be replacing the old ones. Blaming failure on a lack of will power is a self-defeating statement. The process of making new nerve paths in the brain takes hard work and time. It will help to keep reminding oneself of the impending change. By doing this over and over, it makes the process no longer about possible character flaws. The focus is now put on the habit of thought that is being built.

Is it possible to build new nerve pathways in the brain? Yes, it is possible, and it can be done. If more proof is needed, just compare the adult brain to the baby's brain. Every current habit and thought a person has is the direct result of having spent time practicing them over and over until they created a pathway in the brain. New pathways can be created. Think of it this way: they already have. The baby's brain has no idea of anything. It has no thoughts or habits. Every nerve path currently in the brain was practiced until it became a part of the brain. Think of the baby. The baby lies around day after day and does baby things. Then one day the baby notices the shiny rattle that mommy is waving in front of its little face. The baby wants the rattle. As the baby is waving its tiny arms around, the mommy puts the rattle close enough so the baby can touch it with its wavering hand. After a few of these sessions, the baby gets the idea that if the arm is in the air it can touch the rattle. A nerve pathway is beginning to grow. So the baby decides to lift its arm to actively reach for the rattle. The baby will be unsuccessful at first because the arms will wave wildly and will not connect with the rattle. One day, the baby will actually grab the rattle, and the nerve pathway is then complete.

While this may seem like a very simple example, it is exactly how nerve pathways are created in the brain. Every action, thought, or habit has its own nerve pathway. All pathways must be created. No one was born knowing to sit in front of the television and mindlessly eat dip with chips. No one was born lamenting the excess pounds they carry in strange places. No one was born hating their body. All behaviors are learned, good and bad. And the bad ones can be replaced with good ones.

So if the ability to program negative thoughts into the brain exists, then the ability to disrupt those negative thoughts with positive thoughts also exists. The brain can be reprogrammed. It is a powerful tool, and its main function is to turn thoughts into reality. The brain is always working, so why not use the power of the brain to benefit rather than harm? Just because a particular habit or thought has been around all forever does not mean it needs to stay. Use the power of the brain to choose new habits and thoughts to focus on and replace the old, negative thought pathways in the brain.

The new thought needs to be believable; the new habit needs to be doable. It does not real good to try to stick to a habit that is impossible to accomplish or to try to believe a thought that is unbelievable. After years of seeing the reality of an obese body, it would be nearly impossible to suddenly believe that the image in the mirror is that of a skinny person. But the brain will likely accept something that mentions learning to take care of the body or learning to accept the body in order to correct its flaws. The brain will turn a belief in reality. Believing a positive thought will lead to quite a different result than the ending where only negative thoughts are present.

Be prepared to repeat and repeat some more. The primary key to being able to make a new habit stay is repeating it constantly. The more a new, desirable habit is practiced, the more the brain begins to accept it. The nerve path becomes stronger every day. With constant practice, this new nerve path will become the path the brain will prefer to use, and the old one will cease to exist.

In any case, be sure to allow enough time to effectively create a change. Accept the starting point and constantly visualize the ending point. Accept the fact that the path to the goal of a new habit or thought will not be easy or perfect. The path will almost never travel in a straight line. Sometimes people fall completely off the path, and that is okay too. Just get back up and get back on. Do not get sidetracked by the idea that this journey will be easy and carefree because it will not be. Just keep thinking of the new nerve pathway that will be created by the new thought or habit and it will eventually become a reality.

Most of the pathways in the brain are stored in the subconscious mind. This is the part of the mind that is always working without always being thought of. Think of learned skills like tying shoes, zipping a coat, and pouring milk into a glass. These were all learned behavior whose nerve pathways are firmly set in the subconscious part of the mind. This part of the brain is the bank of data for all life functions.

The communication between the conscious mind and the unconscious mind works in both directions. Whenever a person has a memory, and emotion, or an idea, it is rooted in the subconscious mind and translated to the conscious mind through mind power. The subconscious has the power to control just about anything a human does regularly.

For example, during meditation steady, deep breathing is usually practiced. The control of the breath is brought from the subconscious mind and given to the conscious mind to tell it to control the breathing. Once a pattern of deep steady breathing is begun by the conscious mind, the subconscious mind takes over and keeps the set rhythm going until it is told to stop. This is done by a conscious end to the deep breathing or an encounter with an outside stimulus like stress. The subconscious mind also processes the great wealth of information received daily and only passes along to the conscious mind those things that are necessary for the brain to remember.

When sending thoughts from the conscious mind to the subconscious mind, the brain will only send those thoughts that are attached to great emotion. The only thoughts that remain in the subconscious are those that are kept there with strong emotions. Unfortunately, the brain does not know the difference between positive emotions and negative emotions. Any strong emotion will work. Both negative emotions and positive emotions can be quite strong. Also, unfortunately, negative emotions tend to be stronger than positive emotions.

Step one in learning to use the power of the subconscious part of the mind will be to eliminate any thoughts that come with negative emotions. Also, negative mental comments will also need to cease. Fears will usually come true, specifically because they are drowning in negative emotion. This is why negative ideas need to be eliminated because they can be very harmful roadblocks on the road to harnessing brain power.

One best practice to use to get rid of negative thoughts is to counter them with positive thoughts. This will take time and practice, but it is a very powerful and useful technique. Whenever a negative thought pops in the conscious mind, immediately counter it with a positive thought that is dripping with strong emotion. The actual truth will come out somewhere in between the two thoughts.

Another way to counter negative emotions is to delete them, just like using a remote control. When a negative thought comes into the conscious mind, imagine destroying it. Imagine writing that thought on paper and burning it. Imagine pointing a remote control at the thought and pressing a huge delete button. Whatever form used to imagine deleting the thought, the important thing is to get rid of it before it can take hold in the subconscious mind.

Find something energizing and use it to reach a goal. Those things that are found to be energizing bring boundless energy to positive thoughts. It is often necessary to invent motivation, at least in the beginning, to learn to create new habits and thoughts. But with a bit of practice and a lot of positive thought, new positive habits will soon be burned into the subconscious mind and the old negative thoughts and habit will fade away.

More Effective Techniques To Influence Others

Along with all the techniques that you have learnt so far, here are a few more, which if you work on committedly will help you achieve the desired results and always achieve success when it comes to manipulating others.

Generate Urgency

To influence, you need to create urgency. Unless you do that, oftentimes, people will not respond as positively as you hope them to. Creating urgency means that you create a scenario or paint a picture of the problem at hand in a manner that it appears as a pressing issue making the other person feel he/she must act as you want. If you want your friend to file for medical insurance, make her feel how urgent that is and how she must not wait another minute to act on it.

Here are some tactics you can use to create urgency in order to manipulate others.

Ask Probing Questions: Asking the right and often probing questions is just the trick that can help you create earnestness in someone to act as desired. If you are tired of your partner not taking his debt issues seriously, ask questions such as 'What problems are we suffering because of financial issues?', 'What are your concerns about your ever-increasing debt?' and 'Is your debt the reason your self-esteem is dwindling?' Make sure to ask the questions with concern in your tone and facial expressions so the other person feels your apprehension and then becomes stimulated to take the desired action.

Give Examples: Another effective tactic to create urgency is to illustrate examples of other people who went through similar experiences, and ended up suffering in the end because they failed to take the right action at the right time. If you wish for your best friend going through depression to get therapy instead of staying engulfed in the darkness all alone, talk to him about how another friend went through the same traumatic episode, but recovered soon after because she had a therapist by her side. Reinforce the urgency by talking about the problem and sharing relevant examples.

Make them Visualize: Visualization is an incredibly effective technique that does not only help you become more invested in your work and put in extra effort to achieve your goals, but also helps you in influencing others as well.

When you wish for someone to oblige to your commands, paint them a beautiful picture of how doing that chore will benefit them. Make them visualize the end outcome and have all their senses involved in the experience so they become fully immersed in the visualization and are then motivated to take the required action.

If you want your students to do well in a certain internship they have signed up for, help them visualize how doing it well will benefit them in the long run and help them land a great job. Make them visualize the sights, sounds, expressions, feelings, sensations and even tastes associated with success. For instance, you can ask them to think of their most favorite ice cream and think of having that when they are successful. Similarly, you can make them think of the sound the ATM makes when your money is about to come out and how you would hear those sounds and feel the touch of crisp dollar bills when you land a fantastic, well paid job.

When you make someone completely involved in an imagination, it targets and influences their subconscious and imbeds relevant suggestions in it. When your subconscious mind becomes focused on a certain outcome, it then makes you work towards achieving that outcome.

Pinpoint the Scarcity: Earnestness can easily be created by using the principle of scarcity. If you want someone to oblige to your demands, let them know how a certain thing is scarce or an offer is only available for a limited time. For instance, if you wish your friend to apply for a scholarship grant for her M.Phil. thesis as soon as possible, let her know how the offer ends in 2 days and how she will miss out on a wonderful opportunity by missing it out. If you want your friends to go out on a food festival with you, inform them of how it ends tonight and how all of you will miss a lifetime experience if you do not go today.

While creating urgency, try not to force the other person into doing something. People who are smart enough to realize this tactic are likely to feel offended by it and then distance themselves from you for a while. Thus, do employ the tactics, but very cautiously so people do not feel upset by anything.

Be Aware of Your BATNA

BATNA refers to your 'best alternative to a negotiated agreement' and is your preferred fallback option that you resort to when things do not go, as you want. It is different from the bottom line, which refers to a fixed position that limits the options available to you and keeps you from discovering new actions.

Knowing your BATNA means that you think through a certain situation to come up with different scenarios wherein things do not happen as desired and then opt for a settlement that appeals to you the most. You need to assess the different alternatives available to you and then opt for the most promising substitute that suits you the most.

If, however, you begin negotiation with a bottom line in your demand, you are likely not to explore any other promising options and may have to settle only for it if the negotiations do not go through as planned. Let us share with you an example to explain this better.

If you are trying to get your charity program funded by some big MNC's and are in talks with a few potential sponsors, you need to begin with asking for complete 100% sponsorship that includes every aspect of the event. Your plan B can be to cut it down by 10% or by eliminating one activity from the package instead of asking for only 50% funds as soon as the sponsors reject your initial proposal. If you present different alternatives, it is likely you can get 70% funds and some added benefits instead of just settling for a small amount of funds.

Similarly, if you wish for a colleague to help you out with a project, give him different options instead of withdrawing your request or asking him to do just a little bit if the first initial request of help is unacceptable to him.

Always be aware of your BATNA and present it in an interesting way while offering benefits of doing that to the concerned individual.

Make Use of Objective Criteria

When trying to persuade someone to carry out a certain task, make use of objective criteria. Settle on a framework based on objective criteria using facts, figures, statements and underlying interests, needs, goals and opinions.

For instance, while having an interdepartmental discussion in the company regarding the launch event of a new service, you become quite convinced that you need to rush it to the market as soon as you can. Now if you wish for the entire team to understand that, you need to provide evidence in form of marketing data and tie it in with how all the team members will benefit from incentives and promotions if the launch goes as planned and receives an overwhelmingly positive response as desired.

When choosing objective criteria for a certain matter, take into consideration factors such as market value, legal standards, contractual terms, mission and objectives, vision and other factors according to the nature of the problem.

Be the Authority on the Matter

People like listening and following someone they perceive as an authority figure. If you wish for others to listen to you attentively and dance to your tune, you need to come off as an authority figure on a certain subject matter. If you want someone to take action against physical abuse and end the vicious cycle of codependency she/he is involved in, tells her/him how you have been through the same or dealt with people who underwent that trauma and how putting an end to that pain is crucial for their betterment right now.

To be an authority, you need to have command over the topic and be fully aware of the ins and outs related with it so you have complete knowledge on the issue and can convince others about it easily. If you want your business partner to buy certain software for your small business, become convinced about it first and use your knowledge about it to persuade him then.

Carry out an in depth research on the issue to collect as much data on it as possible and then study it on your own to brush your knowledge of it. It is only when you are well versed on it that you can share it with others, educate others about it and influence them in the desired manner.

Bring in the Element of Empathy

Empathy never goes to waste and always does the trick of winning people over. When being empathetic towards people, remember not to do it just to fulfill your ulterior motives. Empathy is about feeling the pain of others as your own and is something so beautiful that it needs to be incorporated positively in all your actions.

Be your compassionate, loving self with others and be as empathetic as you can with people you genuinely care about. Feel the pain of others, be around them to show your support and do not push anyone to do something he/she feels uncomfortable about. You will build a fantastic rapport with people once you become empathetic towards them and this will only make it easier for you to inspire them.

Remember the Names and Faces of People

An effective way to shower attention on someone especially someone you have only met once or twice is to remember their face and name. People love to build connection with others and when they do, they quickly feel drawn towards that very person. When you meet someone, ask his/her name and use it a couple of times during the conversation so you imbed it in your subconscious mind. Also, pick any prominent facial feature and tie it with that person's name so you remember it easily.

The next time you meet him/her, greet him/her using their name affectionately and it will definitely cheer him/her up drawing them towards you.

Try to make written notes of all the practices you try and how each works out in your favor. Certain tactics work well with certain people while some don't. Therefore, write down about how you implement each tactic so you can keep track of your performance and improve on it the next time.

Chapter 10: Assuming Success

So far in the book, we have covered the various types of manipulation, the kind of certain individuals who would repeatedly, and sometimes consciously, do this behavior and how to counter them for protection. You may have gotten the impression that any or all manipulation is harmful, not worth the damage of any kind and should be avoided at all times. That is a tough front to break down, especially since not many, but plenty of, common figures are used as examples of said behavior. Rightfully so, as it has harmed millions of people. That is not always the cause as this chapter will surely show you that this can be used for greatness for one's self and, at most, be used as a tool for utilitarianism. Throughout time and human history, there are numerous examples of the world's most cunning leaders and the most infamous rulers, known and unknown, who have shown that manipulation for the people and nation is a greater gain than for one's self. It is never an easy path for these kinds of people, but the rewards are tremendous and it will have rippling effects. The outcomes of these tactics, used with care, have created prosperous civilizations and brought innovations and machinery we still use and marvel over today. This shows that when used for good, manipulation can give one prosperous wealth and large amounts of power all for the greater good. On the other hand, when these skills are misused and utilized by those with an overly ambitious mind and malicious intent, the resulting consequences have caused the genocides of million and have led to the creation of men with armies with an unstoppable force at their disposal. Because of some of the negative connotations associated with these things, the stigma will no doubt arise yet some of it can be untrue. We will go over the benefits of benevolent manipulation and the success of it and how you can use it to help benefit you and perhaps use it to even try to help other people. They made even like you more amongst the prominent figures, Julius Caesar is one who was able to use his manipulation to become a dictator and do good by his lower-working people of Rome. Little is known about his childhood but we knew he first started his career in the military, making a great name for himself because of the enemies he defeated and battles won. His greatest achievement in the military was the invasion of the galleries, which he knew there, was internal tensions in the tribes and took advantage of them. This also helped him in the political aspect of Rome because of all the strategizing he did in the field. He progressed through all of the ranks in almost a decade, until he became consul of the Roman republic, the highest political office. Once he was in office, many changes came about. One of them was the integration of those who lived outside of Rome. Since they weren't born in Italy, they were not granted full citizenship, which also restricts their rights. Caesar gave them full citizenship and they were able to contribute to society. During his dictatorship, there were numerous families with 2 or 3 kids who were not working and living in poor conditions. Caesar distributed jobs to the families and also allowed pieces of land to them, some of them even working as Freeman for landowners. He also cleared a whole year of debt for low to moderate dwellers, giving them relief. It is unfortunate that his assassination came to fruition by those closest to him. The main reason behind the betrayal is because the Senate disagreed with Caesar's political campaign, in spite of the good it has done for the republic. Caesar himself wasn't fond the title of "king", but that did not persuade the betrayers from executing their plan. On the ides of March, Caesar was lead to his demise as his friends stabbed him 23 times, leaving him to die from blood loss. He was a tremendous loss to Rome and history and shows an example of how power can make those around envious.

Many tragic examples such as Caesar have been told before and there are many others that are the opposite. Long after it's time and likely the most prominent example in manipulation history would be Niccolò Machiavelli and his renowned book **the Prince**. If his name sounds familiar, then you may have heard of Machiavellianism, a political theory based off of him that views any means can be used if its intent is to maintain power. This central crux of the Prince has formed the basis of many modern political doctrines such as Realpolitik the idea in politics of removing morals and fake ideologies and removing all other preconceived notions from a political argument or debate. **The Prince** touches on ways to manipulate politicians and organizations through means of military, persuading powerful figures and making those who are soldiers to you fear you by means of how you conduct yourself. For instance, if one were to come across an evil man, he should not show any good to him for it will do him harm in the end. What this means is that in a room full of liars, what sense or good does it do to be morally good? By always telling the truth, you can never be on the advantage and your opponents will always plan ahead because of your cards. In this situation, where you are a high authority in a city, you must always be ruthless in your dealings with others. Never give a benefit of the doubt and never show mercy.

Another instance, Niccolò proclaims that lying and deceit should always be at one's disposal and home if needed. Always look as if you are truthful and forgiving, and people around you will see you as benevolent. In spite of this, those who are particularly immoral, who you also deal with, one should always be ready to cheat. A person should have the appearance of, let alone actually being, virtues so that one can have the least amount of suspicion. Nevertheless, he should always be ready to cheat or lie, to gain the upper hand to his contemporaries.

Even to this day, whenever **the prince** gets brought up, it brings both praises for how timeless and innovative it was in the 16th century and controversies for how ruthless and heartless the contents described. Like **the 48 laws of power**, people have criticized it for the lack of humanity and encouragement of ruthless behavior. It also doesn't help its case when most of the readers of these books are criminal, both in jail/prison and out. Of course the book cannot be utilized at its fullest for an average citizen; however, there are plenty of truths in the book that can help one maneuver in a workplace. As Niccolò makes clear, if someone is out to do you harm, it would be in your best interest to cheat them to protect yourself and your team.

Like many instruments, either created or founded, by humanity are amoral in essence. They alone cannot do evil or good to others; it is all dependent on the user. This applies just as much to manipulation for there are many examples of great figures rising to the top or inspiring others, such as Martin Luther King Jr and Adolf Hitler. It may not be well known in the current year, but these two men share many common traits of thinking and manipulation yet only one has been deemed as the most despicable person in all the history books. The reason these two are being brought up as examples is that they contrast very greatly from their backgrounds, ethnicities, where their problems lie, and what they did as rising figures of their respective nations. It will also help you to understand just how influential one can be and how one can be just as influential to; hopefully, help others to be seen and to bring light to problems that are profoundly overlooked.

A common observation is a fact that both figures are charismatic men who had a magnetic pull that people were drawn to. For both men, their respective groups were oppressed one way or another, with Hitler's nation under poverty and reparations and MLK Jr. People abused in nearly every establishment. This would allow them to make empathic connections with their people. In the case of Hitler, he was able to connect with the heart of Germany due to how the Versailles treaty crippled the nation. When he spoke, he appealed to their hopes, fears, and deepest desires, offering salvation and redemption from those who put them in this devastating state. As you know the rest, this would pave the way to his rise as chancellor and forming the national-socialist party. The slaughter of more than 6 million people was done by the very same people who would obey and die for the führer. Even after 1945, there were hunts for the remaining Nazi who was hardcore.

At the same time, it is hard to deny the striking similarities to Martin Luther King Jr's upbringing. Far before he was born, black Americans have suffered a long history of oppression in the forms of slavery and violent racism, such as lynching, cross-burnings, blatant discrimination, etc. By the time MLK Jr was born, he could have easily been jaded or cynical towards his oppressors and call for the genocide of all white Americans, however, he didn't. Instead, he pursued education and took an interest in politics from his schools and public organizations. He was a top student at his college and graduated with many degrees. With all the debating knowledge and skills he acquired, he took an active stand against oppression not just in the Montgomery bus boycott, but in his speeches as well. He spoke with articulated conviction in his voice and addressed broader issues, such as poverty and economic injustice, rather than limiting it to just racial issues. Many people of his color, church and other organizations recognized this in him and were rallying behind him in no time. It was astonishing how the people rally with him and the cause awhile protesting peaceful and demonstrating how the police are the ones to be aggressive first. MLK Jr. was a courageous speaker who was able to send powerful messages across all people. Of course, similar to Julius Caesar's fall, MLK Jr was killed outside his motel room despite all the justice he was bringing to the people.

All in all, two men from vastly different backgrounds and with different goals have utilized the power of manipulation and historically will never be forgotten. The large groups who were behind the men were, in a sense, manipulated because Hitler and Junior appealed to their emotions and frustration. But one of them used manipulation as a tool for good, to rally against the injustice using peaceful means, while the other used it from the righteous fury he had for those who wronged him and of burning passion. Manipulation, like many things, will always be at the disposal of anyone who has a goal in mind and rigid beliefs. In business, your company can't thrive if the competition has a better profit. You'll naturally want your team to win and will try to get to the top. In social circles, there may be a toxic person who is spreading misery among others. Naturally, you'll convince your friends to help this person or kick them out. It will always be up to the person what they will do.

Conclusion

We finally have come to the last chapter of the book and it holds a very important question. Throughout this book, we have covered many different topics regarding manipulation and what they are or could look like and how to avoid them. But the question of why people manipulate others is still being answered today, with interesting answers. To begin this subject let's look at antiquity. People have been manipulating each other, according to historical records and the earliest bibliography, since the dawn of humans. From as far back as the first Roman emperors, people have been using tricks to play on simple innate human emotions to get what they want from others. By other promising false things, or playing on primal human fears, people have attained a certain great power, via using these simple psychological tricks to their advantage. The problems begin to arise when people use these techniques start to commit immoral acts on humanity, i.e. Joseph Stalin, Adolf Hitler. Individuals like the ones mentioned prior are the types who use manipulation out of personal conviction. The same reason can be applied to benevolent people, such as Gandhi, John F Kennedy. In simple terms, this means that a strong and rigid idea or belief is one of the main drives for them to use any means necessary to accomplish it.   For example, in the case of Joseph Stalin, Communism drove him to exterminate millions of people without care. Or Hitler who killed millions of minorities all in the sake of a profound belief he conjured up; "Arian purity". Hitler, for example, gained his power by taking advantage of a country that, at the time was gripped by fear and extreme economic downturn. Of course, he seized the opportunity and took these fears and said to the people "if we do not do something drastic than these things will only get worse". This was accomplished by blaming people like Jews, or Jews who were Communists. He once said, "My beloved people, we must exterminate them, for a look at the disastrous state of our country; it has been caused by these monsters".

Everyone who gave Hitler the time was enchanted by his conviction and attention-grabbing aura. This was all done subtly; of course, it was a prime example of victimization multiplied by a massive magnitude. By telling the German people that they had been extremely victimized by both the world and the allies, which while true to a certain degree, he was able to assemble a massive force of angry individuals behind him. It is a powerful tool when emotions and time are aligned right. Now shifting our focus to the modern world in modern individuals who utilize manipulation such as abusive lovers, powerful men, salespeople, and agencies. Their reasoning for doing these things is the same in the past. See modern psychology, according to Maslow, states that a human being must sustain various needs through whatever resources they can get all to attain the highest state of function. This high state is something akin to transcendence, internal peace if you will. This is recognized as self-actualization. It is the top of Maslow's hierarchy, which is when a person realizes their own talents and potential. That alone is what will drive a person to achieve what they want or need with ease. Attaining a great worry free life is something that all people obviously and subconsciously strive for, but for some people, a missed wiring inside the human brain can lead them to take these goals much too far. By this, I mean that in the pursuit of pleasure, whether that be sexual or sadism, and wealth some people will do whatever is required to attain that goal, even if it means damaging and destroying another person in the process. Sometimes victims of this behavior tend to believe they can fix these types of people, or they themselves can change, which results in Stockholm syndrome.

Many real-life examples are because of this relationship and it can stem far back as childhood. This behavior can reach a point where it will even become self-sabotaging, leading to the individual destroying themselves in the goal of reaching something. In others, past trauma can lead to these behaviors. Take the individual who due to growing up in an environment full of abuse and violence that had to lie and be manipulative to survive for example. They may end up entering a romantic relationship and begin using manipulative tactics such as playing the victim or use intimidation to get what they want out of their partner. Out the simple virtue that it what was the kind of behavior, they saw growing up, so as a result, they have come to believe that this is the only way to do something since this kind of stuff has become so normalized to them. People who use manipulation, for this reason, are not people who can easily be helped. As their reason for using manipulation tactics is due to mental illness or past trauma, which is something that some people never recover from. Thankfully it is fairly easy to spot these kinds of individuals when you first encounter them. People who are overly needy of praise or need constant validation or who always sees himself as the victim in any situation they are in or straight up ignore you whenever they don't need you. These kinds of people have learned that manipulation can get them the feelings that they crave so badly with as minimum effort needed. As a result, ranging from things like poor parenting or experiences which validate these kinds of behaviors. As a result, they will be very unlikely to break these negative behavior habits and in fact, as a result, are more likely to continually do the same thing even if it destroys them. On the entirely opposite side of the spectrum, there are entities that utilize manipulation to gain the things that they want. News agencies, political parties, stores, salespeople, etc. Use the power of manipulation to usually further financial or power objectives that take priority first. Not too dissimilar from dictators or despots who did the same thing in the past. This kind of manipulation, while also more common, tends to also happen on a much larger scale. The way the news media or any reporting outlet, for instance, uses manipulation is by trying to only tell you what you want to hear as opposed to telling you the truth. They omit particular details about an event to invoke an emotion. This always has to be done subtly by only reporting on certain news stories or events. While the iPhone ad that may play on the same news channel will try and get you to purchase a brand new product by virtue of it seeming cool or flashy, and playing on the fact that people like things that make them feel exclusive or special while lastly getting into that innate fear of missing out on the big parade. The way a salesperson for an example will agree or reinforce any foolish or stupid preconceives notion a potential buyer may have about a car all in the desire to sell said car while in it neither malicious nor good. It is still a tricky tactic that not many people are aware of. This blatant unawareness is what these people feed on they know that most people are unaware of the fact that they are getting ripped off or falling under the spell of a manipulation. And as a result, they are able to continue using this kind of behavior to get us to buy their products no matter our life routines or the consequences. The main thing to keep in mind when realizing all of this is that no one ever thinks they are the villain in a situation, they will always assume that they are in the right regardless of the result of their actions. And as a result when you try and show them the toxicity of how they are behaving it is highly likely that instead of in fact listening and regarding what you are saying, it will only further embolden them and push them to move on to a better target. And get them to further behavior. This is the number one problem with the manipulation that forgets. Manipulators can be experts at presenting themselves as beautiful and engaging individuals. Dualistic thought it is the same aspect that allows them to reap so much destruction their ability to glib and charm you with fake promises and threats creates a perfect storm. While for some it may be trauma, the idea of gaining power or wealth that drives them to manipulate. For the very select few, they manipulate simply because they like to hurt people and like to see pain inflicted on them. This leads to a whole new breed of manipulation, which can be called psychopathy. Psychopaths are IMMENSELY dangerous beings yet they are few in numbers today in the United States. These kinds of people are extremely hard to detect which is a large part of what leads to the difficulty in dealing with them, how you can defend against something if you do not know what you're guarding yourself against. While manipulation has been used in extremely negative ways by quite a few people. As mentioned previously it can also be used in survival situations or for your own good. With this I mean when manipulation is used in cases like negotiation or certain forms of policy making the net benefit can become better than the cost. I.E lying to an opposing county to avert a war that could lead to a large amount of death and destruction. Diplomats and ambassadors are created for this sole purpose and serve a great role for the nation. As shown in chapter 4, respected individuals have demonstrated how this tool that had the stigma of immoral intent behind it can be used for the greater good. It is warranted, in spite of the good it can do. Numerous events and things in the world always require the correct timeframe and the precise execution to successfully manipulate others. Sometimes you may be worried about how others will view you or will change the way they think about you. This may be the case, however, you can always state your purpose in doing so and hopefully, if they are a sensible person, they'll understand. If they do not, you have to wonder if it's because of a lack of understanding and not wanting to connect or they had other plans which you foiled before they can enact them. You can never know what kind of people you hang around with. Your parents may have told you time and again "don't let others get control over you". There will always be those who are natural born leaders, who are able to bring others up and help towards a common goal. On the other hand, there are people who are deceitful masters and see others as pets for their amusement and tools to increase their gains. You can never know, only anticipate. If you had the thought "what if I am able to prevent any of this from happening?" you should know there isn't a way. It's only when you can plan ahead yourself that you can prevent it. If you ever need a reference to a book, you can use this.

DARK PSYCHOLOGY

Learn Persuasion and Manipulation Secrets. Use the Art of Reading People and Influence Human Behavior with Deception, Hypnotism, Covert NLP & Manipulative Mind Control Techniques

Introduction

Is someone making your life miserable?

How do you recognize if someone is being manipulative, or persuasive?

Is a salesperson manipulating you to buy his wares, for his own profit? Or, is he persuading you because he genuinely believes in his product?

Manipulation can come at you in many forms, from a colleague or a partner to someone you don't know. We are often pressured into making social changes in our lives. There is nothing wrong with that if you are the one to make the decision for the sake of your own wellbeing. If though, someone makes you do something that you don't want to do, then it has become a form of bullying. It can be difficult to stand up to bullies, at any age. Though, if you want to be free of them, then you need to learn how to take back control.

Dark Psychology is an area of psychology, the study of the human mind, which few people are aware of. Dark psychology includes many topics, such as seduction, persuasion, deception, and manipulation. It is effectively the underbelly of what we know about how human beings operate what drives us, and why we sometimes do unsavory, or even unspeakable things, in order to achieve our goals. There are people all over who exhibit dangerous qualities and may try to harm you. Most of the time, we are so blind to what is happening to us, until we have incurred emotional or physical damage that we realize we have been manipulated or abused.

It is also important to keep in mind that each and every one of us has a dark or "evil" side of our own psychology. Recognizing that you are a victim of coercion and manipulation, is important. If you can achieve this, then you are on your way to resolving the problem. By reading this book you will come to realize that you do have the power to change the situation.

With this book, you'll be able to get hold of the secrets that only a few possess and really understand. Also, you'll be able to decipher deep psychologies about 'dark psychology' because book contains tactics and principles that have been employed by the world's most powerful, diabolical, and devious minds and influencers, to manipulate others.

Being a victim of manipulation is very intimidating. It makes you feel powerless because you don't have the confidence to stand up to the perpetrator. It is hurtful and emotionally draining, causing many to become socially reclusive.

This is a book that will show you the way to take yourself forward, with the tips provided. I hope you find this book useful in your future interactions with others and find yourself prepared to deal with even the cruelest and shadiest people.

Chapter 1: Emotional Influence and types of Emotions

Covert emotional manipulation is very important to the art of dark psychology. Many of the tactics that are used with dark psychology are going to use this type of emotional manipulation, whether in part or completely. As you start to learn a bit more about the world of dark psychology and its different manifestations, you will soon start to see the signs of CEM. This is why it is so important to understand what CEM is exactly so that you can watch out for it in your daily life.

Covert refers to the way that a manipulator is able to hide their intentions. They want to be able to hide the true nature of all their actions. Remember that not all types of influence and emotional manipulation will be categorized as covert. The victims of the type that is covert though will typically not realize they are being manipulated and will not be able to understand the way the manipulation is carried out. In some cases, they are not even able to look and figure out the motivation of their manipulator. This is why CEM is such a stealth bomber in the world of dark psychology. Its point is to avoid detection and defense until it is too late for the victim.

Being able to manipulate the emotions of the other person is key. If a person has emotional control over the other person, then they are going to have full control over them.

With an influencer, they are going to go into this with the idea of "I want to help you make a decision that is good for you." But with the manipulator, they have the thoughts of "I want to secretly control you in order to provide benefit to myself." As you can see, both of these are quite a bit different, so understanding the intention behind any given behavior is going to be a large part in deciding whether the situation is covert emotional manipulation or not.

There are four main scenarios in which CEM is able to take place. These include the family, romantic, personal, and professional parts of your life. One of the most common forms of CEM is romantic, and it can sometimes be the deadliest. There are some less obvious forms of CEM that you are able to find anywhere, and because they are less common, they can sometimes be the most dangerous.

If the manipulator is successful, then their wife or their girlfriend will continue to be a victim of emotional manipulation, and they may have a hard time realizing that it is going on. This allows the manipulator to keep the control that they want without any risk of being discovered and losing the other person for good.

This can also happen with a friend who would use CEM in order to get the outcomes they want when they have a relationship with another person. In this group, one of the common types of manipulators is going to be someone who covertly induced feelings of obligation, sympathy, and guilt in a friend. The friend is being manipulated in this way without being aware that they are being influenced.

Basic types of Emotions

Anger

Anger is one of the most unwanted emotions yet it is frequently manifested. One of the causes of anger is when an individual feels entitled to something. For instance, if you feel that you deserve an award, respect, and attention then you are on the path of attracting anger when you get disappointment. Most people that tend to be temperamental also show low self-esteem suggesting that each disappointment they get makes them think they are destined to be failures. If unmanaged, anger can cost your health, social life, work, and finances.

Fear/Discomfort

Whenever we try something new, we experience anxiety. We are afraid of the unknown. This is why we like to maintain our daily routine and stay within our comfort zones. From our brain's point of view, this makes perfect sense. If our current habits allow us to be safe and avoid any potential threat to our survival (or the survival of our ego) why bother changing them? This explains why we often keep the same routine, or have the same thoughts over and over. It is also why we may experience a lot of internal resistance when trying to change ourselves.

Grief

It is important to grieve the loss of someone or something important in your life, but grief can snowball into a debilitating emotion if it isn't managed correctly. If you find yourself overwhelmed by grief, try to be more active. It is easy while grieving to withdraw socially and stop doing productive activities. Force yourself to engage with others and seek the emotional support that you need from the people you are close to. Don't let your life stagnate. Keep practicing mindfulness, exercising, eating right, and everything else that makes you feel good.

Understand that you don't have to feel guilty for moving on from a loss. Just because you have accepted the loss of that thing or person doesn't mean you've forgotten.

Happiness

As one of the most sought after feelings, happiness regards what we wish to feel in an appealing manner. There are numerous efforts and strategies at personal, community, and governmental levels to enhance levels of happiness as it directly impacts the health of people. Happiness as an emotion is manifested through body languages such as a relaxed stance, facial expressions like smiling, and an upbeat illustrated by a pleasant tone of voice.

Like any other emotion, the emotion of happiness is largely created by human experience and the belief system. For instance, if scoring sixty marks is regarded as desirable then a student is likely to feel happy to attain or surpass the mark. If riding in a train with family members is regarded as being happy then an individual that never had that experience might feel happy and eager at the prospect of boarding a train. Fortunately, we can optimize happiness by enhancing our emotional intelligence levels.

Sadness

As an emotion, sadness is a transient emotional state whose attributes include hopelessness, grief, disappointment, dampened mood, and disinterest. There are several ways to manifest sadness as emotion and these include:

- Withdrawal from others

- Dampened mood

- Lethargy

- Crying

- Quietness

Envy

Envy commonly happens at the workplace where an employee admires to be accomplished just like the popular colleague. A human entertains and pursues ambitions routinely and this allowed. The problem starts when one becomes uneasy with the accomplishments of others to the point of being affected mentally and physically the person is feeling envious. As expected, persons with a feeling of envy will rarely acknowledge that they are manifesting the negative emotion. At the workplace, envy affects an individual negatively. While the limited and occasional form of envy is necessary to spur one to improve and strive for more, it becomes a problem if it is not managed. Feelings of envy are likely to commonly manifest at the workplace as workplaces appraise employees and reward those accomplished ones.

Anxiety

Feeling worried is important to enabling one to visualize and plan for the worst-case scenarios. For instance, being worried about passing exams enables you to address the risk of failing by working harder, consulting, or planning for failure as a possible outcome of the test that you took. However, worry becomes a bad emotion when it takes over you and prevents one from routine activities and routine interactions. For instance, when you constantly feel worried about failure making you study until you get burnout then worry as emotion becomes a negative emotion. As earlier on indicated, feelings emanate from human experience and system of beliefs and this implies that if the society does not accommodate failure then you will get the emotion of worry. The emotion is manifesting because of past experiences and the current system of beliefs regarding exams and not necessarily about how you feel internally.

Self-criticism

Self-judgment happens when we critic ourselves and found ourselves inadequate. Self-criticism is necessary as a way of self-evaluation and can help one improve performance, social skills, and communication. A fortunate aspect of human beings is that they can reflect over their experiences, detach from their self and evaluate themselves, and speak to oneself. Limited self-judgment can help increase personal accountability which can increase the professionalism and appeal of an individual at the workplace and in society. However, self-criticism becomes an issue when one gets stuck at it and feels worthless before society.

Frustration

This is when you feel trapped but can't do anything about it. Frustration in the workplace is the most common cause of burnout.

Worry

With so many layoffs, it's natural to be worried about losing your job. However, instead of feeling anxious, try to focus on your job and think about ways of improving your performance, to you make yourself more employable. Nervous people usually have low self-confidence.

Disappointment

Repeated disappointments always negatively affect efficiency and productivity, and if unaddressed, can lead to burnout and high staff turnover.

The key thing about nurturing negative emotions in the workplace be it feelings about your colleagues, management, working environment, salary, or something else is that these feelings are contagious, and this kind of resentment easily spreads and demoralizes others. This is why a negative person is more likely to be fired, if for no other reason than to prevent their negativity and resentment from spreading to others.

Chapter 2: How Emotional Influence Works Against a Victim

Humans are emotional beings with little concern for logic and rationality. That means humanity is motivated by their emotions more than the reasoning faculty. That is the rule employed by the media in broadcasting, as they tend to portray or report incidences with emotional biases that can provoke similar reactions from the public as the case may be.

One of the most critical factors in analyzing how people respond to persuasiveness is through their emotions. Emotions release abundant energy to complete any set task. Even in selling, a prospect cannot buy any product from you based on all the logic you have to present. He responds to the force of emotional stimuli, which you were able to ignite in him during your presentations.

On the other hand, logic is based on facts and figures. That is the rationality and reasoning behind the issues at hand. Moreover, a salesperson may not be able to sell anything based on any facts about the product or the clear logic presented by the marketer concerning his firm and their services. Nevertheless, if such sales executive hinges his philosophy based on emotions, he will succeed and make sales.

Do you think humans are rational beings? Are decisions and opinions based on logic? How do human beings react to facts all the time? These are arrays of questions a curious person needs to answer to be able to carefully juxtapose the relationship between emotions and logic and how a person can apply these two great psychological and intellectual phenomena in influencing other human beings positively.

Your ability to convey logical information emotionally will spike of responses in your audience while a message full of facts and logic with no emotional appeal will inevitably end without a positive reaction from the listeners. Logics and reasoning persuade men but emotion is the motion that compels someone to take a decisive action, which will yield a great result.

Let us analyze some of the ways you can influence others through a blend of emotions and logic such as:

Establishing a Common Identity with the Other Person

One of the means of controlling people is by creating common ground with the others as you build rapport as much as possible. There is a saying "It takes two persons to tangle" before tangling together, both of you must share common goals, experiences, and ideas. This way, it becomes easier to influence the person. Common grounds in a partnership or relationship is more comfortable among persons with the same identity other than people with different culture. By establishing similarity of character, we are united by the same goals and objectives, and then our emotions and feelings become the bond holding us together based on logic and rationale of our collective beliefs that is our collective vision and mission.

Profoundly Exploring Your Partner's Belief System

You cannot maintain a deep relationship or mutually satisfying association with someone you do not know regarding his personality traits and other necessary human psychological tendencies. Nevertheless, by profoundly exploring your partner's belief system, you can understand the person and then positively influence him or her slightly to your advantage.

Looking for Ways to Captivate his Bias

Influencing a person with a different belief system is very difficult, no matter the soundness of your logic. Instead, look for ways of captivating his biases by playing the bias card efficiently. How do you play the bias card? By looking for some ideas and points, he likes so much and presenting them to him. With this approach, he will be relaxed and comfortable with you and eventually give you undue access to his or her private life.

Avoiding Instances of Flight or Fight in Your Discussions

Influencing people based on logic and emotions works best if you carefully avoid instances of flight or fight during your meetings and discussions. This is because whenever there are conflicts and misunderstandings in relationships, rationality and reasoning are misconstrued and objectives are thwarted. At this point, no matter the emotional inclination on a subject or the logical notion expressing the pros and cons, it will not make any headway in an ambiance of fight or flight.

Chapter 3: What is mind control?

Mind control

Mind control involves using influence and persuasion to change the behaviors and beliefs in someone. That someone might be the person themselves or it might be someone else. Mind control has also been referred to as brainwashing, thought reform, coercive persuasion, mental control, and manipulation, just to name a few. Some people feel that everything is done by manipulation. But if that is true or to be believed, then important points about manipulation will be lost. Influence is much better thought of as a mental continuum with two extremes. One side has influences that are respectful and ethical and work to improve the individual while showing respect for them and their basic human rights. The other side contains influences that are dark and destructive that work to remove basic human rights from a person, such as independence, the ability for rational thought, and sometimes their total identity.

When thinking of mind control, it is better to see it as a way to use influence on other people that will disrupt something in them, like their way of thinking or living. Influence works on the very basis of what makes people human, such as their behaviors, beliefs, and values. It can disrupt the very way they chose personal preferences or make critical decisions. Mind control is nothing more than using words and ideas to convince someone to say or do something they might never have thought of saying or doing on their own.

Mind control uses the idea that someone's decisions and emotions can be controlled using psychological means. It is using powers of negotiation or mental influence to ensure the outcome of the interaction is more favorable to one person over the other. This is basically what marketing is: convincing someone to do something particular or buy something in particular. Being able to control someone else's mind merely means understanding the power of human emotion and being able to play upon those emotions. It is easier to have a mental impact on people if there is a basic understanding of human emotions.

A lot of the forms of mind control are considered to be rooted in dark psychology because many believe that mind control is an impure strategy used by those who cannot be bothered to do things themselves. They believe that it is a form of evil hence why it is called "dark" psychology. While we certainly do not want to alleviate the blame from true

458

criminals, you should understand that you are not a criminal for using mind control strategies.

Mind control in this day and age can be a powerful way to encourage people to do the things you need or want them to do. Obviously, this type of powerful strategy can not only be used to have people do bad things or to create criminal results, but it can also be used to encourage positive results. Mind control is a technique whereby you use various psychological techniques to alter someone's mind. In doing so, you can change the way they think about various things so that their thought processes work in your favor. This technique can enable you to achieve virtually anything you want with the help of virtually anyone you want. It truly puts you in the driver's seat of reality and allows you to have an effortless ability to live your desired life with your desired outcomes.

Brainwashing

Brainwashing is basically the procedure where somebody will be connived to abandon ideas that they had in the past in order to take new perfects and also worth's. There is a great deal of manner ins which this can be done although not every one of them will certainly be taken into consideration bad. For example, if you are from an African nation and then relocate to America, you will certainly usually be required to change your worth's and ideals in order to fit in with the new culture and environments that you remain in. On the various other hand, those in prisoner-of-war camp or when a brand-new totalitarian government is taking over, they will certainly commonly undergo the process of indoctrination in order to persuade people to follow along in harmony.

Lots of people have misunderstandings of what brainwashing is. Some individuals have extra paranoid concepts concerning the technique consisting of mind control devices that are funded by the federal government and that are believed to be conveniently turned on like a push-button control. On the other side of points, there are skeptics that do not think that indoctrination is feasible in any way which any individual who asserts it has actually happened is lying. Generally, the practice of brainwashing will certainly land someplace in the center of these two concepts.

Throughout the practice of brainwashing, the subject will certainly be persuaded to transform their beliefs concerning something with a mix of different tactics. There is not just one method that can be utilized throughout this process so it can be challenging to place the method right into a cool little box. Essentially, the topic will be divided from every one of the important things that they understand. From there, they will certainly be damaged down into an emotional state that makes them vulnerable prior to the new principles are presented. As the subject absorbs this brand-new details, they will certainly be compensated for sharing ideas and ideas which support these new ideas. The rewarding is what will certainly be utilized in order to reinforce the brainwashing that is occurring.

This is one of the most famous large scale CEM tactics. We hear about it happening in religions, cults, oppressive governments, and captive kidnapping victims. It is an intense form of social influence that can change someone's behavior and thoughts without his or her consent, and often against their will.

Brainwashing requires the manipulator's total control over their victim, which is why is often requires total isolation of the victim such that their sleeping, eating, and basic needs are interrupted. The complete control required to brainwash someone is exactly the reason it occurs in cults and prison camps. In these settings, leaders have unfettered access to their vulnerable victims and can carry out their brainwashing techniques. In addition, those who join cults or are in prison camps are ideal candidates for brainwashing—they are vulnerable and because of their circumstances, are already prone to trying to find new ways of thinking. Due to the victim's circumstantial flexibility of thought, brainwashing can take effect.

Who uses mind control

Media Producers

Just as our five senses are our guides in life, they can also be our enemies and traitors. Our sense of sight and the visual processing areas of the brain are very powerful. We almost always dream visually, even if another sense is missing, and we usually picture someone we are remembering rather than associating some other sensory input with them. This makes imagery and visual manipulation a particularly powerful technique of media mind control.

Traditionally, media production was in the hands of companies and institutions. These manipulative entities were able to pioneer the use of visual, subliminal mind control. Examples include split-second pictures of a product or person inserted into a seemingly innocent movie. Such split-second images, which the person perceives as nothing more than a flash of light, are able to take powerful control of a person's emotions. They have been used as recently as 21st century Presidential elections.

Sound is another way in which a person is vulnerable to undetected mind control. Both experiments and personal experience will confirm this to you. Have you ever had a song stuck in your head? How easy was it to get rid of? The sound had a powerful influence over you, even though you knew it was present. The power of audio manipulation is even greater when it is undetected. Experiments have shown that if restaurant customers are exposed to music from a particular region, they are more likely to order wine from that country. When questioned, they had no idea that something as simple as sound had steered their decision.

Lovers

People are often a product of their environment, whether they want to be or not. The way people are raised directly affects the way they act in later life. Someone who is raised by alcoholics has a greater chance of becoming alcoholics in adult life, or they may choose never to drink at all. People who are raised in a house where everything is forbidden may cut loose and go a bit crazy when they are finally out on their own. People who are raised in total disorganization may grow up to be totally obsessive about household cleanliness.

Nurture affects people in other, less severe ways, too. Many people believe that Mom's meatloaf is the absolute best and no other recipe exists. People come from different religious and economic backgrounds. People have different beliefs about what is good and bad, what is acceptable and unacceptable. The problem comes when two people are trying to have a relationship, but neither wants to change their way of thinking. When that happens there is no relationship. There are just two people living together under the same roof.

Achieving success in love is just like achieving success in anything else. It is mostly a function of developing good relationships with other people in order to be better able to influence them. Those people who are successful in creating and keeping good, mutually satisfactory relationships with others usually enjoy much more success than people who do not do this. The ability to grow and maintain satisfactory relationships is a trait that is easier for some people. But even if the ability does not come naturally it is easy enough to learn. And Neuro-Linguistic Programming (NLP) makes this skill easier to learn by offering tools and ideas to enable almost anyone to learn the ability to develop great relationships.

461

Sales people

If a salesperson asks a regular customer to write a brief endorsement of the product they buy, hopefully, they will say yes. If someone asks their significant other to take some of the business cards to pass out at work, hopefully, they will say yes. If you write any kind of blog and ask another blogger to provide a link to yours on their blog, hopefully, they will say yes. When enough people say yes, the business or blog will begin to grow. With even more yesses, it will continue to grow and thrive. This is the very simple basis of marketing. Marketing is nothing more than using mind control to get other people to buy something or to do something beneficial for someone else. And the techniques can easily be learned.

Writers

Think of writing a guest spot for someone else who has their own blog. By sending in the entire manuscript first, there is a greater risk of rejection. Begin small. Send them a paragraph or two discussing them the idea. Then make an outline of the idea and send that in an email. Then write the complete draft you would like them too use and send it along. When asking a customer for a testimonial, start by asking for a few lines in an email. Then ask the customer to expand those few lines into a testimonial that covers at least half a typed page. Soon the customer will be ready for an hour-long webcast extolling the virtues of the product and your great customer service skills.

Everything must have a deadline that really exists. The important word here is the word 'real'. Everyone has heard the salesperson who said to decide quickly because the deal might not be available later or another customer was coming in and they might get it. That is a total fabrication and everyone knows it to be true. There are no impending other customers and the deal is not going to disappear. There is no real sense of urgency involved. But everyone does it. There are too many situations where people are given a totally fake deadline by someone who thinks it will instill a great sense of urgency for completion of the task. It is not only totally not effective but completely unneeded. It is a simple matter to create true urgency. Only leave free things available for a finite amount of time. When asking customers for testimonials be certain to mention the last possible day for it to be received to be able to be used. Some people will be unable to assist, but having people unable to participate is better than never being able to begin.

In Education

By educating impressionable children, society essentially teaches them to become "ideal" members of society. They are taught and trained in certain ways that fulfil the desires of the government and authorities, and most people don't even think twice about it.

Advertising and Propaganda

By putting advertising and propaganda everywhere, those in control are capable of eliminating people's feeling of self-worth and encourage them to **need** what is being sold, as opposed to just wanting it. This is essentially a subliminal strategy to make people feel poorly about themselves so that they will purchase whatever is being advertised to increase their feelings of self-worth.

Sports, Politics, Religion

The idea of these strategies is to "divide and conquer". Ultimately, each one has people placed into various categories, where they feel very strongly. As a result, they don't come together and support one another, but rather they are against each other. This means that they are divided, and so the authority can conquer.

Chapter 4: Deception and its Types

What is Deception?

It is the act of causing someone to believe something that is untrue. We all practice deception in one form or another. Some lies are bigger than others, telling your partner that you could never cheat on them is a big one for example. Telling your friend that she looks great in those jeans could just be a way of sparing her feelings.

Deception is not always practiced on other people. We can often self-deceive to preserve our self-esteem. Telling ourselves that we can achieve certain goals when all the evidence points to the fact that we can't is a healthy form of deception, but self-deception can lead to serious delusions.

Deception is an art employed by an agent to spread beliefs in the subject which are untrue, or truths coated with lies. Deception involves numerous things, example dissimulation, sleight of mind, suppression, cover-up, propaganda **etc.** The agents win the favor of the subjects, they trust him and are unsuspecting of his propensity to be dubious. He is able to control the subject's mind having won their confidence and trust. The subjects have no doubts on the agent's words, in fact the subjects trust the agent completely and possibly plan their affairs based on the agent's statements.

The deception practiced by the agent can have grave consequential effects if discovered by the subjects. How? The subjects will not be disposed to hearing his words, neither will they accept them anymore, no wonder the agent must be skilled at the deception technique. He must create an escape route to cover up if things boomerang and still retain the trust his subjects have in him.

Deception breaks the laws that govern relationships and it has been known to affect negatively the hopes that come with relationships. Deception does occur every now and then and this could result in feelings of doubt as well as disloyalty among the two people who are in the relationship. Nearly everyone desires to have an honest discussion with their partner; if they find out that their partner has however been dishonest, they, in turn, need to find out how to make use of confusion and distraction so as to get the dependable and honest information that they are in need of. Trust, on the other hand, would be lost in the relationship, making it hard to restore the relationship to its former glory.

The individual on the receiving end of both dishonesty and betrayal would always wonder about the things their partner was telling them, thinking about whether the story was true or false. As a result of this new doubt, most relationships will be brought to an end once the agent realizes their partner's dishonesty.

While it is an accepted fact that we all use deception, it is a personal choice as to the nature of your lies. The trick is to be able to recognize deception in others. This means that if we know the giveaway signs that tell us we are being lied to, we can avoid displaying them if we choose to practice deception.

Deception is another key aspect that comes with dark psychology. Like many other tactics that come with dark psychology, it is sometimes difficult to tell whether one instance of deception is considered dark or not. But before we explore more into this, we need to first understand what deception is all about in our world.

Deception is going to be any word or action that is capable of making someone believe something that is not true. Fraudulently providing evidence for something that is false, implying falsehood, omitting the truth, and lying are all examples of deception.

Deception is going to become dark any time when it is carried out with an indifferent or negative intention towards the victim. Dark deception is an understanding that the truth is not going to serve the deceptive aims of the deceiver. The deceiver is going to take the truth and either ignore, hide, or change it in favor of a version of events that suits their purpose a little bit better. Those who employ dark deception mean to do it as a way to harm, rather than to help. They want to help out their own interests, but they don't care who gets hurt in the process.

The deception practiced by the agent can have grave consequential effects if discovered by the subjects. How? The subjects will not be disposed to hearing his words, neither will they accept them anymore, no wonder the agent must be skilled at the deception technique. He must create an escape route to cover up if things boomerang and still retain the trust his subjects have in him.

Deception breaks the laws that govern relationships and it has been known to affect negatively the hopes that come with relationships. Deception does occur every now and then and this could result in feelings of doubt as well as disloyalty among the two people who are in the relationship. Nearly everyone desires to have an honest discussion with their partner; if they find out that their partner has however been dishonest, they, in turn, need to find out how to make use of confusion and distraction so as to get the dependable and honest information that they are in need of. Trust, on the other hand, would be lost in the relationship, making it hard to restore the relationship to its former glory.

Types of Deception

Exists

This is when the representative comprises details or offers details that is totally various from what is the fact. They will certainly provide this details to the topic as reality as well as the topic will certainly see it as the fact. This can be unsafe because the topic will certainly not recognize that they are being fed incorrect info; if the subject recognized the details was incorrect, they would certainly not likely be speaking with the representative as well as no deceptiveness would certainly take place.

Misrepresentations

This is when the representative will certainly make inconsistent, unclear, or indirect declarations. This is done to lead the based on obtain overwhelmed as well as to not comprehend what is taking place. It can likewise assist the representative to preserve one's honor if the topic returns later on and also attempts responsible them for the incorrect details.

Camouflages

This is just one of one of the most typical sorts of deceptiveness that are utilized. Cover-ups are when the representative leaves out info that matters or essential to the context, deliberately, or they take part in any kind of actions that would certainly conceal details that relates to the topic for that specific context. The representative will certainly not have actually straight existed to the topic, however they will certainly have seen to it that the essential details that is required never ever makes it to the topic.

Lies

This occurs when the agent manufactures information or provides information that is not similar to the truth. They will give this information to the unsuspecting individual as the truth and the individual will then see this lie to be fact indeed. However, this can be unsafe as the person being given this false information would have no idea about the falsehood; most likely, if the subject understood that they were being given information that was not true, they would not be on talking terms with the agent and no deception would have occurred;

Equivocations

This is the point at which the agent will make statements that are differing, unclear, or not direct, such that the subject becomes confused and does not understand what is going on. Also, it can help the agent to preserve their reputation, saving face if the subject later returns to blame them for the falsehood;

Concealments

It is the most frequently used form of deception. It refers to when the agent leaves out information that is related or critical to the situation on purpose, or they display any such behavior that would cover up information that is of importance to the subject for that exact situation. The agent won't have lied straightforwardly to the subject, they will, however, have ensured that the vital information required never gets to the subject;

Exaggeration

Exaggeration occurs when the agent emphasizes too much on a fact, or stretch the truth just a little so as to twist the story to suit them. Although the agent may not directly be lying to the subject, they will manipulate the situation such that it appears as though it is a bigger deal than it actually is, or they may twist the truth to make the subject do whatever they need them to do;

Understatements

This is the inverse of the exaggeration tool in the sense that the agent will present part of the fact as less important, telling the subject that an event is less of a deal than it actually is when in it really could be what decides whether the subject gets the opportunity to graduate or gets a huge promotion. As such, the agent will be able to return to the subject saying they had no idea how huge a deal their omission was, they get to keep their reputation leaving the subject to look petty if they protest.

Disguise

Camouflage is an additional element that can be located in the procedure of deceptiveness. When this happens, the representative is functioning to develop an impact of being something or someone else. This is when the representative is concealing something regarding themselves from the subject such as their actual name, what they provide for a work, that they have actually been with, and also what they depend on when they head out. This goes better than simply transforming the attire that somebody uses in a play or a film; when camouflage is utilized in the procedure of deceptiveness, the representative is attempting to alter their entire character in order to method as well as trick the topic.

Simulation

Simulation involves presenting false information to the subject. Three methods that can be used in simulation include; mimicry, fabrication, and distraction.

In mimicry, otherwise defined as the copying of another model, the agent will without thinking be giving a picture of something that is like themselves. They may have a plan that is like another person's and rather than giving credit to the other person, they will say that the plan is all their doing. This type of simulation can happen regularly through sound-related, visual, and other methods.

Fabrication is yet another means of deception. Here, the agent takes something found in reality and changes it until it becomes different. They may tell a tale that did not take place or add to a true story to make it better or worse. While the heart of the story might be true, agreed they got a poor score on a test, it will have some additional things put in, for example the teacher gave them a poor score intentionally. While in reality, the agent got a poor score because they failed to read.

Lastly, distraction is another type of simulation in deception. In this case, the agent makes an effort to get the subject to concentrate on other things, but not the truth; usually done by offering the subject with something that may be more tempting than the truth that has been hidden from them. For instance, if a cheating spouse thinks the wife is beginning to suspect, he may bring home a precious stone ring to distract her from the matter even for a short while. The problem with this method is that it is not usually long-lasting and as such, the agent has to look for a new way to trick the subject if they are to keep the process going.

Overestimation

This is when the representative will certainly overemphasize a truth or extend the fact a little in order to transform the tale the manner in which they would certainly such as. While the representative might not be straight existing to the topic, they are mostly likely to make the circumstance appear like a larger offer than it truly is or they might alter the fact a bit to make sure that the topic will certainly do what they desire.

Exaggerations

An exaggeration is the specific reverse of the overestimation device because the representative is mostly likely to minimize or lessen facets of the reality. They will certainly inform the topic that an occasion is not that huge of offer when as a matter of fact maybe the important things that establishes if the subject reaches finish or obtains that huge promo. The representative will certainly have the ability to return later on as well as state just how they did not recognize just how huge of a bargain it was, leaving them to look great and also the based on look virtually minor if they grumble.

How to use deception

Deception is used in order to propagate in the subject beliefs in occasions as well as things that just are not true, whether they are complete lies or just partial lies. Deception can entail a great deal of various things consisting of sleight of hand, propaganda, as well as dissimulation, camouflage, camouflage, interruption. This form of mind control is so hazardous because the subject typically does not recognize that any kind of mind control is taking place in all. They have been persuaded that a person point holds true when the complete opposite is right. This can get dangerous when the deception is hiding information that can keep the subject risk-free.

Frequently, deceptiveness is seen during relationships as well as will generally result in sensations of mistrust and betrayal between both companions. When deception occurs, there has actually been a violation of the relational regulations and can make it challenging for the partner to rely on the other for a very long time. It can be especially harmful since the majority of people are usage to trusting those around them, especially relational partners as well as good friends, as well as expect them to be honest to them for the most part. When they discover that somebody they are close to is tricking them, they may have concerns with trusting others and also will certainly not have the complacency that they are utilized to.

Deception can create a great deal of problems in a partnership or within the representative as well as subject. The topic will have a great deal of concerns relying on the representative in the future once they learn about the deceptiveness. There will certainly be times when the deception will be performed in order to help out the partnership. These would certainly consist of points such as not telling a spouse when a person claims something implies about them. Various other times the deceptiveness is a lot more spiteful or unsafe in nature such as when the agent is hiding vital info from the subject or is even tricking in the person that they really are. Regardless of what kind of deception is being deployed, most individuals agree that deceptiveness is damaging as well as ought to not be done.

Chapter 5: The Power of Persuasion

The power of persuasion means nothing more than using mental abilities to form words and feelings used to convince other people to do things they may or may not want to do. Some people are better able to persuade than other people. And some people are easier to persuade then other people.

The ease of persuading other people is directly tied to their current mental or emotional state. Someone who is lonely or tired is easier to persuade, simply because their defenses are lowered. Someone who is momentarily needy may be easier to persuade than someone who has a strong sense of self-worth. People who are at a low point in their lives are easy prey for others who might try to persuade them to do something they might not usually do.

The first step in persuasion involves the idea of reciprocating. If a person does something nice for someone else, then the receiving person usually feels the need to do something good in return. If someone helps their elderly neighbor carry in groceries from the car, that neighbor might feel obligated to bake homemade cookies for that person. A coworker who helps complete a project is more likely to receive assistance when it is needed. Many people do nice things for others all the time without expecting anything in return. The person who does nice things for people and then mentions some little favor that can be done in return may be someone to watch closely.

Nonprofit organizations use this tactic to gain more contributions to their causes. They will often send some little trinket or gift to prompt people to donate larger sums of money, or even just to donate where they might not have originally. The idea behind this is that the person opening the letter has received a little gift for no reason, so they might feel obligated to give something in return.

Some people are automatically tempted to follow authority. People in positions of authority can command blind respect to their authority simply by acting a certain way or putting on a uniform. The problem with this is that authority figures or those that look like authority figures, can cause some people to do extraordinary things they would not normally do had a person in a position of authority not been the one asking. And it is not simply held to people in uniform. People who carry themselves a certain way or speak a certain way can give the impression that they are something they are not.

For someone or something to be considered a credible authority, it must be familiar and people must have trust in the person or organization. Someone who knows all there is to know about a subject is considered an expert and is more likely to be trusted than someone who has limited knowledge of the subject. But the information must also make sense to the people hearing it. If there is not some semblance of accuracy and intelligence, then the authority figure loses credibility. Even the person who is acknowledged as an expert will lack persuasive abilities if they are seen as not being trustworthy.

The worst part of the power that goes along with persuasion is that things that are scarce or hard to get are seen as much more valuable. People value diamonds because they are expensive and beautiful. If they were merely pretty stones, they would not be as interesting. Inconsistent rewards are a lot more interesting than consistent rewards. If a cookie falls every time a person rings a bell, then they are less likely to spend a lot of time ringing the bell because they know the cookie reward will always appear. If, however, the cookie only appears sometimes, people will spend much more time ringing the bell just in case this is the time the cookie will fall.

There are ways to improve the power of persuasion. Just like any other trait, it can be made stronger by following a few strategies and by regular practice.

Persuasion is a powerful tool in the game of life. Persuasive people know that they have an amazing power, and they know how to use it correctly. They know how to listen and really hear what other people have to say. They are very good at making a connection with other people, and this makes them seem even more honest and friendly. They make others feel that they are knowledgeable and can offer a certain sense of satisfaction. They also know when to momentarily retreat and regroup. They are not pushy. They are persuasive.

Did you know that your body speaks more eloquently than words? Body language is at work constantly whether you are aware of it or not. When you want to master the art of persuasion, you need not only understand (and read accurately) body language, but also learn to use it to drive your point home.

Body language is a mix of hand and facial gestures, posture and overall appearance. Using these to your advantage you can get people to do what you want without them realizing that you are actually controlling the outcome of the discussion.

Why people are persuasive

What makes a person convincing? Why are they persuasive, and you aren't? This is the answer we're going to pursue in this e-book, but I'm telling you now, there is no single, short answer to that question.

What makes this persuasive influence so difficult to pin down and elusive is precisely this almost mosaic quality it has. It's the result, the perfect merger of several important aspects that you wouldn't normally attribute to such an influence.

These aspects of their being don't only affect them, but affect us, as well. That's the fascination around it. It's all psychological, it's an overwhelming and sometimes unintentional psychological influence on the people around them.

Confidence is the absolute most important aspect when it comes to persuasion. There's no doubt it's been scientifically proven that it's easier to persuade people when you're confident. That's because it's just assumed you're an authority on the topic and they'll listen to you, because they have no knowledge or experience, but you seem to have both.

It's also crucial to understand that humans are doubtful creatures. We're not very confident and we don't really believe in our own abilities or even experience, so when someone comes along and appears to be confident and to know more, we follow them like a herd of dim sheep.

Persuasion is just as much about the impression you leave upon people as it is about your actual skill. Like many other times in life, appearances are more "real" than actual reality, because it's all other people will ever know about you. It doesn't matter if deep inside, you're insecure or you don't really think you know what you're doing.

On the outside, you're this dazzling, confident creature that can persuade anyone into anything because you've mastered all the important contributing factors: confidence, eye contact, body language, manner of speaking, tone, facial expressions, as well as your general demeanor.

Confidence

How do you think so many scammers make a living? No, that sketchy guy selling you snake oil isn't really a doctor, but he speaks like he is one, so people believe him and throw money at him, genuinely believing he will solve their problems.

Now, I'm not advocating that you try to trick people, but I am telling you that you need to work on your confidence. You'll notice that every single person you find convincing has some sort of authoritative stance. It's like their presence demands attention and respect.

Eye contact

Eye contact is a classic, natural display of dominance. It's a technique that's even present in the animal kingdom, and if a lion doesn't intimidate you, I don't know who can. It's true that the goal isn't to intimidate? Eye contact can do that very effectively.

Body language

Do you know how often people underestimate body language, or just ignore it outright? I don't know why, because body language is an amazing tool for persuasion. People are always advised to display open body language, like facing your audience, making sure not to keep your arms crossed against your chest, keep your palms open, and all sorts of little tips that we'll discuss at length later.

What you maybe haven't heard is that in order to be effectively persuasive, you also need to take note of and use the body language of the person you're talking to.

Manner of speaking

Your choice of words is overwhelmingly important when attempting to convince someone, because it must be very deliberate. There's a clear strategy behind verbal persuasion, and it relies on appealing to the person's emotions.

The way you speak and what you say are both equally important, because even though your message may be perfect, if the delivery is lacking, it won't do much good. We've already established that speaking with authority is half the battle, but you also have to speak the right words, in order to win it.

Tone

Continuing on the idea that the way you say things is vastly important, let's talk about tone and why it matters. In fact, I lied when I said tone and message are equally important: tone weighs much more on a person's impression.

If someone has a very somber voice, a serious, measured tone, and an equally severe facial expression, it almost doesn't matter what they're saying – you're going to assume it's grave and important; the actual words or what they mean matters less. A joke told with a serious tone isn't funny at all.

Facial expressions

Facial expression goes hand in hand with body language and eye contact and is similarly important to tonality. Creating the impression that you mean what you say involves your face, because it will be the very first to betray you or, on the contrary, help you enforce your message.

General demeanor

Now, a lot of different aspects of your being can fall under "demeanor". In a way, it's a sum of everything we've discussed so far – body language, facial expression, tone, **etc.** General demeanor is actually one of the main things you need to master and it has one major rule: mirror the demeanor of the person you're trying to persuade.

What you can obtain through persuasion

Persuasion is a very powerful and very valuable skill that not everyone has, but that everyone should have. It comes in handy throughout your life in virtually any aspect of your existence, from sweet-talking your way into free movie tickets to convincing your boss you deserve a raise.

Your relationship with your spouse

Far from being unfair or manipulative, having the ability to convince your significant other can actually improve your relationship because you have fewer fights about your disagreements and lack of compromise. Now you can use all that extra time and energy implementing your superior decisions.

Your relationship with your kids

Having the persuasion skills and indisputable power and authority to convince your kids to actually do what you tell them to is as close to magic as you can possibly get. If you don't believe me, try it!

Your relationship with your friends

We all have that one friend who always makes terrible life choices and no one can get through to them and steer them towards the right path...except you, that is. If you have influence and persuasion skills, don't keep them for yourself. Use them for good, not evil.

Get paid what you deserve

Negotiating absolutely falls under persuasion, so really, absolutely everyone should have this skill. No matter if you're haggling at the market or discussing a higher salary, you need to have the ability to convince your 'opponent' that you deserve this and you should have it.

It's mostly applicable in the workplace, where – let's be real – no boss will ever willingly part with their money and hand it over to you. So it's your job to convince them to do it. You've earned it, you deserve it, and it's rightfully yours. You have to ask for it, but you have to know how, and persuasive skills help with that.

Earn the trust and respect of your boss

You can accomplish that by becoming their go-to person. Offer your bright ideas, come up with solutions to problems the company is facing, persuade them to implement your suggestions and that they're the contribution the company needs right now. In time, you will reap the rewards when your boss comes to consult with your first.

Be a good leader to your colleagues

Obviously, your persuasive abilities will prove to be invaluable to a position like this if you want people to respect you, your work, and your ideas. It should be obvious for everyone that your way is the right way and there will be minimal dissent if you have the necessary influence over them.

Get out of paying tickets

Legally, a ticket is a mandatory consequence of breaking the law in some way, by speeding, failing to wear your seatbelt, talking on your cell while driving, **etc.** Practically, however...a ticket can be a negotiation, as long as you have the necessary skills.

Get into coveted clubs or restaurants

If you're persuasive enough, you can influence any menial gatekeeper and convince them to just let you through without needing to jump through fiery hoops or grease the well-meaning palms of anyone. Talk about some sweet perks!

Get important information

If you can talk the talk well enough, you can basically convince anyone to tell you anything. Gossip from your friend, preferred customer sales dates from sales attendants, where they keep the extra free peanuts from the flight attendant...you get the idea. Sweet talk yourself into perks and valuable info.

How to Persuade People

The ability to influence someone during a conversation and make a decision is necessary in order to become one of the most important people in the world today. This ability is useful in business negotiations, and in everyday life.

In general, the impact on people is not so obvious. The basic idea is that people's behavior is often guided by their subconscious simple desires. And to achieve your goals, you need to understand the simple desires of people, and then make your interlocutor passionately wish for something.

It should be noted that in order to influence people you should NOT try to impose or force them to make a hasty decision. It may seem incredible, but the person that wants to reach a mutually beneficial cooperation becomes a huge advantage compared to those that are trying to impose something on others. If you are willing to put yourself in the shoes of another person from whom you want to get something and understand his/her thoughts, then you do not have to worry about your relationship with the person.

The secret lies in the ability to help the self-affirmation of the interlocutor. It is necessary to make sure that your companion looks decent in his own eyes. First things first, there are six basic principles that will absolutely affect any of your interlocutors.

To achieve their goals, people often use the influence of psychology, which helps to manipulate man. Even in ancient times it can be seen that priests ruled the people, instilling in them that religion is harsh, and everyone will be punished if they cannot follow the established rules and practices. Psychological influence strongly acts on the subconscious, causing the victim being influenced to be led by a skilled manipulator.

If you want to succeed and learn how to manage people, these words of the great American entrepreneur should be your credo. You will grow your personality only when you are in close cooperation with the community. From childhood we develop the basic patterns of behavior and outlook, produced by the long historical, biological and mental development of humankind.

In order to have influence and control over another person, it is required that you know their personality and behavioral traits. Most importantly, learn how to use this knowledge to master the specific methods and techniques of influence and control the behavior of the other, on the basis of his outlook, character, personality type and other important psychological features.

If you want to learn how to manage people, secret techniques in this article will let you know not only the theoretical aspect of the question but also allow the use of this knowledge in real life.

To help people to look beyond the limits of consciousness, professionals use a variety of methods and techniques. One of the most effective of these is hypnosis. This method of direct influence on the psyche, whose essence consists of the introduction of human narrowed state of consciousness, makes it is easy to control someone else's suggestion and management.

The ability to manage people, primarily, is to combine the knowledge of human psychology and their personal characteristics. They help to change their own behavior so that this change will cause the desired reaction in others. Try to be more observant while communicating; it will help you better understand the individual psychological characteristics of the interlocutor. Based on this knowledge, try using the following methods and techniques that will help you manage people correctly and efficiently.

To learn how to manipulate people, you must know how it feels to be on both sides. After all, you need to understand the feelings and emotions experienced by each side. This section of the learning process will be much more efficient!

Just focus on the moral side of the issue. If you are ashamed to receive from people that are important to you, you do not accept selfish purposes - better close and do not hurt their highly moral consciousness of the information received.

Chapter 6: What is manipulation?

Manipulation is a form of intentional influence, characterized as an attempt, by a person or party (the manipulator), to change the behavior of another person or party (the target), typically with a view to achieving a goal in the manipulator's interests.

Two problems remain, however. The first relates to "intended influence." Intent is difficult because it implies responsibility. In actual fact, everyone manipulates everyone around them all the time, even from a young age. It would be wrong to exclude a child's temper tantrum from the umbrella of manipulation, just because they aren't old enough to rationalize their behavior. The same applies to adult temper tantrums, for that matter. Intent, therefore, does not imply conscious behavior – it can also be instinctive. This also allows for the, very real, presence of "naturally manipulative" persons.

The second problem is the disappointingly vague ending: "typically to achieve a goal in the manipulator's interests." Not only is it problematic to define "the manipulator's interests," there is a catch-all ambiguity in the inclusion of "typically." This part serves only to create a normalized idea of manipulation for the purposes of this book and absolutely wouldn't suit a more general definition. After all, how can someone perfectly know their own interests? It is of course possible to successfully manipulate someone, and for the result to still be one's own demise.

How will a manipulator target?

Human beings have various personality traits and types such as warm, passionate, adventurous, loyal and dependable, idealistic, analytical, fun-loving personalities, and many others. Our personality traits are greatly influenced by the biochemical processes ongoing in our bodies. These processes affect how we behave at a given time making some persons to have unpredictable natures and sudden mood swings. Despite all these inconsistencies of the human characters and lives, you still need to learn ways to manipulate and persuade people to get what you want from them.

There are various ways of manipulating a person through persuasion, but you can persuade and influence using your body language and manners of speech respectively. Let us look at some ways to manage and control people like

Polishing and improving your manipulation strategies

You can clean your skills for effective manipulation of others through mastering the art of public speaking, theatrical displays, creating parallels and correspondences, exhibiting charismatic traits by displaying self-confidence, and learning from the experts.

Applying various methods of manipulation

Getting what you want, will not be possible if you do not know how to use some techniques of manipulating people like using rationality and logic to present your requests to a person, you can even act like a scapegoat and the victim in dangerous situations. These tactics will subconsciously compel your target to give you what you desire without any restraint. Another way to get what you want from a person is by using bribing pattern like offering a person something in exchange for what you want from him or her.

Using Manipulation Techniques on your friends and Acquaintances

Your friends and acquaintances are the best persons to manipulate to get whatever you want. This is because they must have known you and your personality traits and probably despite your faults will continue to stick to you no matter what happens. To achieve this, you will play on their emotions because your friends should have feelings for you and most importantly, they commit to help you and make you happy or comfortable if it is in their power to do it. Play on their conscience by reminding them how you have been helpful in the past, and this will motivate them to offer you whatever you desire.

Theories on successful manipulation

If you get caught, you will not only completely blow your chances at success in that conversation, but you could end up spoiling your reputation. People do not tend to take lightly to this type of situation, as no one likes the idea of being under mind control or brainwashed. In order to avoid this type of disaster, you need to know how to prevent yourself from getting caught. Getting caught can potentially destroy your success at mind control, as well as any relationships you have used this strategy in. When people catch wind that you are attempting to brainwash them, or that you have effectively done so, they will no longer trust you and this mistrust will spread across your network extremely quickly. People do not appreciate being subjected to brainwashing and mind control, and so they do not want to know that someone they have grown to trust is using it on them.

Practice Regularly

The more you practice, the stronger your mind control game is going to become. You want to make sure that you practice often, preferably in every single conversation you have. Even if you don't actually want anything significant from someone, knowing how to get them to say or do certain things you want will help you practice brushing up on your technique. It could be something as easy as getting someone to touch a certain area on their body, say something in particular, or do anything else small and seemingly unimportant. The more you learn to use these techniques to get what you want, the better.

Take Your Time Expanding Your Skill

It cannot be stressed enough how important it is for you to slow down when it comes to practicing your skill. It may seem like a good idea to embrace many of these techniques at once and create a conversation that will help you get what you want, but this can lead to you being caught, quickly. When you put this type of pressure on yourself in a conversation without having any practice, you essentially infuse the conversation with a lot of unnatural and uncomfortable feeling. This is because you are not practiced at the techniques, so you are attempting to recall them and use them on the spot, and you are doing it with too many at once. People are going to see through you, and they are going to catch you in the act.

Start Small

Sometimes, starting with large goals is honorable. When it comes to learning how to use mind control and not getting caught in the process, it is actually inefficient and an excellent way to get caught, quickly. The best thing you can do is start small with things that are seemingly unimportant and irrelevant. This allows you to practice getting people to say yes or do what you want them to do, with very little pressure on the situation overall. Once you get regular results in getting your smaller goals met, you can start practicing getting larger goals met. This will give you the best opportunity to really get natural in your talent and feel confident when it comes to setting out larger goals and accomplishing them.

Be Choosy About Who You Brainwash

It is very important that you are choosy about who you brainwash. Remember, just as you have the opportunity to learn about mind control, so do others. Many people in this day and age are somewhat knowledgeable about the art of mind control. While they may not be masters of it, they may have general knowledge around some tactics such as deceit and manipulation. It is important that you learn to identify those who are more likely to comply with your attempts and those who are more likely to be resistant against mind control.

Be Selective About Phrasing and Actions

It is very important that you are careful about the phrasing you use and the actions you carry when you are using mind control strategies. If you use the wrong phrasing, are too forceful or obvious in your phrasing, or have fidgety or otherwise uncontrolled physical movements, you are more likely to be caught. People will recognize that you have something "off" about you, and will be less likely to trust you or believe you. This means that you are going to ruin your attempts and even more people will be less likely to believe you, because mind control and manipulative types of reputations tend to be exposed and shared on a mass level to prevent other people from becoming manipulated. You need to be very careful in your actions and phrasing, ensuring that you are intentional and that you are behaving in a way that is not going to expose you and let others know what you are doing.

What are some of the motivations of a manipulator?

Your Goals

Given that you're probably already manipulating the people around you to some degree, and being manipulated yourself, the first significant step in achieving effective manipulation is to understand and define your goals. Without defining goals, it's impossible to measure the effectiveness of your current manipulation efforts.

That's not to say you aren't already manipulating with some level of effectiveness. Some people are naturally more manipulative and some people are natural manipulators; however, the two don't always overlap.

Start by thinking about your actions, and your behavior around others. Consider who you view positively at work, or in your social circle, and who you view negatively. Consider, further, how you behave around different people and whether it aligns perfectly to your opinion of them. There is a good chance that it doesn't. In fact, what you are probably already doing is working to earn the good opinion of others who you believe to hold power and influence.

The Goals of Others

While your own goals are the way to measure the success of your efforts, the goals of others are key to forming a successful manipulation strategy.

The key to manipulation is using the goals of others to further your own.

This is the most all-encompassing theory of manipulation and the core of this book's approach to manipulation.

At times, you might hold the cards and can help someone to achieve their own goals. This might be as an employee who possesses vital assets for your boss to achieve success in their role. It might be the case that you are the boss and have the power to promote people... not discounting the power you have to help those people achieve their goals by **not firing** them.

Having what it takes to help other people achieve their goals gives you inherent value to them.

Understanding goals provides the necessary information for effectively manipulating others. Tools, on the other hand, are the raw materials you have at your disposal for affecting those goals, or the actions taken by others to achieve them.

Power

Power is the ability to help other people succeed. This is an interesting definition because it appears to subvert the normal idea of power as an ability to exert force over others. However, breaking it down, the two are closely related. Having the ability to exert force over others can mean not harming them, not invading their country, not throwing them in jail, not creating laws which negatively impact them; these are all forms of power – the power to help other people succeed is much the same as the power to make other people fail, left unexercised.

These are just positive and negative perspectives of the same thing. The difference is often negligible.

What can you provide people that will help other people achieve their goals? The most obvious thing is extraordinary abilities. Talent is valuable in every aspect of life, from sports competitions, to business, to raising children. If you have talents that other people can use, that's a powerful thing.

Another form of power is authority. The boss gets to decide who is promoted and who is fired. A police officer can arrest you or let you off with a warning, thanks to their legally sanctioned authority. A judge may decide your sentence, based on certain constraints, and their opinion of your nature.

When would I need to manipulate someone

Most times, you may not get what you want in life if you are not ready to take some necessary steps in manipulating other people involved in the process. It is challenging to get what you desire if you are not exactly a careful manipulator. Therefore, you need to learn the necessary steps to use in manipulating people. These steps will surely give you an edge over others because you will know how to appeal to their conscience and mentality without being caught in the act, which may annoy them.

Let us make an analysis of these steps, which involves using some body language expressions and spoken words such as:

Manipulative Looks and Stares

Manipulative looks and stares include wearing of stony faces suggesting displeasure and anger over an incidence or something else, death stares used for intimidating others, sexy looks and stares intended to seduce and lure a person into sexual intimacy, maintaining eye contact with someone without saying anything, rolling of eyes, and many others.

Shouting Down on Someone or Yelling

Insidious or manipulative persons have a way of using these tactics to cow and frighten their victims. Shouting down on someone or yelling at people is a manipulative tendency aimed at making the other person or persons shut up in fear and condescend to your whims and caprices unconsciously. Mostly, bosses use this manipulative tendency or traits in the offices to suppress staffs anger and maintain control or leadership of the firm. In some cases, the staffs are never comfortable whenever the boss is around; everybody whisks away in fear of the next reprimanding action that may happen.

Manipulations by Avoiding you at All Means

When someone avoids or ignores you, by all means, something is possibly wrong in your relationship with that person. This type of attitude manifests in so many ways such as when someone leaves a meeting when you enter, if a person does not acknowledge your presence in a place but acknowledges others, no response to your e-mails, phone calls, and messages. Moreover, if a person avoids eye contact with you, you should know that something is fishing and beware of interactions with such persons.

Preferential or Silent Treatment

One of the ways to manipulate someone to give what you want is by showing them unusual, preferred, or silent treatment. After giving them this type of attention and care, the chances are that they must succumb to your wishes and desires.

Playing on the Emotions

Master manipulators like to play on your emotions to coerce you to give them what they want from you. They know that if they can make you have a feeling for them, you will surely respond to their requests. Therefore, they look for words and expressions that can captivate your feelings and thoughts to give them a leeway into your heart. These manipulators may use words such as "I love you," or anything that can endear them to you. This attitude is to get what they want from you.

Cold Behaviors

This is another good tactic of manipulation, but as the behavior is severe, it does not show up boldly and directly. It manifests subtly and merely displaying aggression and anger as inert frustrations. They are angry but maintaining coolness and calmness. With this mindset, they will surely ignore their responsibilities; they will always arrive late for duties, avoid interacting with other persons, and neglecting to perform their functions purposefully. Additionally, they will be carrying out their jobs poorly and shabbily, unnecessary delays of routines, making sarcastic remarks, acting deaf and dumb to instructions, and many other ugly behavioral traits.

Undue Obstinacy and Difficult

Crafty manipulators are unduly obstinate and challenging. They have a purposeful resolution to be hard and stubborn, always disagreeing with everyone and not condescending to any form of concession. They are crafty negotiators but never arrive at a meaningful agreement or conclusion. This class of persons is very argumentative and quarrelsome. Most of the time, people tend to ignore them in order not to have a headache arguing on simple matters and even quarreling.

Unnecessary Deadline Pressures

Giving unnecessary deadlines is a tactic of some bosses and employers to purposely manipulate their subordinates and even victimize them at the place of work. With this approach, the worker does not have enough time to think and may be under pressure to coordinate himself properly and may miss deadlines and other salient requirements, thereby incurring punishments as the case may be.

Suspending Sex, Food, and other Gratifications

A careful manipulator may in a relationship such as between husband and wife decide to discontinue offering sex, food, and other forms of gratification to their partner to induce or coerce him or her to approve something or agree to do something. It could even be done tactically, to get help, money, and other pleasantries from the spouse.

Unsolicited Treats, Gifts, and Favors

When someone decides to offer you unwanted gifts, treats, and favors, it could portend that such one is looking for a leeway into your life to get something they have been expecting. People usually say, "There is no free lunch anywhere." This saying means that 'nothing goes for nothing' and anything someone gives to you is bait for something 'bigger or equivalent' to what they have given to you.

Manipulation Using Compliments and Flattery

Some persons can manipulate you using unnecessary compliments and flattery, which is intended to get a favor from you. They tend to influence you with their words as they shower you with praises in an attempt to appeal to your conscience and reasoning.

How to Deal with Manipulative People

Walking away

What happens when you cannot walk? What if the dark one is your friend or possibly your child? Taking into consideration that we are all social, we all eventually come in contact with a practitioner of the dark. There are ways to protect us and those around us.

Fear is a motivation tool in dark psychology. From the fear of being killed to the fear of losing your heart in love, the practitioner uses fear as a way to manipulate, intentional or not.

We are creatures of fear. It is the primary emotion that goes off when we are in trouble. We feel it all the time. This emotion is valid because it is our survival technique.

The thing about dark psychology is that it is mostly mental. Our physical lives are only in danger if things truly get out of hand. Sometimes they do. Normally, when the dark smell fear, they know that what they are doing is working. Then they ramp up the volume.

Staying calm.

Breathing and knowing that you are really not going to die because you are scared. Knowing what causes this fear is essential to figuring out what is happening.

The best advice? Stay calm and examine what is going on. Back off if needed, of course. The only way you will know about the individual who is trying to manipulate you with fear is to remain calm and do not let them scare you.

If you do not want to be controlled by fear, then you need to get control over it.

Another thing we forget is that the individual who is using dark psychology is also human. They have a life, just as we do. They may not feel or have morals like everyone else. They are not a beast. They are a person. It takes people to do the horrible things that happen around us.

When we confront them as people, and not as rulers or hunters, we begin to see something happen. It is like a child when you take away the most favorite toy. They settle down. Practitioners of dark psychology are individuals and we need to remember that we can give them direction as much as they try to give us direction. We are not defenseless.

So, we have control of fear. This can be the removal of the tool of fear, and we have one to one, person to person, ability to communicate. Fearless.

Utilize logic. Knowledge is paramount.

It is in this logic we can begin to calm the dark. Explanation of almost everything needs to take place. Left to their own devices, the dark will go out and break things to see how they work. It is best to show them knowledge beforehand to make it so that they have another option to figure things out.

When confronted with darkness, one must be almost always diligent. This is yet another way to be around those who cannot process like everyone else. They are special and need to be treated as such. Not all darkly psychological individuals are killers. There are some who are just not sure how to process things that you may take for granted.

Please reciprocate.

There may not be morals amongst the dark, there is one thing that you can use to touch them and move them.

They have a sense of honor. From the introverted weirdo in the corner to the serial killer who collects trophies of their victims, there is honor. The honor of being weird is in itself respect. Those trophies are also deserving of respect.

Honor is, of course, a respect of what is right. We all want to know what is right and wrong. Life and the mysteries of it do not allow us to have a solid view of what is right and wrong. Taking this into account, there is a way to understand the honor of the dark and discuss it.

You were manipulated by media? Turn it off.

The practice of dark psychology is not a gentle thing, and it deserves a balanced reply. The more vicious an individual is in their darkness, the more work and diligence and logic it will take to get them to shift so that you are both safe.

Respect is one of your best weapons. Asking often, and remembering to actually listen to the answer with an open mind and ears, is respect earned here.

Observe a manipulator before you label them.

It is not unusual in a workplace to have people telling you what to do. So long as they ask in the correct manner and they have the authority. Authority comes in many guises. It could be because they are your managers, or they are close work colleagues. If the request is genuine, then it should not be a problem. If someone is constantly demanding you to do things with aggressive coercion, then you are right to be suspicious. Don't jump the gun though, take your time. You don't want to overreact and ruin a workplace relationship unnecessarily.

Never let them see your own weaknesses.

If you recognize someone to be a controlling manipulative person, it might be best that you have as little contact with them as possible. This can be difficult in a working environment, but try to restrict personal contact with them. That way, you are not likely to ever divulge your personal life or any problems you may be having. The last thing you want is for them to recognize any of your own weaknesses. They may use that information to gain a hold over you.

Never allow them to put you down, especially in front of others.

A common psychological phenomenon often exploited by manipulator's is Imposter syndrome. This is a phenomenon that has been well studied. At least 70% of people will suffer from Imposter syndrome at some time in their life. It includes that dreaded feeling of inadequacy at whatever you attempt to do. Even if there is evidence that shows you otherwise, such as your own success at your work.

Begin with building up a support network.

It is vital that you have support from friends and family. This can be a difficult one though. It could be that the very partner you have just left, browbeat you to severing all personal ties. If this is your situation and you are unable to pick up those ties, then there are organizations that you can turn to. These agencies can guide you on dealing with your situation.

Accept that you will feel scared.

If your partner has sensed anything, they could revert to being overly nice to you. Don't be fooled, you know without anyone having to tell you that it will not last. It will only be natural to hesitate in your actions, whether it is out of fondness, pity, or fear. Fear of being on your own is natural. Fear of your partner's violence is not. If that's something you feel, then you are most certainly making the right choice. If you do leave, then you must make it quick and clean, leaving no trace of where you are going. Manipulative, obsessive partners will attempt to track down fleeing partners, even if only to punish them. You have broken their self-ego and now they have no one left to control. If they do find you, they may try the extra-nice approach and beg you to return, or they may be violent and angry. You don't want to be there for any confrontations whatsoever.

Observe a manipulator before you label them.

Observe their behavior whenever you can, without them realizing what you are doing. Keep your distance because you don't want to attract this character's attention. It is important to identify this person for what they are, so you to keep them at a distance in the future.

Never let them see your own weaknesses.

If you recognize someone to be a controlling manipulative person, it might be best that you have as little contact with them as possible. This can be difficult in a working environment, but try to restrict personal contact with them. That way, you are not likely to ever divulge your personal life or any problems you may be having. The last thing you want is for them to recognize any of your own weaknesses. They may use that information to gain a hold over you.

Never allow them to put you down, especially in front of others.

When you stand up to a manipulator, they can become abusive. A forceful manipulator will not let people stand in the way of their primary objective. Everyone is fair game in their attempts at power-play. If there is one in your work environment, it will only be a matter of time before they turn their attention to you.

How to leave a control freak?

For many people, especially women, this can happen in the family home. For such victims, trying to break free is the most difficult. Not the least because the victim may, in fact, love their toxic partner or parent. If you are in such an unhappy situation, then you must consider your own wellbeing and safety. Only if the perpetrator can admit that they have a problem and seek help, can they begin to mend. If they learn to compromise and accept your input, then it will be a great step forward. Such an openness may save a two-way partnership.

Begin with building up a support network.

It is vital that you have support from friends and family. This can be a difficult one though. It could be that the very partner you have just left, browbeat you to severing all personal ties. If this is your situation and you are unable to pick up those ties, then there are organizations that you can turn to. These agencies can guide you on dealing with your situation.

Don't forget your own health needs.

Do things that help you relax, if possible. Get outside and take short walks. You need personal space so you can consider your situation.

493

Listening to music you like or immersing yourself in a book or a TV program, is good if it helps you to switch off. Avoid overeating or drinking too much alcohol. Your problem will become tenfold if you take that route. All these points are double stressed if you have children. You need to stay strong for them, and for yourself.

Accept that you will feel scared.

If your partner has sensed anything, they could revert to being overly nice to you. Don't be fooled, you know without anyone having to tell you that it will not last. It will only be natural to hesitate in your actions, whether it is out of fondness, pity, or fear. Fear of being on your own is natural. Fear of your partner's violence is not. If that's something you feel, then you are most certainly making the right choice.

Build up your courage.

Once you have built up your courage and self-esteem, you can then face the world head-on. We all approach this one in a different way. The first rule must be, not to compare yourself to others.

There will come a time when you must begin to take risks. That is after the huge risk you have put yourself through by leaving. You have taken a huge leap forward, no need to jump in feet first, give it time to settle.

Build up your courage.

Once you have built up your courage and self-esteem, you can then face the world head-on. We all approach this one in a different way. The first rule must be, not to compare yourself to others. It is not an easy rule to follow, but nonetheless, you are new to freedom. That is exactly what you are, free. Forget other people. Of course, be polite, but concentrate on your needs and not anyone else's, unless you have children.

How and why does manipulation works

Body language is a potent tool needed for mastering how to manipulate people. If you can honestly understand how body language works and be able to analyze it, then you will be in control of the other person, though in a tactical manner.

The way body language works as a compass is by telling you very important things about how the person is feeling and what they are thinking in the present. This information will help you understand how they feel about their environment and what is going on around them, as well as how they feel about you and their interactions with you, or anyone else with whom they may be sharing interactions. Knowing this information means that you have an incredible upper hand when it comes to interacting with the person. With it, you now know when you should approach them and how, which manipulation and persuasion strategies you should use, what wording would likely work best on them, and even the exact timing of when you should be able to completely tip them in your favor.

As you can clearly tell, body language is an essential compass in helping you effectively manipulate people. This is the very first step before you move toward anything else. For that reason, it is vital that you understand the "reading formula," or how you will assess the three types of body language that you will be reading on the person in front of you. This formula is basic, and can even be crafted into an easy-to-remember sentence, just like the one you use to remember the three steps of manipulation.

As you now know, basic body language is the part of the body language you are reading to get a general understanding of what a person is thinking and feeling at the moment. This is the first thing you want to read before you approach a person or begin manipulating them, as this will give you an understanding of where they stand and what path you need to take to get to where you want to go. After you have gained this general understanding, you typically do not want to find yourself focused excessively on basic body language.

When you are reading complex body language signals, you want to look at two primary areas: their hands and their feet. The location and actions being taken with these two parts of the body will tell you more than almost anywhere else on the entire body.

By reading the signs being given to you by the hands and feet, you can get an idea of what the person is thinking and how they are feeling. In general, you want to watch the movements taking place in the hands and feet during your conversation with the person you are talking to and wanting to manipulate. Use them to determine whether you are successfully driving the person into the emotion that you need them to be in for manipulation to happen, or if you need to adjust your tactics to get them there. Pay attention to them during the course of the entire conversation, especially when you use a specific manipulation tactic. These complex signals will act as a form of compass to guide you through the conversation step-by-step, on their terms that are secretly orchestrated by you.

Let us analyze some of the possible ways a person can manipulate others using his body language.

Manipulation by Mirroring the Other Person

When you consciously and deliberately change your body language to fit into another person's class and even behave like the person by learning the tone of voice, posture, facial expressions, including micro-expressions. This merely is mimicry or imitation aimed at impressing someone else.

Although, this process could be risky because the other person may get to know you are just trying to make a false impression and it could cost you the relationship or other valuable details. It is better to maintain your natural body language than mirroring another person's traits, which has the potentials of backfiring at the end, leaving you in pieces.

Exciting and Captivating their Emotions

This step is a beneficial method of manipulating people easily by exciting and captivating their minds through their emotions. Finding out the issue troubling their heart and using it as bait in luring them into doing what will be an advantage to you.

Make People to Like You

You may want to ask me, what shall I do to make people like me? No matter the intrigues and tactics, you want to use in manipulating people, it may not work if they don't like you naturally. Therefore, endeavor to make yourself a likable person. The character is one of the criteria that will cause people to quickly and gullibly accept whatever you say to them.

Howbeit, remember that your ultimate goal is to make everything work to your advantage, nothing less than that.

Present Yourself as a Trustworthy Person

Trust is the crucial thing in every relationship. If your friend does not trust you, he will not commit salient details to you. One of the criteria to win the trust of your friend is to share a very private issue with him or her, and that will make him open his or her heart for you too. With this gesture, you may win the confidence of your partner, as he is poised to confide in you.

Use Your Emotions to manipulate them

The very first step to analyzing anyone is to analyze their body language. Body language is something that virtually every master manipulator has learned how to read, and it is essential that you learn how, too. Body language is a level of language that we use to communicate beyond the spoken word. You have likely heard about, and maybe even learned about body language in the past. Still, it is vital that you understand how to read body language from a manipulator's point of view if you want to effectively analyze a person.

Set a Baseline

When you have a baseline about people, reading body language and other nonverbal clues becomes more accurate. Tune in to people completely to figure out their baseline or essential behavior. This will help you relate nonverbal clues more effectively. How does someone react to different circumstances and situations? What is their inherent personality? How are their communication skills? How is their speech and choice of words? What about the voice? Are they essentially confident or anxious?

Look for a Group of Clues

Read clues in clusters, which offer a more accurate analysis of what a person is thinking or feeling. Do not make quick and sporadic conclusions based on isolated nonverbal signals.

Spotting Lies and Deception

While reading people for deception, it is crucial to keep their baseline behavior and the physical setting and culture/religion into context too. Reading or analyzing people through body language is not an overnight process, but it keeps getting accurate with practice. Try deciphering what people are thinking or feeling by practicing people reading skills at the airport, in the train to work, at the doctor's clinic, or cafe. You'll learn to tune in to their actions and behavior accurately over a period of time.

General Body Language Signs

If you are speaking and someone is leaning in your direction, he or she is clearly interested in what you are saying or keenly listening to you. Likewise, crossed arms and legs are a huge sign of switching off or being completely closed to what you are trying to communicate. The person does not really subscribe to your views or isn't confident about what you are saying. Sometimes, people offer wide smiles yet cross their arms while listening to you.

Smile

This information can be extremely valuable considering smile is the single largest weapon people use to conceal their real thoughts, emotions, and feelings. It is a widely established conclusion among psychological experts that a smile is tough to fake. There has to be a genuine experience of joy or happiness for creating that specific expression. When you aren't really happy, the expressions will not settle into their place.

Chapter 7: The Techniques to Make Dark Seduction Work

Seduction and Dark Psychology

Seduction is persuading someone to have sex with you or make them more excited to do so. Seduction is often simply part of attraction between two people, as it sets the stage for the sex to come. It may include a woman wearing lingerie to greet her partner after his long day at work, or a man buying his date a fancy dinner and whispering in her ear how beautiful she looks in her dress. Among good-intentioned people, seduction is a normal, specific mode of communication appropriate for indicating desire and hoping the person of interest feels the same way. Ideally, the process of seduction is never dishonest or misleading. The person being seduced knows what their pursuer wants, and they can have a mutually satisfying sexual encounter or start a romantic relationship.

How does seduction fit into dark psychology then? Seduction can be to help the person being seduced, to hurt that person, or to benefit the person doing the seducing. All three of these motives have one thing in common though; all seduction, to some degree or another, requires at least some affection of the desired person's mental state.

Seduction and sexual desires are such common motives and features of dark psychology and Many people have been seduced using dark Psychology principles. The human sex drive is one of the most powerful urges and an inability to fulfill it can lead to great stress, worry, and unhappiness in a person's life. Conversely, some of the most famous historical figures are known for the frequent and full fulfillment of their sexual urges. Kings and emperors have often been afforded the finest women in the world as a reward for their elevated social status.

So is all seduction dark psychological seduction? No. All seduction involves the pursue of another human being. Most people who are not adept at the skills of dark psychological manipulators do this in a very clumsy and unstructured way. To illustrate this idea, think of the classic romantic comedy setup with a clumsy guy making mistake after mistake in his pursuit of the girl. A skilled psychological seducer is more like Ryan Gosling in Crazy, Stupid Love, or Will Smith in Hitch. They know what they want and know how to get it.

Reinforcement - A CEM Stacked Sequence

In this technique the victim is controlled without realizing. It involves a sequence of love bombing followed by positive reinforcement.

It causes a deep, subconscious craving for positive attention on behalf of the victim, without the victim ever having conscious knowledge of what is happening. The victim will then begin to chase a good reaction from the manipulator by any means possible. The manipulator has their victim behaving in a certain way and the victim will have no awareness whatsoever of what they are doing or why they are doing it.

Flattery

Most people would detect this quickly and point it out to the seducer. But, if it is done subtly and the insecurities of the victim are taken into account, it just might go unnoticed. No one is without these insecurities. We all have, at least, one area on our lives where we feel inadequate and seek someone or something to validate us. Seducers who use flattery to get their way are quite observant and would prey on such weaknesses. They are often skilled at not being obvious, either with their choice of words or mannerisms. The reassurance they give to their victims is often very effective at gaining their trust. Sale marketers do not shy away from using flattery to convince their audience that a particular product is the best fit for them.

Fantasy

We all have imaginations of what the perfect romantic partner would be. The manner in which they would behave towards us, the words they will say to us their sense of style, their goals, etc. The seducer, in an effort to execute their desire, may go out of their way to bring their victims dreams and fantasies to life. They would get the needed information from studying their target or asking the person's close friends and family members. Then the seducer proceeds to become the victim's person of fantasy. They do the roses on the staircase, lights, music, show interest in the victim's children if they have any, offer to fix certain things in the house, and so on. If done right, the victim, for that moment in time, feels like they have hit the jackpot. They are forthcoming with whatever is asked of them by the seducer. Some especially dark individuals may take this a bit further and derive some enjoyment from shattering the fantasy they had created. After all, it is all a game to them, and there were no actual emotions involved on their part.

Gaslighting

In a relationship with a narcissist, the other partner's reality is constantly called into question and altered. Conversations when recalled at a later date will be completely misremembered. If the victim said once "you are hurting me" to a narcissist, the narcissist could easily twist this into a darker adaptation of the actual conversation, and claim the victim said, verbatim, "I enjoy **hurting you.**" There are many elements that go into the devastating process of gaslighting. One of these is the sheer audacity the victim observes in the narcissist. However, shock soon turns into despair, because the narcissist will never back down; she is relentless in her attempt to undermine the confidence, as well as the **sanity**, of her partner, friend, family member, or child.

Shaming

Should the seducer not get their way, they might resort to guilt-tripping and shaming techniques. Unlike the method of flattery where the seducer enforces the ego of their victims and makes them feel good, shaming does the opposite. The inadequacies and faults of the victim are brought to light, and they are made to believe that their choices or decisions would only lead to unfortunate results, whether in the near or far future. This works quite effectively on people with low self-esteem. At that point, they may be willing to do anything just to please their seducer and feel worthy again.

Logical fallacy

These are errors committed during arguments whereby the reasoning of a person arguing is faulty. It may be done deliberately or unintentionally to misdirect, confuse, or make an argument seem more solid and whole than it actually is. It is done quite often by seducers, especially when they are being resisted. For example, a seducer might pose that their victims would yield to their advances if they, indeed, loved them. This is not exactly accurate, as many unrelated factors could account for why a person may refuse to give in to any request, sexual or not. The seducer could also argue that denying their desires at that particular point in time may result in a domino effect, which would ultimately cause the end of the relationship. This is called the slippery slope fallacy and is one of the most common types. These fallacious arguments are often delivered with such conviction of tone and mannerisms that it appears true and factual.

False control of decision

Have you been accosted by a salesperson who, after some minutes of telling you all you stand to gain and lose depending on your decision, still says, in the end, that it still your choice to make? In truth, it is your choice to make. But their earlier proposal, if successful, had done the job of swaying your mind in the direction of choice most favorable to them. This false sense of control makes the person being seduced feel like they are in charge, even as they give in to the request of their seducer.

Minimizing

This is another common tactic used by seducers in the convincing of their targets. They try to make a situation which holds great importance seem trivial. They would say things like, "this is not such a big deal" (this involves a fallacy called hasty generalization) and "everyone does this" in an attempt to make their victims believe there really is nothing to be wary of. They might also go further to minimize the fears of the individual being seduced, by telling them that it is normal and expected for them to worry and that it does not betray the seriousness of the situation whatsoever.

Vilification

Usually, when someone is trying to manipulate another into doing something against their own personal choices, it is the seducer who seems like the bad guy. But, to get their way, the seducer might turn this around on their victim and make them feel like the villain for saying no. If the victim is a neurotic or one who is a people-pleaser, this tactic would work quite well in getting them to give in to their seducers. The seducer would pretend to be hurt and act the victim. This would place the actual victim in the position of the villain. A role I'm which neurotics and people-pleasers are uncomfortable in.

Pretending to be innocent

This seduction technique bears some similarities to playing the victim, but it differs in that the actual victim is not vilified and the seducer does not pretend to be hurt. Instead, the pretense is one of naiveté, near cluelessness, and innocence. When it has to do with sex, they might tell their victims that they are virgins, and have only been keeping themselves for the right person. They make them appear unlike 'every other guy or girl' who only wants the victim for sex or some other type of material gain. The victim may also feel closer to their seducer if they are novices on the subject.

Seduction is a game that has been played throughout the ages, and one that continues to be a weapon in the arsenal of so many. The methods listed here are nothing new, but they expose the dark psychology at play during such manipulative activities.

Love Flooding

This is when someone is buttering you up to get you to do something that they know you won't want to do. They may come and lather you with affection. Sweet kisses, hugs, nuzzles. "Baby, I love you. Can you get up and do my laundry really quick so I can stay in bed and sleep?"

Normally, you might be nice and do it. But last night you were up with the baby six times. And you've got an appointment with the dentist that you're not looking forward too after lunch. You don't want to get up and even start your day, much less someone else's – even if you truly love that other person.

Withdrawal

This is a hard one. When someone gives you the cold-shoulder or shuts themselves off to you just because you won't do what they want, then it hurts. I don't care who you are or how tough you might be. When someone turns away from you only because you won't do what they want, it's a terrible manipulation and the epitome of emotional exploitation.

It's easy to say, just don't let them get to you, but man, that's right at impossible. That is until you realize why they're doing it. They want you to feel terrible for not giving in to them. They want to make you hurt. And for what?

Love Denial

Much like Withdrawal, love denial is when a person who loves you holds back that attention because you won't do something, they want you to. You can use the same type of scene from above to deal with that person. You will still talk calmly to them and let them know that what they are doing is only hurting them and not you. They are the ones who are missing out on love and attention by acting the way they are. You have to stay strong here and remain calm. They learned this. It was done to them. Have empathy for that, but don't tolerate it. Don't give in to it. They will learn that at least you won't be manipulated by this action.

Projecting

One of the most extraordinary, long-term effects that survivors of relationships with narcissists exhibit is the fact that they wonder if they, in fact, were or still are the narcissist.

How does a person go from being an observer and victim of the devastating harm a narcissist commits to believing that they, themselves, are capable of such cruelty? The answer to that question is called "projecting".

In the wooing or love-bomb phase of a relationship with a narcissist, the would-be victim often spills the contents of their hearts to the narcissist, talking about past heartbreak, being cheated on, being lied to, having things stolen from them. Whatever negative thing happened in the victim's past, if it's shared with the narcissist then he will definitely save that intelligence for later in the relationship, and it will re-emerge, in the form of projection.

Name Calling

Whenever the voice is involved in a way that is mean to hurt or demean you, you are being verbally abused. This includes comments that are meant to hurt, such as belittling, disparaging remarks, or yelling at you. While some people may say things that are critical but to use them in a legitimate manner to help better you, the narcissist uses his voice to keep you down. Oftentimes, verbal abuse goes ignored because it does not leave a mark on you but the constant name-calling or insults can wear down on you and do lasting damage to your mental welfare.

Verbal abuse includes any sort of verbal harm, such as threats, demands, guilt trips, sarcasm, yelling, calling names, insulting, or anything else that involves the voice that you consider intentional and harmful.

Mirroring

Mirroring is one of the most effective manipulation techniques. It has two stages. The first stage is where you mirror the person you are talking with. The second stage is where he or she is the one who is mirroring you. Mirroring is an excellent way to build a connection.

So, how does it work? As the name implies, you have to mirror the other person. This is the first step. To do this, pay attention to how he positions his body, as well as the gestures that he makes. You should apply mirroring while you are engaged in a conversation. Simply mirror or copy how the other person positions his physical body. For example, if his hand is on his lap, then place your hand on your lap. If his hands are both raised to his chin, then mimic the same posture. Simply put, be a mirror of the person with whom you are conversing with. Be sure to do this casually, so that the other person will not notice it.

Once you mirror the other person while talking, a connection is made. The next step is to continue with the flow of conversation. This is also the time when you use other manipulation techniques. If it works, what will happen is that the other person will be the one who will be copying your movements or position. In other words, he will be the one who will be mirroring you.

Mirroring is an excellent way to create rapport and trust with a person. Also, by copying another person, you get to view the situation from their perspective — and this will allow you to have a better understanding of how the other person thinks and feels. Once you have a good understanding of these things, then it will be easier for you to know how to control the other person more effectively.

The more that you mirror a person, the more effective it will be. Therefore, you are not limited to just mirroring gestures and positions of the body. You should also mirror the tone of voice and how the person projects himself. In other words, mirror the other person as much as you can. This is an effective way to establish empathy with the person. Once this empathic link is made, you can then take advantage of it by using other manipulation techniques, which can then lead to the other person to do what you want.

Victim Blaming

In victim blaming, the manipulator tries to convince their victim that a problem in the relationship is their fault. Victim blaming may make the victim feel guilty for harm that befell them or ashamed of themselves.

This tactic sound as though it would be completely obvious when it happens, but it can be more subtle than boldly shifting blame over to the victim. Accidentally forgetting to take precautions does not justify that a crime has been committed against someone. In victim blaming, the victim is meant to wonder or feel that they brought their harm onto themselves. This is common in domestic abuse situations and rape. Victims will become depressed and isolated by their shame that they did not prevent themselves from becoming victims of abuse or crime, and may become so ashamed that they stay silent, and do not tell anyone of what they have endured.

Mind games

Mind games are a small-scale version of CEM, so they usually occur between two people, or one person turning two people against each other. The objective of a manipulator's mind games is to control your thoughts or actions using passive-aggression.

Although directly expressing feelings in an open and honest conversation is usually the best route to take in a conflict, people who play mind games actually have a lot of trouble with this. They may have grown up in emotionally repressive households or feel afraid of causing conflicts. Playing mind games often feels safer to the manipulator, who knows their victim will have trouble holding them accountable for their CEM tactics.

Chapter 8: How to Detect When Manipulation Is Being Used Against You

How to Spot Manipulative and Deceptive People?

An individual that has interest in preventing deception to avoid the mind games that come with it should learn how to detect deception when it is occurring. It is not usually easy to know when deception is going on as there are really no pointers to rely on; except the agent makes a mistake and either tells an obvious lie or says something that the subject knows to be false. While it might be difficult for the agent to mislead the subject for a long period of time, it is something that will usually happen regularly between individuals who know one another.

Deception can place a heavy weight on the cognitive thinking of the agent because they will need to find a way to bring to remembrance all the conversations they have had with the subject on the situation, so the story stays believable and dependable. Any mistake will bring the subject to the realization they are being deceived. The stress involved in keeping the story believable, is much, and as such, the agent is very much likely to spill out details that will give the subject a clue that they are being deceived either through nonverbal or verbal signs.

For better or worse, we can usually tell what others are thinking with or without the aid of what they are actually saying. The words are often just the tip of the iceberg when it comes to what is actually going on within other people's minds. When most hear the term "mind reading" they tend to think of psychics, witches, and other people of this sort, but great steps can be taken by anyone to better understand the thoughts of others. With just a little guidance and a lot of practice, anyone can become just as proficient in the art of telling what others are thinking as the more mystical figures among us.

So much of interpersonal human connection is dependent upon our ability to guess at and respond to the thoughts and actions of others appropriately that we often have difficulty reconciling what is actually being said by others with what impressions we are getting from them. In order to understand the thoughts of others, we must first delve into our own. It is all too easy for an attempt at understanding what another person is thinking to quickly turn into a judgment. We jump to conclusions about the people we meet and often run into errors as a result.

One of the greatest obstacles we face we trying to mind read is that of dishonesty or a lack of expression in the words or the nonverbal cues of those who we are talking to. When we come across people with good poker faces and or dishonest people, our tendency gauge language and nonverbal cues are of little use to us. There are, however, many ways in which we can dig beneath the superficial aspects of the communication and get a glimpse at what it really going on within our partner's minds.

In order to read minds, we must first trust our own intuition. This involves developing a more trustworthy intuition though, which is a task that is always becoming and never being. Here we should avoid some of the magical thinking that often goes into the habit of mind reading and only use our reason. A willingness to look into the places that we least want to and to challenge our own beliefs is also crucial here because if we go into trying to read the minds of others already anchored to our own beliefs our findings will always be less fruitful.

Mindfulness is one of the greatest skills that we can home in on in order to read minds more effectively. This practice allows us to clear our minds of any needless distractions and worries, enabling us to pay greater attention to those who we are speaking with. When we have our heads fully grated on our own inner worries and problems we can never delve into what is going on with others fully. Any ability that we may have had in the way of understanding other people's thoughts falls by the wayside as we try to pick up our own pieces with cluttered and anxiety riddled psyches. Here it becomes clear that if we want to determine what is going on within other people's inner lives we are first going to have to look at our own. Doing so will give us the clarity and the energy necessary for reading the minds of others.

The first step towards better reading the minds of others is always to maintain an open spirit for doing so. Without this openness, we will never reap the full rewards of what other people are communicating to us. This openness does necessarily have to come with a certain degree of intolerance though, intolerance directed at anything that does not immediately serve whatever purposes we have in the present moment. When we try to take in all things, including those things that have nothing to do with us, we always get overwhelmed and feel as though we are making no progress toward our goals, because we probably are not. When we instead remain open only to the things that are affecting us directly we usually find that we have much more energy to understand others and to work with what we have accordingly.

Again, mindfulness training of some kind is the best practice we have to foster this sense of openness. Stress and distraction cause us to not only extract less information out of others but to also misinterpret what little that we do get. Any interpretations of other people's thoughts that we make when under stress are inherently ill conceived and hindered by our own issues. As Kant believed, it is only the judgments of the unprejudiced that should be taken into account, so mindfulness is a necessary practice for all those who want to better read minds.

If we are going to make further progress on reading the thoughts of others we are going to have to analyze them holistically. This is where some problems will always arise because no two people are exactly the same. People are complicated, and just when we think we have figured out another fully, yet another layer of the onion that is their personality is peeled away, asking us to strip away axiomatic preconceptions and other facets of our integrated knowledge structure in order to adapt to the changes that we are met with.

Many times, this kind of dark persuasion is going to show up in a relationship. Often one but sometimes both partners are going to be inclined towards trying to use dark persuasion on each other. If these attempts are persistent and endure, then this type of relationship is going to be classified as psychologically abusive, and that is not healthy for the victim in that relationship. Often, they will not realize that there is something going on or that they are darkly persuaded until it is too late, and they are stuck there.

Methods you can use to effectively Analyze people

Facial profiling

Our face is the most obvious and visible reflection of our personality. Faces don't just help in remembering an old long-lost friend or keep us different from each other. They also help in understanding the underlying personality traits and characteristics of people. Facial profiling or face reading techniques are very useful to read and understand a person's nature and character. With sustained practice and patience, you can learn to notice facial structure and more or less come to a reasonably correct conclusion about a person's character. There is a lot of history and literature covering the subject of facial profiling.

Body Language

The power of body language is so huge that what your body says is always taken as right when there is a conflict between your words and your actions. It mostly only during extremely pleasant or unpleasant experiences, that our body language comes to the fore. Our brain understands our intentions and transfers those understandings through our body systems to reveal them via body language.

Learning to read body language will help you understand what and how others are feeling about us which will help us understand how our relationships are evolving. It is common for people to realize things are not going well in their love relationships based on body language. It is easy to sense changes.

Know When You Are the Target

Financial Gain

This is one of the major motives for manipulation. That motive is not only limited to the commercial world. Manipulation in a personal relationship may be for financial reasons too. It could come in the form of family trying to force an elderly relative to change their will in their favor. Even an abusive partner who controls everything about your life, including your personal finances.

Sexual Gain

For some, there is a sexual element to their manipulation. They use their overpowering control over their victims to gain sexual favors. Some may even use physical force, in effect rape, to satisfy their sexual urges. Others may be subtler in their approach. This can begin in the form of extreme praise and flattery, lavishing their target with gifts and false promises. They will come across as the perfect attentive partner. Watch out! Once they have you where they want you, they can quickly turn too controlling, and even become violent. It is their goal to keep you trapped in the relationship. Emotional blackmail is their game. The use of fear begins, making you feel obliged and guilty for not complying to their requests.

Chapter 9: Being Proactive: How to Defend Against Dark Manipulation

Why You Need to Protect Yourself and Loved Ones Against Dark Psychology

Though manipulation does not cause any harm or put the subject in any immediate danger, it is designed to deceive and change the attitude, reasoning and understanding of the intended subject regarding a particular situation or topic and is good to protect yourself and your loved ones against it.

Social influence, such as a teenager inducted into a culture or a society to interact with different people either at home or at work, is admirable. Any social influence that regards the privilege and right of individuals to decide, without been intimidated, is usually seen as something that is helpful.

Then again, social influence is despised when people beguile others to maneuver their way against other people's will. The impact can be very destructive and generally looked down upon as very weak in nature.

We have been groomed to show strength, to not give in and to never let anyone see our fears. In sum, we are being taught that going contrary to these instructions would result in people reading you as weak and vulnerable. Ironically, it is the very thing that separates us from other creatures that have also become the very source of both our strength and weakness. And that thing is our humanity. We are vulnerable simply because we are human. Our desires, our hopes, our aspirations, our quests for living transcendent lives reflect some of the things that make us vulnerable.

But the day we cease to possess any of these things, we cease to be human: and when we are no longer human, we become the thing that we are trying to protect ourselves against becoming. When we stop believing, when we stop caring, or when we stop being vulnerable, we become these seemingly soulless individuals whose sole mission is to satisfy their wanton lusts with ruthlessness regardless who would be hurt in the process. That said, while we acknowledge that our humanity makes us vulnerable, we must not forget that we can also draw strength from it.

This brings me to the biologically ingrained need for humans to connect with others. Recognize that this need is a healthy emotional human need.

Without a connection with another human being, we fail to function properly.

Why you should protect yourself from Dark Seducers?

A dark seducer can be a formidable foe. They know exactly how to get the other person, their victim, to fall in love with them. But the problem comes with the fact that the dark seducer really isn't in love with the other person. There is something that the dark seducer wants out of the relationship. This could be companionship because they don't like to be alone, sex, or something else. But they are usually not looking for love at all.

As soon as the victim of this seduction doesn't provide the thing that their seducer wants, the seducer is going to leave. So, if the victim starts to feel that they are being used and withholds sex from the seducer, the seducer will simply leave the relationship and move on to their next victim.

The seducer has no worries about the other partner in the relationship. A true seducer is only going to see the other person as a tool, something that helps the seducer get the pleasure that they want. As soon as that tool stops doing the job that it's supposed to, the seducer will move on to find a new person to do the work for them.

A dark seducer may move quickly between one relationship to the next, or they may even stay in a relationship for a long time. It all depends on the situation and how long the seducer is able to keep the victim under their control. Some victims stand up for themselves pretty quickly. The longer the victim is under the control of the dark seducer, the harder it is for them to leave.

This doesn't mean that the dark seducer has learned how to love their victim. It simply means that the dark seducer has become used to the way that things are, and they will use their powers and their mind control techniques in order to keep the victim right where they are.

It is important for you to be aware of dark seduction. While some men may choose to use some of the ideas of dark seduction in order to help them gain some confidence, avoid some issues with their fear of rejection, and make it easier for them to meet women, there are many that will use these techniques because they don't really care about the other person at all. They have specific goals that they want to reach in the relationship, and they will get there, no matter who gets hurt in the process.

If you do end up getting into one of these relationships, it can be devastating. The dark manipulator is really skilled at using the dark seduction techniques to get what they want. They will find a victim who is vulnerable, and they will present the right solution that the victim needs at that time. For example, they may find a victim who just got out of a major relationship, and they will step in to feel the need of that victim to not be lonely any longer.

The seducer is going to be charming, fun, and the perfect person for that victim. The victim may feel like they have found their soul mate, but the seducer is just there to get what they want out of the relationship. Sure, it may last for some time, but as soon as the victim is no longer meeting the needs of the seducer, the seducer will be gone.

This will leave the victim hurt and broken. They may have overly trusted the seducer (because the seducer is skilled at reading the victim and knew exactly what to do and say to gain that trust and get what they want), and now they are broken. They may go through depression and anxiety and even have trouble trusting others in the future.

Because of all these negatives that come with dark seduction, it is important to watch out for the signs. If you run into dark seduction with a narcissist or with a psychopath, it is even more important to watch for the signs. These individuals are not there to care about what the other person wants. They simply look out for themselves, they feel that they deserve what they want, and they don't have the capacity to care about how it is going to harm the other person.

Due to the way that the relationship was started, including the romance, attraction, the mutual feeling that you found a soul mate (all created by the seducer to get what they want), when things start to take a lot of wrong turns, it is likely to be too late for you, the victim, to walk away. This can be especially true if you went into that particular picture without a good idea of what you wanted in the relationship. Without this clear picture, you would not have the determination to walk away from that relationship when it didn't meet your expectations.

This is why you must always make sure that you know what you want to get out of the relationship before one begins. This will help you be prepared if the relationship becomes something else because you will be able to see when it is going away from your chosen course. You will give yourself a chance to see it for what it is before you damage your self-worth so much where you will stay in that relationship and accept the bad treatment.

This can be hard. Many times we feel that we need a relationship like we are not worth anything unless we are in a relationship with someone else. Then, when we are not in a relationship, we are going to feel like something is missing, and we jump into the first relationship that comes available. This is where the issues will start.

Before you jump into the next relationship, it is important to take some time to soul search. Remember that there is nothing wrong with not being in a relationship all the time. Taking some time for yourself and really exploring where you are at that time in your life and what you would like to happen in your next relationship can make a difference.

This gives you a good idea of what kind of relationship you want to be in. You won't just jump into the next relationship because you are needy or because you worry about being alone. You will have specific goals in mind, and if you feel the relationship isn't going in the right direction, you will be able to step out before the dark seducer gets too deep and tries to take control over you.

The first thing that you should do here is to start with some deep thinking and even some soul-searching and decide on the details of the relationship that you are looking to enjoy at that time in your life. Describe what you want out of the other person in this partnership. Describe how you want to feel in this relationship. Set out some clear boundaries and then make sure that you understand why you have these boundaries.

Chapter 10: Dark Manipulation Is All Around Us

Individuals using dark manipulation

Narcissists – People clinically diagnosed with narcissism have a bloated sense of self-worth and they are compelled by a need to make others believe that they are superior. In order to realize their deep desires of being adored and worshipped by everybody, narcissists are commonly known to use dark psychology and unethical persuasive tactics.

Sociopaths – Clinically diagnosed sociopaths are persuasive, intelligent, and charming too. However, they lack emotion and they feel no remorse because of which they do not hesitate to use dark psychology tactics to create superficial relationships with others and then take undue advantage of these people.

Attorneys – Driven by a deep passion to win each and every case under their care, attorneys, very often, use dark psychology tactics to get their desired outcomes.

Politicians – Using dark psychology tactics, politicians convince people to cast votes in their favor by convincing them that their view is the perfect view.

Sales People – This set of people are so focused on achieving their sales numbers that they do not think twice about manipulating people using dark persuasion and other unethical tactics to convince people of their dire need for a product or service they are selling.

Leaders – There are many leaders who use dark psychology techniques to get their subordinates and team members to comply more, to work harder or to perform better, **etc.**

Selfish People – This could be anyone who always puts his or her needs above everyone else's. They are willing to let others forego their benefits so that they themselves are benefited. They have no problem with win-lose outcomes where they win and others lose.

This list serves two purposes; one is to make you aware of such people who can manipulate you to do things that you don't want to do and the second one is to help you with self-realization. Are you using tactics that these people use to get what you want? How then can you discern between ethical tactics and dark ones so that there is good for all stakeholders? Also, knowing about these dark psychology tactics and the people who are most prone to using them will put you on guard and make you realize if anyone is using them to cause you harm.

Use of Dark Psychology in the Online Mode

Cyber-stealth is a common criminal activity that law enforcement agencies are grappling to keep under control.

Ease of Deception – It is very easy to deceive people online driven by the veil of anonymity that the Internet provides. Stealth and camouflage are the primary survival instincts of all living beings and unscrupulous people will find it very tempting use these instincts to victimize through the Internet.

No access to the physical person – This enhances the ease of deception as the victim cannot see or read the nonverbal aspects of the communication including body language, facial features, **etc.**

The most confounding part of online deception is the fact that victims are fully aware that there could be something wrong taking place here and yet, they do not hesitate to take the plunge.

Dark manipulation in the Working Environment

Anyone who is vulnerable is a potential target of a manipulator. It is not always the obvious people that can get ensnared. Already we have learned that such a character will initially behave with impeccable manners. This false front is performed to impress and gain trust. If you do not know this person already, it may be hard to recognize that you have become their target. That is until it is too late. On a personal front, this type of relationship can occur at work, or even in intimate relationships.

Consider your place of work. Do you have a boss that makes your life a misery by demanding work at higher and quicker levels constantly? Browbeating you to meet impossible targets. Warning you of a reduction in your salary or canceling any bonuses. Could even threaten to sack you. At that point, you become trapped. This person knows we all have responsibilities, such as mortgages or rents and families to support. We cannot walk away. In such a situation, any of us could become this vulnerable person. This is the victim of a controlling manipulator.

Dark manipulation in Love and relationships

Love is a universal language. It is a primordial emotion that we all instinctively crave. As humans, we are designed for love. We want to love and feel loved. No one is as happy as a man or a woman who is in love and feel loved in return. Some people mate for procreation purposes. Some people mate in order to negate societal pressure. Some even mate to promote the alliance between powerful families. But, the primary reason for relationships aka getting a mate is love. In essence, it is easy for things to degrade to a point where love is used as a bargaining chip for more power over another individual. And this is where elements of dark psychology come to play.

Dark manipulation in Blind faith and religious beliefs

You see a beautiful flower and marvel at how something so exquisite and delicate could just be...without thought, without pattern, it just is. We look at the big expanse of the sky and wonder what lies beyond. Does it just go on forever? Or does it just tapper off into an endless end? When you hear the powerful roar of the waterfall or the earth-shaking sounds made by a thunder blast, even with the advancements and knowledge made available to us, we still quake in fear and awe. Back then, your choices were to either let the fear drive you insane or you rationalize the situation by pinning it on a sovereign being that is bigger than you. Some of the braver folk chose to use science to validate their explanation.

Staying with this same line of thinking, when someone we love dies, we are forced to confront our own mortality. Our grief is compounded by questions regarding life and death. Does the journey end here or does it continue into the afterlife? This has been a strong motivational force behind today's belief systems. The fear and consideration given to the life after this life has spurred many into making the "right choices" here, so that when death comes, the life that we hope continues after us is favorable for us. It is our own way of manipulating the final outcome so to speak because the alternative as it is being portrayed to us is so grim.

Some people prey on our fear of the afterlife, so they use it to manipulate us into getting what they want.

The common tactic is to use the name of the principal deity to twists the words that are drawn from the religion's sacred manual to mean new things that corroborate whatever story they are making up in order to help them successfully manipulate the people. A lot of people have been swindled, physically hurt and even made to commit atrocious crimes under this guise. Another method these false leaders use is claiming to have a vision or spiritual insight into a specific need that the victim has. They create an elaborate story that is a mishmash of lies interspersed with the truth (usually obtained unknowingly from the victim or third parties) and the main goal is to extort the victim for money, favor or just power play. Some victims are coerced to part with more money than they can ever hope to have. In some cases, young impressionable victims are brainwashed into living in fear under occult-like situations.

Dark manipulation in Social Media Networking

Do you use social media to its full potential? Are you prepared to invest time and energy in your online connections? If not, then you are missing a huge opportunity. The potential to reach thousands of people who can help you in your career is invaluable.

Potential investors or customers are all waiting for you to tell your story or promote your product. Social media allows you to solicit ideas from a huge audience all with the click of a mouse. The power of a "like button" is not to be ignored! The evidence of thousands of positive affirmations will only serve to amplify your voice and make more people listen.

Your social life can also thrive online. Groups of like-minded people are all out there waiting for you to join them. Maybe you have a passion for sailing or extreme sports but aren't sure of the facilities near you. Facebook is a great place to start looking for groups in your area, reach out and connect. Use Twitter and Instagram to help your dating life if you are looking for love! Providing you take precautions and always meet for the first time in public you can meet some interesting people!

Social media can also be a brutal place and it is essential you monitor your settings. Before you join a group make sure they can only see the information you are comfortable with.

Dark manipulation in Court Protection

Throughout background, people have been declaring that they devoted terrible wrongs because they had been brainwashed. It was an excuse that several would declare wanting to conserve their very own lives or to get away with a mass murder or a few other criminal offense versus humanity. It could also be something as basic as taking from an additional individual. Whatever the action was, persuading was an easy protection because it took the obligation of the action far from the accused and it was tough to verify whether somebody had been persuaded or not.

Whether teaching pleas can be utilized as a protection in the court is up to some argument. Several experts feel that by enabling this protection right into the court, the courts would end up being overwhelmed with false cases of brainwashing and also the sources for verifying or disproving this protection would certainly be greater than the courts could take care of. Despite this, there have actually been some instances offered court that might show the credibility of indoctrination as a protection for criminal activities devoted.

Dark manipulation in Shaming Others

There are various other choices offered to the manipulator if they want to obtain their based on aid within the last objective. One method that has a fair bit of success is when the manipulator has the ability to take down their topic. In regular situations, if the manipulator makes use of spoken abilities in order to place their topic down, they will certainly run a high threat of making the subject feeling as if an individual strike has actually been put on them. When the subject seems like they are struck, they will certainly bristle and also not agree to help the manipulator in the manner in which they desire. Rather, the topic will certainly not such as the manipulator as well as will certainly remain as away from them as feasible, making it extremely hard for the manipulator to reach their last objective.

This is why the manipulator is not most likely to simply walk around and also take down their topic. They need to be a lot more very discreet concerning the procedure and also discover a method to do it without increasing warnings or making the subject seem like they are being assaulted. One manner in which this can be done is with wit. Wit has the ability to reduced obstacles that may or else appear due to the fact that wit is amusing and also makes individuals really feel great. The manipulator has the ability to transform their disrespect right into a joke. Although that the taken down has actually been become a joke, it will certainly function equally as properly as if the joke were absent without leaving the noticeable marks on the topic.

Frequently, the manipulator will certainly guide their taken down right into the type of 3rd individual. This assists them to mask what they are claiming a lot more conveniently together with supplying a very easy method to reject creating injury if it returns to haunt them later. As an example, they could begin their taken down with "Other individuals assume ..." If the topic is still able to presume that the remarks were made at them, after that the manipulator would certainly finish it with a disposable line that could consist of something like "existing business excepted, naturally."

The suggestion of the taken down is to make the subject seem like they are in some way much less than the manipulator. It increases the manipulator as much as a brand-new degree and also leaves the subject sensation like something is desiring. The topic is most likely to wish to make points far better and also to take care of any type of incorrect that they have actually done. This will certainly place the manipulator in a setting of power, and also they will certainly have the ability to extra conveniently obtain the based on aid them.

Dark manipulation in Seduction

Seductive behaviors have been so popularized by new age media that the average Joe might not identify them as part of dark psychology. It is portrayed as one simply trying to get what they want by any means necessary and, in some cases, might even be seen as a win-win. In reality, such actions that attempt to manipulate an individual and get them to do things against their better judgment stems from the dark continuum. This is because such actions exploit the weaknesses of others, and it only fits that we discuss seduction in this book.

Seduction can be defined in several ways, depending on which angle you view it from. It may be sexual, which is the most common definition. In this case, a person is tempted to engage in sexual intercourse. Often, such an individual may be opposed to this act. A less common definition is, ironically, one that is seen everywhere and every time. It involves enticing an individual or groups of people with any particular offer, which may not be as true as presented, in a bid to influence people to make certain choices that may or may not be in their best interest.

Seduction, both of the sexual and nonsexual kind, is used in marketing with increasing frequency. This is especially noticeable in recent times. Sparsely clad male and female models are used for advertising anything from undergarments to toothbrushes. Hence the common saying that 'sex sells.'

The lack of empathy and manipulative devices utilized during seduction has been some of the reasons why seduction is associated with the dark triad, although these attributes are only observed in short-term seduction, as long-term would require more commitment.

The human sex drive can be a very powerful urge and not being able to fulfill it can sometimes lead to unhappiness, worry, and stress in the person's life. On the other side of things, some of the most famous historical figures are known for their frequent and full fulfillment of sexual urges. For example, emperors and kings have often been afforded the finest women as their reward just because of their status.

But a dark seducer is going to be someone who knows what they want and they know how to get it. They will go after the other person in order to fulfill their own personal needs, and often they don't really care how the other person feels about it. They can be charming and they are not going to be clumsy at all, and they always know the right thing to say and do.

It is important for you to be aware of dark seduction. While some men may choose to use some of the ideas of dark seduction in order to help them gain some confidence, avoid some issues with their fear of rejection, and make it easier for them to meet women, there are many that will use these techniques because they don't really care about the other person at all. They have specific goals that they want to reach in the relationship, and they will get there, no matter who gets hurt in the process.

The seducer is going to be charming, fun, and the perfect person for that victim. The victim may feel like they have found their soul mate, but the seducer is just there to get what they want out of the relationship. Sure, it may last for some time, but as soon as the victim is no longer meeting the needs of the seducer, the seducer will be gone.

This will leave the victim hurt and broken. They may have overly trusted the seducer (because the seducer is skilled at reading the victim and knew exactly what to do and say to gain that trust and get what they want), and now they are broken. They may go through depression and anxiety and even have trouble trusting others in the future.

Dark manipulation in Con Artists Scam

Con artists are a great example of dark psychology at work. This can keep you out of trouble when you run into these scams yourself, and can also teach you a little of the dark psychology behind the con. Some of them are only mildly malicious, but others are quite horrible. We hope this will help to explain a little the mindset behind these dark persuaders so that you may be better equipped to avoid them in your future.

Con artists know that a majority of folks will NOT report the incident, as they will feel embarrassed at having been manipulated by a scammer. If it happens to you, you should report it, because we can guarantee that you are probably not the only one and it might not stop for a very long time without your help.

Con artists know that by mirroring your body language, you are more likely to like and trust them. Be sure to watch out for this technique in order to help protect yourself.

Con artists know that you are more likely to trust someone who is well-dressed than you are to trust someone who looks like they just came in off the street. They will take advantage of this. Watch out when someone very well-dressed starts treating you like a best friend, especially if they are talking about new business opportunities. If you do decide to do business, it can wait, and there is nothing wrong with insisting on a background check.

Con artists will buy you drinks, tell you stories that make them seem more down to earth, and, if you aren't careful, they will win your trust. A con doesn't always occur in the space of an evening, so even if you have known someone for a month or two, you should still be careful where money is concerned. Anyone whom you barely know that asks "Do you want to make some money?" should be viewed with suspicion at the very least.

As dark manipulators, con artists know that people like you more if you get them to talk about themselves. They also know that this gives them information which they can use against you in order to get what they want. Pay attention to their body language and remember the background check advice that we gave you. It gets you information, it's legal, and you can throw it away once you've protected yourself by checking. It's not popular advice, but it is good advice.

The scams that con artists like to employ the most are those that play on your greed. They usually involve buying items or investing in something that is going to have an unrealistic turnaround time and profit. Be especially wary if there is a time limit or it's a 'one-time offer.' If it sounds too good to be true, it probably is.

Dark manipulation in Job interviews

Dark psychology relates to the unethical ways that people can use to get what we want.

Have you ever lied or exaggerated on your CV to get a job? Sounds innocent enough, but it is a means of dark manipulation to get what you desire. It is a dark tactic used purposefully to mislead another person. We learn from a young age how to get our own way by using manipulative tactics. A new-born baby cries for the attention of its parent, could we accuse a baby of manipulative behavior? Sounds a little unethical to accuse a baby of using dark psychology, but some would argue that it is true. The baby has to survive, so cries out to get what it needs.

Conclusion

Thank you for making it through to the end of this book. We all have a dark side of our psyche whether we admit it or not. Only those who accept and study this dark side can incur the benefits of doing so, and these benefits are some of the greatest we can come across in life, so this book and others like it are some of the greatest resources that we can give ourselves.

This guidebook took some time to explore how dark psychology works as well as some of the methods and techniques that you can use to avoid being manipulated.

This book is intended to teach you to leverage dark psychology tactics, techniques, and strategies to help you become more efficient, more productive, more likable, and, therefore, a better person than you are today.

This book should enlighten you on how to cope with some of the problems you may face in life. It is meant only as a guide on how to deal with controlling manipulative relationships. It cannot give you your freedom. Only courage can do that. Build up your self-confidence. Take care of your health. For the sake of living a happy life, learn how to handle such controlling characters that may pass you by.

So, go ahead and get started on the goodness of dark psychology so that you can you get what you want in your life.

Made in the USA
Las Vegas, NV
22 November 2020

11276912R20289